WRITING SKILLS ACTIVITIES FOR Special Children

Including 135 ready-to-use lessons with reproducible activity sheets to help children master basic writing skills...practice writing for real-life situations...and encourage the exploration of writing as a creative and enjoyable activitiy!

DARLENE MANNIX

JOSSEY-BASS
A Wiley Imprint
www.josseybass.com

Published by Jossey-Bass
A Wiley Imprint
989 Market Street, San Francisco, CA 94103-1741   www.josseybass.com

Jossey-Bass books and products are available through most bookstores. To contact Jossey-Bass directly call our Customer Care Department within the U.S. at (800) 956-7739, outside the U.S. at (317) 572-3986 or fax (317) 572-4002.

Jossey-Bass also publishes its books in a variety of electronic formats. Some content that appears in print may not be available in electronic books.

ISBN 0-7879-7884-1

CIP data is available from the Library of Congress.

FIRST EDITION
PB Printing 10 9 8 7 6 5 4 3 2

About the Author

Darlene Mannix is presently a remedial reading teacher in LaPorte, Indiana. She has previously been a teacher for students of all ages who are at-risk, language disordered, and emotionally, mentally, and learning disabled. She has also taught alternative education classes for middle school students.

Ms. Mannix holds a Bachelor of Science degree from Taylor University and a Master's in Learning Disabilities from Indiana University. She is an active member of the Council for Exceptional Children.

She is the author of several resources published by The Center for Applied Research in Education, including *Oral Language Activities for Special Children* (1987), *Be a Better Student: Lessons and Worksheets for Teaching Behavior Management in Grades 4–9* (1989), *Life Skills Activities for Special Students* (1991), and *Social Skills Activities for Special Children* (1993).

About This Book

Writing Activities for Special Children is for teachers of students in grades 1–6 who need specific instruction for the various skills involved in writing. Some children are natural writers; they seem to speak, read, and write without specific training. Words and ideas simply flow into wonderful stories and reports; they are well-organized, clever, and easy to read. Most children, however, especially those with special needs, benefit more from targeted training on specific writing tasks. This book is written to help them.

Writing as an educational skill involves many subtasks. Writers must have an idea of *what they want to write about*. What do they want to say? What is being communicated? What is the purpose of the writing?

This idea then must be *conveyed to the readers* in a way that will be understood. The words, sentences, and paragraphs must flow together to comprise the author's message. The writing must be legible, the thoughts must be clearly communicated, the grammar must be standard so that it is understood, and spelling should be conventional rather than invented.

There are several main purposes for this book. First of all, it serves as a step-by-step guideline for students to move through basic writing skills. It begins with simpler skills such as copying words and completing sentences, proceeds through the teaching of writing proper sentences for many different purposes, and finally guides students to longer literary projects, such as reports and stories.

Another purpose is to provide students with writing experiences on a practical level. Although the majority of writing tasks may take place within an educational setting, there are life skills which also call upon writing skills. Students will always be faced with tasks such as filling out information on forms, expressing an opinion in writing, and recording information for later use.

The final purpose for this book is to encourage students to explore writing as a creative, enjoyable event. Writing can be perceived as a dreaded, tedious subject for students who have great difficulty organizing, collecting, and expressing their thoughts. Once the basic skills are achieved, young writers can be free to delve into the truly fun aspects of writing. Hopefully, some of the activities noted in this book (writing a play, a poem, a story) will be appealing to even reluctant writers.

Contents

This book is divided into four main sections with a total of 136 lessons. The lessons cover writing skills which are appropriate in part for grades 1 through 6. The earlier lessons begin with copying skills and then progress through more complex writing skills.

Section I, Writing Words, contains 41 lessons that focus on the task of writing at the "word" level. Part 1, *Beginning Writing*, involves skills that demand only the ability to copy words. Part 2, *Writing High-Frequency Words and Phrases*, teaches students how to remember to spell "tricky" words that are very commonly used. Part 3, *Increasing Vocabulary Words*, deals with common words that are found in everyday life (days, months, colors, etc.) as well as words that are important to understand in one's vocabulary (opposites, synonyms, etc.). In Part 4, *Editing Words*, students are given practice in the very simplest of editing tasks: changing only one word in a sentence to make an improvement.

Section II, Writing Sentences, provides 41 lessons that take students past the word stage into a higher level of writing. In this section, students manipulate words to form sentences. Part 1, *Writing a Basic Sentence*, shows students how to recognize and write a complete sentence. In Part 2, *Writing Sentences for a Specific Purpose*, the student must write a sentence that specifically serves a purpose (answering a question, describing something, etc.). Part 3, *Varying Sentences*, demonstrates ways that students can write much more interesting sentences by adding phrases, adjusting the length, using different words, and paraphrasing. The final part, Part 4, is *Proofreading/Editing Sentences*. Editing is more challenging in this part, as students are taught to edit for punctuation, spelling, meaning, and interest.

Section III, Writing Paragraphs, includes 20 lessons that require students to organize sentences into a cohesive paragraph. Part 1, *The "Sandwich" Model for Paragraphs*, lays the foundation for how to organize a basic paragraph (topic sentence, details, conclusion). Part 2, *Types of Paragraphs*, provides practice in writing different types of paragraphs (descriptive, narrative, etc.). Finally, in Part 3, *Multiple Paragraphs*, the students are given examples of how to organize pieces of writing that are longer and require more than one paragraph to convey the information.

Section IV, Other Types of Writing Activities, concludes with 34 lessons that cover many other writing tasks. Part 1, *Writing a Story*, is given quite a bit of attention since this skill covers many other skills. Part 2, *Writing for School Projects*, is a collection of exercises that deal with typical school-related writing assignments (keeping a journal, writing a letter, answering an essay question, writing definitions, etc.). Part 3, *Practical Writing Activities*, attempts to bridge the gap between school and real-life with activities such as taking a phone message, writing notes on a calendar, and completing forms. The last portion of this section, Part 4, is *Creative-Writing Activities*. In this part there are activities that tap into a student's creative thinking. Even in this part, the examples and instruction are still very step-by-step for students who can't seem to think of anything to write about to proceed by following through on a divergent project.

Lessons

There are 136 lessons in the entire book with a total of 269 illustrated worksheets. For each lesson, the following information is provided:

- **To the Teacher:** This is a short commentary that explains the purpose and content of the lesson. There may be a brief rationale why this skill is important.

- **To the Student:** These comments are directed to the students. Teachers may choose to copy these notes for the students, adapt them orally to their own style of teaching, paraphrase the content, or even omit them entirely. Basically, however, these comments convey one way to teach the skill to students.

- **Worksheet:** Each lesson has at least one worksheet activity which can be reproduced for student use. The worksheet is directly related to the skill taught.

- **Follow-up Activity:** At least one follow-up activity is suggested for the classroom. This activity may be helpful for reteaching a skill or to promote further interest in a skill.

How to Use This Book

Because of the many writing skills involved and topics covered, this book serves as a resource for elementary school teachers. Teachers may simply "pick and choose" whatever skills or activities are most appropriate for their grade level. It is noteworthy, however, that the lessons are somewhat sequential in terms of simplicity and higher-order thinking. That is, the earlier lessons are more appropriate for younger, less skilled writers while subsequent lessons assume that prerequisite skills have been met in order for writers to focus on more complex skills.

The lessons vary in length. While one lesson may be completed adequately in a day, others may take a few days or even a week to be thoroughly taught. When writing a story, for example, it will take time to plan the story, carry out the writing, complete the revision, and publish the story. Teachers will have to gauge the time frame according to their own purpose for writing. If the intent is to simply expose students to types of writing, a brief introduction would be fine. If the intent is for students to completely master a skill, more teaching and writing time would be needed.

Final Comments

The best way to become a good writer is to write. The more you can encourage your students to write, write, write, the easier it will become for them and the more they will truly enjoy being authors. Whether they are scribbling words with a stubby pencil or tapping out a thesis on a word processor, students are sharing their thoughts, their ideas, and themselves with their writing. Let's not forget to appreciate that!

Contents

Section II: Writing Sentences...183

Section III Writing Paragraphs...333

Section IV Other Types of Writing Activities...419

Part 4 Creative-Writing Activities

Section 1
Writing Words

Lesson I-1: Matching Words to Pictures (Beginning Writing)

To the Teacher

Students should by now be able to write correctly all 26 letters of the alphabet. The next writing skill involves using those letters to form words. In this lesson, students will match words (by writing) to pictures. Students should use initial consonants to help them select the correct word.

To the Student

You are going to begin using your writing skills to write words. At this point, you will be able to copy the words, but later you will be writing and spelling them on your own. There are pictures of objects or things on this worksheet that are familiar to you. Find the word that matches the picture and copy the word next to it. The pictures and words are in groups of five.

Worksheet

Answers to Worksheet I-1:

1. web;	9. saddle;
2. gate;	10. tiger;
3. nut;	11. mouse;
4. door;	12. pear;
5. ball;	13. table;
6. fox;	14. vase;
7. lamp;	15. yell
8. ring;	

Follow-up Activity

Make a set of cards with a picture on one side and the word printed on the other side. Have students practice reading the word cards and flipping the card over to see the picture. This will build up the students' sight-word vocabulary and make it easier for them to recognize quickly what the sight word "looks" like.

Name _____ Date _____

I-1. Match the Word

Look at each picture, say the word, and use the starting sound to find the word that matches the picture. Then write the word next to the picture.

1. _____ door

2. _____ ball

3. _____ web

4. _____ nut

5. _____ gate

6. _____ ring

7. _____ tiger

8. _____ fox

9. _____ saddle

10. _____ lamp

11. _____ yell

12. _____ mouse

13. _____ vase

14. _____ pear

15. _____ table

Lesson I-2: Completing Sentences by Copying Words
(Beginning Writing)

To the Teacher
Students continue to work on their copying skills by completing sentences. The purpose of this lesson is for students to read sentences along with you and figure out the missing word by using context and pictures. The student then copies the appropriate word.

To the Student
Listen to this: "Yesterday, my brother and I went outside and played with a (blank)." What word could go in that blank? (dog, ball, friend) There are several words that make sense! Now I'm going to give you another clue. (Draw a ball on the board.) Do you know what is the right word? (ball)

On this worksheet, we are going to read some sentences that are missing a word. Use the words and the clues from the picture to help you pick out and copy the correct word for each sentence.

Worksheet
Answers to Worksheet I-2:
1. saddle
2. banana
3. bowl
4. kite
5. ball
6 fish
7. table
8. zebra

Follow-up Activity
Have students practice reading the sentences. Discuss why some of the answers that were not selected could seem to be right if it weren't for the picture clues. Can students think of other answers that would also fit? It is important to use every possible clue to figure out the one specific answer!

Name _____ Date _____

1-2. Completing Sentences by Copying Words

Read the sentences. Using the picture clues, select the word that best completes the sentence and write it on the lines.

1. There is a _____ on the horse.

   boy   saddle   pear

2. Karl can eat a _____.

   banana   fox   jar

3. Amy put the goldfish in a _____.

   jar   bowl   kite

4. I see a _____ in the sky.

   sun   rainbow   kite

5. Let's play with the _____.

   ball   jump rope   monkey

6. This book is about a green _____.

   bicycle   fish   vase

7. The flowers are on the _____.

   vase   table   jar

8. We saw a _____ at the zoo.

   yak   butterfly   zebra

Lesson I-3: Completing Sentences with Picture Clues
(Beginning Writing)

To the Teacher

Students begin to string together several words to complete a sentence. After looking at a picture, students generate several sentences about the picture. These can be stated orally at first, and then in writing with words to be copied. The purpose of this lesson is to provide students with simple sentences to complete, based on a picture.

To the Student

You will see several pictures on the worksheet. I would like you to make up some sentences about each picture. They don't have to be long, but they should tell something about the picture. Then you can complete some sentences by using some words that make sense. I will write the sentences that we come up with on the board, and you can copy the words on the worksheet.

Worksheet

Answers to Worksheet I-3:

Answers will vary. Here are examples.

Picture #1: running after the mouse; running after the cat; going to fall

Picture #2: swimming in the bowl; thinking about dinner

Picture #3: sleeping at the table; going to wake him up

Picture #4: get on the horse; ride him over the jump

Follow-up Activity

Have students find interesting pictures or photos for the class to see. Offer the students some "sentence starters" and have them complete the sentences orally and by copying them.

Name _____ Date _____

I-3. Completing Sentences with Picture Clues

Finish the sentences that tell about the pictures.

Picture #1

The cat is _____.

The dog is _____.

The lamp is _____.

Picture #2

The goldfish is _____.

The cat is _____.

Picture #3

The king is _____.

The queen is _____.

Picture. #4

The girl will _____.

Then she will _____.

Lesson I-4: Sentence Starters (Beginning Writing)

To the Teacher

Sentence starters are a good way to get students thinking about their individual experiences with situations. They also encourage divergent thinking, as students see you enthused about their creative answers. The purpose of this lesson is to get students thinking about their individual responses to unfinished sentences, as well as to have students select which response they will choose to copy to finish the sentence.

To the Student

Finish this sentence for me: "If I had $100, I would… ." (buy a pizza, buy a lot of toys, give it to my mother, etc.) I can see that there are a lot of different answers. There are lots of things you can do with $100. There is certainly no one correct answer, is there?

I would like you to read a list of unfinished sentences. You may complete the sentence with words that make sense and explain how you think about each sentence. As we read them out loud together, give me your answers and I will write them on the board. You might like someone else's answer better after you hear a lot of answers. Feel free to choose, and copy, whatever answer you like.

Worksheet

Answers to Worksheet I-4:

Answers will vary. Here are examples.

1. read, sleep, play outside

2. a puppy, money, a car

3. the moon, Florida, a tree

4. give me his guitar, move out

5. pick it up, take it home, name it

6. call the police, take it home, draw a picture of it

7. call the police, scream, let the dogs out

8. I watch cartoons, someone tickles me, I feel happy

9. ride horses, go camping, play video games

10. hit the wall, go to my room, yell a lot

Follow-up Activity

Keep a list of good sentence starters. Students may come up with some good ideas. This can be a first-thing-in-the-morning activity or a two-minute-right-before-lunch activity.

Name _____ Date _____

I-4. Sentence Starters

Complete the sentences with your own words.

1. On a rainy day, I like to _____

_____.

2. I wish someone would give me _____

_____.

3. If I could fly, I'd go to _____

_____.

4. I wish my brother/sister would _____

_____.

5. If I saw a kitten, I would _____

_____.

6. If I saw a dinosaur, I would _____

_____.

7. If I saw a burglar, I would _____

_____.

8. I laugh when _____

_____.

9. My best friend and I like to _____

_____.

10. When I'm really angry, I _____

_____

_____

_____.

Lesson I-5: Completing Sentences
to Make a Short Story (Beginning Writing)

To the Teacher

Students are given a topic or theme to think about. Several sentences are started for the students, and they are to complete the sentences. At this point, words can be written down for students to copy. If this is done orally at first, students may suggest several answers. You can write their answers on the board and students can select which ones they want to use by copying the words. The purpose of this lesson is to provide a somewhat longer piece of writing for students to work on, with a related theme for all sentences. (*NOTE:* Two additional worksheets, "My Pool" and "My Dog," are given.)

To the Student

What's your favorite winter activity? (sledding, tubing, skiing, snowboarding, etc.) I want you to think about sledding. Tell me about a time when you had fun sledding. I am going to give you a big drawing of a sled. There are some unfinished sentences that go with the drawing, but you get to finish them in any way you want. I'll read them to you, and then I'll write everyone's answers on the board/on paper. When you're ready to do this on your own, just look up here to find your words.

Worksheet

Answers to Worksheet I-5:

Answers will vary. Here are examples.

1. my friend Bob, my sister
2. the park, the big hill
3. scared, excited, happy
4. I'd have a hat and mittens on
5. trees, other people
6. laugh, get up again
7. have hot chocolate, go to bed

Follow-up Activity

Seasonal drawings can be used for further activities of this type. Drawing a snowman, a mountain, a person swimming or any picture that would depict an enjoyable activity can be used. Add some starter sentences and have students complete them.

Name _____ Date _____

I-5A. My Red Sled

Complete the sentences that tell about the red sled.

1. I would go sledding with _____

_____.

2. We would take the sled to _____

_____.

3. I would feel so _____

_____.

4. I wouldn't be cold because _____

_____.

5. We would have to look out for _____

_____.

6. If we fell off the sled, we would _____

_____.

7. When we got home, we would _____

_____.

Name _____ Date _____

I-5B. My Pool

1. It is fun to play with _____

_____ .

2. My favorite pool toy is _____

_____ .

3. The diving board is _____

_____ .

4. I like to swim with _____

_____ .

5. Sometimes the water is _____

_____ .

6. When I open my eyes underwater _____

_____ .

Name _____ Date _____

I-5C. My Dog

1. My dog's name is _____

   _____.

2. He looks like _____

   _____.

3. He likes to_____

   _____.

4. When we play together, we _____

   _____.

5. Sometimes I tell him to _____

   _____.

6. The best thing about my dog is _____

   _____.

Lesson I-6: Composing and Copying a
Class Story (Beginning Writing)

To the Teacher

The class can work together to follow story prompts to compose a short story that can be written on the board and then transferred to individual student's papers. Composing the story together can be fun for the class, especially as students brainstorm and come up with lots of ideas. The purpose of this lesson is to encourage students to orally generate ideas and come to a consensus as to how the story will progress; followed by capturing the story in writing and copying the sentences on individual student's papers.

To the Student

Today we're going to do a prompted story. I am going to ask you questions about what will happen in the story. Because there are many of us who probably have different ideas, we'll have to listen to everyone's ideas and then come up with our story. I might call on individuals to give me their ideas or we might toss around some ideas and take a class vote on what should happen.

I will write down the sentences that tell about the story. A sentence starts with a capital letter and ends with a period, so make sure I don't forget to do those things while I'm writing your story here on the board.

Answers will vary:

1. "Alice was a great inventor."

2. "Alice had a car that was blue and had stripes."

3. "Alice wanted her car to fly."

4. "She put on an extra motor to make it fly."

5. "The invention worked great."

6. "Alice wanted to sell her invention to a lot of people."

7. "The invention sold for one million dollars."

8. "You can buy a flying car at a department store."

Worksheet

As you lead students through the prompted questions, ask for their ideas (either individual students or students at random who have their hands up!). Guide them toward picking reasonable responses that could keep the story going. Write the sentences that follow the questions on the board. When the story is finished, have the class read the story out loud. Students can then copy the story in their personal notebooks or on paper.

Follow-up Activities

1. Students may want to draw a picture of the great invention that the class wrote about.

2. If the class enjoyed this activity, you may want to continue with other class stories.

I-6. The Great Invention

1. What will the name of our great inventor be? _____

_____

2. This inventor had a car. What did the car look like? _____

_____

3. What did the inventor want the car to do? _____

_____

4. What did the inventor do to the car to make it different?_____

_____

5. Did the invention work well? _____

_____

6. Did the inventor want to sell the invention? _____

_____

7. How much did the invention sell for? _____

_____

8. Where can you go to buy this invention? _____

_____

Lesson I-7: Twenty Little Words

(Writing High-Frequency Words and Phrases)

To the Teacher

There are many lists of sight words or high-frequency words that will help students get started on independent writing. This section will focus on 100 common sight words that are important for reading and writing. The purpose of this lesson is to acquaint students with 20 sight words that can be immediately helpful in writing short sentences.

To the Student

Certain words in the English language are very common. There are hardly any sentences that don't contain some of these little words. Some of these words are: *the, a, in, at.* They are very small words, but they are common and very useful.

First, of course, you have to be able to read the words. Once you know what the word is, you can work on learning to spell it.

Here is the word list of the first 20 words that you need to know how to spell:

1. a	5. come	9. in	13. said	17. two
2. and	6. get	10. look	14. the	18. want
3. at	7. here	11. ride	15. this	19. we
4. can	8. I	12. run	16. to	20. well

One way to get in some practice writing these words is to use them in sentences. As you copy the words in sentences, try to look at how the word is spelled. I want you to be able to write the words two different ways: (1) from a word list that I call, and (2) in a sentence using the word.

Worksheets

Answers to Worksheet I-7A:

1. and	5. can	9. in	13. ride	17. want
2. come	6. look	10. get	14. run	18. two
3. a	7. here	11. said	15. the	19. to
4. at	8. I	12. this	16. will	20. we

Answers to Worksheet I-7B:

Part One:

a, and, at, can, come

Make corrections if you need to so that you can copy them/write them correctly in Part Two.

Part Two:

1. can come   2. and a   3. come at   4. can a   5. and can

Part Three:

1. (*Prompt*: What time should we come to the party?) come at

2. (*Prompt*: Do you think Bob can come with us?) can come

3. (*Prompt*: Do you have a dog and a cat?) and a

4. (*Prompt*: Ask Sue if a kangaroo can hop.) can a

5. (*Prompt*: Yes! A kangaroo can also eat.) and can

Part Four:

Students write these words:

1. come   2. a   3. and   4. can   5. at

Answers to Worksheet I-7C:

Part One:

get, here, I, in, look

Part Two:

1. get in   2. here at   3. I can come   4. come in   5. and look at

Part Three:

1. (*Prompt*: Sammy is standing outside the door.) come in
2. (*Prompt*: Can you come to the game?) I can come
3. (*Prompt*: What time will Aunt Sarah be here?) here at
4. (*Prompt*: It's raining outside.) get in
5. (*Prompt*: This is an interesting insect.) and look at

Part Four:

1. here   2. I   3. in   4. get   5. look

Answers to Worksheet I-7D:

Part One:

ride, run, said, the, this

Part Two:

1. ride in the   2. run and   3. I said   4. and the   5. in this

Part Three:

1. (*Prompt*: You look tired. What did you say to your mother?) I said
2. (*Prompt*: Would you like to ride in the airplane?) ride in the
3. (*Prompt*: What are the animals doing?) and the
4. (*Prompt*: Where should you put the pencil?) in the
5. (*Prompt*: What do children like to do outside?) run and

Part Four:

1. said   2. ride   3. this   4. the   5. run

Answers to Worksheet I-7E:

Part One:

to, two, want, we, well

Part Two:

1. to the   2. in two   3. want to get   4. we can   5. well and

Part Three:

1. (*Prompt*: How fast can you be here?) in two
2. (*Prompt*: Do you think we can finish this in a hurry?) we can
3. (*Prompt*: Where is Carla going?) to the
4. (*Prompt*: What kind of book do you want to get?) want to get

5. (*Prompt*: How is Alex feeling now?) well and

Part Four:

1. well   2. two   3. want   4. we   5. to

Follow-up Activity

Give students ample opportunity to use these words in their writing. You may put up a "word wall" with cards containing these words for reading and spelling. Arrange the word cards alphabetically, if desired, or start an actual wall with these words on the bottom. As you continue to add new words, add new cards as "bricks" on top of the first layer of cards.

Name _____ Date _____

I-7A. Fill in the Blanks on Words 1–20

Read each of the five words in each group. Write the word that best completes each sentence. Make sure you write each word correctly.

1. I have a dog _____ a cat.

2. Can you _____ over to my house?

3. I see _____ boy.

4. We are _____ school.

5. I _____ go for a walk.

a   and   at   can   come

6. I want you to _____ at this book!

7. Will you come over _____?

8. My mother says that _____ am pretty.

9. There is a kitten _____ the box.

10. Come with me to_____the apple.

get   here   I   in   look

11. My father _____ that I have to go home now.

12. I think _____ is my best drawing.

13. Can you _____ a horse?

14. I like to _____ home.

15. I have a picture of _____ big dog.

ride   run   said   the   this

16. I hope we _____ go outside today.

17. What do you _____ to do?

18. I have_____ dogs.

19. I want _____ go for a ride.

20. My sister said that _____ will go out to eat.

to   two   want   we   will

Name _____ Date _____

I-7B. More Practice on Words 1–5

Part One: **Writing Words**

_____   _____   _____   _____   _____

Part Two: **Writing Phrases**

1. _____   _____

2. _____   _____

3. _____   _____

4. _____   _____

5. _____   _____

Part Three: **Completing Sentences with Phrases**

1. We should _____ _____ 3 o'clock.

2. Bob _____ _____ with us.

3. I have a dog _____ _____ cat.

4. Sue, _____ _____ kangaroo hop?

5. A kangaroo can eat _____ _____ hop, too!

Part Four: **Check Again**

1. _____

2. _____

3. _____

4. _____

5. _____

Name _____ Date _____

I-7C. More Practice on Words 6–10

Part One: **Writing Words**

_____   _____   _____   _____   _____

Part Two: **Writing Phrases**

    1. _____ _____

    2. _____ _____

    3. _____ _____ _____

    4. _____ _____

    5. _____ _____ _____

Part Three: **Completing Sentences with Phrases**

    1. Tell Sammy to _____ _____ the house.

    2. Yes, _____ _____ _____ to the game.

    3. Aunt Sarah will be _____ _____ noon.

    4. Hurry and _____ _____ the car before you get wet!

    5. Come over here _____ _____ _____ this bug.

Part Four: **Check Again**

    1. _____

    2. _____

    3. _____

    4. _____

    5. _____

Name _____ Date _____

I-7D. More Practice on Words 11–15

Part One: **Writing Words**

_____ _____ _____ _____ _____

Part Two: **Writing Phrases**

1. _____ _____ _____

2. _____ _____

3. _____ _____

4. _____ _____

5. _____ _____

Part Three: **Completing Sentences with Phrases**

1. _____ _____ that I am going to bed now.

2. I want to _____ _____ _____ airplane.

3. The dog _____ _____ cat are playing.

4. Put your pencil _____ _____ can.

5. The children like to _____ _____ play outside.

Part Four: **Check Again**

1. _____

2. _____

3. _____

4. _____

5. _____

Name _____ Date _____

I-7E. More Practice on Words 16–20

Part One: **Writing Words**

_____ _____ _____ _____ _____

Part Two: **Writing Phrases**

1. _____ _____

2. _____ _____

3. _____ _____ _____

4. _____ _____

5. _____ _____

Part Three: **Completing Sentences with Phrases**

1. I will be right there _____ _____ minutes!

2. I think _____ _____ finish this quickly.

3. Carla is going _____ _____ store.

4. I _____ _____ _____ a book about hurricanes.

5. Alex is feeling very _____ _____ happy now.

Part Four: **Check Again**

1. _____

2. _____

3. _____

4. _____

5. _____

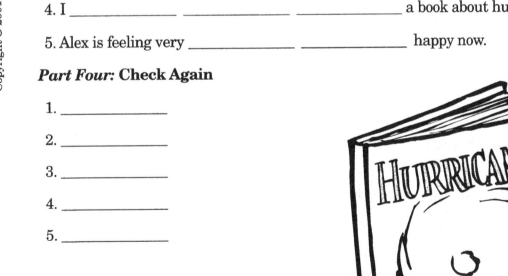

Lesson I-8: Twenty More Words (21–40)

(Writing High-Frequency Words and Phrases)

To the Teacher

This lesson extends Lesson I-7 by introducing students to another group of 20 high-frequency or sight words to read and write. Students may still begin by copying the words, but with practice they should be able to start writing them independently and spelling them correctly. The purpose of this lesson is to give students practice in working with additional sight words.

To the Student

Are you ready for more sight words to write? Here is the list we will be working with in the activities for this lesson:

21. did	25. help	29. me	33. play	37. up
22. fast	26. is	30. no	34. red	38. will
23. for	27. it	31. not	35. see	39. with
24. go	28. little	32. one	36. that	40. work

Remember, you will have to be able to write the word from a word list and also write it correctly when you use it in a sentence.

Worksheets

Answers to Worksheet I-8A:

1. for	5. go	9. it	13. one	17. with
2. help	6. is	10. no	14. see	18. that
3. did	7. little	11. red	15. play	19. up
4. fast	8. me	12. not	16. work	20. will

Answers to Worksheet I-8B:

Part One:

did, fast, for, go, help

Part Two:

1. did it fast	2. go for	3. did help	4. it did	5. go fast

Part Three:

1. (*Prompt*: Fred was having trouble writing with a broken pencil. Would it help him to use a new one?) did help
2. (*Prompt*: Do you think Mark can win the math race worksheet?) did it fast
3. (*Prompt*: Can this car go fast?) go fast
4. (*Prompt*: Do you think the lawn mower cut the grass pretty well?) it did
5. (*Prompt*: What will you and your dog do?) go for

Part Four:

1. fast	2. go	3. help	4. did	5. for

Answers to Worksheet 1-8C:

Part One:

is, it, little, me, no

Part Two:

1. is it   2. is little   3. no little   4. is me   5. it is

Part Three:

1. (*Prompt*: I wonder if it is snowing outside.) it is

2. (*Prompt*: This costume is a real disguise.) is me

3. (*Prompt*: Do you have any little dogs?) no little

4. (*Prompt*: Do you think your parents will let you keep that dog?) is little

5. (*Prompt*: I think this math page is difficult.) Is/is it

Part Four:

1. me   2. little   3. is   4. it   5. no

Answers to Worksheet 1-8D:

Part One:

not, one, play, red, see

Part Two:

1. not see   2. one red   3. not red   4. see and play   5. see a red

Part Three:

1. (*Prompt*: Why are your socks two different colors?) one red

2. (*Prompt*: I can't find my car in the parking lot. Can you see it?) see a red

3. (*Prompt*: Andy is too short to see the television.) not see

4. (*Prompt*: Do you have red hair like your father?) not red

5. (*Prompt*: Are your cousins coming over this weekend?) see and play

Part Four:

1. one   2. see   3. red   4. not   5. play

Answers to Worksheet 1-8E:

Part One:

that, up, will, with, work

Part Two:

1. that will   2. with me   3. will work fast   4. will go up   5. that is a

Part Three:

1. (*Prompt*: What do you think of a clown coming to your birthday party?) that will

2. (*Prompt*: Will the airplane fly high?) will go up

3. (*Prompt*: Will you work quickly?) will work fast

4. (*Prompt*: I don't want to go to the playground alone.) with me

5. (*Prompt*: Do you like my drawing of a horse?) that is a

Part Four:

1. work   2. with   3. that   4. up   5. will

Follow-up Activity

See Lesson I-7.

Name _____ Date _____

I-8A. Fill in the Blanks on Words 21–40

Read each of the five words in each group. Write the word that best completes each sentence. Make sure you write each word correctly.

1. Let's go _____ a walk.

| did   fast   for   go   help |

2. I need _____ on this.

3. Who _____ all of their homework?

4. My dog can run _____.

5. I wish we could _____ swimming.

6. What _____ this a picture of?

| is   it   little   me   no |

7. See the cute _____ kitten!

8. This is a picture of _____.

9. Do you think _____ will rain today?

10. There is _____ one who has a dollar today.

11. I like my new _____ wagon.

| not   one   play   red   see |

12. You are _____ supposed to climb on the chair.

13. I have _____ sister.

14. I can not _____ out of the window.

15. Let's _____ with our new toys.

16. We have to do our _____ at school.

| that   up   will   with   work |

17. Will you play _____ me?

18. My mom said _____ we should come right home.

19. The nest is _____ in the tree.

20. Do you think Dad _____ come to the game?

Name _____ Date _____

I-8B. More Practice on Words 21–25

Part One: Writing Words

_____ _____ _____ _____ _____

Part Two: Writing Phrases

1. _____ _____ _____

2. _____ _____

3. _____ _____

4. _____ _____

5. _____ _____

Part Three: Completing Sentences with Phrases

1. It _____ _____ Fred to use a new pencil.

2. Mark _____ _____ _____ so he won.

3. This car can _____ _____.

4. I think _____ _____ a good job.

5. My dog and I will _____ _____ a nice long walk.

Part Four: Check Again

1. _____

2. _____

3. _____

4. _____

5. _____

Name _____ Date _____

I-8C. More Practice on Words 26–30

Part One: **Writing Words**

_____   _____   _____   _____   _____

Part Two: **Writing Phrases**

1. _____ _____

2. _____ _____

3. _____ _____

4. _____ _____

5. _____ _____

Part Three: **Completing Sentences with Phrases**

1. Tell me if _____ _____ snowing outside.

2. No one will know it _____ _____ in this costume.

3. There are _____ _____ dogs in this house.

4. We can keep that dog if it _____ _____.

5. This math is hard. _____ _____ too hard for you?

Part Four: **Check Again**

1. _____

2. _____

3. _____

4. _____

5. _____

Name _____ Date _____

I-8D. More Practice on Words 31–35

Part One: **Writing Words**

_____ _____ _____ _____ _____

Part Two: **Writing Phrases**

1. _____ _____

2. _____ _____

3. _____ _____

4. _____ _____ _____

5. _____ _____ _____

Part Three: **Completing Sentences with Phrases**

1. I have only _____ _____ sock.

2. I can _____ _____ _____ car in the parking lot.

3. Andy can _____ _____ the TV.

4. My hair is _____ _____.

5. This weekend we are going to _____ _____ _____ with my cousins.

Part Four: **Check Again**

1. _____

2. _____

3. _____

4. _____

5. _____

I-8E. More Practice on Words 36–40

Part One: **Writing Words**

_____ _____ _____ _____ _____

Part Two: **Writing Phrases**

1. _____ _____

2. _____ _____

3. _____ _____ _____

4. _____ _____ _____

5. _____ _____ _____

Part Three: **Completing Sentences with Phrases**

1. I think _____ _____ be a lot of fun!

2. The airplane _____ _____ _____ very high.

3. I promise we _____ _____ so we can play.

4. Please go _____ _____ to the playground.

5. I think _____ _____ _____ nice drawing of a horse!

Part Four: **Check Again**

1. _____

2. _____

3. _____

4. _____

5. _____

Lesson I-9: Another Group of Twenty Words (41–60)

(Writing High-Frequency Words and Phrases)

To the Teacher

This lesson basically follows the same format as the previous two lessons. The emphasis is on writing and spelling the targeted words correctly; however, being able to read the words quickly will assist with writing them. Students who are good readers will quickly recognize when a word "looks" right, and this will help them with their writing. The purpose of this lesson is to provide students with activities to use these high-frequency words.

To the Student

We have another group of 20 important words to learn how to write. They are:

41. are	45. do	49. good	53. my	57. what
42. away	46. down	50. he	54. now	58. who
43. big	47. eat	51. jump	55. she	59. yes
44. but	48. funny	52. make	56. went	60. you

Worksheets

Answers to Worksheet I-9A:

1. do	5. big	9. down	13. my	17. you
2. away	6. good	10. eat	14. jump	18. yes
3. but	7. he	11. make	15. now	19. who
4. are	8. funny	12. she	16. went	20. what

Answers to Worksheet I-9B:

Part One:

are, away, big, but, do

Part Two:

1. are away	2. ride the big	3. but we can	4. do it	5. the big red

Part Three:

1. (*Prompt:* It's hard; do you think we can do it?) do it
2. (*Prompt:* Which sled do you want to ride on?) the big red
3. (*Prompt:* Where are your parents?) are away
4. (*Prompt:* Which pony do you want to ride?) ride the big
5. (*Prompt:* Where can we play?) but we can

Part Four:

1. big	2. but	3. do	4. away	5. are

Answers to Worksheet I-9C:

Part One:

down, eat, funny, good, he

Part Two:

1. down to eat	2. is a funny	3. is a good	4. he can help	5. eat a little

Part Three:

1. (*Prompt*: Do I have to eat everything on my plate?) eat a little

2. (*Prompt*: What is your little brother doing?) he can help

3. (*Prompt*: Does your family eat together?) down to eat

4. (*Prompt*: What is that clown's name?) is a funny

5. (*Prompt*: Do you like that book?) is a good

Part Four:

| 1. down | 2. funny | 3. he | 4. good | 5. eat |

Answers to Worksheet I-9D:

Part One:

jump, make, my, now, she

Part Two:

| 1. jump in | 2. make a big | 3. my two | 4. now we can | 5. she is away |

Part Three:

1. (*Prompt*: Do you want to go in the pool?) jump in

2. (*Prompt*: Do you like the way you look?) my two

3. (*Prompt*: What will you do in the pool?) make a big

4. (*Prompt*: What are you going to do while your mother is gone?) she is away

5. (*Prompt*: When do you get to play?) now we can

Part Four:

| 1. she | 2. now | 3. jump | 4. make | 5. my |

Answers to Worksheet I-9E:

Part One:

went, what, who, you, are

Part Two:

| 1. went for help | 2. what I can | 3. who said | 4. you can come | 5. yes I will |

Part Three:

1. (*Prompt*: What did the police officer do when he saw the accident?) went for help

2. (*Prompt*: Someone told everyone to come in.) who said

3. (*Prompt*: Can we come over after school?) you can come

4. (*Prompt*: Are you having trouble with something?) what I can

5. (*Prompt*: Debby, are you worried that I won't bring you a present for your birthday?) yes, I will

Part Four:

| 1. who | 2. what | 3. yes | 4. went | 5. you |

Follow-up Activity

See Lesson I-7.

Name _____ Date _____

I-9A. Fill-in-the-Blank on Words 41–60

Read each of the five words in each group. Write the word that best completes each sentence. Make sure you write each word correctly.

1. Did you _____ all of your homework?

are away big but do

2. My cat ran _____ again.

3. I would like to come over, _____ I can't.

4. How _____ you today?

5. That is a _____ book for you to read.

6. This is a _____ dinner.

down eat funny good he

7. My father said that _____ would play with me.

8. That is a very _____ clown.

9. Make the dog get _____ from the couch.

10. I love to _____ pizza.

11. I hope my mom will _____ a cake for dinner.

jump make my now she

12. I hope _____ will hurry with that cake.

13. I like it when _____ mom cooks.

14. I can _____ really high.

15. Is it time to eat _____?

16. My brother _____ to the store.

went what who you yes

17. I told _____ the answer.

18. Can you come over—_____ or no?

19. Tell me _____ is my secret pal.

20. Please tell me _____ is in the box.

Name _____ Date _____

I-9B. More Practice on Words 41–45

Part One: **Writing Words**

_____ _____ _____ _____ _____

Part Two: **Writing Phrases**

1. _____ _____

2. _____ _____ _____

3. _____ _____ _____

4. _____ _____

5. _____ _____ _____

Part Three: **Completing Sentences with Phrases**

1. We can _____ _____ if we try.

2. I want to ride on _____ _____ _____ sled.

3. My mom and dad _____ _____ on a trip.

4. I want to _____ _____ _____ pony.

5. We can not go outside, _____ _____ _____ still play inside.

Part Four: **Check Again**

1. _____

2. _____

3. _____

4. _____

5. _____

Name _____ Date _____

I-9C. More Practice on Words 46–50

Part One: **Writing Words**

_____ _____ _____ _____ _____

Part Two: **Writing Phrases**

1. _____ _____ _____

2. _____ _____ _____

3. _____ _____ _____

4. _____ _____ _____

5. _____ _____ _____

Part Three: **Completing Sentences with Phrases**

1. You should _____ _____ _____ of everything on your plate.

2. My little brother thinks _____ _____ _____ my dad.

3. My whole family sat _____ _____ _____ dinner.

4. Big Happy Face _____ _____ _____ name for a clown.

5. This _____ _____ _____ book to read.

Part Four: **Check Again**

1. _____

2. _____

3. _____

4. _____

5. _____

Name _____ Date _____

I-9D. More Practice on Words 51–55

Part One: **Writing Words**

_____ _____ _____ _____ _____

Part Two: **Writing Phrases**

1. _____ _____

2. _____ _____ _____

3. _____ _____

4. _____ _____ _____

5. _____ _____ _____

Part Three: **Completing Sentences with Phrases**

1. I hope we can _____ _____ the pool.

2. Sometimes I don't like _____ _____ ears.

3. We are going to _____ _____ _____ splash!

4. My mother said while _____ _____ _____ we must be good.

5. We did our homework, so _____ _____ _____ play.

Part Four: **Check Again**

1. _____

2. _____

3. _____

4. _____

5. _____

Name _____ Date _____

I-9E. More Practice on Words 56–60

Part One: **Writing Words**

_____ _____ _____ _____ _____

Part Two: **Writing Phrases**

1. _____ _____ _____

2. _____ _____ _____

3. _____ _____

4. _____ _____ _____

5. _____ _____ _____

Part Three: **Completing Sentences with Phrases**

1. The police officer _____ _____ _____.

2. I want to know _____ _____ we should come in now.

3. My mother said that _____ _____ _____ over after school.

4. I want to know _____ _____ _____ do to help you.

5. Debby, _____, _____ _____ bring you a present.

Part Four: **Check Again**

1. _____

2. _____

3. _____

4. _____

5. _____

Part Three:

1. (*Prompt:* What do you like to do in winter?) like to make
2. (*Prompt:* Where did your sister go?) had to go
3. (*Prompt:* Do you think the movie will make you laugh?) laugh at the
4. (*Prompt:* How will Sharon help with the story?) has a good
5. (*Prompt:* Why isn't your aunt here?) but she

Part Four:

1. laugh	2. like	3. had	4. has	5. but

Answers to Worksheet I-10D:

Part One:

pretty, put, ran, saw, soon

Part Two:

1. did a pretty good	2. put it down	3. ran to the	4. saw a big	5. soon we will

Part Three:

1. (*Prompt:* What did you see at the zoo?) saw a big
2. (*Prompt:* How did the students do on the test?) did a pretty good
3. (*Prompt:* Where did your sister go in such a hurry?) ran to the
4. (*Prompt:* When are we going home?) soon we will
5. (*Prompt:* What does the dog have in his mouth?) put it down

Part Four:

1. pretty	2. soon	3. ran	4. put	5. saw

Answers to Worksheet I-10E:

Part One:

there, they, walk, was, white

Part Two:

1. go there	2. they have a	3. walk to the	4. was funny	5. big white

Part Three:

1. (*Prompt:* Where is the class going?) walk to the
2. (*Prompt:* Why are your neighbors nice?) they have a
3. (*Prompt:* Where do you go in the summer?) go there
4. (*Prompt:* Why are you laughing?) was funny
5. (*Prompt:* What are you looking at?) big white

Part Four:

1. white	2. there	3. they	4. was	5. walk

Follow-up Activity

See Lesson I-7.

Lesson I-10: Yet Another Group of Twenty Words
(61–80) (Writing High-Frequency Words and Phrases)

To the Teacher

This is the fourth group of sight words for students to work on. Students continue to read the words in lists and become familiar with how they look. The purpose of this lesson is to provide students with more opportunities to write useful words and phrases.

To the Student

This group of sight words is:

61. all	65. got	69. like	73. ran	77. they
62. as	66. had	70. but	74. saw	78. walk
63. by	67. has	71. pretty	75. soon	79. was
64. come	68. laugh	72. put	76. there	80. white

Worksheets

Answers to Worksheet I-10A:

1. as	5. by	9. has	13. saw	17. walk
2. all	6. laugh	10. like	14. pretty	18. there
3. come	7. but	11. ran	15. put	19. was
4. got	8. had	12. soon	16. white	20. they

Answers to Worksheet I-10B:

Part One:

all, as, by, come, got

Part Two:

1. all of you	2. as big as	3. by the	4. come to the	5. got in the

Part Three:

1. (*Prompt:* We're going to a game. Want to join us?) come to the
2. (*Prompt:* What did Mom say to you before she left?) all of you
3. (*Prompt:* How tall are you?) as big as
4. (*Prompt:* Where is the flower pot?) by the
5. (*Prompt:* What got your car all dirty?) got in the

Part Four:

1. got	2. come	3. all	4. by	5. as

Answers to Worksheet I-10C:

Part One:

had, has, laugh, like, but

Part Two:

1. had to go	2. has a good	3. laugh at the	4. like to make	5. but she

Name _____ Date _____

I-10A. Fill in the Blanks on Words 61–80

Read each of the five words in each group. Write the word that best completes each sentence. Make sure you write each word correctly.

1. I am almost _____ tall as my brother.

2. We can't leave until we are _____ here.

3. What time will you _____ home?

4. I never _____ the letter you mailed.

5. Please be home _____ 5 o'clock.

all   as   by   come   got

6. The clown made me _____ .

7. I would like to buy the toy, _____ I don't have enough money.

8. The boy _____ fun at the party.

9. No one here _____ a pencil.

10. I _____ you!

but   had   has   laugh   like

11. My dog _____ away.

12. I hope he will come home _____ .

13. I _____ a good movie last night.

14. You are very _____ .

15. My mother _____ the milk in the refrigerator.

pretty   put   ran   saw   soon

16. My favorite cake is _____ .

17. Let's go for a _____ in the park.

18. Put your books over _____ .

19. My sister _____ taking a nap.

20. My mother and father think _____ are lucky.

there   they   walk   was   white

Name _____ Date _____

I-10B. More Practice on Words 61–65

Part One: **Writing Words**

_____ _____ _____ _____ _____

Part Two: **Writing Phrases**

1. _____ _____ _____

2. _____ _____ _____

3. _____ _____

4. _____ _____ _____

5. _____ _____ _____

Part Three: **Completing Sentences with Phrases**

1. I hope you will _____ _____ _____ game with us.

2. I want _____ _____ _____ to be good while I am gone.

3. Are you _____ _____ _____ your father now?

4. The flowerpot is _____ _____ back steps.

5. My muddy dog _____ _____ _____ car.

Part Four: **Check Again**

1. _____

2. _____

3. _____

4. _____

5. _____

Name _____ Date _____

I-10C. More Practice on Words 66–70

Part One: **Writing Words**

_____ _____ _____ _____ _____

Part Two: **Writing Phrases**

1. _____ _____ _____

2. _____ _____ _____

3. _____ _____ _____

4. _____ _____ _____

5. _____ _____

Part Three: **Completing Sentences with Phrases**

1. I would _____ _____ _____ a snowman.

2. My sister _____ _____ _____ to the dentist.

3. We are going to _____ _____ _____ funny movie.

4. Sharon _____ _____ _____ idea for a story.

5. My aunt was going to come, _____ _____ had a flat tire on her car.

Part Four: **Check Again**

1. _____

2. _____

3. _____

4. _____

5. _____

Name _____ Date _____

I-10D. More Practice on Words 71–75

Part One: **Writing Words**

_____ _____ _____ _____ _____

Part Two: **Writing Phrases**

1. _____ _____ _____ _____

2. _____ _____ _____

3. _____ _____ _____

4. _____ _____ _____

5. _____ _____ _____

Part Three: **Completing Sentences with Phrases**

1. We _____ _____ _____ elephant at the zoo.

2. The students _____ _____ _____ _____ job on the test.

3. My sister _____ _____ _____ store to get an apple.

4. Very _____ _____ _____ be going home.

5. Make the dog _____ _____ _____.

Part Four: **Check Again**

1. _____

2. _____

3. _____

4. _____

5. _____

Name _____ Date _____

I-10E. More Practice on Words 76–80

Part One: **Writing Words**

_____ _____ _____ _____ _____

Part Two: **Writing Phrases**

1. _____ _____

2. _____ _____ _____

3. _____ _____ _____

4. _____ _____

5. _____ _____

Part Three: **Completing Sentences with Phrases**

1. Our class will _____ _____ _____ library.

2. My neighbors are nice because _____ _____ _____ pool we can use.

3. We like to _____ _____ in the summer.

4. The clown _____ _____.

5. I like that _____ _____ cloud in the sky.

Part Four: **Check Again**

1. _____

2. _____

3. _____

4. _____

5. _____

Lesson I-11: A Final Group of Twenty Words (81–100)

(Writing High-Frequency Words and Phrases)

To the Teacher

Here is another group of important, useful sight words for students to write and use. The purpose of this lesson is to provide students with activities to use these words.

To the Student

This group of words consists of:

81. am	85. give	89. his	93. old	97. thank
82. an	86. going	90. know	94. please	98. then
83. black	87. her	91. let	95. so	99. too
84. call	88. him	92. new	96. take	100. yellow

Worksheets

Answers to Worksheet I-11A:

1. give	5. an	9. her	13. let	17. yellow
2. black	6. going	10. him	14. old	18. too
3. call	7. his	11. please	15. new	19. thank
4. am	8. know	12. so	16. take	20. then

Answers to Worksheet I-11B:

Part One:

am, an, black, call, give

Part Two:

1. am a good	2. make an	3. black and white	4. call me	5. give it to me

Part Three:

1. (*Prompt:* Will you talk to someone tonight?) call me
2. (*Prompt:* Are you a good runner?) am a good
3. (*Prompt:* Do you think Mom will cook something good tonight?) make an
4. (*Prompt:* What does your new kitten look like?) black and white
5. (*Prompt:* I am missing my pencil.) give it to me

Part Four:

1. give	2. black	3. an	4. am	5. call

Answers to Worksheet I-11C:

Part One:

going, her, him, his, know

Part Two:

1. going to get	2. has her	3. go with him	4. one of us	5. know if we

Part Three:

1. (*Prompt:* Why are you holding John's shoe?) one of his
2. (*Prompt:* What time are we leaving?) know if we
3. (*Prompt:* Where does Dad want us to go?) go with him
4. (*Prompt:* Is Mom driving a new car?) has her
5. (*Prompt:* What are you going shopping for?) going to get

Part Four:

1. going   2. know   3. her   4. him   5. his

Answers to Worksheet I-11D:

Part One:

let, new, old, please, so

Part Two:

1. let me   2. a new one   3. an old   4. please do not   5. so we can

Part Three:

1. (*Prompt:* That box looks very heavy.) let me
2. (*Prompt:* Which book would you like?) a new one
3. (*Prompt:* What rule did the bus driver tell you?) please do not
4. (*Prompt:* What is your house like?) an old
5. (*Prompt:* Why are we supposed to write neatly?) so we can

Part Four:

1. old   2. new   3. so   4. please   5. let

Answers to Worksheet I-11E:

Part One:

take, thank, then, too, yellow

Part Two:

1. take it   2. thank you   3. then we will   4. too far   5. white and yellow

Part Three:

1. (*Prompt:* Why is your teacher so happy?) white and yellow
2. (*Prompt:* Where is that note supposed to go?) take it
3. (*Prompt:* How can you be polite?) thank you
4. (*Prompt:* Do you live close to school?) too far
5. (*Prompt:* Are we going outside after lunch?) then we will

Part Four:

1. take   2. too   3. thank   4. then   5. yellow

Follow-up Activity

See Lesson I-7.

I-11A. Fill in the Blanks on Words 81–100

Read each of the five words in each group. Write the word that best completes each sentence. Make sure you write each word correctly.

am   an   black   call   give

1. Please _____ me a minute to get my stuff.

2. That is a beautiful _____ cat.

3. I hope my friend will _____ me tonight.

4. I _____ so sleepy!

5. Do you have _____ apple that I can eat?

going   her   him   his   know

6. We are all _____ on a field trip to Chicago.

7. Tell John that _____ mother is here to get him.

8. I _____ how to spell all of my spelling words this week.

9. My mother thinks that _____ dress is too old.

10. Someone told Pete that this jacket belongs to _____.

let   new   old   please   so

11. Would you _____ pass the carrots?

12. I am _____ tired, I think I will go to bed.

13. I will _____ you use my bicycle if you are careful.

14. This game is very _____, so I'll throw it away.

15. I hope we can buy a _____ game now.

take thank then too yellow

16. I have to _____ my library books back.

17. What a pretty _____ flower.

18. May my little brother go with us to the movies, _____?

19. I must be sure to _____ my aunt for the money.

20. First we have to do our work, and _____ we can play.

Name _____ Date _____

I-11B. More Practice on Words 81–85

Part One: **Writing Words**

_____ _____ _____ _____ _____

Part Two: **Writing Phrases**

1. _____ _____ _____

2. _____ _____

3. _____ _____ _____

4. _____ _____

5. _____ _____ _____ _____

Part Three: **Completing Sentences with Phrases**

1. I hope my friend will _____ _____ tonight.

2. I _____ _____ _____ runner.

3. Maybe Mom will _____ _____ apple pie.

4. My new kitten is _____ _____ _____.

5. If you have my pencil, please _____ _____ _____ _____.

Part Four: **Check Again**

1. _____

2. _____

3. _____

4. _____

5. _____

Name _____ Date _____

I-11C. More Practice on Words 86–90

Part One: **Writing Words**

_____ _____ _____ _____ _____

Part Two: **Writing Phrases**

1. _____ _____ _____

2. _____ _____

3. _____ _____ _____

4. _____ _____ _____

5. _____ _____ _____

Part Three: **Completing Sentences with Phrases**

1. This is _____ _____ _____ shoes.

2. Do you _____ _____ _____ are leaving at 3 o'clock?

3. Dad wants us to _____ _____ _____ to the store.

4. Mom _____ _____ new car today.

5. I am _____ _____ _____ a new basketball.

Part Four: **Check Again**

1. _____

2. _____

3. _____

4. _____

5. _____

Name _____ Date _____

I-11D. More Practice on Words 91–95

Part One: **Writing Words**

_____ _____ _____ _____ _____

Part Two: **Writing Phrases**

1. _____ _____

2. _____ _____ _____

3. _____ _____

4. _____ _____ _____

5. _____ _____ _____

Part Three: **Completing Sentences with Phrases**

1. I wish you would _____ _____ help you carry that box.

2. Would you like an old book or _____ _____ _____?

3. The bus driver said, "_____ _____ _____ stand up."

4. We live in _____ _____ house.

5. Please write neatly _____ _____ _____ read what you
   wrote.

Part Four: **Check Again**

1. _____

2. _____

3. _____

4. _____

5. _____

Name _____ Date _____

I-11E. More Practice on Words 96–100

Part One: **Writing Words**

_____ _____ _____ _____ _____

Part Two: **Writing Phrases**

1. _____ _____

2. _____ _____

3. _____ _____ _____

4. _____ _____

5. _____ _____ _____

Part Three: **Completing Sentences with Phrases**

1. My teacher loves the _____ _____ _____ flowers.

2. I see that you have a note. Would you _____ _____ to the office?

3. Always say please and _____ _____ to people.

4. My family lives _____ _____ from school to walk there.

5. We will eat lunch inside, and _____ _____ _____ go outdoors
   for recess.

Part Four: **Check Again**

1. _____

2. _____

3. _____

4. _____

5. _____

Lesson I-12: Dictated Sentences with High-Frequency Words (Writing High-Frequency Words and Phrases)

To the Teacher

Students should now feel they have the ability to write many common words. While our hope is that they will take this ability and write, write, write, the reality is that many students need confidence-building activities to gain a feeling of competency in their writing. While dictated sentences may seem stiff ("Who really talks like that?"), it is a way for students to drill and practice those commonly used words. The purpose of this lesson is to provide both students and teacher with sample sentences that students can learn by drill or rote to use high-frequency words in their writing.

To the Student

You know how to spell and write a lot of common words. When you put a group of words together to make sense or say something, you have made a sentence. Soon you will be writing your own sentences, and you may be writing your own right now, but I would like you to be able to write some dictated sentences that use these common words. **The rule is: Every word has to be spelled correctly!**

There are different ways to learn how to write and spell words. Some people learn best when they can see the word. Others like to spell and say each letter out loud. Some people need to write the word over and over so that their hands can write the words practically all by themselves. Maybe you need to move around while you are spelling and make the letters in the air. Find out how you are best able to learn to spell and write words.

Here is another rule: Once you learn to spell or write a word correctly, you have to spell or write it correctly all the time. That means you can't spell it correctly on a spelling test on Friday and then on Saturday forget you ever saw it. That means you can't only spell it in these sentences; you have to spell it correctly *whenever* you write that word. Once you learn to spell a word, make your brain take a picture of it and drill it into your head! Now you *know* that word! It's a word you know how to spell—forever!

With those rules in mind, I would like to challenge you to learn to write these sentences correctly. Maybe you want to learn them in groups of three or five; maybe you can pass half of them right now; maybe there are a few words that are "sticky" for you and you need to learn how to spell them. We will come up with a plan for you to conquer these sentences!

Worksheets

Answers to Worksheet I-12A:

Part One:

1. look, the	3. want two	5. said, can run	7. can, here
2. Come, get this	4. run, the ride	6. Look in, well	

Answers to Worksheet I-12B:

Part One:

1. will work, you	3. will, for	5. is, little red	7. See, up
2. did go fast	4. will not play	6. No, play	

Answers to Worksheet I-12C:

Part One:

1. are, funny
2. Who, away
3. are big, are good
4. He, eat
5. What, she
6. Make, jump
7. Yes, funny

Answers to Worksheet I-12D:

Part One:

1. put, pretty white, there
2. come as fast
3. They, laugh
4. walk by, the
5. saw, got it
6. one, pretty, but
7. ran fast
8. was little but, am big

Answers to Worksheet I-12E:

Part One:

1. going with her
2. Give, call, know
3. Please take, black, go
4. Thank, new yellow
5. him, too old, play
6. Eat an, then, jump

Follow-up Activity

As students add more words to their written vocabulary, have them come up with their own "silly sentences" using these words. As long as the sentence makes sense grammatically, it will be okay for a learning sentence. Students will enjoy writing their own and sharing them with each other. (Obviously, these 100 high-frequency words compose only a small fraction of the words students will need to express themselves and continue to mature as writers. Consider these lessons of 100 words only a brief sample of how activities can be written and adapted to help students learn to write these words.)

I-12A. Sentences to Read, Copy, and Write (Words 1–20)

Part One:

1. I can look at the cat.

   I can _____ at _____ cat.

2. Come here and get this.

   _____ here and_____ _____.

3. I want two dogs.

   I _____ _____ dogs.

4. I can run to the ride.

   I can _____ to _____ _____.

5. I said we can run.

   I _____ we _____ _____.

6. Look in the well.

   _____ _____ the _____.

7. A cat can come here.

   A cat _____ come _____.

Word Bank:	**cat**	**dogs**

Part Two: Cover the top. Be ready to write the sentences.

1. _____

2. _____

3. _____

4. _____

5. _____

6. _____

7. _____

I-12B. Sentences to Read, Copy, and Write (Words 21–40)

Part One:

| Word Bank: | **car** | **game** |

1. I will work with you.

   I _____ _____ with _____.

2. The car did go fast.

   The car _____ _____ _____.

3. I will go for help.

   I _____ go_____ help.

4. I will not play that game.

   I _____ _____ _____ that game.

5. It is a little red car.

   It _____ a _____ _____ car.

6. No one will play.

   _____ one will _____.

7. See me go up.

   _____ me go _____.

Part Two: Cover the top. Be ready to write the sentences.

1. _____
2. _____
3. _____
4. _____
5. _____
6. _____
7. _____

I-12C. Sentences to Read, Copy, and Write (Words 41–60)

Part One:

1. You are my funny toy.

   You _____ my _____ toy.

2. Who went away?

   _____ went _____?

3. You are big but you are good.

   You _____ _____ but

   you _____ _____.

4. He can eat now.

   _____ can _____ now.

5. What can she do?

   _____ can _____ do?

6. Make the dog jump down.

   _____ the dog _____ down.

7. Yes, you are funny.

   _____, you are _____.

> **Word Bank:** **toy**

Part Two: Cover the top. Be ready to write the sentences.

1. _____

2. _____

3. _____

4. _____

5. _____

6. _____

7. _____

Name _____ Date _____

I-12D. Sentences to Read, Copy, and Write (Words 61–80)

Part One:

1. I put the pretty white cat there.

   I _____ the _____ _____ cat _____.

2. I will come as fast as I can.

   I will _____ _____ _____ as I can.

3. They like to laugh.

   _____ like to _____.

4. I had to walk by all the trees.

   I had to _____ _____

   all _____ trees.

5. He saw that you got it.

   He _____ that you _____ _____.

6. No one has a pretty cat but you.

   No _____ has a _____

   cat _____ you.

7. He ran fast.

   He _____ _____.

8. I was little but now I am big.

   I _____ _____ _____ now I _____ _____.

Word Bank:	cat	trees

Part Two: Cover the top. Be ready to write the sentences.

1. _____

2. _____

3. _____

4. _____

5. _____

6. _____

7. _____

8. _____

I-12E. Sentences to Read, Copy, and Write (Words 81–100)

Part One:

Word Bank:	**car** **tell** **egg**

1. I am going with her.

   I am _____ _____ _____.

2. Give me a call and let me know.

   _____ me a _____ and

   let me _____.

3. Please take his black car so I can go.

   _____ _____ his _____

   car so I can _____.

4. Thank you for the new yellow car.

   _____ you for the _____

   _____ car.

5. Tell him he is too old to play.

   Tell _____ he is _____ _____ to _____.

6. Eat an egg, then you can jump.

   _____ _____ egg, _____ you can _____.

Part Two: Cover the top. Be ready to write the sentences.

1. _____

2. _____

3. _____

4. _____

5. _____

6. _____

Lesson I-13: -ould and -n't

(Writing High-Frequency Words and Phrases)

To the Teacher

Certain words are difficult for anyone to spell because they are longer than four letters and do not follow phonetic rules. Still, they are useful common words and students should write them correctly. The purpose of this, and the following lessons in Part 2, is to give students "tricks" to help them remember ways to spell these tricky words. This lesson gives ideas for the following words: *would, could, should, wouldn't, couldn't, shouldn't*.

To the Student

Part One: would, could, should

We are going to learn how to spell and write six very troublesome words. They are words you probably will use quite often, but they are tricky to spell because you can't hear all of their letters.

Can someone give me a sentence with the word *would* in it? (I *would* like to eat lunch now.) Let's write that on the board. Pay special attention to the word *would*. How about a sentence with the word *could*? *Should*? It's easy to think of sentences because we use these words all the time.

I want you to remember a little saying. If you do something that makes your mom happy, she might come up to you and squeeze your cheek and say, "Oh, you little dear." That might seem a little silly, but it will help you remember these four letters: Oh—o, You—u, Little—l, Dear—d: O-U-L-D. Those are the four tricky letters in *would, could, should*. When you write these words, stop and make your mother happy!

Part Two: n't

I've got some new things to ask you about. I'll write the answers on the board.

Tell me something that you *shouldn't* do on the playground. (You *shouldn't* throw snowballs.) Tell me something you *couldn't* do when you were two years old. (I *couldn't* talk very well.) Now tell me something that you *would not* ever do in a million years. (I *wouldn't* smoke.)

What do these words have in common? (o-u-l-d) They also have the same ending—n't. We're going to call this little syllable "n't" (oont). Whenever I say, "Write oont," I want you to write it just like this: n, apostrophe, t.

Let's practice: oont, oont, oont. Remember to put the apostrophe in the air between the two letters.

When we tack oont (n't) on the end of *would, could,* and *should*, we get: *wouldn't, couldn't, shouldn't*—three more very useful words.

Worksheet

Part One:

Write the words that I say: *would, could, should*. Write the syllable: *oont (n't)*. Write the words: *shouldn't, couldn't, wouldn't*.

Part Two:

Answers:

1. wouldn't	3. couldn't	5. shouldn't
2. should	4. would	6. couldn't

Have students finish the sentences using one of the six words as you read the questions out loud.

7. What is something you shouldn't do on the bus?

8. What is something you would do to help someone?

9. What is something you could make for a sick friend?

10. What is something you could not do if you had a broken arm?

Follow-up Activity

Have a question of the day that encourages students to use these words in response. These words would be good for journal activities because they are so open-ended!

Name _____ Date _____

I-13. Tricks for Tricky Words: ould, n't

***Part One:* Writing Words and Syllables**
Write the words that I say:

_____ _____ _____ _____

_____ _____

***Part Two:* Completing Sentences**
Use the words you wrote above to complete the sentences below.

1. I _____ jump off the roof if someone told me to.

2. He _____ do his homework after school.

3. She _____ drive a car because she's too young.

4. I _____ like to have a puppy.

5. People _____ be mean to other people.

6. Our team _____ make enough baskets to win the game.

Answer the questions that I will ask you.

7. _____

8. _____

9. _____

10. _____

Lesson I-14: More n't Words
(Writing High-Frequency Words and Phrases)

To the Teacher

Lesson I-35 will explain contracted words more thoroughly (he + is = he's, etc.); but a few more words can be learned quickly if students are familiar with *n't* (oont). The purpose of this lesson is to give students practice in hearing and then writing the words *didn't, can't, won't, don't.*

To the Student

Say these words slowly: *wouldn't, couldn't, shouldn't.* What is that syllable you hear at the end? (n't) Who remembers how we write that syllable? (n, apostrophe, t) Here are a few more words that end like that. You might have to listen carefully to hear it, but it's there: *didn't, won't, don't, can't.*

Didn't is easy: did + n't. *Can't* is easy; you know how to write the word *can*: can +'t (Don't put two n's there.) *Won't* and *don't* are rhyming words. If you can write wō as w-o, and dō as d-o, then just add the oont at the end: we + n't, do + n't.

Worksheet

Part One:

Write the words and syllables that I say: did, can, dō, wō, n't, didn't, can't, don't, won't

Part Two:
Answers:

1. don't	3. can't
2. won't	4. didn't

Have students answer the questions you will ask.

5. Did you have homework yesterday? I did…; I didn't…

6. Did you have homework in the summer? I didn't…

7. What is something you can do in the winter?

8. What is something you can't (do in the winter?

9. What is something your teacher will not let you do?

10. What is something you don't have in your desk?

Name _____ Date _____

I-14. Tricks for Tricky Words: n't

Part One: **Writing Words and Syllables**
Write the words that I say:

_____ _____ _____ _____ _____

_____ _____ _____ _____

Part Two: **Completing Sentences**
Use the words you wrote above to complete the sentences below.

1. I _____ have enough money to buy the toy.

2. My mother _____ let me go to the zoo alone.

3. The boy _____ reach the toy car on the top shelf.

4. We _____ have enough time yesterday to watch TV.

Answer the questions that I will ask you.

5. _____

6. _____

7. _____

8. _____

9. _____

10. _____

Lesson I-15: ough (Writing High-Frequency Words and Phrases)

To the Teacher

These are common *ough* words: *thought, through, enough.* There are others, of course, such as *though* and *rough*, but the first three are probably the most commonly used ones in students' writing. The purpose of this lesson is to give students a technique and practice in spelling these words.

To the Student

Here are three more words that are tricky to write, but you will use them a lot in your writing. Does anyone know these words: *thought, through, enough*? When you read them and then look at them, you can see that they are going to be difficult to figure out if you just sound them out.

Here's a clue that might help you to remember the o-u-g-h combination: Remember how you felt when your mom called you a little dear? Well, in this lesson she's going to call you a good helper: Oh—o, You—u, Good—g, Helper—h.

Let's try it: Write the word while I give you the sentence. I *thought* you did a good job. Th—that's easy. Now the four letters: oh you good helper. Then you hear a /t/ at the end, so add the t: th—ough—t. There you go!

The dog jumped *through* the door. Thr—you hear that part. Now the four letters: oh you good helper. That's it.

You can never have *enough* chocolate. E—that's easy. n—you hear that letter. Then the four letters. Good.

Practice writing these words. You may want to take a highlighter and find the 4-letter combination that is hiding in these words.

Worksheet

Part One:

Write the sound combinations and words that I say:

| ough | th | thr | thought | enough | through |
| thr | th | ough | enough | through | thought |

Part Two:

Write each of the target words five times. Then highlight the 4-letter combination in each word.

Part Three:

Answers:

| 1. enough | 3. enough | 5. through |
| 2. through | 4. thought | 6. enough |

Have students answer the questions you will ask.

7. What is something you can't get enough of?

8. What is something that will go through water?

9. What is something you can read through very quickly?

10. What is something you thought would be fun to do?

Follow-up Activity

Encourage students to play "Hangman." They now have some really good words to use!

Name _____ Date _____

I-15. Tricks for Tricky Words: ough

Part One: **Writing Words and Word Parts**

Write the words or parts that I say:

_____ _____ _____ _____ _____

_____ _____ _____ _____ _____

_____ _____

Part Two: **Writing Practice**

Write each of the three words above five times. Highlight the 4-letter combinations.

_____

_____

_____

Part Three: **Completing Sentences**

Use the three words to complete the sentences below.

1. Did you get _____ to eat?

2. The ball went _____ the window.

3. I have had _____ school for one day.

4. I _____ I saw you at the movie.

5. The lion jumped _____ the hoop.

6. We are early _____ to get good seats.

Answer the questions that I will ask you.

7. _____

8. _____

9. _____

10. _____

Lesson I-16: a, e (Writing High-Frequency Words and Phrases)

To the Teacher

This lesson covers seven common words whose primary problem is the vowel sound *a* and *e*. Students want to write *vary* for *very*, *meny* for *many*, *thay* for *they*, and *eny* for *any* with good reason! *Want* and *went* are other confusing words. The purpose of this lesson is to give students memory techniques and practice in writing these words.

To the Student

These are the tricky words we are going to work on today: *any, many, want, went, they, very, every.*

The reason these are tricky words is because of the *a* and the *e*. Sometimes the word will sound like it should have the other letter. We are going to learn them as a string of seven words—the first three will have an *a* in them; the last four will have an *e* in them.

Here we go.

Start with *a*: a. Add an *n*: an. Add a *y*: any. M in front: many.

Tricky *want*. (Think: Do you want an ant? Well, why not!) w + ant.

Change the vowel to *e*: w + e + nt. Now we're into *e* words. *They*, with no *a*: they. *Very*, with no *a*: very. *E* in front: every (Think: *Every* word is *very* hard!)

Let's do a practice run. Number your paper 1–10.

1. Write the word *a*.
2. Write the word *an*.
3. Write the word *any*.
4. Write the word *many*.
5. Write the word *ant*.
6. Write the word *want*. (Do you want an ant? No!) No more *a*'s!
7. Write the word *went*.
8. Write the word *they*.
9. Write the word *very*.
10. Write the word *every*. (Every word is very hard!)

Here are some sentences that will help you practice these words:

1. Every boy is very glad they went.
2. Many girls don't want any candy.
3. ~~They went very fast to get many ants that I want.~~

The many ants went very fast

Worksheet

Part Two: Completing Sentences

Answers:

1. many	3. enough	5. went	7. they
2. very	4. want	6. every	

Part Three: Writing Dictated Sentences

Answers:

1. Every boy is very glad they went.
2. Many girls don't want any candy.
3. They went very fast to get many ants that I want.

Name _____ Date _____

I-16. Tricks for Tricky Words: a, e

Part One: Ten-Word Sequence

1. _____ 2. _____ 3. _____ 4. _____ 5. _____

6. _____ 7. _____ 8. _____ 9. _____ 10. _____

Part Two: Completing Sentences
Use the words you wrote above to complete the sentences below.

1. I hope that _____ people will come to the party.

2. I am _____ glad to see you.

3. I don't have _____ candy to give you.

4. I sure _____ some candy!

5. My mom and dad _____ for a walk.

6. I think _____ student should get good grades.

7. My brothers said that _____ will get me a present.

Part Three: Writing Dictated Sentences

1. _____

2. _____

3. _____

Lesson I-17: igh (Writing High-Frequency Words and Phrases)

To the Teacher

Now that you know about the little dears and the good helpers, can you figure out a trick for words like *might, right, night, high*? How about "I'm a good helper": I'm—I (a), good—g, helper—h. The purpose of this lesson is to give students additional practice in writing difficult but useful words.

To the Student

Remember the *ough* words? What was the trick? (Oh you good helper.) You can use the helper to help you with these words: *might, right, night, light, fight, high.* These words have a helper, too—I'm a good helper!

I'm a = i

good = g

helper = h

The rest of the word is easy to write because you can hear the letters. *Might* is easy: m + igh + t; *right, night, light, fight*—same thing. *high*—just the *h* in front.

Worksheet

Part One:

Write the words and parts that I say:

m, n, r, h, f, l, igh, right, high, might, night, light, fight

Part Two:

1. night	3. high	5. light
2. might	4. right	6. fight

Have students answer the questions you will ask.

7. What do you like to do at night?

8. What might you do at a party?

9. What will happen to you if you fight at school?

10. How do you feel when you know the right answer?

11. What makes it light outside?

12. What is something that is up very high?

Name _____ Date _____

I-17. Tricks for Tricky Words: igh

***Part One:* Writing Words and Parts**
Write the words and parts that I say:

_____ _____ _____ _____ _____

_____ _____ _____ _____ _____

_____ _____ _____

***Part Two:* Completing Sentences**
Use the words you wrote above to complete the sentences below.

1. I'm afraid of the dark at _____.

2. My father said he _____ take us to the game.

3. The bird is up very _____ in the tree.

4. Turn _____ at the comer.

5. Turn on the _____ so we can see.

6. You shouldn't _____ over toys.

Answer the questions that I will ask you.

7. _____

8. _____

9. _____

10. _____

11. _____

12. _____

Lesson I-18: Pronouncing Words "Funny"

(Writing High-Frequency Words and Phrases)

To the Teacher

There are certain words that will "stick" in a student's mind if you simply pronounce them the way they look. One example of this is the word *people*. If you say, "pee-oh-pull" and then add, "That's what it looks like, but we don't spell it that way," students will start to pronounce it so that they can spell it. As long as students know that you are just using tricks to help spell the word, this technique can be helpful. When students start using odd pronunciations when they speak, however, remind them that it's just a trick! The purpose of this lesson is to give students ideas for spelling some words correctly by using the actual letters and the sounds they make.

To the Student

Today I have several words that I want you to pronounce wrong. Yes, you heard me correctly; pronouncing them wrong will help you spell them right. You have to remember, though, that we are just using these funny pronunciations to help spell the words; you know that we don't really talk like that!

Here are the words:

people: Let's talk funny by saying "pee-oh-pull" *Spell it:* pe-o-ple.

answer: Let's talk funny by saying "tell me the an-swer." *Spell it:* an-swer. It has a silly W in there!

together: Let's talk funny by saying "to-get-her" *Spell it:* to-get-her.

friend: Let's talk fumy by saying "fri-end." Here's another trick: We'll meet our friends on *Fri*-day (starts the same); and we will always be friends until the *end* (ends the same way). *Spell it:* fri-end.

was: Let's talk funny by saying "waaaaz." This word might make you cry because it's so weird, so you can put a baby crying in the middle of it ("Wahhhh"). *Spell it:* was.

again: Let's talk funny by saying "a-gain." *Spell it:* a-gain.

Worksheet

Part One:

I'm going to pronounce these words in a "funny" way. But you should write them the way they should be spelled: friend, was, people, answer, together, again.

Part Two:

Answers:

1. was	3. again	5. friend
2. together	4. people	6. answer

Part Three:

Answers:

1. Many people were together.
2. I was with my friend again.
3. People like to tell the answer.
4. He was with many people.
5. We will get together with my friend.

I-18. Tricks for Tricky Words: "Funny Words"

Part One: **Writing Words**

Write the word that I pronounce "funny," but write it correctly!

_____ _____ _____

_____ _____ _____

Part Two: **Completing Sentences**

Use the words you wrote above to complete the sentences below.

1. I _____ very glad to see you.

2. Let's go for a walk _____.

3. I have to write this paper all over _____.

4. Lots of _____ came to watch the circus.

5. You are my best _____.

6. What is the _____ to this math problem?

Part Three: **Writing Dictated Sentences**

1. _____

2. _____

3. _____

4. _____

5. _____

6. _____

Lesson I-19: Question Words
(Writing High-Frequency Words and Phrases)

To the Teacher

Students will find the question words *who, what, when, where, why,* and *how* to be very useful in their writing. There are a few commonalities among these words that can help students write them correctly. The purpose of this lesson is to give students practice in writing these words.

To the Student

Some really important words that you will use often in writing are words that ask and answer questions. They are commonly known as the "question words" and they are: *who, what, when, where, why, how.*

With the exception of *how,* the other five words all begin with *wh.* The tricky thing about this is that it is often pronounced as a *w* sound. The words *who* and *how* are often confused in reading as well as writing. We will work on using and writing these six words as a group.

Use these phrases to help you remember how to spell the words.

who: start with the *wh*; add ooooo like an owl.

what: *What* is on your head? Oh, it's a *hat*!

when: *When* are you going to feed the *hen*?

where: *Where* did you put it? Over *here.*

why: Start with the *wh*; add "y" (says the letter).

how: The /ow/ makes you say "owww!" when it pinches you. (Think of the *h* as a vice!)

Worksheet

Part One:

Write the words that I say: who, what, when, where, why, how

Part Two:
Answers:

1. why	3. when	5. who
2. where	4. how	6. what

Part Three:
Answers:

1. Who told you how to do that?
2. What is that hat for?
3. When is the hen going to eat?
4. Here is where you should be.
5. This is why we try.

Follow-up Activity

Students can write questions beginning with these question words. They may come up with sentences such as: Who has red hair? Where is your favorite place to go? How many people ride the bus to school? And so on.

Name _____ Date _____

I-19. Tricks for Tricky Words: Question Words

Part One: **Writing Words**

Write the words that I say:

_____ _____ _____ _____

_____ _____

Part Two: **Completing Sentences**

Use the words you wrote above to complete the sentences below.

1. Do you know _____ we have to leave right now?

2. I don't remember _____ we were supposed to meet my mom. Was it at the park or at the zoo?

3. We had a good time _____ we went to the zoo.

4. Please show me _____ to make a painting like yours.

5. Everyone _____ has a birthday in February should stand up!

6. I don't know _____ animal is making that noise.

Part Three: **Writing Dictated Sentences**

1. _____

2. _____

3. _____

4. _____

5. _____

Lesson I-20: Confusing Words
(Writing High-Frequency Words and Phrases)

To the Teacher

Certain pairs of words can be very confusing to students, because they sound alike (homonyms: their, there); look very much alike (here, her; where, were); are confusing in their usage (our, are); or are all three (to, too, two)! The purpose of this lesson is to give students strategies to distinguish between confusing groups of words and practice in writing these 19 words correctly.

To the Student

The next group of words that we will work on are pairs of words (except for the *to*'s and the *there*'s which are triplets!) that can be confusing because the words sound alike, look alike, or are used mistakenly—using one when you really should be using the other.

These words are: know/no; knew/new; right/write; here/her; here/hear; where/were; their/they're/there; our/are; to/too/two.

Here are some tricks that might help you.

no—This is easy; opposite of *yes*; easy to write.

know—Whenever it starts with *kn*, it means it's "in your head."

new—This is easy; opposite of old.

knew—Remember, the *kn* means it's "in your head."

write—Think of the *w* at the beginning being written by a big pencil; this word means the pencil is writing something.

right—This word means the other kinds of right (being correct, direction).

hear—This word has a little "ear" in it; that's what you hear with.

here—This is the "other" here; a *place*; put the two *e*'s in the right place.

her—This is the word most likely to be written by mistake when the other two are intended; it's the word that is not a place and doesn't have an ear in it; short little word.

where—This is a *place*; put the two *e*'s in the right place.

were—No *h* in this word; it's not a place.

there—This is a *place*; put the two *e*'s in the right place.

their—This word is talking about people; that little *i* could be a person (the dot is his head).

they're—That apostrophe tells you it's really two words crushed together (more on this in Lesson I-35 on contractions); say the two words slowly: they + are; say them quickly: they're.

are—You can hear the "ar" sound in this word; this is the word you're most likely to use.

our—This word is talking about people; put a smiley face in the *o* to help you remember it's a person.

to—This is the easy one; use this word for "to" unless you have a reason to use something else!

two—This is the numeral 2; think of this as the "to" with a *w* in the middle to split it into two parts; in fact, you can cut the *w* into two parts, too.

too—This is a "to" gone crazy, meaning it's more and more (too fast, too much, too tired); OR it means "also" with that extra "o" hanging around because it wants to come along, too!

Worksheet

Part One:

I will give you some clues to help you write these words correctly.

1. no—opposite of yes (no); 2. the easy "to"—going to the store (to); 3. know, like you know something in your head (know); 4. they're—two words crushed into one: they are (they're); 5. our—talking about a group of people with a smiley face at the beginning (our); 6. the number two—remember to cut the middle letter into two parts (two); 7. are—you can hear the "ar" (are); 8. here—the place, come over here (here); 9. there—the place, go sit over there (there); 10. where—the place, I know where you live (where); 11. too—like too much of something or with the extra *o* that wants to come too (too); 12. hear—you have an ear to hear this word (ear); 13. write—grab your pencil to start writing (write); 14. her—easy, no tricks (her); 15. right—the correct answer or turning right (right); 16. were—looks like *where* but it's not a place so don't put in an *h* (were); 17. their—talking about people, so make sure you see a little person in there (their); 18. new—opposite of old (new); 19. knew—you knew it in your head (knew)

Part Two:

Answers:

1. know	11. right	21. where	31. they're	41. to
2. know	12. write	22. where	32. there	42. two
3. no	13. write	23. were	33. they're	43. too
4. know	14. right	24. where	34. are	44. two
5. no	15. her	25. were	35. are	45. too
6. new	16. here	26. there	36. our	46. to
7. knew	17. hear	27. their	37. our	47. two
8. knew	18. her	28. their	38. are	48. too
9. new	19. hear	29. their	39. our	49. too
10. write	20. here	30. there	40. are	50. too

Part Three:

Answers:

1. They're going to write to us.
2. Her two cars are here.
3. I know our new car was right here.
4. I knew where they put their things.
5. Mine are there, too.
6. No, I can't hear you.
7. Where were you?

Follow-up Activity

These are words that will require practice, practice, and more practice in order for students to become comfortable with writing them and determining which word is used correctly. Daily dictated sentences using these words can be very helpful. Try to have students remember the entire sentence instead of writing them word by word. Don't be afraid to have students repeat writing them often. If a student gets stuck on a particular word, try having him or her recall the entire sentence to put it into a familiar context and jog the memory. Also, having students teach memory tricks to each other or to another student can be helpful to imprint that word.

Name _____ Date _____

I-20. Tricks for Tricky Words: Confusing Words

Part One: Writing Words

I will give you some clues to help you write these words correctly:

1. _____ 2. _____ 3. _____ 4. _____ 5. _____

6. _____ 7. _____ 8. _____ 9. _____ 10. _____

11. _____ 12. _____ 13. _____ 14. _____ 15. _____

16. _____ 17. _____ 18. _____ 19. _____

Part Two: Completing Sentences

Use the words at the top of each group to complete the sentences.

| no   know |

1. I _____ where you live.

2. I don't _____ how to drive a truck.

3. There is _____ person in this room who has an elephant.

4. I think my parents _____ everything about cars.

5. My mother said _____ to my going to the pool.

| knew   new |

6. This is a _____ car.

7. Andrew _____ the answer to the problem.

8. I never _____ you were so smart.

9. Would you like a _____ pencil?

| write   right |

10. Get a pencil and _____ this down.

11. I got the _____ answer.

12. Do you know how to _____ in cursive?

13. I like to _____ letters.

14. Turn _____ when you get up the stairs.

here	hear	her

15. My grandmother likes to listen to _____ radio.

16. Come over _____ right now, please.

17. I can't _____ you.

18. My mother said that _____ favorite food is pizza.

19. I like to _____ you sing.

20. Put that book down right _____ beside me.

where	were

21. I don't know _____ I put my glasses.

22. This is _____ we come to play.

23. I think you _____ late to school.

24. I walk my dog _____ he has room to run.

25. We _____ all laughing at the joke.

they're	there	their

26. Put the book over _____.

27. My neighbors like _____ new boat.

28. The basketball players like _____ new shoes.

29. My parents took _____ new car for a ride.

30. The flowers are _____ by the window.

31. The kids in class think _____ pretty smart.

32. The desk over _____ is mine.

33. I like puppies because _____ so cute.

are	our

34. We _____ going to swim outside.

35. The neighbors next door _____ very nice.

36. This is _____ house.

37. I think _____ dog is going through your garbage.

38. We _____ going to pick it up.

39. I don't want people to see _____ stuff.

40. We _____ going to be more careful next time.

to	too	two

41. I am going _____ the mall tonight.

42. I have only _____ dollars to spend.

43. Would you like to come _____?

44. We will have to leave at _____ o'clock.

45. I hope you are not _____ tired.

46. It's fun _____ shop.

47. I will buy _____ gifts for my friends.

48. I need some shoes, _____.

49. My mother thinks she is _____ tall.

50. This worksheet is _____ long.

Part Three: **Writing Dictated Sentences**

1. _____

2. _____

3. _____

4. _____

5. _____

6. _____

7. _____

Lesson I-21: Having Enough Letters

(Writing High-Frequency Words and Phrases)

To the Teacher

With some longer words, the child may hear and write most of the letters (and even put them in the right order), but may miss a vowel or a doubled consonant. With some of these words, it helps to first "frame the word" by knowing how many letters to expect that word to contain, and then fill in the missing letters and sounds with good guesses. The purpose of this lesson is to provide students with practice in the strategy of considering the word as a whole and then writing the letters. (*Note*: You may need to group the words and teach them over several days as a 6-letter group; 7-letter group, etc. Students may become confused if too much information is presented too quickly.)

To the Student

Some longer words are hard to remember to spell and write correctly because they may have an extra syllable or sound that you don't hear clearly. Instead of trying to listen for each sound and then add the letters, I'm going to give you some ways to remember some commonly used words that might help you remember when to add another letter.

Here are the words we will work with.

Words with 6 letters: *mother, father, animal, around*

Words with 7 letters: *because, picture, watched*

Words with 8 letters: *children*

Words with 9 letters: *important, different*

I will pronounce a word for you and tell you how many letters are in the word. Before you write it, though, draw a blank for each letter. Then add the letters.

mother: 6 letters __ __ __ __ __ __

(Students may begin with the "m," end with "er," and then add other letters.) Remember to put a smile on your mother's face on the letter "o." (Some students will erase the *u* and change it to an *o*, then add the smile!)

father: 6 letters __ __ __ __ __ __

(If students spelled mother correctly, they will probably get most of these letters right.) Remember to thank your father for that nice aaaaaaapple that he gave you! (Check to see if students wrote an *a* instead of an *o* for the second blank!)

animal: 6 letters __ __ __ __ __ __

As you write the word, remember that "i" love animals. When you are done, circle the last two letters of the word and you will find the name of my dog (AL). Check to make sure you have two *a*'s in the word.

around: 6 letters __ __ __ __ __ __

Think of a letter that goes around (the letter o). It might make a loop like a roller coaster. Now, who likes to go around on a roller coaster? (you—u) Finish the word.

Here are some 7-letter words:

because: Watch for two *e*'s; one is at the end.

picture: Think about a camera. I am going to use the letter *t* to remind me to push the button to take the picture. Then, I see that you are (u-r) in my picture.

watched: Think about a stopwatch. Pretend I'm going to start timing you when you get to the letter *t*. (Pretend to click down.) Circle the last two letters of *watched*. Do you see the name of one of my cats? (ED)

Here is my favorite 8-letter word:

children: You can hear these letters if you say the word slowly.

I have two 9-letter words for you:

important: Circle the three letters at the very end and you will find a little creature (ANT). Remember that a tiny little ant is important, especially to another ant.

different: This word sounds like it ends like *important*, but it doesn't; it's different, and ends in a different way. Remember to say all three syllables—diff-er-ent. Check to make sure you have two *e*'s in the word.

Here are some dictated sentences to help you remember to write these words:

1. My mother and father don't want that animal around.

2. We watched the picture because it was good.

3. It is important for children to be different.

Let's do a practice run. Number your paper from 1–10. Make the blanks first, then fill in the words:

(Words with 6 letters) 1. mother, 2. father, 3. animal, 4. around

(Words with 7 letters) 5. because, 6. picture, 7. watched

(Word with 8 letters) 8. children

(Words with 9 letters) 9. important, 10. different

Worksheet

Part One:

Write the words that I say. I will give you a clue as to how many letters: father (6), watched (7), different (9), children (8), important (9), mother (6), picture (7), animal (6), because (7), around (6).

Part Two:

Answers:

1. picture	3. mother	5. around	7. important	9. watched
2. animal	4. father	6. because	8. different	10. children

Part Three:

Answers:

(*Hint*: Watch for 6-letter words.) 1. My mother and father don't want that animal around.

(*Hint*: Watch for 7-letter words.) 2. We watched the picture because it was good.

(*Hint*: Watch for my favorite 8-letter word and 9-letter words.) 3. It is important for children to be different.

Follow-up Activity

Because these words are somewhat longer, every single letter needs to be carefully noted to make sure it's there, first of all, and it is in the right order. These words are good for activities such as crossword puzzles and word searches. Students may enjoy making up their own word-search puzzles with these words hidden inside.

I-21. Tricks for Tricky Words: Having Enough Letters

Part One: **Writing Words**
Write the words that I say.

____ ____ ____ ____ ____ ____

____ ____ ____ ____ ____ ____

____ ____ ____ ____ ____ ____ ____

____ ____ ____ ____ ____ ____ ____

____ ____ ____ ____ ____ ____ ____

____ ____ ____ ____ ____ ____

____ ____ ____ ____ ____ ____

____ ____ ____ ____ ____ ____

____ ____ ____ ____ ____ ____

____ ____ ____ ____ ____

Part Two: **Completing Sentences**
Use the words above to complete the sentences below.

1. I will take a _____ with my camera.

2. An eagle is a beautiful _____.

3. My _____ is a nice lady.

4. I love my _____, too.

5. Let's walk _____ that puddle.

6. I like you _____ you are nice to me.

7. It's very _____ to do your homework.

8. A dog is very _____ from a cat.

9. We _____ the basketball game last night.

10. Many _____ went to the party.

Part Three: **Dictated Sentences**

1. _____

2. _____

3. _____

Lesson I-22: A Few More Tricky Words
(Writing High-Frequency Words and Phrases)

To the Teacher

Once students get used to writing and using high-frequency words in their formal (dictated) and informal (creative) writing, it should become easier and more natural for them to use them correctly in writing. A few more tricky words are now presented with which students seem to have a lot of trouble. The purpose of this lesson is to give students practice in using these words.

To the Student

Here are six more tricky words for you to learn to spell and write correctly.

The first three words are things you do in school: *work, read, and learn*. The next word is how you are doing: *great*. The next one is a word that tells something that everybody has: *birthday*. The last is a word that you can laugh about if you spell it wrong: *girl*. If you spell it *gril*, then you are talking about something on which to cook hamburgers. That could be very embarrassing if you are going to take a grill out on a date or if you call yourself a grill!

Here are some tricks to help you remember how to spell and write these words:

work: Would you like to work *or* go outside and play?

read: I'm not going to read the letter *a* because it's quiet. Then I can figure out the rest of the word. r-e(a)-d

learn: We can learn to spell by using our *ear*.

great: It's great when it's time to *eat*!

girl: I am a girl/I know a girl. Watch for the *i* to come first. (Students will hear the "r" and want to write that first.)

birthday: I love it when I have a birthday. Watch for the *i* to come first.

Worksheet

Part One:

Write the words that I say. I will give you a clue in the sentence. *work* (Would you rather work OR play?), *read* (I am going to read one of the letters VERY QUIETLY), *learn* (I can learn if I use my EAR), *great* (It's great when we get to EAT), *girl* (I am a girl), *birthday* (I have a birthday every year).

Part Two:

Answers:

1. birthday	3. read	5. girl
2. work	4. learn	6. great

Part Three:

Answers:

1. The girl had a birthday.

2. We can all learn to read.

3. This is great work.

Name _____ Date _____

I-22. Tricks for Tricky Words: A Few More Tricky Words

Part One: **Writing Words**

Write the words that I say. I will give you a clue in the sentence.

_____   _____   _____

_____   _____   _____

Part Two: **Completing Sentences**

Use the words above to complete the sentences below.

1. I will wish you a very happy _____.

2. My mother and father both go to _____ every day.

3. I want to _____ that book when you're done.

4. I wish my dog would _____ to walk on a leash.

5. My sister is a nice _____.

6. You did a _____ job on this!

Part Three: **Writing Dictated Sentences**

1. _____

2. _____

3. _____

Lesson I-23: Personal Words
(Writing High-Frequency Words and Phrases)

To the Teacher

Students will have ther own list of high-frequency words. They will have certain words that are important and useful to them. These words might include names of family members and pets, words that reflect personal interests (horse words, truck words), special people or places, and certain phrases they like to use. The purpose of this lesson is to help students make a "word bank" that shows the correct way to spell and write these words.

To the Student

I'll bet if I asked everyone in here who their favorite athlete is, not everyone would have the same person. What about your favorite place to go on vacation? Or the name of your little brother? Or your dog? You can see that everybody has his or her own special words that are important and useful to that individual.

Today I want you to make a "word bank." This is a place where you can put or deposit words that you know you will use a lot. When you are writing and aren't sure how to spell that word, you can go to your word bank and find out. Pretty soon you will realize you don't have to keep looking up the word—you will know how to write it by yourself.

Worksheet

Fill out (with help) the information on the "Personal Information Sheet."

Follow-up Activity

Have students make a booklet with each page designated by a subject (names of pets, favorite foods, etc.). The title page could read: "My Personal Word Book" or "Personal Dictionary." Students will enjoy decorating this book. Students can add to their list as they encounter new words they will need to use often. The booklet should be kept handy so students can refer to it while they are writing.

Name _____ Date _____

I-23. Personal Information Sheet

Names

your name…

names of family members…

friends…

pets…

other names…

Places

where you live…

special places…

vacation places…

places you'd like to travel to…

places you know a lot about…

Things

favorite things…

I know a lot about _____ and these words
will tell about it…

Lesson I-24: Sight-Word Games

(Writing High-Frequency Words and Phrases)

Sight-Word Bingo

Materials:

- reproducible bingo boards with 12 (or 16) squares (see Worksheet I-24A)
- sight-word cards (keep each list separated in an envelope)

Directions:

1. Select 12 (or 16) words from each list and have students write them in random order on the bingo board.
2. Pull a card at random from the envelope. Students should circle, X out, or otherwise highlight each word.
3. A student wins when he or she has 3 (or 4) words across or down. You may want to play for second place or until all students have bingo.
4. Here is a sample group of words: a, and, at, can, come, get, here, I, in, look, ride, run, said, the, this, to, two, want, we, well.

here	I	and	look
come	run	a	get
said	the	at	ride

I-24A. Sight-Word Bingo Boards

Race to the Finish

Materials:

- small drawing of a race car or hot rod for each student (or students can pick a small object to be their marker—a penny, a cute eraser, etc.)
- game board of a race track (see Worksheet I-24B)
- one die
- sight-word cards
- "Oh, No!" cards

Directions:

1. All students begin at the "Start." They take turns rolling the die to move the race car or marker that number of spaces.

2. At every stop, the student has to read and spell three sight-words cards and then return the cards to the pile.

3. If a student lands on an "Oh, no!" space, he or she reads something funny from the "Oh, No!" card pile, laughs, then returns it to the pile.

4. The first student to cross the finish line wins. You can play until all students finish.

"Oh, No" Cards (*Feel free to add your own!*):

1. You run out of gas!

2. You stop to wave to your mom in the stands.

3. You have to slow down for a squirrel.

4. You spin out!

5. Your tire blows out!

6. You roll the car into a ditch.

7. You stop to get a hot dog.

8. You slow down to wave to a friend.

9. You slow down because smoke is coming out of your engine.

10. Your muffler is making funny noises!

Name _____   Date _____

I-24B. Race to the Finish

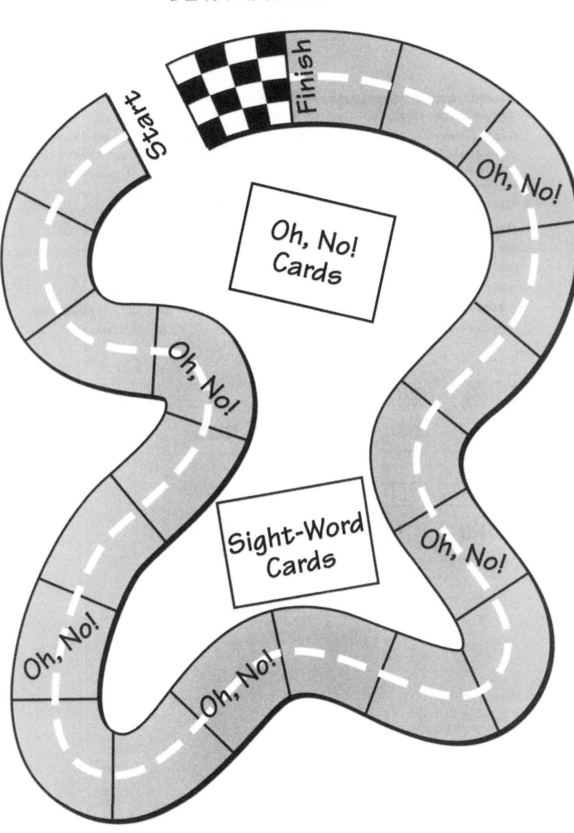

Start

Finish

Oh, No!
Cards

Sight-Word
Cards

Oh, No!

Oh, No!

Oh, No!

Oh, No!

Oh, No!

Sight-Word Shapes
Materials:

- sight-word cards
- reproducible worksheet with shapes of the words for each group of words selected (see Worksheet I-24C)

Directions:

1. Students circle 10 shapes on the worksheet that are going to be their "active" shapes to search. The remaining 10 are not in play for that round.
2. A card is selected from the sight-word pile. Students who have circled a shape that matches that word's shape can go ahead and write the word in the outline. (There may be several possibilities for words and shapes; e.g., *him, her, his* all have the same outline shape.)
3. The first student to have all 10 circled shapes filled in correctly is the winner.
4. You can play to second place or until all students are finished with 10 words.
5. For example: *words*: are, away, big, but, do, down, eat, funny, good, he, jump, make, my, now, she, went, what, who, you, yes.

If you call *big*, the student can write the word because that shape is circled.

If you call *funny*, the student cannot use that word because that shape is not circled.

If you call *he*, the student can write the word. The word *do* could also be used.

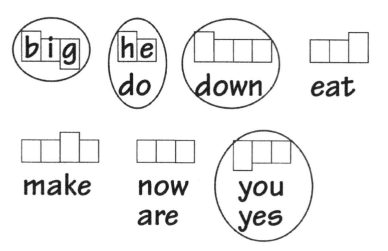

I-24C. Sight-Word Shapes

are	away	big	but	do
down	eat	funny	good	he
jump	make	my	now	she
went	what	who	you	yes

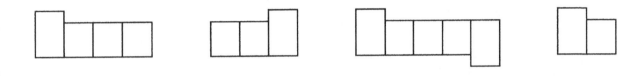

Fill Up the Card

Materials:

- reproducible scorecard (see Worksheet I-24D)
- sight-word cards (can combine several groups of 20 to make a large pool of cards)

Directions:

1. Students fill out blanks (one for each letter) on their scorecards for 6 words. Because there are only two words having one letter (I, a), students probably will assign 2–6 blanks for each word.

2. Sight-word cards are shuffled and placed in the middle. Each player takes a turn picking a card off the top. If he or she can "use" the card to fill in the blanks for one word, he or she writes the word on the card.

3. Play continues to the next person.

4. The winner or winners are the players who have their scorecards completed at the end of each round. This can be played several times with a point going to the winner of each round. The first player to reach 5 points is the "Ultimate Winner."

5. An alternative way to play is to have all players select a card from a pile (spread in a big circle) at the same time. This way the winner or winners are announced at the same time.

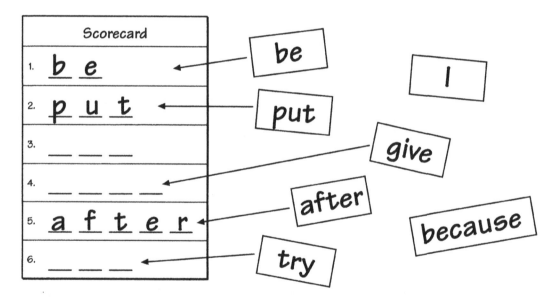

Name _____   Date _____

I-24D. Fill Up the Card: Scorecard

Draw blanks for letters in the spaces below. You should draw between two and six blanks for each word.

Scorecard
1.
2.
3.
4.
5.
6.

Sight-Word Search

Materials:

- newspaper, magazine, or any printed material that can be written on and consumed
- colored highlighters
- list of 20 high-frequency words

Directions:

1. Give each student the same list of words, a highlighter, and a source to search through.

2. Set a timer for 3–5 minutes. Have each student search through his or her magazine to find each word on the list. As students find each word, they should highlight the word and check it off their list.

3. The winner is the first student to find and highlight all 20 of his or her words.

4. An alternative way to play is to have all students search for the same word and record how many times they can find that word in 2 minutes.

5. This can also be played with teams, having students rip out the highlighted word on a page and put it in a central location, calling out what word they found (I found "another"! I found "because"!) The first team to find all the words is the winning team.

6. For example: a ✓ and ✓ at can some get here ✓ I in look

The students (in) Ms. Garcia's science class know all about pressure—not to mention temperature, humidity (and) the other aspects of meteorology—because Ms. Garcia has turned these students into full-fledged weather forecasters.

Ms. Garcia had her students take all they learned (in) class about weather fronts, (and) how pressure systems affect things like temperature and barometric readings, and put it to work. Dividing the class into small groups, she had each pick (a) location across the country and attempt to accurately predict the weather.

Lesson I-25: Writing Color Words

(Increasing Vocabulary Words)

To the Teacher

Students may be able to readily read common color words, but writing them correctly is a different matter. The purpose of this lesson is to provide the students with activities involving basic color words: red, green, yellow, blue, brown, black, pink, white, orange, and purple.

To the Student

Our next series of worksheets and activities is going to be about common color words. I am thinking of ten common colors. Can you help me fill out this chart?

r—red; g—green; y—yellow; bl—blue; br—brown; bl—black; p—pink; p—purple; wh—white; o—orange

Some of these words will be pretty easy to spell and write (red, green, black, pink, etc.), but others will be a little trickier. I bet we can find ways to remember how to spell these tricky words correctly.

First of all, we're going to find one main picture to go with each color. I'll bet you can figure out what I'm thinking by these clues:

red—It's a fruit! (*apple*)

yellow—It's the color of something very hot. (*sun*)

blue—You'd like to dive into this water. (*pool*)

green—Something horses like to eat. (*grass*)

black—Some people think this color is unlucky on this animal. (*cat*)

pink—It's a beautiful color for a bouquet of these. (*flowers*)

orange—It's the name of the color and something you can eat. (*orange*)

purple—The two p's in this word remind me of this purple fruit. (*grapes*)

brown—It's something good to eat for dessert. (*chocolate cake*)

white—This white thing might scare people at Halloween. (*ghost*)

Worksheet

Answers to Worksheet I-25A:

1. pink	4. yellow	7. brown	10. blue
2. white	5. green	8. purple	
3. red	6. black	9. orange	

Answers to Worksheet I-25B:

1. red, apple	4. green, green	7. orange, orange	10. white, ghost
2. yellow, yellow	5. black, black	8. purple, grapes	
3. blue, pool	6. pink, pink	9. cake, brown	

Answers to Worksheet I-25C:

1. pool	3. sun, yellow	5. orange, orange
2. apple	4. grass, green	6. cat

Students' answers for other items will vary.

Answers to Worksheet I-25D:

1. pink	4. green	7. yellow	10. red
2. white	5. blue	8. brown	
3. black	6. orange	9. purple	

Answers to Worksheet I-25E:

```
b  h  y  b  r  o  w  n  l  g  d  m
u  r  e  d  n  t  x  b  b  r  c  p
v  i  l  j  j  c  w  l  o  e  k  u
k  b  l  a  c  k  r  u  s  e  n  r
d  t  o  r  a  n  g  e  q  n  e  p
e  o  w  h  i  t  e  p  y  z  a  l
l  f  m  u  p  i  n  k  f  h  g  e
r  s  t  a  w  x  g  i  y  v  q  p
```

Follow-up Activity

There are many activities students can create and exchange for additional practice. One example is having students design a simple picture and then label what parts should be colored a certain color (e.g., write the word "yellow" on the sun, "brown" on a dog, "red" on a house, and so on). You may want to copy some (those that are clearly labeled and easy to color) for the class.

Name _____ Date _____

I-25A. Associating Colors with Pictures or Symbols

Write the color word to go with each picture.

1. ___ ___ ___ ___ ___ ___

2.  ___ ___ ___ ___ ___

3.  ___ ___ ___

4.  ___ ___ ___ ___ ___ ___

5.  ___ ___ ___ ___ ___

6.  ___ ___ ___ ___ ___

7. ___ ___ ___ ___ ___ ___

8. ___ ___ ___ ___ ___

9. ___ ___ ___ ___ ___ ___

10. ___ ___ ___ ___

yellow

green

pink

black

blue

white

red

brown

orange

purple

I-25B. Writing Color Words in Contex

Write the missing word in each little story. Remember! It won't always be a color word, so read and think carefully.

1. An apple is red.

   I like the _____ apple. An _____ is red.

2. The sun is yellow.

   The _____ sun is hot. The hot sun is _____.

3. The pool is blue.

   I swim in the _____ pool. The _____ is blue.

4. The grass is green.

   I cut the _____ grass. The grass is _____.

5. The cat is black.

   I like the _____ cat. The _____ cat is nice.

6. The flower is pink.

   The _____ flower is pretty. I like the pretty _____ flower.

7. The orange is orange.

   I can eat the _____. The _____ is orange.

8. The grapes are purple.

   I like _____ grapes. I can eat the purple _____.

9. The cake is brown.

   We eat the brown _____. I like the _____ cake.

10. The ghost is white.

    I like the _____ ghost. The white _____ is funny.

Name _____ Date _____

I-25C. What Are These Colors?

Think of different things that are these colors. The word/picture bank will help you get started.

1. What is blue? A _____ is blue.

   A _____

2. What is red? An _____ is red.

   A _____

3. What is yellow? The _____ is _____.

   A _____

4. What is green? The _____ is _____.

   A _____

5. What is orange? An _____ is _____.

   A _____

6. What is black? A _____ is black.

   A _____

Pick two more colors and write your own sentences for them. Use the other side of this sheet for your answers.

grapes   sun   orange   pool   flower   ghost   grass   cake   apple   cat

Name _____ Date _____

I-25D. Complete the Sentence

Circle the word that completes each sentence and write it on the line.

1. A flower is _____.   pynk   bink   pink

2. A ghost is _____.   white   wite   with

3. A cat is _____.   blak   back   black

4. The grass is _____.   gren   green   grene

5. The pool is _____.   bloo   blu   blue

6. An orange is _____.   orang   arange   orange

7. The sun is _____.   yelo   yellow   yello

8. The cake is _____.   bown   borwe   brown

9. The grapes are _____.   perple   purple   pirpel

10. The apple is _____.   red   rade   ride

I-25E. Color Word Search

Find and circle these color words in the grid below. The words go sideways or up-and-down.

green	yellow	pink	black	purple
blue	red	white	brown	orange

b	h	y	b	r	o	w	n	l	g	d	m
u	r	e	d	n	t	x	b	b	r	c	p
v	i	l	j	j	c	w	l	o	e	k	u
k	b	l	a	c	k	r	u	s	e	n	r
d	t	o	r	a	n	g	e	q	n	e	p
e	o	w	h	i	t	e	p	y	z	a	l
l	f	m	u	p	i	n	k	f	h	g	e
r	s	t	a	w	x	g	i	y	v	q	p

Lesson I-26: Writing Number Words

(Increasing Vocabulary Words)

To the Teacher

Writing the number words zero through ten is probably the most useful for students, at least in the beginning stages of writing. The purpose of this lesson is to provide students with practice in writing and using the number words in isolation and context.

To the Student

Who can count to ten? (Let students respond.) I'm going to ask you some questions, and I would like you to give me the number that answers the question.

How many clocks are in the room?

How many boys are in the first row?

How many flags are in the room?

How many live gorillas are in the room? (probably zero)

How many fingers and thumbs are on your hands?

How many eyes do you have?

You can see that numbers are going to be very useful words to know how to write. Again, some of the numbers are really tricky, but we're going to try to figure out ways to write them correctly.

Notice:

In "zero"—there is a "zero" at the end.

One—As you say the letters o-n-e, it makes the phrase "owe any?" (Do you owe any money?)

Two—Split the sneaky W into two parts.

Three—There are three letters before you get to the *ee*'s.

Four—Four letters in four.

Five—Look for the "I"; then give a "high five" to your neighbor.

Six—This ends with the "kissing sound" letter "x."

Seven—This has a "v" in the middle, which is a 7 on its side.

Eight—This is crazy eight! It makes no sense whatsoever! (The *g* looks like an 8.)

Nine—Look for the "I"; then give a "high nine" with your left hand.

Ten—Sound it out.

Worksheets

Answers to Worksheet I-26A:

zero, one, two, three, four, five, six, seven, eight, nine, ten

Answers to Worksheet I-26B:

Students' answers will vary. Here are some examples:

zero—3-headed teachers, number of gorillas in the room

one—your nose, you

two—twins, eyes, socks, pigtails, wheels on a bike

three—The 3 Stooges, 3 little pigs, triplets, poison ivy leaves

four—legs on a table, legs on a dog, tires on a car, 4-leaf clover

five—fingers on a hand, Jeep with a spare tire on the back, pennies in a nickel

six—1/2 dozen eggs or cookies or roses, insect's legs

seven—days of the week, The Seven Dwarfs

eight—Santa's eight reindeer, package of hot dog buns, spider legs, octopus arms

nine—players on a baseball team, planets

ten—all of your fingers and toes, bowling pins, pennies in a dime

Answers to Worksheet I-26C:

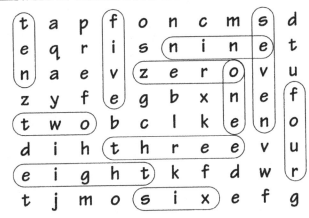

Answers to Worksheet I-26D:

1. two	4. eight	7. ten	10. six
2. seven	5. five	8. four	11. nine
3. three	6. one	9. zero	

Follow-up Activities

1. **Funny Pictures:** Write the number words (zero through ten) on separate cards. Write words that are associated with each number on eleven other cards (space aliens for zero, head for one, eyes for two, etc.). Then shuffle each set of cards. Students select one from each group. Whatever cards they have indicate what they are to draw. For example, if a student picked the cards *seven* and *toes*, she would draw a foot with seven toes. If a student picked the cards *four* and *eyes*, he would draw a picture of someone with four eyes.

2. **Number Hangman:** This quick game reinforces spelling the number words correctly. Tell students that the words can only be number words that they have studied.

3. **Match Game:** This card game can be adapted for numbers. Students match the number word with the corresponding number of dots, objects, or a sentence that gives a clue (*eight*: number of Santa's reindeer; *four*: leaves on a clover, etc.).

I-26A. Writing the Numbers

Use the lines below to write out the number words **zero** through **ten**. Look at the clues to help you with the tricky numbers.

_____ _____ _____ o

o _____ _____

t _____ o

_____ _____ _____ ee

_____ _____ u _____

_____ i _____ _____

_____ _____ _____

_____ v _____ _____

_____ _____ g _____ _____

n _____ _____ _____

_____ _____ _____

Copyright © 2001 by John Wiley & Sons, Inc.

Name _____ Date _____

I-26B. Number Concepts

Think about things that come in one's, two's, etc. List as many as you can. Think hard! Draw pictures on the back of this sheet, if you can.

_____

zero

_____

one

_____

two

_____

three

_____

four

_____

five

_____

six

_____

seven

_____

eight

_____

nine

_____

ten

_____

I-26C. Word Search

Find the number words **zero** through **ten**. First, write the number word correctly, then check them off as you find them. The words can be found across and down.

0 _____ 1 _____ 2 _____ 3 _____

4 _____ 5 _____ 6 _____ 7 _____

8 _____ 9 _____ 10 _____

t	a	p	f	o	n	c	m	s	d
e	q	r	i	s	n	i	n	e	t
n	a	e	v	z	e	r	o	v	u
z	y	f	e	g	b	x	n	e	f
t	w	o	b	c	l	k	e	n	o
d	i	h	t	h	r	e	e	v	u
e	i	g	h	t	k	f	d	w	r
t	j	m	o	s	i	x	e	f	g

Name _____ Date _____

I-26D. Complete the Sentences

Read each sentence. Complete the missing word by filling in the number word.

1. I have _____ eyes.

2. There are _____ days in the week.

3. A shamrock has _____ leaves.

4. Let's play Crazy _____ s.

5. I have _____ fingers on one hand.

6. I have _____ head.

7. I have _____ toes.

8. A lucky clover has _____ leaves.

9. There are _____ space aliens in the room.

10. Mom has _____ pink roses in the vase.

11. There are _____ planets.

Lesson I-27: Writing Common Nouns
(Increasing Vocabulary Words)

To the Teacher

When students are asked to write "about" something, most likely they will need to have a noun in mind. In fact, entire sentences, paragraphs, and reports can be written based entirely on a simple common noun. In this lesson, students are given examples of what a noun is and are then given practice in using nouns to complete writing activities.

To the Student

Look around the room. Help me list ten things in the room. (Proceed to list items.) Most likely our list consists of things you can see, touch, or hold (e.g., calendar, desk, flag, boy, girl). These are really important words because they are good sentence starters when you are talking or writing. Words that describe these sorts of things are called *nouns*. A very simple definition of a noun is a person, place, or a thing.

Let's come up with some lists of people, places, and things. I will give you some clues.

People

1. a person who examines your teeth (*dentist*)
2. a person who is your mother's mother (*grandmother*)
3. the person who is in charge of the school (*principal*)
4. the person who got you to school today (*bus driver, mother, father*)
5. another child who lives in your home (*brother, sister, baby*)

Places

1. where you go to learn things (*school*)
2. where you go for recess (*playground, gym*)
3. where you go to eat lunch (*cafeteria*)
4. where you sleep (*bedroom*)
5. where you could go swimming (*pool*)

Things

1. something you use to brush your teeth (*toothbrush, toothpaste*)
2. something you might eat for breakfast (*bacon, toast, cereal*)
3. something that provides music (*radio, CD, tape player*)
4. something you need to write (*pen, pencil, chalk*)
5. something you wear on your feet (*socks, shoes, sandals*)

Now we are going to work on some activities that involve using nouns.

Worksheets

Answers to Worksheet I-27A:

Students' answers will vary. Here are examples.

1. car, truck, wagon
2. chair, couch, table
3. mother, father, sister, brother
4. dog, cat, hamster, gerbil, bird

   5. pants, shirt, socks, hat

   6. knife, cutting board, bowl

   7. ball, jump rope, football

   8. corn, beans, carrots

   9. river, lake, goldfish bowl

   10. sun, corn, lemons

Answers to Worksheet I-27B:

   Students' answers will vary. Here are examples.

   1. red, wheels, toy

   2. legs, soft, wooden

   3. boy, noisy, tall

   4. furry, wiggly, cute

   5. blue, baseball team, funny

   6. good smells, hot, pizza cooking

   7. milk, cold, eggs

   8. yellow, on the cob, sweet

   9. swimming, water skiing, fish

   10. hot, yellow, round

Answers to Worksheet I-27C:

   Students' answers will vary.

Answers to Worksheet I-27D:

   Students' answers will vary. Here are examples.

   a—alligator, b—boat, c—cat, d—dentist, e—elephant, f—frog, g—gate, h—horse, i—ice cream cone, j—jump rope, k—kite, l—lamp, m—monkey, n—nut, o—octopus, p—pony, q—quilt, r—raccoon, s—snake, t—television, u—umbrella, v—violin, w—wagon, x—x-ray, y—yarn, z—zebra

Answers to Worksheet I-27E:

   Students' answers will vary.

Follow-up Activities

   1. **Matching Nouns:** Make "Match Game" cards with words and pictures. Students may want to draw their own pictures.

   2. **Category Game:** Each day give students a category to think about (animals, toys, clothing, etc.). Have them write as many words as they can think of that would go in the category. Challenge them to think of 10–20 words for each group.

I-27A. Build a Word Wall of Nouns

Complete the word wall with nouns that fit the description given.

1. Things with wheels

6. Kitchen things

2. Furniture

7. Toys

3. People in a family

8. Vegetables

4. Kinds of pets

9. Things with water

5. Clothing

10. Things that are yellow

I-27B. Making a Word Web

For every noun given, add more words that tell something about it in each of the bubbles that makes a "web" around the word.

Example:

8 legs

spider

spins web   black

1. **wagon**

2. **chair**

3. **brother**

4. **puppy**

5. **hat**

I-27B. Making a Word Web (continued)

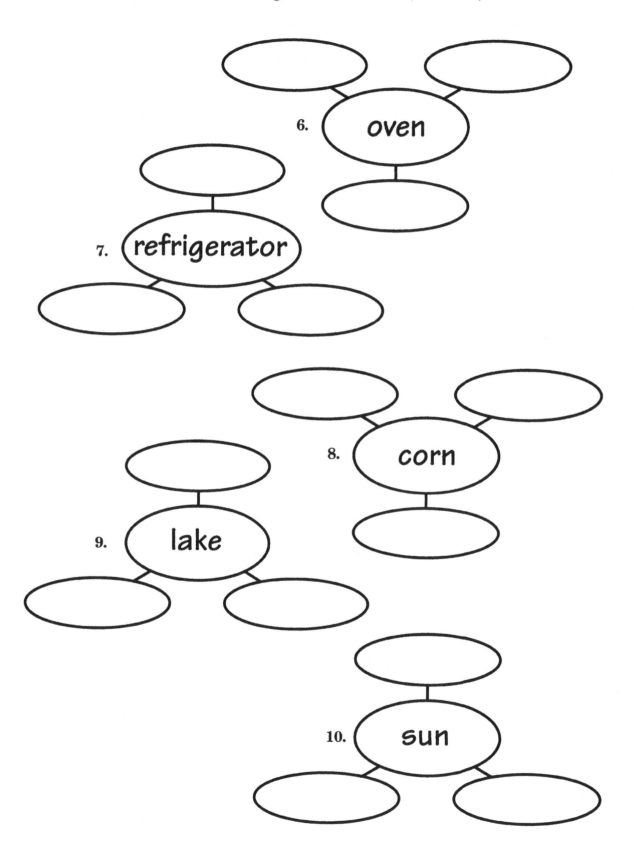

I-27C. Word Web Sentences

Use the word webs you made in Worksheet I-27B to complete the sentences below.

1. My favorite toy is a _____. It is the color _____. I can put many things inside it. I can put a _____ and a _____ inside it.

2. I like to sit on a _____. When I am sitting, I can also read a _____. It feels very _____. It makes me feel _____.

3. I have a _____. He is a _____ who likes to do a lot of different things. He is _____. He likes to _____.

4. It is fun to have a _____. You should put a _____ around his neck. Puppies like to _____. They are very _____.

5. I wear a _____ on my head. It is the color _____. I wear it when I go _____. My hat makes me feel _____.

6. There is a good smell coming out of the _____. I hope it is _____. Don't touch the oven when it is _____.

7. When I open the _____, I see food. There might be a carton of _____. Maybe there are some _____. You should put _____ in the refrigerator.

8. I like to eat _____. You can get corn on the cob at a _____. I like to put _____ on my corn. It is the color _____.

9. There are many things to do at a _____. You can go _____. You can take a _____ out, too. Sometimes the water might be _____.

10. The _____ is up in the sky. It is very _____. The sun makes things _____. A sunny day makes me feel _____.

I-27D. Nouns A to Z

Can you think of a noun that starts with each letter of the alphabet? (You may want to work in teams!)

a _____   n _____

b _____   o _____

c _____   p _____

d _____   q _____

e _____   r _____

f _____   s _____

g _____   t _____

h _____   u _____

i _____   v _____

j _____   w _____

k _____   x _____

l _____   y _____

m _____   z _____

I-27E. Guess My Noun

Select a noun. Write three clues that would help someone guess
your noun.

Example: ice cream cone

   1. It is something to eat.

   2. It is cold.

   3. You use a scoop.

My noun is _____

Clue #1: _____

_____

_____

_____

_____

Clue #2: _____

_____

_____

_____

_____

Clue #3: _____

_____

_____

_____

_____

Lesson I-28: The Days of the Week

(Increasing Vocabulary Words)

To the Teacher

A task that confronts students daily is being able to correctly write the days of the week. Students can use these words to date their assignments, homework sheets, and calendars. The purpose of this lesson is to provide cues and practice in correctly writing the days of the week.

To the Student

Who can name the days of the week? (Call on students.) These are very special words. For one thing, they are a group of words that are very common, as you will probably use some of them every day. They are also very useful, in that you will find you need to know something about the days to give information about something.

Because they are special words, each day of the week starts with an upper-case (capital) letter.

Let's take a look at some ways to remember how to spell these words. We will group them this way: the first five days will be the days you go to school (Monday through Friday), and the last two days are the weekend days (Saturday and Sunday).

Monday—"Day" is easy. Use this sentence to help you spell it correctly: I wear red *on* Mo*n*day.

Tuesday—"Day" is easy. Use this sentence to help you with the rest: I wear bl*ue* on T*ue*sday.

Wednesday—"Day" is easy. Think of the other six letters in two parts (wed/nes) and use this sentence to help you: I go to a *wed*ding on *Wed*-nes-day.

Thursday—"Day" is easy. Then use this sentence: You are (*u-r*) going to school on Th*ur*sday.

Friday—"Day" is easy. Then use this sentence: I will see my *friend* on *Fri*day, the *end* of the school week.

Saturday—"Day" is easy. Use this sentence: You are (*u-r*) coming over to play on Sat*ur*day.

Sunday—"Day" is easy. Use this sentence: The *sun* is out on *Sun*day.

Worksheets

Answers to Worksheet I-28A:

Part One:

1. Friday	3. Tuesday	5. Wednesday	7. Thursday
2. Sunday	4. Monday	6. Saturday	

Part Two:

1. Answers will vary.	5. Monday	9. Answers will vary.
2. Answers will vary.	6. Friday	10. Answers will vary.
3. Answers will vary.	7. Wednesday	
4. Saturday, Sunday	8. Answers will vary.	

Answers to Worksheet I-28B:

Part One:

1. Monday	3. Wednesday	5. Friday	7. Sunday
2. Tuesday	4 Thursday	6. Saturday	

Part Two:

1. Wednesday	3. Monday	5. Saturday	7. Tuesday
2. Sunday	4. Thursday	6. Friday	

Follow-up Activities

1. **Write Each Day:** Make sure students write the day of the week on their written work each day, especially while they are acquiring these words in their written vocabulary. You may have students start out with writing their name, then follow immediately with the day of the week.

2. **What We Do On...:** Write a class story in which each day of the week is characterized in some day. Perhaps your class has a special activity (art, counselor, music, etc.) on a certain day. Certain routines might be performed on certain days (Pledge of Allegiance on Monday morning, cleaning the chalkboards on Friday, etc.). Include whatever is special about that day in your class composition.

Name _____ Date _____

I-28A. Using the Prompted Sentences

Part One: Answer the questions using the days of the week and the helping sentences.

1. What day is your **friend** coming over? _____

2. What day is the **sun** out? _____

3. On what day do you wear **blue**? _____

4. **On** what day do you wear red? _____

5. What day is the **wedding** day? _____

6. What day **are you** coming over to **play**? _____

7. What day **are you** going to **school**? _____

Part Two: Complete the Sentences
Use a day of the week to complete these sentences.

1. Today is _____.

2. Tomorrow is _____.

3. Yesterday was _____.

4. The weekend days are _____ and _____.

5. The first school day is _____.

6. The last school day is _____.

7. The middle school day is _____.

8. We have art on _____.

9. We have music on _____.

10. The next holiday is on _____.

Add your own on the back of this sheet.

I-28B. Writing and Recognizing the Days of the Week

Part One: Write the days of the week in order.

1. ____ ____ ____ ____ ____ ____

2. ____ ____ ____ ____ ____ ____ ____

3. ____ ____ ____ ____ ____ ____ ____ ____ ____

4. ____ ____ ____ ____ ____ ____ ____ ____

5. ____ ____ ____ ____ ____ ____

6. ____ ____ ____ ____ ____ ____ ____

7. ____ ____ ____ ____ ____ ____

Part Two: Circle the day of the week that is spelled correctly in each row.

1. Wensday   Wednesday   Wenisday

2. Sunday   Sunda   Sundae

3. Moonday   Mondaey   Monday

4. Thursday   Tursday   Thersday

5. Saterday   Saderday   Saturday

6. Fryday   Friday   Firday

7. Tusday   Teusday   Tuesday

January

	1	2	3	4	5	6
7	8	9	10	11	12	13
14	15	16	17	18	19	20
21	22	23	24	25	26	27
28	29	30	31			

Lesson I-29: The Months of the Year

(Increasing Vocabulary Words)

To the Teacher

As with the days of the week, being able to write the months of the year is another task that confronts students on a daily basis. The purpose of this lesson is to provide cues and practice activities for students to use to help them write the months of the year.

To the Student

Who knows how many months of the year there are? (12) Who can name all of the months in order? What month is your birthday in? What is this month? What is a summer month? What is a winter month?

I can see you know a lot about the months. These are special words, like the days of the week, so they will need an upper-case letter (capital) to start them.

Some of these words are long, but if we break them down into parts, it will be easier to remember how to write them. There are certain parts of the words, or syllables, that are the same in some of the months. If you learn how to write the syllable, then it will be easier to hear it and spell it when you have to write the whole month.

Here are the syllables to know: u, ru, ch, ril, gust, to, ary, ber, vem, cem, tem, Jan, Feb, Mar, Ap, Au, Sep, Oc, No, De.

Let's go through the months and try to hear the parts:

January = Jan + u + ary

February = Feb + ru + ary ("Are" you looking for the tricky "r"?)

March = Mar + ch

April = Ap + ril

May = this one is easy

June = this one is easy, too

July = just remember the tricky "y" at the end

August = Au + gust

September = Sep + tem + ber

October = Oc + to + ber

November = No + vem + ber

December = De + cem + ber

Worksheets

Answers to Worksheet I-29A:

Jan/u/ary; Feb/ru/ary; Mar/ch; Ap/ril; May; June; July; Au/gust; Sep/tem/ber; Oc/to/ber; No/vem/ber; De/cem/ber

Answers to Worksheet I-29B:

1. Answers will vary.
2. Answers will vary.
3. Answers will vary.
4. February
5. December
6. July
7. June, July, August
8. March
9. Answers will vary.
10. Answers will vary.

Answers to Worksheet I-29C:

Part One:

Answers will vary.

Part Two:

1. February 6, 1994
2. August 11, 2001
3. May 15, 1996

4. March 8, 1999
5. July 4, 1776
6. January 1, 2000

Follow-up Activities

1. Have students write the correct date on their daily written assignments or journals. By the end of each month, students should be able to spell that word correctly after so much practice!

2. Make a months-of-the-year book in which special events that occur during a month (holidays, traditions, school events, etc.) are highlighted. This would also make a nice calendar to decorate for a parent or grandparent.

3. A simple puzzle or game can be made by having students copy the months of the year on individual cards or strips of paper. Have students shuffle the set of cards and then "race" to put them in correct sequential order.

4. The months of the year make good "Hangman" words as well.

I-29A. Months by Syllables or Parts

Write the months in order. Use the syllable parts at the top to help you write the words.

u	ru	ch	ril	gust	to	ary	ber	vem	cem
tem	Jan	Feb	Mar	Ap	Aug	Sep	Oc	No	De

Name _____ Date _____

I-29B. What's the Month?

Write the month that answers each question.

1. What month is it right now? _____

2. What was last month? _____

3. What is next month? _____

4. In what month is Valentine's Day? _____

5. In what month is Christmas and (usually) Hanukkah? _____

6. In what month is our Independence Day? _____

7. What are the three summer months? _____

_____

8. In what month is St. Patrick's Day? _____

9. In what month is your birthday? _____

10. Which is your favorite month? _____

Name _____ Date _____

I-29C. Writing the Date

When you write the date, start with the month, then the number of the day, then a comma, and finally the year.

Example: October 16, 2001

Part One: Write the correct date for the following items:

1. Write the date on which you were born. _____

2. Write today's date. _____

3. Write the date for the 10th day of February last year. _____

_____

4. Write the date that school started. _____

5. Write the date for the first day of next month. _____

_____

6. Write the date for the next holiday. _____

7. Write the date for your brother's or sister's birthday. _____

_____

8. Write the date for Christmas or the start of Hanukkah. _____

_____

9. Write the date for the third month, sixth day, and the year 1975. _____

_____

10. Write tomorrow's date. _____

Part Two: Write the dates that I say:

1. _____

2. _____

3. _____

4. _____

5. _____

6. _____

Lesson I-30: Abbreviations and Titles

(Increasing Vocabulary Words)

To the Teacher

It is important for students to be familiar with writing the months of the year and days of the week, but most likely students will use common abbreviations when referring to these items. The purpose of this lesson is to introduce students to common abbreviations.

To the Student

It takes a long time to write out some of the words you have been working on—for example, the words *December*, or *Wednesday*, or *February*. Instead of writing out the entire word, you can often use abbreviations. That simply means a shortcut to writing the entire word.

Here are some common abbreviations. You can see that most of the abbreviations are simply the first few letters of the word.

Months

January—Jan.	May—(no abbreviation needed)	September—Sept.
February—Feb.	June—(no abbreviation needed)	October—Oct.
March—Mar.	July—(no abbreviation needed)	November—Nov.
April—Apr.	August—Aug.	December—Dec.

Days

Monday—Mon.	Thursday—Thurs.	Sunday—Sun.
Tuesday—Tues.	Friday—Fri.	
Wednesday—Wed.	Saturday—Sat.	

Abbreviations for states: (Be sure to include your state and surrounding states.)
(Examples)

Indiana—IN	New York—NY
Wisconsin—WI	California—CA

Addresses:
(Examples)

Avenue—Ave.	Parkway—Pkwy.	Boulevard—Blvd.	Post Office Box—P.O. Box
Street—St.	Apartment—Apt.	Circle—Cir.	
Lane—La.	Road—Rd.	Trail—Tr.	

Directions:

North—N.	South—S.	East—E.	West—W.

Finally, another group of words that is shortened is called a title. When you are talking to an adult or someone you don't know very well, you would or should use a title of respect. These are words like: Mister—Mr. (a man); Misses—Mrs. (a married woman); Ms. (a woman—may be married or unmarried); Doctor—Dr. Also, Junior (a man whose name is the same as his father's name)—Jr.

Worksheets

Answers to Worksheet I-30A:

Part One:

1. Answers will vary.	4. Answers will vary.	7. Jan.	10. Nov.
2. Answers will vary.	5. Answers will vary.	8. Oct.	
3. Aug.	6. Answers will vary.	9. Mar.	

Part Two:

1. Answers will vary.   4. Fri.   7. Sat. or Sun.   10. Thurs.
2. Answers will vary.   5. Mon.   8. Sat. or Sun.
3. Answers will vary.   6. Wed.   9. Tues.

Answers to Worksheet I-30B:

Part One:

1. Answers will vary.   4. NY   7. HI   10. NV
2. Answers will vary.   5. KY   8. CA
3. FL   6. IN   9. Answers will vary.

Part Two:

1. 206 E. Brown Rd.   5. 101 S. Marshall Blvd., Apt. 3   9. 599 E. Indian Tr.
2. 32 N. Kingsbury St.   6. 2 W. Orchard Pkwy.   10. 7 Stephenson Ave.
3. 6313 Washington Cir.   7. 18135 Apple La.
4. P.O. Box 26   8. 28 Packard Rd.

Answers to Worksheet I-30C:

Part One:

1. (e) or (i)   4. (k)   7. (d) or (f)   10. (b) or (g) or (h)
2. (f)   5. (a) or (c)   8. (a) or (c) or (j)
3. (g)   6. (e) or (i)   9. (b) or (g) or (h)

Part Two:

Answers will vary.

Follow-up Activities

1. **Months**: Have students use the abbreviations for the months of the year on their headings for written work.

2. **Days**: Have students use the abbreviations for the days of the week when they are writing their homework assignments or routine activities for each day (for example: Mon.—History test; Tues.—remember to bring gym shoes, etc.). Be sure you use the abbreviations also when you are writing assignments for students on the board.

3. **States**: Be sure students are familiar with the abbreviations for their own state and neighboring states. You may try to think of something interesting for students to associate with each state (Florida: Walt Disney World; Texas: The Alamo). Students will learn the abbreviations by using them, rather than memorizing them. It is more important that they recognize the abbreviations for states that are meaningful to them.

4. **Street Directions:** Make sure students can correctly write their own street address with and without the abbreviations. You may want to compile a list of all students' addresses in your class (without abbreviations) and use that to have students rewrite them using abbreviations.

5. **Titles:** Talk about the people who work in your school, community, and state. Discuss why each title is the appropriate one for that person.

Name _____ Date _____

I-30A. Abbreviations for Months and Days

Part One: **Months**

Write the abbreviation for the following months:

1. the month of your birthday _____

2. the month of the first day of school _____

3. the month after July _____

4. a summer month _____

5. a winter month _____

6. the month of your favorite holiday _____

7. the month that has New Year's Day _____

8. the month after September _____

9. the month with St. Patrick's Day _____

10. the month with Thanksgiving _____

Part Two: **Days**

Write the abbreviation for the following days:

1. the day you have music _____

2. the day you have art _____

3. the day you have P.E. _____

4. the last day of the school week _____

5. the first day of the school week _____

6. the middle day of the school week _____

7. a weekend day _____

8. a day that begins with "S" _____

9. the day after Monday _____

10. the day before Friday _____

Name _____ Date _____

I-30B. Abbreviations for States and Roads

Part One: **State Abbreviations**

Write the state abbreviation for these clues:

1. the state in which you live _____

2. a nearby state _____

3. the state where you can go to Walt Disney World _____

4. the state where you can go to New York City _____

5. the state that has the Kentucky Derby _____

6. the state that has the Indianapolis 500 race _____

7. a state where people like to vacation on the beaches and eat pineapples _____

8. the state that has Hollywood and movie stars _____

9. a state that you would like to visit _____

10. the state where you would find Las Vegas _____

Part Two: **Abbreviations for Addresses**

Rewrite these addresses using the correct abbreviations:

1. 206 East Brown Road _____

2. 32 North Kingsbury Street _____

3. 6313 Washington Circle _____

4. Post Office Box 26 _____

5. 101 South Marshall Boulevard _____

6. 2 West Orchard Parkway _____

7. 18135 Apple Lane _____

8. 28 Packard Road _____

9. 599 East Indian Trail _____

10. 7 Stephenson Avenue _____

Name _____ Date _____

I-30C. Titles of Respect

Part One: Match the name with the description of the person. There may be more than one correct answer.

(a) Dr. Ellen Romez	**(e) Dr. Peter Vlami**	**(i) Dr. Richard Peteri**
(b) Mr. Bob Mackel	**(f) Ms. Ann Carbon**	**(j) Dr. Linda Master**
(c) Dr. Susan Ionian	**(g) Mr. Thomas Jones, Jr.**	**(k) Mrs. Kathleen Kelley**
(d) Miss Christine Lloyd	**(h) Mr. Akeem Morrison**	

1. This person is a man who is a doctor. _____

2. This person is a woman, but you don't know if she is married or not. _____

3. This person is a man, and he has the same name as his father. _____

4. This person is a woman who is married. _____

5. This person is a woman and she is a dentist. _____

6. This person is a man and he is a dentist. _____

7. This person is a woman who is not married. _____

8. This person is a woman who could be married and she is a doctor. _____

9. This person is a man who is not a doctor. _____

10. This person is a man who is a teacher. _____

Part Two: Write the names of these people including their titles.

1. your mother's name _____

2. your father's name _____

3. the name of your doctor _____

4. the name of your teacher _____

5. the name of your principal _____

6. the name of your dentist _____

7. the name of your neighbor _____

8. the name of your aunt _____

9. the name of your uncle _____

10. the name of an adult you like _____

Lesson I-31: Proper Nouns (Increasing Vocabulary Words)

To the Teacher

Students have been exposed to certain groups of words that require upper-case letters (the days of the week, the months of the year, titles, etc.). In this lesson, they will be given practice in determining nouns that are "specific" enough to require a capital letter—proper nouns.

To the Student

What are some types of words that have to have a capital letter? (days of the week, months of the year, names, titles, etc.)

We have already talked about what a noun is—a person, place, or thing. Nouns like *dog, cat, boy, lake, book* are words that could refer to a lot of different things within that group. Can you think of some names of dogs that you know? (Barney, Rover, Spot, etc.) If you are referring to a *specific* dog, you would use a capital letter to let the reader know that it is not just any dog, it's a special dog. It's the same with the word *girl*. Can you give me the name of a specific girl? (Caroline, Anna, Jasmine, etc.) If you are thinking of just one specific girl, you use a capital letter.

Let's try some examples. I'll give you a general noun, and you tell me one specific example of that noun.

boy—Tommy

lake—Lake Michigan

cola—Coca-Cola

teacher—Mr. Parker

cat—Fluffy

Here's the rule to remember: If you are using a general or common noun, use a lower-case letter. If you are referring to one specific special noun, use a capital letter.

Worksheets

Answers to Worksheet I-31A:

Students' answers will vary. Here are examples.

1. President Washington, President Clinton, President Reagan
2. Grand Canyon National Park, Yellowstone National Park, Luhr Park
3. Snickers, Nestles' Crunch, Milky Way
4. Monopoly, Payday, Clue
5. Mr. Smith, Dr. Jones, Mr. Roberts
6. Mrs. Carlson, Dr. White, Miss Ray
7. *Huckleberry Finn, Old Yeller, Across Five Aprils*
8. Florida, Wisconsin, North Dakota
9. Mississippi River, Snake River, Hudson River
10. Riley School, Lakeview School, North School

Answers to Worksheet I-31B:

1. *common*: lake; *proper*: Lake Laura
2. *common*: brother; *proper*: Tommy
3. *proper*: Pennsylvania; *common*: state

4. *proper*: Boomer; *common*: puppy

5. *common*: book; *proper*: *Harry Potter and the Sorcerer's Stone*

6. *common*: doctor; *proper*: Dr. Cameron

7. *proper*: Harvard; *common*: college

8. *proper*: Stormy; *common*: horse

9. *proper*: Pizza Town; *common*: restaurant

10. *common*: singer; *proper*: Britney Spears

Name _____ Date _____

I-31A. Give an Example

For each common noun, give three examples of a proper noun that goes with it.

Common Noun	**Proper Nouns**		
1. U.S. president	_____	_____	_____
2. park	_____	_____	_____
3. candy bar	_____	_____	_____
4. game	_____	_____	_____
5. man	_____	_____	_____
6. woman	_____	_____	_____
7. book	_____	_____	_____
8. state	_____	_____	_____
9. river	_____	_____	_____
10. school	_____	_____	_____

Can you add two of your own?

_____ _____ _____

_____ _____ _____

Name _____ Date _____

I-31B. Be a Detective

There is a common noun and a proper noun in each sentence. Circle the common noun and underline the proper noun.

Example: <u>Mary</u> is a very nice girl.

1. If you want to swim in a warm lake, go to Lake Laura in the summer.

2. My little brother is named Tommy.

3. My family used to live in Pennsylvania, but then we moved to another state.

4. Boomer is my cute little puppy.

5. My favorite book is *Harry Potter and the Sorcerer's Stone.*

6. My doctor is Dr. Cameron.

7. I would like to go to Harvard someday when I am ready for college.

8. Would you like a ride on Stormy, my favorite horse?

9. I think we are eating at Pizza Town tonight, which is my favorite restaurant.

10. The singer on this tape is Britney Spears.

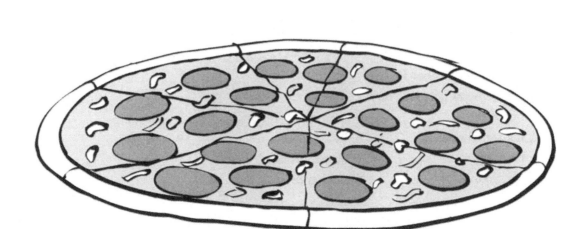

Lesson I-32: Antonyms (Opposites)

(Increasing Vocabulary Words)

To the Teacher

Students seem to "catch on" to the idea of opposites quite readily. It seems obvious to visualize *big* vs. *little, happy* vs. *sad*, and so on. The purpose of this lesson is to provide students with opportunities to find and use antonyms.

To the Student

Help me finish these sentences:

That elephant is really big. The mouse is very… (little).

Don't go so fast! You should go… (slow).

Do you like things that are hot or things that are… (cold)?

How did you know what word to use? The things I was talking about can be very different. When you think of sizes, an elephant is at one extreme (very big) and a mouse is at the other end in terms of size (very small). When you think of speed, fast is one extreme, and the most different you can get from fast is… slow! When you think of temperature, hot is one extreme, and the other extreme is cold.

Words like fast/slow, hot/cold, big/little, and lots of other word pairs are called *opposites*. Another word for opposites is *antonyms*. These words mean the same thing. I bet you know a lot of opposites. Try these: start (finish), up (down), in (out), black (white), yes (no).

In this lesson you will be doing a lot of thinking and working with words that are opposites. A little trick to help you remember opposites is to think about something being most different. Think of a seesaw. At one end is something (let's say an elephant) and at the other end is the most different thing you can find (let's say a mouse). Put your hand down low to show one side of the seesaw; then raise your other hand up high to show the other side. Think about how different things can be. Those are opposites!

Worksheets

Answers to Worksheet I-32A:

big/little; fat/thin; tall/short; noisy/quiet; narrow/wide; dark/light; back/front; kind/mean

Answers to Worksheet I-32B:

1. huge (little)	6. slowly (fast)	11. careless (careful)
2. light (dark)	7. cry (laugh)	12. full (empty)
3. shallow (deep)	8. back (front)	13. mean (nice)
4. hate (love)	9. dull (sharp)	14. never (always)
5. hot (cold)	10. light (heavy)	15. short (long)

Answers to Worksheet I-32C:

Students' sentences will vary.

1. big, little	5. boring, interesting	9. up, down
2. fastest, slowest	6. lost, found	10. hot, cold
3. boys, girls	7. brave, afraid	
4. old, young	8. sick, great	

Follow-up Activities

1. **Drawing Opposites:** Give students a pair of opposites and have them draw a picture (can be humorous) to illustrate the opposites. For example, for the words *fast* and *slow*, students could draw the tortoise and the hare. Encourage them to exaggerate for effect.

2. **Opposite Match:** Make a "Match Game" with opposite cards. Have students play with a partner, alternating turning over two cards at a time. If they get a match, the student takes both cards.

3. **Opposite Day:** Have students write a short story about "Opposite Day" (not to be confused with "backwards"). Have them go through a day in their life in which many things are opposite—sitting backwards instead of forwards at their desk, eating dessert and then the main meal, turning the alarm clock on first thing in the morning, etc. This may make a good group activity.

Name _____ Date _____

I-32A. Find My Opposite

Using 8 different colored crayons, color the matching opposites in the puzzle below.

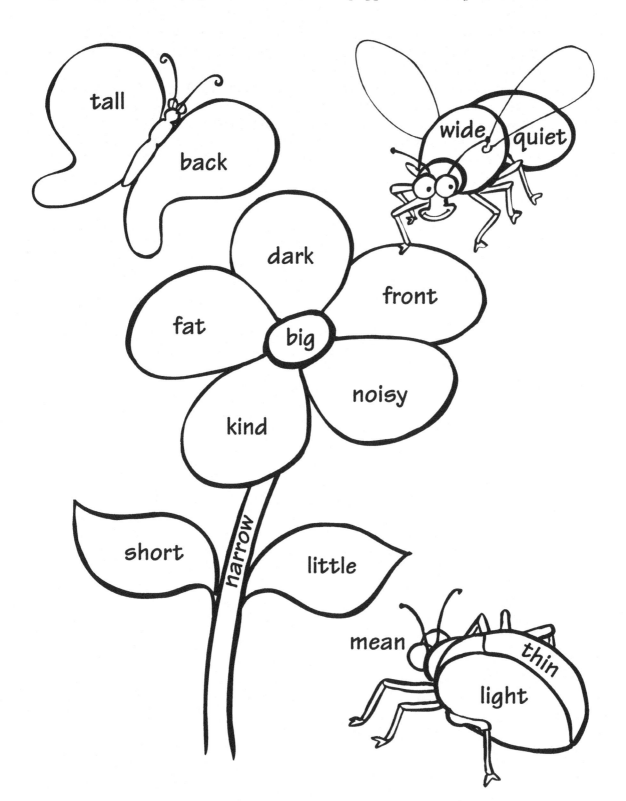

tall

back

wide

quiet

dark

front

fat

big

noisy

kind

short

narrow

little

mean

thin

light

Name _____   Date _____

I-32B. Make a Change

Read each sentence and underline the one word that doesn't make sense in the sentence. Change it to an opposite.

1. I like the huge dog because she fits on my lap. _____

2. It was so light out, I couldn't see anything. _____

3. I'm afraid to swim in the shallow water because my feet don't touch the bottom.

   _____

4. I hate chocolate chip cookies, fresh and warm from the oven. _____

5. On a summer day, I like to eat hot ice cream. _____

6. My brother is a track star because he is slow. _____

7. The funny movie made me cry out loud! _____

8. I couldn't see the board, so I sat in the back of the room closer to the chalkboard.

   _____

9. Don't touch that baby lion in the mouth because she has dull teeth. _____

   _____

10. I can't lift that very light box. _____

11. The beautiful dress was very expensive so I will be careless with it. _____

12. My car stopped because the gas tank was full. _____

13. I love my father because he is such a mean man. _____

14. You should never tell the truth. _____

15. I can tie my shoes with this lace if it is short

    enough.  _____

Name _____ Date _____

I-32C. Finish the Sentence

Think about using opposites as you finish these sentences. Then circle the opposite pairs in each sentence.

1. If I want a big pet, I would get a horse; if I want a little pet, I would get _____

2. The fastest runner got first place. The slowest runner _____

3. The boys in the class got swimming suits and Frisbees because they wanted to play outside at the party. The girls in the class _____

4. The old people thought the room was too cold, so they got blankets. The young kids thought the room was too hot, so _____

5. The long movie was boring so I fell asleep, but my friend thought it was interesting so he _____

6. I lost my lunch money in the cafeteria, but I found _____

7. The brave bird tried to fly high, but he was afraid _____

8. I felt sick when I realized I had lost my homework, but I felt great when _____

   _____

9. We took the elevator up to the top floor to see the view, and then we took it down to

   _____

10. I wanted to drink a hot chocolate, but I changed my mind and ordered a cold _____

   _____

Lesson I-33: Synonyms (Increasing Vocabulary Words)

To the Teacher

Recognizing and using specific words can make a student's writing much more precise and interesting. The correct use of synonyms is a skill that young writers need to practice and perfect. The purpose of this lesson is to provide a pool of synonym pairs that students should be familiar with and to provide practice in choosing appropriate words.

To the Student

I am going to say something in several different ways. Listen:

That is a *cute puppy.*

That is a *beautiful dog.*

That is a *nice-looking canine.*

That is a *gorgeous German shepherd.*

Think about the words that were different in each sentence: *cute, beautiful, nice-looking, gorgeous*—they all mean about the same thing, but they might make you have a little different picture in your mind. *Puppy, dog, canine, German shepherd*—these words are all "dog" words, but your mental picture of a puppy might not be a German shepherd. By using different words, the writer can help the reader make a picture in his mind of what the writer wants you to see.

Words that mean almost the same thing are called *synonyms*. Can you think of a synonym for these words?

big (large, huge, enormous)

fast (quick, swift)

beautiful (cute, pretty)

easy (simple, a "cinch")

A way to help you think about synonyms is to use your hands—put your left hand out while you say the main word, then put your right hand out to say a matching word. The words are "equal"; they mean about the same thing.

Worksheets

Answers to Worksheet I-33A:

Students' answers may vary. Here are examples.

1. present (gift)
2. weep (cry)
3. leap (jump)
4. huge (big, large)
5. unusual (odd, interesting)
6. ached (hurt)
7. halt (stop)
8. delicious (yummy, good)
9. tardy (late)
10. rush (hurry)

Answers to Worksheet I-33B:

1. **thin: slender, tiny, skinny**, fat
2. **nice: sweet, considerate**, mean, **kind**
3. **happy: joyful, excited, pleased**, angry
4. **destroyed:** built, **wrecked, ruined**, liked
5. **on sale: cheap, inexpensive**, broken, **discounted**
6. **slippery: slick, icy**, creamy, rough
7. **cold: bitter**, warm, **freezing, chilly**
8. **afraid:** happy, **scared, nervous**, sleepy
9. **running: working, driving**, spinning, **going**
10. **children: people, students**, adults, **kids**

Follow-up Activities

1. **Password:** Divide students into two teams. Two players from each team play at the same time, taking turns. One member from each team is given a target word, the other member must give words (a synonym) to help the student guess the target word. Make sure students can read the words. Choose words that have several available synonyms!

2. **Change One Word:** Write a sentence on the board and underline one word. Have students rewrite the sentence, putting in a synonym for the underlined word. Later in the day or on another day, write the same sentence, but change a different word. Day by day the, sentence will evolve into a completely different (yet the same in meaning!) sentence. For example:

The **child** saw a huge dark dog running down the street.

The boy saw a huge dark **dog** running down the street.

The boy saw a huge dark lab running down the **street**.

The boy saw a huge dark lab **running** down the boulevard.

The boy saw a huge dark lab dashing **down** the boulevard.

etc.

Name _____ Date _____

I-33A. Think of a Synonym

Read each group of sentences. Write a synonym in the second sentence for the bold word in the first sentence.

1. I have a **present** for you. You will really like this _____.

2. This book will make you **weep**. The ending is so sad you will want to _____.

3. I hope this horse will **leap** over the fence. I know that he likes to _____.

4. I was so hungry I ate the **huge** pizza. Then I had to have a _____ drink.

5. This purple hair makes you look very **unusual**. The tattoo is kind of _____, too.

6. Todd ran ten miles and then stopped when his legs **ached**. His side _____, too.

7. The teacher told the class to **halt** at the end of the hall. I hope everyone remembered

   to _____.

8. Grandma's chocolate cake is **delicious**. I have never eaten anything that tasted quite

   so _____.

9. Oh, no! We are going to be **tardy** for class. I hate to be _____.

10. If you **rush** through your math assignment, you might get some problems wrong. Try

    not to _____ so much.

I-33B. Pick Out the Synonyms

There are several words that would make sense in each sentence. Circle all of the synonyms.
Put an X on any that are not synonyms. Can you add a synonym of your own?

1. The model was very **thin**.

   slender, tiny, skinny, fat, _____

2. What a **nice** person you are!

   sweet, considerate, mean, kind, _____

3. I was so **happy** to win $10,000!

   joyful, excited, pleased, angry, _____

4. The monster **destroyed** the city.

   built, wrecked, ruined, liked, _____

5. This game didn't cost much because it was **on sale**.

   cheap, inexpensive, broken, discounted, _____

6. The **slippery** sidewalk made me fall.

   slick, icy, creamy, rough, _____

7. I don't want to go outside because it's too **cold**.

   bitter, warm, freezing, chilly, _____

8. The little boy was **afraid** of the dark.

   happy, scared, nervous, sleepy, _____

9. My old car quit **running** yesterday.

   working, driving, spinning, going,

   _____

10. Many **children** go to this school.

    people, students, adults, kids,

    _____

Lesson I-34: Homonyms (Increasing Vocabulary Words)

To the Teacher

Another group of confusing words is *homonyms*. These are words that are pronounced alike, but have different meanings (blue, blew; to, too, two; creek, creak; etc.). Students need to be able to visually distinguish between these pairs of words and have experience in knowing the words' meanings as well. The purpose of this lesson is to provide practice for students in determining which of a pair of words is the appropriate word to be used in sentence context. (*Note*: The homonyms *to/too/two* and *they're/their/there* are specifically taught in Lesson I-20.

To the Student

Listen to these sentences:

I blew out my birthday candles.

My favorite color is blue.

What words did you hear in both sentences? (Repeat, if necessary.) Yes, the words "blue/blew." Do both words mean the same thing? (no) What does "blew" mean in the first sentence? (movement of air) What does "blue" mean in the second sentence? (a color) Would you know which word I was talking about if you didn't hear the sentence? (no—need context)

These special words are like twins. They sound alike, but they are spelled differently and they mean different things. Words like that are called *homonyms*. Here are some more examples. Can you think of two meanings for these words that sound alike: heal/heel, pair/pear, sea/see, flu/flew.

Remember that before you really know which word is needed, you need clues from the sentence or from the context. Be sure to read the entire sentence on your worksheet before you choose the answer.

Worksheet

Answers to Worksheet I-34:

creak/creek	**heal/heel**	**groan/grown**
1. creak	1. heal	1. grown
2. creek	2. heel	2. grown
3. creek	3. heel	3. groan
4. creak	4. heal	4. groan
5. creek	5. heal	5. grown
6. creak, creek	6. heel, heal	6. groan, grown
break/brake	**plain/plane**	**blue/blew**
1. brake	1. plane	1. blew
2. break	2. plain	2. blue
3. break	3. plain	3. blue
4. brake	4. plain	4. blew
5. break	5. plane	5. blue
6. break, brake	6. plane, plain	6. blew, blue
flu/flew	**scene/seen**	**which/witch**
1. flew	1. scene	1. witch
2. flew	2. seen	2. which
3. flew	3. seen	3. which
4. flu	4. scene	4. witch
5. flu	5. scene	5. witch
6. flew, flu	6. seen, scene	6. which, witch

steal/steel
1. steel
2. steal
3. steal
4. steel
5. steel
6. steal, steel

fir/fur
1. fir
2. fir
3. fur
4. fur
5. fir
6. fur, fir

piece/peace
1. peace
2. piece
3. piece
4. peace
5. piece
6. peace, piece

pair/pear
1. pear
2. pair
3. pair
4. pear
5. pair
6. pear, pair

loan/lone
1. lone
2. lone
3. loan
4. loan
5. loan
6. lone, loan

hear/here
1. hear
2. here
3. hear
4. here
5. hear
6. hear, here

see/sea
1. see
2. sea
3. sea
4. see
5. see
6. see, sea

for/four
1. for
2. four
3. four
4. for
5. four
6. for, four

new/knew
1. new
2. knew
3. knew
4. new
5. knew
6. knew, new

one/won
1. one
2. one
3. won
4. won
5. won
6. won, one

be/bee
1. be
2. bee
3. be
4. bee
5. bee
6. be, bee

Follow-up Activity

Have students illustrate the two meanings for a pair of homonyms. First write each pair of words at the top of a piece of paper. Draw a line to separate the paper into two parts. You may want to have students use each word in a short sentence and write that sentence under the word. After discussing several examples for each word, have students work either individually or in pairs to come up with a good visual example of each homonym pair. Here is an example:

flu

I have the flu.

flew

We flew in an airplane.

I-34. The Two Meanings

Look at each pair of words. They are pronounced the same, but they mean different things. Use the definitions to write the correct word in each sentence. The last sentence uses both words!

creak—a noise	**creek**—a stream of water

1. Did you hear the old door _____?

2. Don't fall into the _____.

3. The fish are swimming in the _____.

4. This floor will _____ if you walk on it.

5. I got my shoes wet in the _____.

6. If that board makes a _____, we will throw it into the _____.

heal—to get better	**heel**—part of your foot

1. You won't _____ if you don't stay in bed.

2. I stepped on a nail with my _____.

3. I can kick the ball with my _____.

4. The doctor will help the girl _____.

5. Sometimes flowers will _____ some sores.

6. I hope my sore _____ will _____ soon.

groan—a noise	**grown**—got bigger in size

1. My, how you have _____!

2. Have you ever _____ flowers in the yard?

3. My grandfather made a _____ when he saw his phone bill.

4. That sounds like the _____ of a ghost!

5. My sister has _____ two inches.

6. Tom made a _____ when he found out he had only _____ one inch.

I-34. The Two Meanings (continued)

break—come apart	**brake**—make something stop

1. Put your foot on the _____.

2. Don't _____ that vase.

3. My brother will _____ his leg if he falls down.

4. I have to get a new _____ on my bike.

5. Did you ever _____ your arm?

6. The car won't stop if you _____ the _____.

plain—not special or fancy	**plane**—something you fly in

1. We took a _____ to California.

2. This is a very _____ dress.

3. I would like my cheeseburger _____, please.

4. This is just a _____ old dog.

5. We will fly the toy _____ in the backyard.

6. The _____ was just very _____.

blue—a color	**blew**—moving air

1. My little brother _____ out the candles on his cake.

2. The sky is very _____ today.

3. I like your _____ shoes.

4. The wind _____ the leaves all around.

5. You have _____ eyes.

6. The wind _____ the _____ paper all over.

I-34. The Two Meanings (continued)

| **flu**—a sickness | **flew**—made something fly |

1. My dad _____ a plane to Arizona.

2. The birds _____ over our house.

3. Santa _____ his sleigh at Christmas.

4. I have the _____ today.

5. It's no fun to be sick with the _____.

6. My aunt _____ to our house when we all had the _____.

| **scene**—a picture or background | **seen**—looked with your eyes |

1. That painting is a beautiful winter _____.

2. I have never _____ such a nice painting.

3. No one has _____ my dog since yesterday.

4. Let's draw a forest _____ on the wall.

5. In the play, the first _____ takes place outdoors.

6. I have never _____ such a beautiful _____!

| **which**—picking one | **witch**—a magical person |

1. I will dress up as a _____ for Halloween.

2. Tell me _____ candy bar you want.

3. I don't know _____ kitten is the cutest.

4. Can you draw a picture of a _____?

5. The _____ flew across the sky on her broom.

6. _____ _____ has the tallest hat?

I-34. The Two Meanings (continued)

> **steal**—to take something that isn't yours   **steel**—hard material

1. This door is made of _____.

2. Do not _____ my candy.

3. People who _____ should pay back what they take.

4. The car has a lot of _____ in it.

5. Superman can bend a rod of _____ in his bare hands.

6. Who would want to _____ a bunch of _____?

> **fir**—a tree   **fur**—animal skin

1. Let's pick up the cones from that _____ tree.

2. Our Christmas tree is a _____ this year.

3. My mom has a beautiful fake _____ coat.

4. The dog had long _____ that shed all over the place.

5. That's a nice picture of a _____ tree.

6. The dog's _____ sheds and the _____ tree sheds, too!

> **piece**—part of something   **peace**—quiet

1. My mom likes _____ and quiet.

2. May I have a _____ of your pizza?

3. I want a _____ of chocolate cake.

4. I don't want war; I want _____.

5. May I borrow a _____ of paper?

6. If you want to have _____ in the house, give everyone the same

   size _____ of cake!

I-34. The Two Meanings (continued)

pair—two of a kind   pear—a fruit

1. Would you like a _____ for lunch?

2. I have on a new _____ of shoes.

3. I got my mom a nice _____ of earrings.

4. This _____ is yellow.

5. I saw a _____ of birds outside.

6. You may have one _____ or else a _____ of mittens.

loan—to let someone borrow   lone—by yourself

1. There was a _____ wolf in the mountains.

2. A _____ man was walking in the dark.

3. Would you _____ me a pencil?

4. We went to the bank to get a car _____.

5. Don't _____ your comb to anyone.

6. The _____ woman went to the bank to try to get a _____.

hear—with your ears   here—a place

1. Did you _____ the bell ring?

2. Come _____ right now!

3. I can't _____ what you are saying.

4. I put the books over _____.

5. Do you think the dog will _____ me whistle?

6. I can't _____ you unless you stand _____.

I-34. The Two Meanings (continued)

| **see**—with your eyes   **sea**—a body of water |

1. Can you _____ that bird in the tree?

2. We took a boat ride on the rough _____.

3. The men went fishing in the _____.

4. I did not _____ anyone I knew at the party.

5. It's nice to _____ you again.

6. I could not _____ the fish at the bottom of the _____.

| **for**—to get something   **four**—a number |

1. I went to the store _____ milk.

2. There are _____ puppies in the box.

3. My brother is _____ years old.

4. I went _____ a walk around the block.

5. It's almost _____ o'clock.

6. Sally went _____ a long walk at _____ o'clock.

| **new**—opposite of old   **knew**—understood |

1. Do you like my _____ shoes?

2. I thought I _____ the answer to that problem.

3. Robbie _____ who his teacher was going to be.

4. We moved into a _____ house.

5. We _____ how to build a model.

6. My sister _____ who the _____ neighbors were.

I-34. The Two Meanings (continued)

one—only one, the number	won—to win something

1. I have _____ sister.

2. You are the best_____ for this job!

3. Our team _____ the tournament!

4. I hoped I _____ first place.

5. My dog _____ a prize at the dog show.

6. I have only _____ _____ game.

be—to exist	bee—a buzzing insect

1. Where will you _____ after school?

2. Don't get stung by that _____.

3. I will _____ home at 4 o'clock.

4. I sat on a _____.

5. The _____ was on the flower.

6. I'm going to _____ dressed as a _____ for the play.

Lesson I-35: Contractions (Increasing Vocabulary Words)

To the Teacher

Contractions can be confusing to students when reading and writing. Although students may be able to use the words conversationally and read them in text, it is a more complex task to "break apart" the contraction into the two original words and also to combine the words (correctly writing the contracted word). The purpose of this lesson is to provide techniques and practice for students in recognizing, writing, and breaking apart contracted words.

To the Student

Look at these sentences on the board:

I do not want to run a mile outside.
I would not eat a worm.
I cannot bench press 1,000 pounds.
We have not seen Sally since this morning.
She is not here today.

All of these sentences are fine, but we don't always talk like that. (Read each one aloud, emphasizing each word.) Instead of saying "do not," sounding like a robot, what's the normal way we would say that sentence? (I don't want to run a mile outside.) How would we say the other sentences? (I wouldn't eat a worm; I can't bench press…; We haven't seen Sally…; She isn't…)

I will rewrite the words that we changed:

do not = don't
would not = wouldn't
cannot = can't
have not = haven't
is not = isn't

What we did in each case was combine or "crush" two words together to make them one single word. These words are called *contractions*.

When I talk about a "contracted word," I am referring to two words that are crushed together to make one word. A big clue that I am looking at in a contraction is the *apostrophe*. This is a signal that something is missing; a letter (or sometimes more than one letter) was taken out and left an apostrophe in its place. When you write an apostrophe, it's just like writing a comma, only it's up high.

Let's practice figuring out what the two words are that make up these contractions: *Let's* go for a walk. First find the contraction. (let's) Then figure out the two words that were put together. Remember, the sentence still has to make sense and sound right when you substitute the two original words. *Let us* go for a walk.

Try this one: We'll be here until tonight. Find the contraction. (we'll) What two words make sense? (we will)

Now let's try this: *I will* be home tonight. Read each word carefully. Think about how a robot might talk, saying every word. Then read it and say it more normally. If you read it and say it a little faster, what words might you combine to say it a little faster? *I'll* be home tonight. What letters did you take out to make *I will* into *I'll*? (wi)

When you write the contraction, remember that you need parts of both complete words and you will connect them with an apostrophe.

Now, here's one big exception. This is the one that will try to trick you every time. It's the contraction *won't*. Can you think of the two words that go together to make the word *won't*? First, put it in a sentence to give yourself more clues. *I won't be home tonight.* How could you say that using only complete words that make sense? *I will not be home tonight.* What a surprise! Will not = won't.

You'll just have to remember that one, because it doesn't follow the regular pattern. Remember not to get tricked!

Worksheets

Answers to Worksheet I-35A:

1. I'm, I am
2. You're, You are
3. She'd, She would
4. I've, I have
5. He's, He is
6. She's, She is
7. Don't, Do not
8. I won't, will not
9. Let's, Let us
10. We'll, We will

Answers to Worksheet I-35B:

Part One:

1. I will
2. she would
3. will not
4. they are
5. he is
6. they will
7. I am
8. I would
9. we are
10. do not
11. have not
12. does not
13. should not
14. would not
15. could not
16. there is
17. here is
18. we will
19. we are
20. they would

Part Two: Students' sentences will vary.

Answers to Worksheet I-35C:

Part One:

1. I'm
2. he'll
3. they're
4. she's
5. I'd
6. won't
7. can't
8. don't
9. I've
10. we'll
11. we're
12. isn't
13. I've
14. shouldn't
15. let us

Part Two: Students' sentences will vary.

Answers to Worksheet I-35D:

1. We're
2. She'll
3. They've
4. He's
5. We'll
6. isn't
7. Let's
8. wouldn't
9. won't
10. You're

Answers to Worksheet I-35E:

Students' answers will vary.

Answers to Worksheet I-35F:

Be sure students have found the 29 contractions.

Follow-up Activities

1. Make a class list of common contractions. Have students look in a newspaper, magazine, or a story from material used in class. Have them find and circle as many contractions as they can in a certain time limit. You may want to copy a sheet for each student and have students cross off each contraction as it is found. The first student (or team) to cross them all is the winner.

2. Have students find as many contractions as they can in a story. If possible, have them circle each one.

Name _____ Date _____

I-35A. Recognizing a Contraction

Circle the contraction in each sentence. Then circle the two words that make up that contraction.

1. I'm the first one finished.	I am	I have	I will
2. You're my best friend.	You have	You will	You are
3. She'd like to go with us.	She has	She had	She would
4. I've got a secret.	I will	I have	I should
5. He's very funny.	He will	He has	He is
6. She's got the answer key.	She has	She is	She will
7. Don't ring the doorbell.	Do it	Do will	Do not
8. I won't go home now.	would not	we not	will not
9. Let's ride our bikes.	Let us	Let is	Let them
10. We'll be back in a minute.	We have	We should	We will

I-35B. Writing Out Contracted Words

Part One: Write the two words that make up each contraction.

1. I'll   _____   _____

2. she'd   _____   _____

3. won't   _____   _____

4. they're   _____   _____

5. he's   _____   _____

6. they'll   _____   _____

7. I'm   _____   _____

8. I'd   _____   _____

9. we're   _____   _____

10. don't   _____   _____

11. haven't   _____   _____

12. doesn't   _____   _____

13. shouldn't _____   _____

14. wouldn't   _____   _____

15. couldn't   _____   _____

16. there's   _____   _____

17. here's   _____   _____

18. we'll   _____   _____

19. we're   _____   _____

20. they'd   _____   _____

Part Two: Write a sentence for ten of the contractions from Part One. Use another sheet of paper.

Name _____ Date _____

I-35C. Writing a Contraction

Part One: Combine the two words below to make a contraction. Don't forget to put in the apostrophe in the right place!

1. I am _____

2. he will _____

3. they are _____

4. she is _____

5. I would _____

6. will not _____

7. cannot _____

8. do not _____

9. I have _____

10. we will _____

11. we are _____

12. is not _____

13. I have _____

14. should not _____

15. let's _____

Part Two: Write a sentence for ten of the contractions from Part One. Use another sheet of paper.

Name _____ Date _____

I-35D. Recognizing Correct Contractions in Sentences

Circle the correct contraction for each of the bold words in each sentence.

1. **We are** going to the dog show this weekend.	We'r	We'are	We're
2. **She will** go along with us.	She'l	She'll	She'wi
3. **They have** got a lot of puppies to show.	They've	They'v	The've
4. **He is** my best dog.	He'z	He's	He'is
5. **We will** have a lot of fun there.	We'll	We'will	We'l
6. It **is not** raining outside today.	isn't	is'nt	i'snt
7. **Let us** hurry up or we will be late!	Le'ts	Let'us	Let's
8. My dog **would not** chew on a book.	wouldn't	wou'ldnt	would't
9. We **will not** be late if we go right now.	will'nt	wil'nt	won't
10. **You are** the best dog at the show, Rover!	You're	You've	You'r

Name _____ Date _____

I-35E. Answering Questions with Contractions

Answer each question using a complete sentence. Use a contraction in your answer. Then circle the contraction that you used.

1. What is the weather like outside today? _____

_____

2. What is something you should not do on the playground? _____

_____

3. What do you think your parents will get you for your birthday? _____

_____

4. What would you spend $100 on? _____

_____

5. What would your mother do if you brought home all
   A+'s on your report card?

   _____

   _____

   _____

6. What would your father do if you brought home a dog?

_____

_____

7. What will you do this weekend? _____

_____

8. Does your teacher drive a convertible? _____

_____

9. What is something you cannot do at the lunch table? _____

_____

10. What is something kids are not supposed to have at school? _____

_____

I-35F. Finding Contractions in a Story

Read the following story and circle every contraction you find.

My dad came home one night and said, "I've got good news, kids!"

"What?" asked my mother. "What's the good news?"

Dad said, "We're going to take a vacation! Guess where we're going?"

I said, "I don't know! Where are we going?"

My little brother, Bobby, said, "Let's go to Walt Disney World! Is that where we are going?"

Dad laughed. "No," he said. "We can't go to Walt Disney World this year. That isn't where we're going."

"Then tell us," I cried. "I won't be able to sleep until you tell us!"

Dad said, "We'll be on an airplane. We will soon be landing in Florida. Then we'll take a taxi to see your Aunt Jane."

"Oh, no," said Bobby. "That's not going to be fun. I'm not going. I don't want to see Aunt Jane."

Mom said, "Well, if Bobby can't go, then I guess we'll have to let him stay home to take care of the dogs. I know they aren't going!"

I said, "I want to see Aunt Jane. She's got lots of toys in her yard."

Dad said, "There's more news, kids. Aunt Jane is going to take us all to Sea World and Busch Gardens. She's paying for the whole trip!"

Bobby said, "Well, I guess I'll go then. I don't want to take care of the dogs at home by myself."

Mom said, "That's better. Let's get our clothes packed! I'd like to be ready to leave soon."

I said, "It's going to be fun going to Florida. I think flying on an airplane is going to be great. I haven't ever been on an airplane!"

Dad looked at us and smiled. "It's going to be a great vacation. Let's go!"

How many contractions did you find? _____

Lesson I-36 Compound Words (Increasing Vocabulary Words)

To the Teacher

Most children catch on to compound words quite easily, although some may confuse syllables with words (for example: *butter-fly* is a compound word with two separate words joined together; but *light-ning* is two syllables, each part is not a word by itself). The purpose of this lesson is to provide practice for students in identifying, writing, and using compound words.

To the Student

Today you are going to learn about compound words. These are special words that are made up of two words "stuck" or glued together to make one bigger word. Here's an example: *doghouse*. What are the two words that make up *doghouse*? (dog, house)

Let's try some more: *butterfly* (butter, fly); cookbook (cook, book); watermelon (water, melon).

But be careful! Not all longer words are made up of two separate words. Think about the word stapler. Could you break that into two parts? (yes) What are they? (stap-ler) Is a "stape" anything? (no) How about "ler"? (no) These are just two parts of the word, or syllables. Those words don't mean anything by themselves. In a compound word, when you break the word apart, both words can stand alone as a real, complete word. Don't get fooled!

When I think about a compound word, I'm going to pretend to grab one word from over here (reach to the left), and grab another word from over there (reach to the right), and then I'm going to glue them together (pound your fists together one time to make a smacking noise). There! Now I have a compound word—two words stuck together!

Worksheets

Answers to Worksheet I-36A:

Part One:

1. grandmother (grand/mother)
2. weekend (week/end)
3. afternoon (after/noon)
4. basketball (basket/ball)
5. outside (out/side)
6. sidewalk (side/walk)
7. snowball (snow/ball)
8. weatherperson (weather/person)
9. rainbow (rain/bow)
10. bookstore (book/store)

Part Two:

1. grandfather
2. doghouse
3. newspaper
4. snowball
5. firefighter
6. mailbox
7. baseball
8. cowboy

Answers to Worksheet I-36B:

Part One:

1. starfish
2. upstairs
3. basketball
4. mailbox
5. snowman
6. blueberries
7. playground
8. fireplace
9. rattlesnake
10. airplane

Part Two:

1. house
2. ball
3. place
4. drop
5. paper
6. cow
7. foot
8. birth
9. grand
10. rain

Part Three:

1. baseball, football, basketball
2. strawberry, blueberry
3. snowman, snowfort
4. firefighter, policeman
5. rainbow, raindrop, snowflake

Answers to Worksheet I-36C:

Part One:

1. cuppaper (cupcake)
2. rainfoot (raincoat)
3. bareprint (barefoot)
4. fingercake (fingerprint)
5. newscoat (newspaper)

Part Two:

Students' answers will vary.

Follow-up Activities

1. **Compound Word Puzzles:** Have students make simple compound word puzzles by writing the compound word on a card and then cutting the card into two puzzle pieces. Show students how to make swirls or points or jagged edges so that the two puzzle parts easily fit back together.

2. **Silly Sentences:** Some students will be able to write silly sentences in which the compound words are mismatched. Have these students make silly sentences with only half of the word correct; then let them read the sentences to the class and have others try to guess what the word should be.

Name _____ Date _____

I-36A. Identifying a Compound Word

Part One: Circle the compound word in each sentence. Then write the two words that make up the compound word.

1. My grandmother is coming to visit us.   _____

                                                                                  _____

2. We will have fun on the weekend.   _____

                                                                                  _____

3. In the afternoon, we will play together.   _____

                                                                                  _____

4. I like to play basketball.   _____

                                                                                  _____

5. If the weather is nice, we will go outside.   _____

                                                                                  _____

6. Let's jump rope on the sidewalk.   _____

                                                                                  _____

7. Don't throw a snowball at your little sister!   _____

                                                                                  _____

8. The weatherperson said it will be sunny tomorrow. _____

                                                                                  _____

9. There may even be a rainbow in the sky.   _____

                                                                                  _____

10. I bought a book at the bookstore this morning.   _____

Name _____ Date _____

I-36A. Identifying a Compound Word (continued)

Part Two: Circle the compound word that could be an answer to each question.

1. I went to visit my _____.

   sister   mother   grandfather   uncle

2. The dog has wet feet, so he must stay in the _____.

   garage   yard   cage   doghouse

3. My dad likes to come home and read the _____.

   newspaper   magazines   mail   books

4. I threw a _____ at my friend.

   ball   stick   dish   snowball

5. There was an accident so we had to call a _____.

   cop   firefighter   teacher   telephone

6. Is there anything for me in the _____?

   mailbox   box   basement   office

7. Let's play _____.

   tag   baseball   school   video games

8. I watched a movie about a _____.

   robber   tiger   cowboy   mouse

Name _____ Date _____

I-36B. Writing Compound Words

Part One: Make a compound word by combining two words in each row. Circle both parts.

1. star   down   fish   up   6. blue   box   five   berries

2. any   up   stairs   ball   7. park   play   fast   ground

3. basket   blue   ball   toy   8. super   fire   place   berries

4. mail   grand   box   flake   9. doll   rattle   fast   snake

5. snow   man   where   place   10. air   not   birth   plane

Part Two: Finish writing the compound word. Use the clues to help you.

1. where a dog lives: dog _____

2. a game you can play: basket _____

3. a place where you can burn logs: fire _____

4. something wet that comes out of the sky: rain _____

5. something you read to get the news: news _____

6. a person who rides a horse on a ranch: _____ boy

7. what you leave with your shoes after you walk in the mud: _____ print

8. a special day for you: _____day

9. your mother's mother: _____mother

10. something you might see in the sky after a storm: _____bow

Part Three: Write a compound word that fits the clue. There might be more than one correct answer.

1. a game you can play with a ball: _____

2. a flavor of ice cream: _____

3. something made of snow: _____

4. a person in the community who helps you: _____

5. something you would see in the sky: _____

I-36C. A Set of Silly Sentences

Part One: The sentences below are full of mixed-up compound words. Underline the mixed-up compound words. Somewhere in another sentence is the part you are looking for. Rearrange the mixed-up words so they make sense.

1. My grandmother will make a cuppaper for my birthday.

_____

2. Put on your rainfoot because it's raining outside.

_____

3. Don't go around bareprint because there is glass on the floor.

_____

4. Someone left a big fingercake around the fireplace.

_____

5. My grandfather likes to read the newscoat when he eats breakfast.

_____

Part Two: Your turn! Write six compound words. Write a good sentence for each compound word. Then mix up the parts of the compound words and rewrite each sentence with the new, mixed-up compound word. Trade papers with a friend. Can you figure out what the original word is supposed to be?

Lesson I-37: Changing the Noun (Editing Words)

To the Teacher

Students now move toward critical reading of a sentence and making changes of just a word or two. In this lesson, students are to change a noun to make it fit the picture or thought.

To the Student

Listen to this sentence and tell me what's wrong with it: "I am going to write my paper with this apple." (probably will write with a pencil or pen, not an apple) Does one little word make a difference in what you hear and understand? (yes)

Listen to this sentence: "My father drove his new car on the river." What's wrong with that? (you drive a car on a road, not a river)

On these worksheets, you are going to have to read each sentence carefully and decide which word does not make sense.

An editing mark to use is this: Cross out the word that you don't want. Then write your new word choice above it.

Worksheets

Answers to Worksheet I-37A:

1. pencil (book)
2. dog (cat)
3. apples (grapes)
4. trumpet (piano)
5. lake (pool)
6. drawing (painting)
7. shed (cabin)
8. floor (lamp)
9. star (rainbow)
10. zipper (bandage)

Answers to Worksheet I-37B:

Students' answers may vary.

1. kitten (giraffe, ape, etc.)
2. spider (giraffe)
3. toes (legs)
4. paste (cereal, etc.)
5. couch (computer, typewriter)
6. pizza (rain)
7. horn (bubble)
8. dolphins (fish)
9. shoe (ball)
10. rugs (horses)

Follow-up Activity

Have students write five sentences using a common noun at the top of a sheet of paper. Then have them rewrite the sentence at the bottom, leaving a blank for the word. Have students exchange the bottom parts of their sheets and see if they can determine the missing word based on the clues in the rest of the sentence. For example: banana.

I love to eat a _____. (no clues to tell what the word is)

My favorite fruit is a yellow _____. (*clues*: fruit, yellow)

Name _____ Date _____

I-37A. Change the Noun (Picture Clues)

Look at each picture. Then change the word that does not make sense with the picture.

1. I dropped my pencil.

2. The dog is on the house.

3. I enjoy eating apples and bananas.

4. My sister is really good at playing the trumpet.

5. Do you want to swim in the lake with me?

6. The artist made a beautiful drawing of the woods.

7. We had a great vacation in a shed on the mountains.

8. It's dark in here so I will turn on the floor.

9. Look! There is a beautiful star in the sky.

10. I need to put a zipper on my cut.

I-37B. Change the Noun (Word Clues)

Read each sentence. Then change one word so that the sentence makes sense.

1. An interesting zoo animal is a kitten.

2. That spider has a really long neck!

3. A spider has eight toes.

4. At breakfast, my family likes to eat bacon, toast, and paste.

5. It's my turn to type a letter on the couch.

6. You are all wet. Have you been out in the pizza?

7. I am going to blow a big horn with this gum.

8. My brother likes to catch dolphins with his fishing pole.

9. There is a hole in my shoe so it won't bounce anymore.

10. The sleigh is pulled by two beautiful rugs.

Lesson I-38: Changing the Adjective (Describing Word) (Editing Words)

To the Teacher

Adjectives can spice up a sentence to make it more interesting. The purpose of this lesson is for students to edit sentences by replacing a describing word (adjective) with a more interesting or appropriate word.

To the Student

Gather some interesting pictures for students to view. Take a look at these pictures. Who can give me a good sentence that describes each one? (Call on students.)

What if I said: (hold up picture of a huge dog) "This is a big dog." Does the word "big" really indicate how big this dog is? What is another word—a synonym—that you could use to describe this dog? (enormous, gigantic, etc.) Sometimes picking just the right word makes all the difference!

Words that describe how something looks, acts, or appears are called *adjectives*. Here are some examples:

"That is a *fat* man." *Fat* describes the man. What are other words you could use to describe the man's appearance? (hefty, stocky, etc.)

"The *sly* fox sneaked into the chicken house." What word describes the fox? (sly) What other words could you use to describe the fox? (sneaky, cunning, tricky, etc.)

"The *golden* sunset made us run for our cameras." What word describes the sunset? (golden) What other words could you use to describe the rainbow? (shiny, bright, yellowish, etc.)

Some adjectives are used very often—*big, pretty, nice, good,* and so on. Try to use some more interesting words instead of the same ones all the time.

Worksheets

Answers to Worksheet I-38A:

1. clean (muddy, dirty)
2. tiny (high, big, tall)
3. sticky (slippery)
4. boring (exciting, thrilling)
5. chilly (hot)
6. striped (checkered)
7. scary (funny, silly)
8. long (short, curled)
9. soft (loud)
10. friendly (mean, suspicious)

Answers to Worksheet I-38B:

1. nice (wonderful, delicious)
2. big (huge, gigantic)
3. friendly (sweet, affectionate)
4. good (outstanding, excellent)
5. tiny (puny, miniature)
6. nice (exciting, beautiful)
7. cold (freezing, chilly)
8. hard (complicated, elaborate, difficult)
9. interesting (fascinating, intriguing)
10. wet (dripping, damp)

Follow-up Activity

Retirement Ceremony for Overused Adjectives: Once students become familiar with using more interesting adjectives, you can have a "retirement ceremony" for overused adjectives. At the ceremony, officially retire the words by putting them on cards and into a shoebox. Have students make a list of alternative adjectives that can be used instead, and post the list in an obvious spot.

I-38A. Change the Adjective (Picture Clues)

Look at each picture. Then change the word in each sentence that does not make sense with the picture.

1. Please wipe off that clean dog.

2. We climbed the tiny tree.

3. This floor is sticky.

4. The boring football game lasted for an hour.

5. The chilly bath water made me reach for a cold drink.

6. I took the striped towel to the pool.

7. We all laughed at the scary clown.

8. Do you like my hair long like this?

9. Turn down the television! The volume is too soft!

10. You have such a friendly dog.

Name _____ Date _____

I-38B. Add an Interesting Adjective

Read each sentence. Change one common adjective to something more interesting. Check out the words in the word box for some ideas!

delicious	gigantic	excellent	miniature
chilly	complicated	fascinating	dripping
huge	outstanding	affectionate	freezing
complicated	delicious	wonderful	exciting

1. This is a **nice** dinner.

2. I live in a **big** house.

3. That is a **friendly** dog.

4. You did a **good** job on the test.

5. The book was about a **tiny** mouse.

6. There is a **nice** view from the window.

7. It's **cold** outside in the snow.

8. This game is **hard** to understand.

9. I thought the museum exhibit was **interesting**.

10. My hair is **wet**.

Lesson I-39: Changing the Verb (Action Word)

(Editing Words)

To the Teacher

Verbs are another common group of words that can be changed and improved in sentence writing. The purpose of this lesson is to provide students with editing practice in using verbs.

To the Student

Think of a frog. What are some words that tell how a frog moves? (leaps, jumps, hops) Now think of a snake. What are some words that describe how a snake moves? (slides, slithers)

Words that describe action are called *verbs*. There are other types of words that are also verbs, but in this lesson we are concerned with words that tell about something happening. Here are some examples. What verb am I describing?

Something you do at the dinner table. (eat)

Something you do at an amusement park. (ride)

Something you do when you're watching a funny movie. (laugh)

Something you do when you're watching a sad movie. (cry)

Something you do when you're outside. (play, run, climb, etc.)

Just like with nouns and adjectives, some verbs are better or clearer than others. If I said, "The snake moved down the road," this tells you what happened. But if I said, "The snake slithered slowly down the road," this helps give you an even better picture in your head of how the snake moved.

In this lesson you will be working with finding and changing verbs in sentences.

Worksheets

Answers to Worksheet I-39A:

1. walking (running)
2. drinking (eating)
3. crying (laughing)
4. petting (hitting)
5. destroying (fixing, repairing)
6. sleep (ride)
7. jump (slip)
8. ski (surf)
9. ride (paint, build)
10. slip (dive)

Answers to Worksheet I-39B:

1. walk (stroll, amble)
2. hop (leap, jump)
3. tease (torment, trick, bother)
4. look (peek, examine, stare)
5. ate (devoured, gulped, tore into)
6. sleeping (exhausted, worn out)
7. cut (trim, style, shape)
8. run (gallop, race)
9. yell (shout, scream)
10. barking (howling, whining)

Follow-up Activity

Have students begin "collecting" colorful verbs by writing them in a class or individual booklet when they encounter them in their reading or writing activities. At the top of each booklet page, write some common verbs (run, walk, say, make) and, as instances arise, add synonyms to the page. ("Oh, there's a good word we could use instead of *walk*!")

I-39A. Change the Verb (Picture Clues)

Look at each picture. Then change the word in each sentence that does not make sense with the picture.

1. The boy was walking down the hall to get to class.

2. We enjoyed drinking our pizza.

3. We were all crying after we heard the funny joke.

4. Stop petting the cat!

5. My brother is having fun destroying the car.

6. I want to sleep on the horse.

7. Be careful so you don't jump on the banana peel.

8. The woman got her surfboard and began to ski on the waves.

9. My brother likes to ride model airplanes.

10. I am afraid to slip into the pool.

I-39B. Changing the Verb (Word Clues)

Read each sentence. Change one common verb to something more interesting. Check out the words in the word box for some ideas!

examine	**gulped**	**exhausted**	**trim**	**gallop**
howling	**stroll**	**leap**	**torment**	**race**
scream	**peek**	**leap**		

1. I will **walk** to school with my friend.

2. Can you **hop** over the rock?

3. It is not nice to **tease** people.

4. Would you like to **look** at my postcard?

5. The wolf **ate** the raw meat.

6. I was **sleeping** the next day after I stayed up all night.

7. Carla likes to **cut** other people's hair.

8. The horse can **run** fast.

9. I can hear you so don't **yell** so loudly.

10. Make the dog stop **barking**.

Lesson I-40: Changing One Word (Mixed Practice)

(Editing Words)

To the Teacher

Students now have had practice in making changes to one specific type of word (nouns, adjectives, verbs). The purpose of this lesson is to provide mixed practice for students to select one word in a sentence that needs to be changed or improved.

To the Student

You are now getting good at looking for words that don't make sense in a sentence or words that could improve the sentence.

You are going to have some practice now in editing sentences carefully to find a word in each one that should be changed.

Worksheets

Answers to Worksheet I-40A:

1. flower (tree)	6. horse (bike)
2. put (dropped)	7. sad (funny)
3. little (huge)	8. movie (book)
4. eat (drink)	9. mother (father)
5. glass (cup)	10. stir (water)

Answers to Worksheet I-40B:

1. ride (swim)	6. fly (paddle)
2. low (high)	7. luggage (food)
3. blue (yellow, golden)	8. open (close)
4. run (look)	9. early (late)
5. hot (cold)	10. breakfast (or evening) (dinner, or morning)

Follow-up Activity

Provide examples of mixed practice editing for students. You may want to write a sentence a day on the board or select some students who are able to write a "silly sentence" and have others correct it.

Name _____ Date _____

I-40A. Make a Change (Picture Clues)

Look at each picture. Then change one word in each sentence that does not make sense with the picture.

1. The strong man tried to chop down the flower.

2. Bobby put his books and pencils on the floor.

3. I just love my cute little dog.

4. Do you like to eat milk?

5. Please hand me that glass so I can fill it with water.

6. I fell off my new horse.

7. This movie is really sad.

8. This movie is really sad.

9. My mother likes to drive fast in her new car.

10. My grandmother likes to stir her flowers.

Name _____ Date _____

I-40B. Make a Change (Word Clues)

Read each sentence. Change one word in each to make the sentence make sense.

1. In the summer, we like to ride in the lake.

2. We have to cut the grass when it gets too low.

3. I love to look at the blue sun in the sky.

4. The cat likes to sit in front of the window and run out.

5. Penguins live where it is hot.

6. At camp, we can fly our canoes down the river.

7. The ants are carrying luggage to their ant hill.

8. Remember to open your door before the car is moving.

9. I like to get up early on Saturday because we don't have school.

10. What would you like for breakfast this evening?

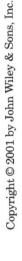

Lesson I-41: Finding Omitted Words

To the Teacher

It is very common among young writers to hastily write a sentence and leave out a word. It is also common for the writer to read the sentence back and put the word in as if it were there all the time. The purpose of this lesson is to make students aware of and to look for omitted words in sentences.

To the Student

Look at this sentence on the board: We had a lot fun this weekend at the beach. Will someone read that for me? You may or may not have noticed the missing word. What is it? ("of" after "We had a lot...") Why do you think some people would forget that word? (it's little; you don't really need it to figure out the sentence)

A lot of times it is easy to forget to write each and every word. When you are thinking of what you want to say in your head, you might be rushing a little bit and writing down the words quickly. It's easy to skip over a word, especially a little word, but it is still important for the sentence to be complete.

In this lesson, you are going to have to be good detectives. I am going to read some things that are missing words. See if you can find them and figure out what they should be.

An editing mark that will be helpful to you is called the "caret" (not carrot, that's something you eat). When you have found the spot where the missing word should be, draw the little caret (∧) and then write the word in the space above it. For example:

You did good job on test.

Worksheets

Answers to Worksheet I-41A:

1. Many people like to a pet.
2. Dogs can wonderful companions.
3. It is fun to get a puppy, but it can be a of work.
4. Many people like have cats.
5. Sometimes cats and dogs do not get with each other.
6. An elephant would be unusual pet.
7. A friend mine has a pet squirrel.
8. Another friend of wants to get a baby raccoon.
9. Look around the next time you to a pet store.
10. Your next best friend might waiting for you.

Answers to Worksheet I-41B:

My favorite winter activity is skiing. I like to (*go*) ice skating, too. They are both a lot of fun. I have been (*to*) the mountains. My family stayed at (*a or the*) hotel at the top of the mountains. Every morning we got to ski down big hills. One morning my sister forgot (*to*) bring her mittens. My mother said that I should go back with her to get them. It (*is or was*) too cold to ski without mittens. The next morning she didn't forget them, but I forgot mine!

Follow-up Activities

1. **Work Samples:** Start collecting students' samples of written work. When you come across sentences with missing words, use them (anonymously) for practice activities. Call students' attention to the type of words to look out for—probably *to*, *and*, *is*, and other little words.

2. **Dictated Sentences:** If students are beginning to write short dictated sentences, have them say the sentences out loud before writing and count how many words they would expect to have in the sentence. After they write the sentence, have them recount to make sure they have enough words.

3. Have students "keep the sentence in their head" and then write the sentence on the board, with a number in mind of how many words there should be. Before evaluating the sentence, have the students count the words to check for any possible missing words.

Name _____ Date _____

I-41A. Find the Missing Word (Sentences)

Read each sentence. Use a caret (^) to insert the missing word.

1. Many people like to a pet.

2. Dogs can wonderful companions.

3. It is fun to get a puppy, but it can be a of work.

4. Other people like have cats.

5. Sometimes cats and dogs do not get with each other.

6. An elephant would be unusual pet.

7. A friend mine has a pet squirrel.

8. Another friend of wants to get a baby raccoon.

9. Look around the next time you to a pet store.

10. Your next best friend might waiting for you.

Name _____ Date _____

I-41B. Find the Missing Words (Paragraph)

Read the story. There are five missing words in the story. Can you figure out all five and write the correct words?

My favorite winter activity is skiing. I like to ice skating, too. They are

both a lot of fun. I have been the mountains. My family stayed at hotel at the

top of the mountains. Every morning we got to ski down big hills. One morning

my sister forgot bring her mittens. My mother said that I should go back with

her to get them. It too cold to ski without mittens. The next morning she didn't

forget them, but I forgot mine!

Section II
Writing Sentences

Lesson II-1: Identifying a Complete Sentence
(Writing a Basic Sentence)

To the Teacher

Students should now be ready to start the basics of writing in sentences. The first step is for students to recognize what a complete sentence "sounds like." Lessons I-1 through I-6 provided activities for students to practice writing sentences ("say the whole thing"). Students may of course need some review. The purpose of this lesson is to give students practice in orally composing and then recognizing what "sounds like" a complete sentence.

A sheet of pictures is used to give students something to begin talking and writing about.

To the Student

Do you remember what a "complete sentence" is? Basically, it's when you say something that sounds complete. For example, if I walked up to you and said, "A brown dog," you wouldn't know what happened to that brown dog, what that brown dog did, or where that brown dog was going. I have to tell you more—to give you the complete thought. How does this sound to you: "A brown dog bit me on the leg." Now you know exactly who did what! Ouch!

Oral Practice: Tell me if these are complete sentences or not. If not, can you figure out what information is missing?

1. The dog. (no—we need to know what the dog did)
2. The big black dog named Rover and the little cat. (no—we don't know what happened to them)
3. The woman sat at a table. (yes)
4. Many dishes were in the sink. (yes)
5. Dirty dishes and glasses. (no—what about them? what's important?)
6. The boy got a box. (yes)
7. The boy had a birthday. (yes)
8. The big beautiful horse. (no—what did the horse do?)
9. The big horse was standing. (yes)
10. The girls were. (no—were what?)
11. The girls raced to the finish line. (yes)
12. The little girl. (no—what about her?)
13. Lost a balloon. (no—who lost a balloon?)
14. The little girl lost her balloon. (yes)
15. The girl had very long hair. (yes)
16. The girls' hair. (no—what about it?)
17. The boy was tipping his. (no—his what?)
18. The boy tipped his chair. (yes)
19. The chair is going to fall. (yes)
20. Falling on the floor. (no—who or what is falling on the floor?)

Worksheet

Look over all eight of the pictures on Worksheet II-1. I am going to tell you a sentence. I want you to find the picture that the sentence is about.

The girl is unhappy because she lost her balloon. (6)

The cat was chased by the dog. (1)

The boy is going to be on the floor in a minute. (8)

The girl is going to be sad because she did not win the race. (5)

The beautiful horse was standing in a field. (4)

The boy was surprised on his birthday. (3)

It will take a long time to wash all that hair. (7)

The woman has a lot of work to do today. (2)

There are lots of different sentences that could each describe the very same picture. Now I want you to think of a complete sentence that could go with each picture and write them on another sheet of paper.

Examples:

1. The dog chased the cat up the tree. The cat is afraid of the dog.

2. The woman is tired. The woman doesn't want to clean her house.

3. The boy is having a birthday party. The boy got a great present.

4. The horse is pretty. The horse is waiting for his owner.

5. The girl is going to win the race. The next girl is going to come in second.

6. The little girl let go of her balloon. The wind carried the balloon away.

7. The girl has long hair. The girl is wearing a wig.

8. The boy is going to tip over in his chair. The boy is going to fall on the floor.

Follow-up Activity

Have students write their sentences about each picture, then share their various perspectives of the pictures. Compare them!

II-1. Understanding Complete Sentences

1.	2.
3.	4.
5.	6.
7.	8.

Lesson II-2: Identifying a Sentence in Print
(Writing a Basic Sentence)

To the Teacher

A complete sentence should tell a complete thought. A sentence in print can be recognized by starting with a capital letter and ending with a punctuation mark. The purpose of this lesson is to make students aware of these qualifications for a string of words acting as a sentence.

To the Student

You wrote some good sentences about the pictures you looked at in the last lesson. Who remembers a good sentence for some of them? (Write them on the board.) Who remembers what a sentence is? (words that make a complete thought) When you say a sentence, you can hear whether or not it is a complete thought. But when you are writing or reading, you can also see whether it is a complete thought. Sentences have a special way to start and a special way to end.

The way to *start* a sentence is with a *capital letter.* The way to *end* a sentence is with *end punctuation.* There are several ways to end a sentence and we will learn more about that later. For this lesson, I want you to look for a *period* at the end of the sentence.

When you are with your parents and they are driving the car, what do they do at a stop sign? (hopefully stop) A period is a stop sign for when you are reading or writing. It lets us know that the complete thought is over. Stop and think about it. When you are writing, remember to put a period when you have said what you wanted to say about your topic.

Worksheet

Answers to Worksheet II-2:

1. yes	5. no	9. no
2. yes, add period	6. yes	10. yes, add period
3. no	7. no	11. no
4. yes, add capital letter and period	8. yes	12. yes

Follow-up Activity

Have students draw a picture of this story.

Name _____ Date _____

II-2. Complete Thought? Written Correctly?

Remember that a sentence tells a complete thought, starts with a capital letter, and ends with a period (in this lesson).

Write yes/no to show which of these tell complete thoughts. However, if the complete thought is not written correctly, correct any mistakes that you find.

1. Once there was a big black dog. _____

2. The dog liked to chase cats _____

3. One day he. _____

4. the cat did not like to be chased _____

5. Scratched the dog with her claws. _____

6. The dog was really mad now. _____

7. The dog growled at. _____

8. The cat scratched right back. _____

9. the dog decided he would leave the _____

10. The cat smiled and drank her bowl of milk _____

11. Learned a lesson _____

12. It is not nice to fight like cats and dogs. _____

Lesson II-3: Writing Short Sentences

(Writing a Basic Sentence)

To the Teacher

Once students have the "ear" for what a sentence sounds like, and are aware of starting with a capital letter and ending with a period, they are ready to start writing good basic sentences. The purpose of this lesson is to give students practice in writing short sentences. For purposes of this lesson, a short sentence is really a "simple" sentence with one subject and one verb: The dog ran. The black cat jumped over the bowl. A man sat down in his chair.

To the Student

Something you will do a lot of is writing simple sentences. Later you will learn things like how to add words to make a sentence more interesting, how to connect sentences to make them longer, and how to choose words carefully to write exactly what you want to say. For now, though, we're just going to work on writing complete basic sentences.

Remember what it takes to write a good sentence? (complete thought, capital letter, period) For this exercise, you will be given a pool of words to use. This worksheet has a lot of short words in it. You should be familiar with how they sound and how to write the starting syllables or parts of the longer words.

You don't have to worry right now about long sentences. Just make sure you follow the three guidelines for making a good short sentence.

Worksheet

Answers to Worksheet II-3:

Students' answers will vary.

Follow-up Activities

1. Have students exchange papers and read each others' sentences. Tell them to be on the lookout for capital letters to start, periods at the end, and complete thoughts.

2. Give students two or three words every day to use in a sentence as a writing warm-up activity.

   Word Pool #1: tablet, ant, answer, taffy, daddy, apple, basket, add

   Word Pool #2: absent, raccoon, alley, cap, saxophone, taxi, ladder, ax

   Word Pool #3: energy, pebble, pencil, elevator, egg, letter, elephant, red

   Word Pool #4: energy, messy, pepper, referee, exit, best, necklace, web

   Word Pool #5: igloo, river, rib, icky, riddle, kitten, iguana, licorice

   Word Pool #6: lipstick, ill, interview, dig, nickel, fin, sister, limp

   Word Pool #7: octopus, odd, costume, lobster, robber, hot, doctor, fox

   Word Pool #8: olive, polliwog, mom, copper, rocket, otter, operate, doll

   Word Pool #9: upstairs, ugly, juggle, funny, umbrella, dusty, butter, tub

   Word Pool #10: underwear, submarine, gull, bun, up, tusk, supper, puddle

Name _____ Date _____

II-3. Write a Sentence

Use each word below to write a complete sentence. Remember
to start with a capital letter and end with a period.

| magazine | fancy | baboon | ladder | accident |
| ambulance | family | attic | passenger | cafeteria |

1. _____

_____

2. _____

_____

3. _____

_____

4. _____

_____

5. _____

_____

6. _____

_____

7. _____

_____

8. _____

_____

9. _____

_____

10. _____

_____

Draw pictures to illustrate some of your sentences. Write the number of the sentence by the
picture!

Lesson II-4: Identifying a Fragment (Writing a Basic Sentence)

To the Teacher

A very common writing error for students is to write incomplete sentences, or a fragment of a sentence. This is especially common when students are answering a question (e.g., Who lives in the White House? This may be answered by "The president" instead of "The president lives in the White House.") or when students have written several sentences about something and "add a thought" that turns out to be a phrase instead of a sentence. The purpose of this lesson is to have students identify fragments of a sentence as answers to questions and in a paragraph or story context.

To the Student

A word that you will need to know and understand is the word "fragment." What this means is a part of something, not the whole thing. When we talked earlier about writing in sentences, we said that a sentence tells a complete thought. We wouldn't say, "A dog." We would say, "I see a dog," or "A dog is outside." It has to tell us enough so we know and understand the complete thought. Remember to test for a fragment by thinking: If someone walked up to me and just said the fragment to me, would it make sense? If someone walked up to me and said, "A dog," would I understand? (no)

In this lesson, you are going to have some practice in picking out those fragments that are supposed to be complete sentences. Don't let one get past you!

Worksheet

Answers to Worksheet II-4:

Part One:

1. X	5. OK	9. OK
2. OK	6. OK	10. OK
3. X	7. X	
4. OK	8. X	

Part Two:

In the gym.

And candy.

And games to play.

To win a big stuffed bear.

But we did not want to because.

Follow-up Activity

Begin collecting student samples of this type of error. After you blank out the student's name, reproduce them and have students analyze the mistakes made.

II-4. Answers to Questions

Part One: Read the questions. Put an X after the answers that are fragments. Put OK if the answer is a complete sentence.

1. Where is the ambulance going? To the hospital. _____

2. Do you know the answer to the math problem? I know the answer. _____

3. Is the apple red or green? Green. _____

4. Who cleaned out the attic? Mother cleaned out the attic yesterday. _____

5. Where is your house? My house is behind the alley. _____

6. What are you reading? I'm reading a magazine. _____

7. How many people are in your family? My mother, my father, and me. _____

8. What are you doing on Saturday? Going to the park to ride my bike. _____

9. Who can play the saxophone? Mike can play the saxophone. _____

10. Who made this strawberry jam? My grandmother made the jam. _____

Part Two: Read this short story. Underline any fragments that you find.

The Fun Fair

My school had a fun fair last Saturday. In the gym. There were lots of fun things to do. There were rides. And candy. And games to play. We bought some tickets for a raffle. To win a big stuffed bear. We didn't win, but it was fun. It was late when we went home. Mom said we had to go right to bed. But we did not want to because. I hope they have the fair next year.

Lesson II-5: Repairing a Fragment (Writing a Basic Sentence)

To the Teacher

After students become adept at identifying a fragment, they need to be able to repair one! The simplest way is to take the fragment and probably add a subject to it, but in some cases the verb may be missing. The purpose of this lesson is to help students practice repairing fragments by applying the "Who—Do" test to each fragment.

To the Student

When you find a fragment in writing, you have to be able to make some quick repairs to fix it and make it into a sentence.

What's wrong with this fragment? (Write it on the board.) "going to the store." We don't know WHO (or what) is going to the store. Every sentence has to have a WHO.

What's wrong with this fragment? "Marvin and Tony." What did Marvin and Tony DO? Every sentence has to have a part that tells what the main subject (the WHO) is up to!

Worksheet

Answers to Worksheet II-5:

Students' answers will vary. Here are examples.

1. My sister ate the rotten egg. The rotten egg was stinky.

2. The circus elephant was huge. The circus elephant gave rides.

3. We rode in the elevator. We had fun jumping in the elevator.

4. I have lots of energy. The children had lots of energy today.

5. Dad put pepper on the meat. I don't like pepper on the meat.

6. My bedroom is a mess. I love my bedroom.

7. The messy desk needs to be cleaned up. I have the messy desk in my class.

8. I wrote a nice letter. This is a nice letter.

9. I wore my mother's necklace. My mother's necklace is black.

10. Dad's telephone is broken. I can use Dad's telephone to call you.

Follow-up Activity

Have students categorize the fragments that they repair into WHO repairs (ones that need a subject) and DO repairs (ones that need a verb).

II-5. Fragment Repair

Read each fragment. You can fix each one any way you want. Make sure you have a WHO (or what) in each sentence. Make sure you have a part that tells what the who is going to DO.

1. The rotten egg. _____

_____

2. The circus elephant. _____

_____

3. In the elevator. _____

_____

4. Lots of energy. _____

_____

5. Pepper on the meat. _____

_____

6. My bedroom. _____

_____

7. The messy desk. _____

_____

8. A nice letter. _____

_____

9. My mother's necklace. _____

_____

_____

10. Dad's telephone. _____

_____

_____

Lesson II-6: Identifying a Run-On (Writing a Basic Sentence)

To the Teacher

Another common mistake when writing sentences is running what should be two separate sentences together without a period. (*The dog is big he jumped on me.*) Students should be taught to pay attention to when the first complete thought has ended, and show the stop by putting a period there (*The dog is big. / He jumped on me.*) The purpose of this lesson is to provide practice for students in identifying when a group of words is actually a run-on sentence and should be two separate sentences.

To the Student

I am going to write some words on the board. It will look like one long sentence, but actually it is two sentences. A period is needed somewhere to end the first sentence. Can you figure out where that period should be?

Melvin and Sandy went to the beach to go swimming and diving / they also had a picnic on the beach.

How did you know that you should stop after the word *diving*? (It sounds like the thought is finished; the second part is talking about something different.)

Worksheet

Answers to Worksheet II-6:

1. igloo / it	5. OK	9. OK
2. OK	6. OK	10. pickle / it
3. today / I	7. river / it	
4. Mittens / she	8. puzzle / I	

Follow-up Activity

Look for examples of run-ons in students' work. Start compiling a collection of anonymous mistakes that can be examined and soon repaired.

Name _____ Date _____

II-6. Find the Run-Ons

Read these groups of words. If it is a run-on sentence, put a slash mark (/) where you think the first sentence should stop. If it is OK, write OK next to it.

1. The eskimos live in the igloo it is very cold up north. _____

2. I have a pet iguana named Sam who is very cute. _____

3. I am not feeling well today I think I am ill. _____

4. My kitten is named Mittens she likes to nibble on my fingers. _____

5. I like this red lipstick because it makes me look like a clown. _____

6. We will have chicken for lunch and pork for dinner. _____

7. My sister and I took a boat down the river it was really fun. _____

8. I cannot figure out this jigsaw puzzle I guess I will give up. _____

9. The movie was very silly when the villain

   lost his hair. _____

10. I do not want this pickle it is too cold

   for me. _____

Lesson II-7: Repairing a Run-On (Writing a Basic Sentence)

To the Teacher

When repairing a run-on sentence, the student needs to remember to do two things: (1) put a period where the first sentence stops; and (2) capitalize the first letter of the second or next sentence. Although a run-on sentence may consist of two sentences, there are cases in which students may need to divide a string of words into three sentences. In this lesson, students are given practice in rewriting run-on sentences correctly.

To the Student

After you have read what seems to be a run-on sentence, you have to do two things to repair this mistake. First, you have to figure out where the first sentence or complete thought ends. What should you do at that point? (put in a period) Then what should you do to indicate that the next sentence is starting? (erase or cross out the lower-case letter and put in a capital letter)

In this activity, you will have some practice in making these repairs to some run-on sentences. Watch out for run-on sentences that are really two or even three sentences in disguise!

Worksheet

Answers to Worksheet II-7:

1. I would like to eat an omelet. I would like one for breakfast.

2. OK

3. OK

4. I can't climb over the obstacle. It is too high.

5. My class does a good job in spelling. We work hard in class. We are smart.

6. Tom threw a copper penny into the pond. He jumped in after it.

7. OK

8. The rocket went high into the sky. The rocket went fast.

9. I have to wear goggles when I swim. The water gets into my eyes.

10. Jimmy found a fossil. He was excited. He took it to school.

Follow-up Activity

Collect examples of run-on sentences in students' written work. You may want to reproduce them exactly as written in the students' own handwriting. For students who still have difficulty making the corrections, try using a colored marker to emphasize the period and new capital letter that is needed.

II-7. Repairing the Run-Ons

Rewrite each sentence that is a run-on sentence. Remember to make all needed repairs! If the sentence is OK, write OK.

1. I would like to eat an omelet I would like one for breakfast. _____

_____

2. When we went to the zoo, we saw an ox. _____

_____

3. The doctor will operate on the patient to take out her gallbladder. _____

_____

4. I can't climb over the obstacle it is too high. _____

_____

5. My class does a good job in spelling we work hard in class we are smart. _____

_____

6. Tom threw a copper penny into the pond he jumped in after it. _____

_____

7. I like the vampire costume because it is really scary. _____

_____

8. The rocket went high into the sky the rocket went fast. _____

_____

9. I have to wear goggles when I swim the water gets into my eyes. _____

_____

10. Jimmy found a fossil he was excited he took it to school. _____

_____

Lesson II-8: Writing a Telling Sentence

(Writing a Basic Sentence)

To the Teacher

This is an introductory lesson for the basic sentence types: telling, asking, exclaiming, and commanding. In this lesson, students are given practice in identifying and writing basic telling sentences.

To the Student

There are many different kinds of sentences. We are going to learn about four basic kinds: *telling, asking, exclaiming,* and *commanding.* The first type is a telling sentence, sometimes called a declarative sentence. This is the easiest kind to write, as most sentences are just telling about something.

You can identify a telling sentence by two things. A telling sentence is just that—it tells you something. Also, a telling sentence ends with a period.

Worksheet

Answers to Worksheet II-8:

Part One:

1. yes	5. yes	9. yes
2. yes	6. no	10. no
3. no	7. yes	
4. no	8. no	

Part Two:

Students' sentences will vary.

Follow-up Activity

This activity can be used with students' spelling word lists. Instruct students to write a telling sentence with each of this week's words.

Name _____ Date _____

II-8. Identifying a Telling Sentence

Part One: Are these telling sentences? Write *yes* or *no* after each one.

1. It is raining outside. _____

2. I lost my umbrella somewhere at school. _____

3. Where is my ugly witch mask? _____

4. Go upstairs right now, young lady! _____

5. This is a beautiful picture of a cow. _____

6. Would you help me cut out this picture? _____

7. I watched the bug crawl up the plant. _____

8. Have you ever ridden in a submarine? _____

9. The duckling was swimming in the pond. _____

10. Would you please pass the butter? _____

Part Two: Write a telling sentence about...

1. bubble gum

2. a lucky clover

3. the mud puddle

4. the funny clown

5. buttered popcorn

6. a little brown puppy

7. my pet iguana

8. the rotten banana

9. four otters

10. an old olive

Lesson II-9: Adding a Sentence (Writing a Basic Sentence)

To the Teacher

Writing one telling sentence is fairly easy. But when students have to write longer pieces, they will need to connect several sentences. The purpose of this lesson is to have students practice "telling more" by adding a second telling sentence to the first.

To the Student

You are probably finding that writing telling sentences is pretty easy. Before we go on to the next sentence type, I would like you to practice just a little bit with adding a telling sentence to your first telling sentence. For example, if your first sentence was: *The funny clown was at the circus…* what could the next sentence be? (He did tricks. He did a cartwheel. He jumped on the trampoline.) There are lots of things that tell more about your first sentence.

On this worksheet, you are going to match a sentence with a picture and then add your own telling sentence to the first one. I will give you a prompt that will help direct you towards what to write about.

Worksheet

Answers to Worksheet II-9:

Students' sentences will vary.

1. The boy is running to his brother.
2. The girl is going to slip on a banana peel.
3. The man is knocking on the door.
4. We are having pizza for dinner.
5. The dog is sleeping on a pillow.
6. The papers blew out of the window.

Follow-up Activity

Give students a prompt to add a third telling sentence to each picture on the worksheet. Students may be able to come up with prompts to share.

II-9. Match and Add

Look at the pictures below. Find the telling sentence that matches the picture and write the number beside the sentence. Then follow the prompt to write another telling sentence next to the picture.

The man is knocking on the door.
(Write why the man looks so sad.)

The boy is running to his brother.
(Write how the little boy feels.)

The girl is going to slip on a banana peel.
(Write what will happen to her books.)

The dog is sleeping on a pillow.
(Write why the dog is so tired.)

The papers blew out of the window.
(Write what the papers were about.)

We are having pizza for dinner.
(Write what kind of pizza it is.)

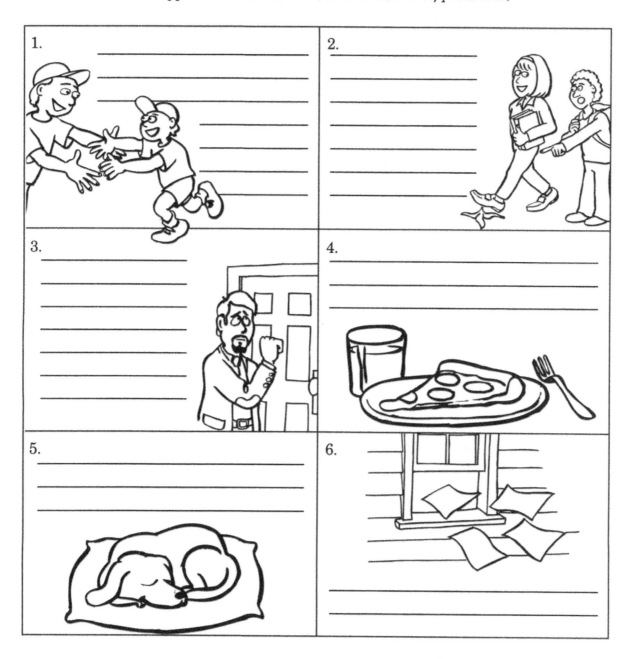

Lesson II-10: Writing a Question (Writing a Basic Sentence)

To the Teacher

The second basic sentence is the question, or interrogative. Students may have difficulty recognizing a question (unless it has the obvious question mark at the end) and changing a statement to question. The purpose of this lesson is to provide practice in both of these skills.

To the Student

What's your name? Where do you live? How old are you? When did you wake up this morning? Why am I asking you all these questions? Well, the reason is that the second sentence type that we will be studying is questions. Who can give me some examples of questions?

Here are some things to help you with questions. First of all, a question is going to end with a question mark. Before you put a question mark at the end of your sentence, however, make sure you are really asking something.

Also remember that a question means you want to know something. A question means you are asking for information about something.

Finally, a question ends with a question mark.

Another hint is that there are several words that are question starters. They are: who, what, where, when, why, how, is, are, can, may, will, would, should, could, did, do. There are others, of course.

On this worksheet, you are going to practice identifying questions and then writing some of your own.

Worksheet

Answers to Worksheet II-10:

Part One:

1. ?	5. .	9. ?
2. ?	6. ?	10. ?
3. ?	7. ?	
4. .	8. .	

Part Two:

Students' answers will vary.

Follow-up Activity

Save these questions for later activities in which students will have to write complete and appropriate answers to questions.

II-10. Identifying a Question

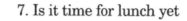

Part One: Are these questions? Put a question mark (?)
at the end of each one that is a question. Put a period (.)
after the telling statements.

1. Do you want a ride home

2. What is the name of your dog

3. Would you like something to eat   7. Is it time for lunch yet

4. I wish I could stay up all night   8. My mother went to the store

5. Many children have pets   9. Does anyone have a pencil

6. What kind of pet would you like   10. Who turned off this computer

Part Two: Write a question that begins with these question words. Then trade with another
student and answer the questions.

1. Who _____

_____

2. Where _____

_____

3. When _____

_____

4. What _____

_____

5. Do you think _____

_____

6. Would _____

_____

7. Could _____

_____

8. Is it time _____

_____

9. Why _____

_____

10. If we _____

_____

Lesson II-11: Writing an Exclamation (Writing a Basic Sentence)

To the Teacher

Exclamations are fun! Students usually enjoy conveying strong emotions and fun expressions, and putting exclamation points at the ends of their exclamatory sentences. The purpose of this lesson is to provide practice for the students in recognizing and writing exclamations.

To the Student

FIRE!! No, just kidding. Did I get your attention? The third type of sentence you need to know is called an exclamation. These sentences, exclamatory sentences, let the reader know that you are really emphasizing what you have written—it means it is very important and you are calling attention to what you wrote.

When you write an exclamation, be sure to pay attention to these hints: Make sure you put an exclamation point at the end of that sentence. Don't overdo your exclamations—use them only when you really want to get someone's attention.

Changing a telling sentence to an exclamation sentence can change the whole meaning. For example, if you write "This is fun," it tells the reader that you think something is OK, but maybe not that exciting. But if you wrote "This is fun!" the reader would know that whatever you were doing is *really* fun and exciting.

Worksheet

Answers to Worksheet II-11:

Part One:

1. !	3. .	5. .	7. !	9. . (or !)
2. .	4. !	6. .	8. !	10. !

Part Two:

Students' sentences will vary.

Follow-up Activity

Have students make cartoons to illustrate the situations in Part Two of the Worksheet. They may also come up with other interesting situations that would evoke strong emotion. They may want to use speech balloons to have the characters talking using exclamations.

II-11. Identifying an Exclamation

Part One: Are these sentences exclamations? Do they show great excitement or feeling? Put an exclamation point (!) at the end of the ones that show exclaiming. Put a period (.) at the end of the ones that are telling about something ordinary.

1. I need help right away

2. This hamburger is pretty good

3. I think the phone is for you

4. You just won the lottery

5. Grandma is coming over again

6. I am going outside with my friends

7. It's raining all over my homework

8. That train is going to hit the car

9. I smell something good

10. I smell something burning

Part Two: Read each situation. Then write a sentence that shows great excitement or feeling. Pretend you are talking to a friend.

1. Your rich uncle just gave you $1,000.

_____

2. You see a fire on the second floor of a building.

_____

3. You are the only one to get an A+ on the vocabulary test.

_____

4. Someone tripped you and you fell to the floor.

_____

5. You are trying to yell loud enough so your brother will hear you.

_____

6. You see a car that is just about to hit a dog.

_____

7. Your team is just about to score a winning basket at a game.

_____

8. You are at a surprise party and your friend just walked in.

_____

9. Your pencil broke for the third time in the middle of a test.

_____

10. You won first place in a race.

_____

Lesson II-12: Other Exclamations (Writing a Basic Sentence)

To the Teacher

When expressing strong emotion in writing, sometimes that feeling is best conveyed with a simple word or phrase rather than a complete sentence. Examples are: *Aha! Oh, no! Yikes!* The purpose of this lesson is to provide students with examples of these uses of an exclamation. These can be called interjections or words of exclamation.

To the Student

What would you say if you opened a box and found a million dollars inside? (*Wow!*) What would you say if a tree was about to fall on someone's head? (*Look out!*) When you are in a hurry to get a message across to someone, you may not want to write an entire sentence—you would get the idea across quickly in just a word or two.

It's the same in writing. Sometimes an exclamatory sentence is just too long to get the impact to your reader. There are little words or phrases that are commonly used as exclamations even though they are not complete sentences. They still need an exclamation point at the end to express your great emotion or feeling, however. Here are some examples: *Help! Wow! Oh, no! Yes! Stop! Help! Run!*

These can be used all by themselves, or you can follow up the short exclamation with an exclamatory sentence. This is like giving the one–two punch! You are telling the reader you are excited about something and, then in the next sentence, you tell the reader what you are so excited about.

Worksheet

Answers to Worksheet II-12:

Students' answers will vary. Here are examples.

1. It's beautiful!
2. Stop! Get away from me!
3. Look out!
4. Help me!
5. Don't splash!
6. Wait!

Follow-up Activity

Students may enjoy drawing pictures of more situations that would require exclamations. Display the pictures and have students add several versions of good interjections or short exclamations that would make sense.

Name _____ Date _____

II-12. Use of Exclamations: Summary Sheet

Exclamations are fun to use in writing because they get attention. Here are some ways you can use exclamations to express what you want to say in writing.

Surprise: "Wow! You bought me a horse!"

Shock: "Oh, no! It's a vampire!"

Fear: "Help me!"

Anger: "I said to stop that right now or you're in big trouble!"

Despair: "The test is going to be tomorrow!"

Warning: "Look out!"

Joy: "I love you!"

Excitement: "We won the game!"

Anticipation: "Ready… get set… GO!"

You can also use special words or phrases with exclamation points to indicate these feelings. They are not complete sentences, but are simply interjections, or words that stand alone to convey a feeling. Examples:

Oh!	Mom!	Aha!
Oh, no!	Yes!	Yikes!
Wow!	Good grief!	No way!

II-12. Use of Exclamations: Summary Sheet (continued)

Write an exclamation for each picture.

Lesson II-13: Writing Commands (Writing a Basic Sentence)

To the Teacher

The fourth sentence type is the imperative—a command. The part that is difficult for students to understand about this sentence type is that there is no stated subject; it is understood (you). The purpose of this lesson is to give students practice in recognizing and writing commands.

To the Student

Raise your hand if you have ever heard someone say this to you:

Sit down.

Raise your hand.

Make your bed.

Turn left at the end of the hallway.

These are types of sentences called commands, or imperatives. When you give a command, you might use the person's name (Mark, give me that pen), but even if you don't, you can recognize a command because it starts with a word asking or telling someone to do something.

Commands are common when you are giving instructions for something (how to get to your house) or working with training a dog (Sit down, Roll over), or being in charge of someone or something (Turn in your paper). Basically, commands are given because a situation needs to change or be different.

Commands usually end with a period, but they can also end with an exclamation point if the situation is one that makes you feel great emotion or feeling (Call the police! *vs.* Call the dog.).

Worksheets

Answers to Worksheet II-13A:

Part One:

1. yes	5. yes	9. yes
2. no	6. no	10. no
3. yes	7. yes	
4. no	8. yes	

Part Two:

Students' answers will vary. Here are examples.

1. Clean up your room.	6. Toss that ball to me.
2. Shake hands.	7. Turn on Washington Circle.
3. Get some water!	8. Buckle your seat belt.
4. Sit down for just a minute.	9. Throw me the ball!
5. Water the plants carefully.	10. Stay right with me!

Answers to Worksheet II-13B:

Part One:

Students' answers will vary.

Part Two:

Students' answers will vary.

Follow-up Activity

King or Queen for a Day: Have students assume the role of being the king or queen of their own invented country. As the royal ruler, what commands would he or she give to the subjects? Have them make a royal list of royal commands and share with the other students. It might help to give them the starter phrase: "Royal subjects, you are hereby commanded to" (bring me pizza for breakfast; exercise my royal horses; polish my coach, etc.).

Name _____   Date _____

II-13A. Commands

Part One: *Identifying a Command*

Are these commands? Write yes or no after each sentence.

1. Sit down over there. _____

2. I hope you will give me that book. _____

3. Go quietly to your bedroom. _____

4. Tommy walked quietly down the hall. _____

5. Steve, be quiet. _____

6. Everyone has a pencil today. _____

7. Take out your gym shoes. _____

8. Stop talking. _____

9. Do your best work on this test. _____

10. It is too far to walk home. _____

Part Two: *Writing a Command*

Read each situation and then write a command for it. You might use a period or an exclamation point.

1. Your sister's room is really a mess. _____

2. You want your dog to shake hands. _____

3. You see a fire starting on the stove. _____

4. A friend of your mother's comes to visit and has to wait. _____

5. You are leaving all of your plants with your friend while you are gone. _____

6. You are in the swimming pool and want someone to throw you a ball. _____

7. You are telling someone how to get to your house. _____

8. You are ready to leave in the car but someone hasn't buckled up. _____

9. You can make a basket if your teammate will get the ball to you. _____

10. You are baby sitting and don't want your little friend to stray too far. _____

Name _____ Date _____

II-13B. More Practice

Part One: Write a command that the first person might give to the second person or thing.

1. A king to his servant: _____

_____

2. A teacher to his student: _____

_____

3. A scientist to her robot: _____

_____

4. A dog trainer to his dog: _____

_____

5. A father or mother to a child: _____

_____

6. A bus driver to a rider: _____

_____

7. A coach to a player in a game: _____

_____

8. A police officer to a driver: _____

_____

Part Two: On another sheet of paper, draw pictures to illustrate three of your commands from Part One.

Lesson II-14: Sentences with Quotation Marks

(Writing a Basic Sentence)

To the Teacher

When students begin writing stories, they will need to use conversation between characters. This will involve using quotation marks. The purpose of this lesson is to give students practice in (1) identifying direct discourse, and (2) correctly punctuating the spoken words.

To the Student

What did Little Red Riding Hood say to the Big Bad Wolf disguised as Grandma? ("What big teeth you have.") What's the last thing your mother said to you today? ("Have a good day.") What do you say to someone at his or her birthday party? ("Happy birthday.") What do you say to someone at a surprise birthday party? ("Surprise!")

All of these are examples of things people say. You can show this in writing with special marks called *quotation marks*. You have to mark where the person started talking and where the person stopped talking. Look at this sentence I will write on the board.

Tom said, "Please give me the keys to your car."

The word *said* is a clue—a big clue—that talking is coming very soon in the sentence. Right after the word *said*, I'm going to put a comma to alert me that the next few words are going to be talking.

Then I'm going to imagine Tom getting ready to talk. I can picture him with his mouth open, ready to speak. Because he's going to speak his first sentence, I'm going to make sure it starts with a capital letter. Now I'm going to put quotation marks around every word that comes out of his mouth. When he starts talking, I'll put the quotation marks around the beginning of what he says. When he stops talking, I'll put the quotation marks around the last word—after the period—to enclose that part. When you look at it, it should look almost like a pair of hands "holding" the words that were spoken.

Sometimes the talking comes at the beginning of the sentence and the *said* comes at the *end* of the sentence. Here's an example.

"Please give me the keys to your car," said Tom.

You have to start the first set of quotation marks at the beginning of the sentence. Keep reading until the person has stopped talking. Now you need to make a decision before you put the ending quotation marks. Did the person ask a question? Put a question mark; then the quotation marks. Did the person say something with great emotion or feeling? Put an exclamation point. Did the person just say something ordinary that would be a telling sentence? *Don't put a period!* Put a comma, then your ending quotation marks, and then notice who was talking.

How would you punctuate these sentences?

"I would like to have some ice cream," said Martha.

Father said, "Let's build a birdhouse today."

John asked, "Could we go outside today?"

"I will not go!" screamed the little boy.

Here are some clue words to let you know that talking is coming up: *yelled, screamed, exclaimed, whispered, shouted, cried, asked, laughed, sang.* Can you think of some others?

Worksheets
Answers to Worksheet II-14A:

Part One:

1. said	5. sang	9. —
2. —	6. —	10. exclaimed
3. exclaimed	7. whispered	
4. asked	8. screamed	

Part Two:

1. "We got a new computer."
2. "I wonder what kind of computer you got."
3. "Does it have games on it?"
4. "I love to play games!"
5. "I do, too,"
6. "Why don't we try it out?"
7. "That's a great idea."
8. "You have to be quiet now."
9. "Why?"
10. "This game is really loud,"

Part Three:

1. Alison said, "Let's have a party for Mark."
2. Jill cried, "Help me with this painting!"
3. "Throw the ball to me," Tyrone called.
4. "Don't forget to write!" yelled the boy.
5. The girl screamed, "I don't want to go to camp."
6. "It will be fun," insisted her sister.
7. "Come here, little puppy," called Debbie.
8. Michael said, "I'm going sailing on my boat."
9. "Could I go with you?" asked Michelle.
10. "I moved to this state last year," explained Carlos.

Answers to Worksheet II-14B:

Students' answers will vary. Here are examples.

1. "Mom, could we have a dog?" "No, I like the cats."
2. "Kick the ball to me," said Amanda. "Here it comes," yelled Tony.
3. "This is great pizza," exclaimed Mr. Marshall. "Could you pass the cheese?" asked Sally.
4. "Hold still," said Rick. "Does it look like me?" asked Skyler.

Follow-up Activity

Take some colored comic strips from the Sunday paper and have students practice writing the conversations that take place between familiar characters in the strips. Some students may want to write their own comic strips and fill in the conversation in comic balloons.

Name _____   Date _____

II-14A. Quotation Marks

Part One: *Find the Clue Words*

Be a good detective and find the clue words that let you know someone is talking. Circle each clue word you find. Be careful! Not every sentence will have one.

1. Bob said, "My car won't start."

2. Andrew will help me with this hard work.

3. "Oh, no!" exclaimed Mom.

4. "May I borrow some money?" asked Melissa.

5. "Happy birthday to you," sang the children at the party.

6. This is really a nice gift.

7. "Pass that pencil, please," whispered Jack to his friend.

8. "Give me that!" screamed the little boy.

9. It is too far to drive to the market today.

10. "It is too far to drive to the market today," exclaimed Dad.

Part Two: *Finding the Talking*

Someone is talking in each of these sentences. Circle all of the words that come out of someone's mouth in each sentence below.

1. "We got a new computer," said Cindy.

2. Bob said, "I wonder what kind of computer you got."

3. "Does it have games on it?" he asked.

4. "I love to play games!" exclaimed Cindy.

5. "I do, too," laughed Bob.

6. Cindy said, "Why don't we try it out?"

7. Bob said, "That's a great idea."

8. Her father whispered, "You have to be quiet now."

9. Cindy said, "Why?"

10. "This game is really loud," explained her father.

II-14A. Quotation Marks (continued)

Part Three: *Adding Quotation Marks*

These sentences are missing quotation marks. Put in the beginning and ending quotation marks.

1. Alison said,   Let's have a party for Mark.

2. Jill cried,   Help me with this painting!

3. Throw the ball to me,   Tyrone called.

4. Don't forget to write!   yelled the boy.

5. The girl screamed,   I don't want to go to camp.

6. It will be fun,   insisted her sister.

7. Come here, little puppy,   called Debbie.

8. Michael said,   I'm going sailing on my boat.

9. Could I go with you?   asked Michelle.

10. I moved to this state last year,   explained Carlos.

II-14B. Writing Sentences with Quotations

What do you think each person is saying in the pictures below? Write the sentences with quotations on the lines below each picture.

1. Jack and Mother at the pet store.

2. Amanda and Tony playing soccer.

3. The Marshall family eating pizza.

4. Rick painting a picture of Skyler.

Lesson II-15: Writing to Describe

(Writing Sentences for a Specific Purpose)

To the Teacher

A descriptive sentence is one that puts words together to describe something. This can be as basic as telling who did what. (The dog drank out of a bowl. The horse jumped over a fence.) These sentences can also describe more complicated ideas. (The thirsty dog was grateful for the cold water. The champion horse leaped boldly over the huge fence.)

Descriptive sentences can be used to convey descriptions of all the senses—how something looks, sounds, feels, tastes, or smells. For beginning writers, using a picture to prompt a sentence may be helpful. A word box with common word choices will also make the student feel more successful and independent. The purpose of this lesson is to provide students with opportunities to write descriptive sentences for all senses.

To the Student

Look at this picture (hold up a picture or a poster with an interesting idea). What's a good sentence that you could write to describe this? (The dog is holding a newspaper in his mouth. The girl is hang gliding over a mountain. etc.) You probably described how the person looked, or what he or she was doing.

A good descriptive sentence will tell the reader exactly what you see, hear, feel, taste, or smell. Give me a good descriptive sentence that would help me understand what a rainbow looks like. (The rainbow has beautiful colors in it.) Give me a good descriptive sentence that would help me understand how a chocolate chip cookie tastes. (The cookie is soft and warm.) How about what your favorite rock group sounds like? (The band is loud!) Describe what a rotten egg smells like. (The egg smells awful and makes me want to plug up my nose.) Describe what a puppy feels like. (The puppy's fur is soft and fuzzy.)

Worksheets

Answers to Worksheet II-15A:

Students' answers may vary slightly. Here are examples.

Part One:

1. The boy is diving into a swimming pool.
2. The girl is reading a book.
3. The girl is flying a kite.
4. The puppy is playing with a ball.
5. The family is camping.
6. The butterfly is going to land on a flower.

Part Two:

1. The phone is ringing.
2. The mother is calling for her child.
3. The boy is playing the drums.
4. The dishes are going to crash all over the floor.
5. The dog is howling.
6. The students are cheering for their team.

Answers to Worksheet II-15B:

Students' answers may vary slightly. Here are examples.

Part Three:

1. The pizza is cheesy.

2. The cake is sweet.

3. The lemon is very sour.

4. The ice cream is cold.

5. The soup is hot.

6. The popcorn is salty and full of butter.

Part Four:

1. The water is freezing!

2. The rocks are rough.

3. The ice is slippery.

4. The fire is very hot!

5. The lamb's fur is soft.

6. The road is bumpy.

Answers to Worksheet II-15C:

Students' answers may vary slightly. Here are examples.

Part Five:

1. The skunk smells really bad!

2. The cookies smell great!

3. This perfume smells really strong.

4. The flowers smell so sweet.

5. The garbage smells rotten.

6. The pizza smells delicious.

Follow-up Activities

1. Start a collection of interesting pictures, photos, or drawings that can be used to jump-start good descriptive sentences.

2. Have students read their sentences out loud and then have other students guess which picture is being described.

3. Write one descriptive sentence on the board and have all students draw a picture to go with it. It will be fun to see how one sentence can trigger different responses.

Name _____   Date _____

II-15A. Writing to Describe

Part One: On a separate sheet of paper, write a sentence that describes what you **see** happening in each picture.

> ***Word Box:*** diving   camping   flower

Part Two: On a separate sheet of paper, write a sentence that describes what you might **hear** in each picture.

> ***Word Box:*** phone   crash   howling   cheering

II-15B. Writing to Describe

Part Three: On a separate sheet of paper, write a sentence that describes how something might **taste** in each picture.

> **Word Box:** cheesy sweet salty sour

Part Four: On a separate sheet of paper, write a sentence that describes how something might **feel** in each picture.

> **Word Box:** rough soft bumpy slippery

II-15C. Writing to Describe

Part Five: On the lines below, write a sentence that describes how something might **smell** in each picture.

Word Box: skunk perfume strong rotten delicious

1.	2.	3.
4.	5.	6.

1. _____

_____

2. _____

_____

3. _____

_____

4. _____

_____

5. _____

_____

6. _____

_____

Lesson II-16: Writing a Reaction
(Writing Sentences for a Specific Purpose)

To the Teacher

Another purpose for writing is for the student to give a reaction or response to something. Students may have an opinion they wish to express or may feel strongly about something. The purpose of this lesson is to provide students with opportunities to convey their feelings by reacting to a given situation.

To the Student

I am going to ask you some questions. I would like you to give me your reaction out loud in one sentence. (Call on various students.)

How would you feel if I said we were all going to go swimming after school? (happy, not pleased)

What would you do if you found a little lost kitten? (take it home, call the animal shelter)

How does a rainy day make you feel? (sad, lazy)

What do you think about riding the bus to school? (like, don't like)

Where is the best place to get pizza in town? (Pizza Hut, local restaurant)

Do you think everyone would have the same answers to these questions? (no) Why or why not? (people have different opinions, different experiences)

Today we're going to work on writing sentences that give your opinion or strong feeling about something. Remember, your answers might very well be different from someone else's. Just give your own answers.

Worksheet

Answers to Worksheet II-16:

Students' answers will vary.

Follow-up Activity

Save these papers because they can be used later to develop into paragraphs. Have students share their ideas. Note how students had different reactions to the questions.

II-16. Write Your Reaction

Write your reaction to each question.

1. What is the best ride at an amusement park?

2. What is the hardest subject in school?

3. What is your favorite dessert?

4. How do you feel about winter?

5. What is a really good book to read?

6. How does being in the dark make you feel?

7. What would you do if you found a wallet with $100 in it and no name?

8. Do you think girls play as many sports as boys do?

9. What is the worst thing about Saturday?

10. Why is it important to be clean?

11. Do you think students should be paid to do their homework?

12. What do you do when you are scared?

13. What's the best way to make someone laugh?

14. What would your father/mother say about your report card?

15. What makes a person a good friend?

Lesson II-17: Writing to Give Information

(Writing Sentences for a Specific Purpose)

To the Teacher

Students are usually knowledgeable about hobbies, celebrities, sports, or other topics of interest to them. Eventually, they will be writing paragraphs about topics they know something about. The purpose of this lesson is to have students write factual statements (compared with opinion statements in Lesson II-16).

To the Student

Who has an interesting hobby? (call on various students) Can you tell me three things that you know for sure about your hobby? I will list them on the board.

Things that you know *for sure* are called *facts*. In the previous lesson, you wrote sentences that gave your opinion about things, or told how you felt. Remember that not everyone had the same answer. But when you are talking about facts, it means that something is true and it is the same for everyone.

This is a fact: *Horses have four legs.* (Always true—under most circumstances.) This is an opinion: *Horses are the best animals in the world.* (But someone else might think dogs are better. That is their opinion.)

This is a fact: *It is sunny outside today.* (True at this moment.) This is an opinion: *I like sunny days.* (But maybe someone else doesn't!)

What you are going to be writing today are sentences that tell facts, something that is true.

Worksheets

Answers to Worksheet II-17A:

Students' sentences will vary. Here are examples.

1. The dog is chasing a ball.
2. The boy is playing a game.
3. The kite is high in the sky.
4. The girls are playing on the swings.
5. The family is eating from the picnic basket.
6. The people are in a boat.
7. The children are throwing a ball.
8. The girl is riding a horse.
9. The swimmers are in the water.
10. The little girl is building a sand castle.

Answers to Worksheet II-17B:

Students' answers will vary. Here are examples.

1. A turtle has a hard shell.
2. A giraffe has a long neck.
3. An ant can dig a tunnel.
4. A bicycle has two wheels.
5. A skunk is black and white.
6. Bumblebees can sting people.
7. An igloo is made of ice.
8. Apples can be red.
9. An octopus has eight arms.
10. A fire is hot.

Answers to Worksheet II-17C:

Students' answers will vary.

Follow-up Activity

Students take turns having 5 minutes "in the spotlight" to share their knowledge about something with the class. This could be done over several days, and does not need to be elaborate at this point.

Name _____ Date _____

II-17A. A Day in the Park

On a separate sheet of paper, write ten sentences that are true about this picture. (If you need help getting started, focus on: the dog, the boy, the kite, the swings, the picnic basket, the boat, the ball, the horse, the swimmers, the sand castle.)

Name _____ Date _____

II-17B. Fun Facts

Write a sentence that tells something you know for sure about each topic.

1. **a turtle:** _____

_____

2. **a giraffe:** _____

_____

3. **an ant:** _____

_____

4. **a bicycle:** _____

_____

5. **a skunk:** _____

_____

6. **bumblebees:** _____

_____

7. **an igloo:** _____

_____

8. **apples:** _____

_____

9. **an octopus:** _____

_____

10. **a fire:** _____

_____

Name _____ Date _____

II-17C. Personal Topic

Think of something you know a lot about. It may be a hobby, something you collect, a sport that you are good at, or a topic you know a lot about. List ten facts about your topic that you can tell others.

1. _____

_____

2. _____

_____

3. _____

_____

4. _____

_____

5. _____

_____

6. _____

_____

7. _____

_____

8. _____

_____

9. _____

_____

10. _____

_____

Lesson II-18: Writing to Explain/Give Instructions

(Writing Sentences for a Specific Purpose)

To the Teacher

Students can use sentences to give directions or explain a sequential event. Each sentence needs to be clear enough to give the reader an idea of what is happening, and the sentences need to be in correct order to make sense. The purpose of this lesson is to provide practice activities for students to write sentences that give directions.

To the Student

If someone asked you how to get to the office from your classroom, could you give them good directions? (Let students try.) Why is it important to give good directions? (so the person ends up where she or he is supposed to go) What would happen if you gave the directions in the wrong order? (the person would be off track and lost)

If I told you there was a hidden treasure in this building, would you listen carefully to find it?

Today we are going to work on writing clear directions so that someone would be able to follow what you wrote and have it make sense.

Worksheets

Answers to Worksheet II-18A:

Students' answers will vary. Here are examples.

1. Start at the shack by the tree.

2. Walk to the river and get in the boat at the dock.

3. Take the boat to the next dock.

4. Follow the path up the little mountain.

5. Get on the helicopter that is waiting for you.

6. Fly in the helicopter to the castle (land at the landing pad).

7. Go inside the castle and slip out the trap door. (through the underground tunnel).

8. Sneak along the brick wall to the stable.

9. Grab the black horse and ride to the closest edge of the big woods.

10. Follow five stone steps to the opening of the cave.

11. The treasure is inside the cave.

Note: Students may want to hide their "treasure" in other spots in the town (e.g., in the hay loft, on top of a mountain, at the bottom of a lake, etc.). Students can add their own features to the town and label them. After students write their directions, have them copy their directions and map, and exchange with other students.

Answers to Worksheet II-18B:

Students' answers will vary. Here are examples.

1. Murphy ran into the woods and chased some birds.

2. Then he chased a cat up a tree.

3. Next he tore up some flowers in a flower bed.

4. Then he swam across the little river.

5. He strolled through a neighborhood and got into some garbage.

6. He stopped to bury a bone.

7. Then he ran to visit another dog in a fenced-in yard.

8. He saw some children playing in a park and chased the ball with them.

9. Then he got into someone's lunch on a picnic table.

10. He ran along the hills.

11. He rolled in some mud by a little pond.

12. He swam across the pond.

13. He chased some cars.

14. He went home.

Follow-up Activity

Have students make their own Treasure Maps and Adventure Maps. They can write a suggested answer key for each and exchange with classmates.

II-18A. Hide the Treasure

On a separate sheet of paper, write the directions on how to find the treasure chest of gold.

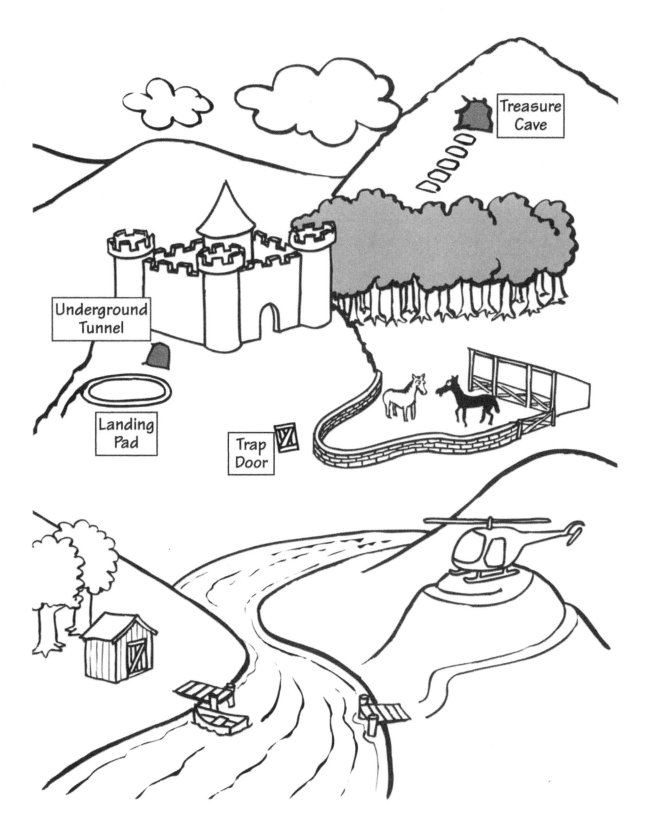

Treasure Cave

Underground Tunnel

Landing Pad

Trap Door

II-18B. Murphy's Travels

Murphy the dog had an adventure one day! Follow his footprints and, on a separate sheet of paper, write what happened to Murphy before he returned home.

Lesson II-19: Answering a Question with Appropriate
Information (Writing Sentences for a Specific Purpose)

To the Teacher

The phrasing of a question usually indicates what type of answer is desired. Some may require a yes/no response, others a one-word answer, and still others may ask for a specific piece of information. The purpose of this lesson is to provide students with practice in answering different types of questions.

To the Student

I am going to ask you some questions. (Call on various students.)

What is your name? (name) Do you have a hat on? (yes/no) What is the name of your dog? (name) What day is it today? (day) Do you have a pet elephant? (yes/no) What color is an elephant? (color)

You can see that I wanted to know some very specific things by the questions that I asked you.

If I asked you, "What is your name?" and you said, "No," does that make any sense? If I asked you, "Do you have a pet elephant?" and you said, "Thursday," does that make any sense? You have to give an answer that fits the question.

If I asked you, "What is the name of a fruit?" is there only one correct answer? (No, there are lots of correct answers.) If I asked you, "What is a good game to play?" is there only one correct answer? (No, there are lots of good games.) If I asked you, "What is the name of the president?" is there only one correct answer? (Yes, only one president at a time.)

So you have to be sure you understand the question before you give your answer!

Worksheets

Answers to Worksheet II-19A:

1. Tom, Jeff, Michael
2. blue, yellow, black, pink
3. yes, maybe, no
4. yes, no
5. Rocky, Pete, Flakey
6. cats, hamsters, dogs
7. October, February, December
8. yes, no

Answers to Worksheet II-19B:

Students' answers will vary.

Follow-up Activity

Play "Question Game." Make game cards as follows:

yes/no questions   name questions   number questions   place questions

Write up to ten questions for each category. Divide students into two teams. Have students randomly pick questions and point values (1 point, 2 points, 5 points, 10 points). If the question is answered correctly, that team gets the assigned points. For example, if Team A answers a 5-point question for the name category ("What is the name of our mayor?"), it would get 5 points.

The categories can be changed to fit any subject or topic studied. The point is that students must answer the questions correctly. Here are sample questions:

Yes/No Questions

Is the temperature today above 50 degrees?

Is anyone in the class absent today?

Do crocodiles have webbed feet?

Number Questions

What time does school end?

How many days are in this month?

How many minutes are in two hours?

Name Questions

Who is our principal?

Who is our president?

What is a breed of dog?

Place Questions

Where would I go to see a camel?

What is the capital of Florida?

Name _____ Date _____

II-19A. Find the Possible Answers

Read each question carefully. Circle EVERY answer that might make sense!

1. What is the name of that boy?

   Tom   Ellen   Jeff   Sally   Cathy   Michael

2. What is a good color for the background of this painting?

   no   blue   yellow   Tom   Tuesday   black   pink

3. Are you going to take a vacation this summer?

   June   yes   maybe   Mr. Smith   green   Canada   no

4. Do you have a pet iguana at home?

   Flakey   yes   Rocky   no   white   scaley

5. What is the name of your pet iguana?

   Rocky   Pete   white   pink   Flakey   no

6. What pets do you like?

   cats   blue   green   hamsters   dogs   Speedy   no

7. What month is your birthday in?

   October   Thursday   February   Saturday   December

8. Do you have any brothers?

   five   yes   sisters   no   Tony

II-19B. Answer the Questions

1. What is your name? _____

2. What month is your birthday in? _____

3. Do you have any pets? _____

4. What is your mother's first name? _____

5. What color is the sun? _____

6. Do you like pizza? _____

7. What time does school start? _____

8. What is your favorite school subject? _____

9. Have you ever ridden a horse? _____

10. Do you like to swim? _____

11. What kinds of pets do you like? _____

12. How old are you? _____

Lesson II-20: Answering a Question with Complete Sentences (Writing Sentences for a Specific Purpose)

To the Teacher

Sometimes a short answer (yes/no, one word) is sufficient to answer a question. At other times, such as on an essay test, it is necessary for the student to use complete sentences. The purpose of this lesson is to give students opportunities to recognize and write complete sentences when answering a question.

To the Student

Get ready to answer some questions: What is your name? What color are your eyes? What state do you live in?

You probably answered these questions by using only one word. A lot of times that is perfectly fine. When you are talking to someone, most of the time your answer may be short—just a word or two. But when you are answering other questions, particularly in writing, it might be necessary for you to use a complete sentence to answer the question.

Let's try those sentences again, but this time use a complete sentence. What is your name? ("My name is...") What color are your eyes? ("My eyes are...") What state do you live in? ("I live in...")

We're going to practice two skills: (1) recognizing when an answer is a complete sentence, and (2) writing complete sentences to written questions.

Worksheets

Answers to Worksheet II-20A:

1. no	5. yes	9. yes
2. yes	6. no	10. yes
3. yes	7. yes	
4. no	8. no	

Answers to Worksheet II-20B:

Students' sentences will vary.

Follow-up Activities

1. Each morning for a week or so, write a question on the board that must be answered in a complete sentence. You can make this part of the students' daily boardwork or morning activity.

2. Have students exchange their papers (or even leave names off their papers) and proofread each others' answers. Check for (a) complete sentences, and (b) giving a response that correctly answers the question or makes sense.

Name _____ Date _____

II-20A. Complete Sentence Answers

Read each question and the answer that is written. Is the answer in a complete sentence? Write *yes* or *no* in the box after the sentence.

1. How many arms does an octopus have?

   Eight.

2. Do crocodiles have webbed feet?

   Crocodiles have webbed feet.

3. What color is your pencil?

   My pencil is yellow.

4. How many planets are there?

   Nine.

5. Is the canoe in the water?

   The canoe is in the water.

6. Is the digital camera working?

   Yes.

7. What do monkeys like to eat?

   Monkeys like bananas.

8. When did the Civil War begin?

   A long time ago.

9. How many people can ride on your bus?

   There is room for 55 people on my bus.

10. Who invented an early plane?

    The Wright brothers invented a very early plane.

II-20B. Write Your Answers

Use complete sentences to answer these questions.

1. What is your full name?

_____

2. How many brothers do you have?

_____

3. How many sisters do you have?

_____

4. Do you live in a big house?

_____

5. Where do you like to go for fun?

_____

6. When is your birthday?

_____

7. Do you play any sports?

_____

8. Who is your favorite singer or band?

_____

_____

9. When do you get up in the morning?

_____

_____

10. What do you like to do on Saturdays?

_____

_____

Lesson II-21: Turning a Statement into a Question

(Writing Sentences for a Specific Purpose)

To the Teacher

Answering a question is rather straightforward. Changing a statement into a question is a more difficult task. This skill can be helpful in future tasks, such as writing a report (deciding on questions to answer), learning how to request information from others (writing to a pen pal), or playing Jeopardy-type games. The purpose of this lesson is to provide practice for students in changing statements into questions.

To the Student

Here is the answer: *A banana.* What could be the question? (What is a yellow fruit? What do monkeys like to eat? What is in your lunch box?)

Here's another answer: *Charlie Brown, Lucy, and Snoopy.* What could be the question? (What are some Peanuts characters?)

Now I'm going to give you a sentence: *I dreamed that I could fly.* Can you make that into a question? (What did you dream about? Did you ever dream that you could fly?)

Here's another sentence: *Some camels have two humps.* Can you make that into a question? (How many humps do some camels have?)

Today you're going to practice two skills: (1) making a question that fits the short answer you are given, and (2) changing a sentence into a question.

Worksheets

Answers to Worksheet II-21A:

Students' answers will vary. Here are examples.

1. Who lives in a jungle and swings from a tree?
2. What is a really good dessert?
3. What is a good breakfast food?
4. What do you need to go skating in the winter?
5. What is green and worth 100 pennies?
6. What time do you go to bed?
7. What is your favorite children's book?
8. What is a good summer sport?
9. What is a good board game?
10. What color is your birthday cake?

Answers to Worksheet II-21B:

Students' answers will vary. Here are examples.

1. What's the weather like today?
2. What did your dog run off with?
3. Where did the king and queen live?
4. How did Marsha break her leg?
5. Where did the pirates bury the treasure?
6. What is the capital of Kentucky?

7. What did the children dress up as?

8. What planet did the rocket land on?

9. How long is a marathon?

10. How many colors are in the rainbow?

Follow-up Activity

A quick Jeopardy-type game can be made by selecting 10–20 common nouns, interesting words or phrases, or vocabulary/spelling words. Write them on individual index cards, then tape them (blank side up) on the board in 5 columns. Assign each row a point value (10 points for the first row, 20 for the second, and so on depending on how many rows and words you use). Divide students into two teams (one red, one blue) and have them alternate picking a category and point value. When a card is selected, read the word and give the student/team 10 seconds to come up with an oral question. Give points to the team if it is successful and color-code that card or space to show that team's points. Then play goes to the other team. The idea is for one team to get a complete row or column to win. Adaptations to this game can be made as needed.

Name _____ Date _____

II-21A. The Answer Is...

Read each word or phrase that answers a question. Then write a question (there may be more than one possibility) that uses that word or phrase as the answer.

1. **Tarzan:** _____

_____

2. **ice cream sundae:** _____

_____

3. **pancakes:** _____

_____

4. **ice skates:** _____

_____

5. **a dollar bill:** _____

_____

6. **midnight:** _____

_____

7. **Green Eggs and Ham:** _____

_____

8. **swimming:** _____

_____

9. **"Monopoly":** _____

_____

_____

10. **pink:** _____

_____

_____

II-21B. From Statement to Question

Read each sentence below. Then change it into a question.

1. The weather is sunny today.

   _____

   _____

2. My dog ran off with my socks.

   _____

   _____

3. The king and queen lived in a castle.

   _____

   _____

4. Marsha broke her leg skiing.

   _____

   _____

5. The pirates buried the treasure in a cave.

   _____

   _____

6. The capital of Kentucky is Frankfort.

   _____

   _____

7. The children dressed up as clowns.

   _____

   _____

8. The rocket landed on Mars.

   _____

   _____

9. A marathon is a 26-mile run.

   _____

   _____

10. There are seven colors in the rainbow.

   _____

   _____

Lesson II-22: Varying the Beginning (Varying Sentences)

To the Teacher

Inevitably, students will want to begin many of their sentences with "The," or "I," or "We." While these are good sentence starters, they can become boring. This lesson provides activities for students to vary the way they start their sentences.

To the Student

(Write on the board or read to students.) Here are some sentences. Tell me what you think of them:

I am ten years old.

I like to eat pizza.

I have a dog.

I have my own room at home.

I like to go swimming.

I read comic books.

What's the same about all of those sentences? (They all start with "I.")

Here are some more sentences. Tell me what you think of this group:

The cat is big.

The horse is brown and white.

The man is going to the store.

The kids are playing baseball.

The dog is going through the garbage.

What's the same about all of those sentences? (They all start with "The.")

There's nothing wrong with starting a sentence with "I" or "The"; in fact, these are common sentence starters. But when *every* sentence starts the same way, or when you overdo it by using the same word too many times, it gets boring for the reader and the writer. We're going to try to work through some ways to vary or change the way you start sentences.

Worksheets

Answers to Worksheet II-22A:

Students' sentences will vary.

Answers to Worksheet II-22B:

Students' sentences will vary.

Follow-up Activity

Use students' spelling word lists (probably new ones every week) as the target words for sentence writing. It may seem hard at first for students to think of new words to begin their sentences, but with practice it should come easier and easier.

II-22A. One Time Only

Write a complete sentence using each target word below. You can only use each word one time.

mail sail trail train pail main stain bait brain hailing

Try using the target word as the first word in the sentence. For example:

mail—Mail comes every day to our city.

hailing—Hailing is when frozen rain hits the ground.

1. (mail) _____

_____

2. (sail) _____

_____

3. (trail) _____

_____

4. (train) _____

_____

5. (pail) _____

_____

6. (main) _____

_____

7. (stain) _____

_____

8. (bait) _____

_____

9. (brain) _____

_____

10. (hailing) _____

_____

Name _____   Date _____

II-22B. More Practice

Continue practicing writing sentences with new target starting words. Use other sheets of paper for your sentences.

Set #1 (long *a* words):

   May   play   fade   hay   rake   cake   baking   staple   raining   way

Set #2 (long *e* words):

   heal   meat   neat   read   bee   seem   deeper   leak   leaning   peas

Set #3 (long *i* words):

   high   frighten   wide   hide   riding   hike   fight   night   wild   ice cream

Set #4 (long *o* words):

   hold   row   moan   roll   home   hoping   load   float   bowling   go

Set #5 (long *u* words):

   jukebox   Luke   music   cute   cube   tube   tune   ruined   duty   future

Set #6 (*ar* words):

   far   partner   hard   car   darkness   park   star   farmer   barn   yard

Set #7 (*er* words):

   person   serve   term   cooler   her   summer   herd   winter   teacher   fern

Set #8 (*ir* words):

   fir   whirling   bird   girl   firm   third   first   dirty   stirring   sir

Set #9 (*or* words):

   fork   more   for   born   pork   horse   corn   storm   short   cork

Set #10 (*ur* words):

   hurting   purr   purchase   burn   curling   church   turn   nurse   purse   fur

Lesson II-23: Lengthening Sentences (Varying Sentences)

To the Teacher

Beginning writers often write the shortest possible sentence that will still technically be a sentence. (I see a cat.) To make sentences more interesting and readable, students can learn different techniques to lengthen a sentence. The purpose of this lesson is to provide students with several means of lengthening sentences.

To the Student

Here's a sentence. How do you like this one?

I have a dog.

Well, that's pretty basic, isn't it? How many words are in that sentence? (4) Do you think we could make that sentence more interesting? How? (add more details, tell more about the dog, start with a better beginning, etc.)

When you are writing, there are ways to make a sentence more interesting both for the reader and the writer—you. In this lesson, we're going to work on ways to make a sentence longer by adding some details.

Here are some details that would help make the original sentence longer: What kind of dog is it? What color is the dog? What size is the dog? How do you feel about the dog?

Using those details as prompts, how could you improve the sentence?

I have a big, sweet Golden Retriever that I love very much.

Just because a sentence is longer doesn't mean it is better. You have to be careful not to just add words to make the sentence longer. You have to add things that make the sentence clearer, more interesting, and more readable.

Let's try another example. Here's a basic short sentence. Let's try to think of ways to lengthen it by adding details.

The girl is happy.

Why is the girl happy? Can you tell me more about the girl? What is she doing that makes you know she is happy?

What can you come up with?

The little girl is very happy because it is her birthday.

Remember: When you start with a short sentence and want to lengthen it, try asking yourself more details about what's happening in the sentence that other people might want to know.

Worksheets

Answers to Worksheet II-23A:

Students' sentences will vary.

Answers to Worksheet II-23B:

Students' sentences will vary.

Follow-up Activities

Have students examine a writing sample they produced earlier in the year (perhaps sentences from spelling words or a journal entry). Have them rewrite the same basic sentences, but now add interesting details to make the sentences longer. Compare by counting the number of words used in sentences (you can calculate the average, if you like) at the beginning of the grading period, semester, or year—and then after working on these lessons.

Name _____ Date _____

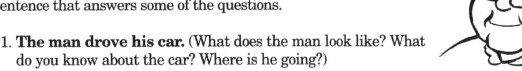

II-23A. Adding Details

Read each sentence. Then read the question prompts. Write a longer sentence that answers some of the questions.

1. **The man drove his car.** (What does the man look like? What do you know about the car? Where is he going?)

   _____

2. **We live in a house.** (What size house is it? What does the house look like? Where is the house? Who lives in the house?)

   _____

3. **We had fun on Saturday.** (What did you do? Who had fun? Why was it fun? Where did you go?)

   _____

4. **My sister rode her bike.** (What does the bike look like? Where did your sister go? How did your sister feel about the bike ride?)

   _____

5. **My favorite meal is at the pizza place.** (What things do you like to eat? What do you get on your pizza? Why is the pizza place so good?)

   _____

6. **The kitten is happy.** (What does the kitten look like? How do you know the kitten is happy? What is the kitten doing?)

   _____

7. **My grandmother is nice.** (What does your grandmother look like? What did she do that was so nice? How do you feel about your grandmother?)

   _____

8. **Today is boring.** (Why is today boring? What do you wish you were doing instead? How do you feel about today?)

   _____

Name _____ Date _____

II-23B. On Your Own

Read these short sentences. Add words and details to make them longer and more interesting.

1. The water is hot. _____

_____

2. The horse is brown. _____

_____

3. I'm tired. _____

_____

4. My bike had a flat tire. _____

_____

5. I fell over a rock. _____

_____

6. My mother is mad at me. _____

_____

7. The sky is blue. _____

_____

8. I don't like beans. _____

_____

9. I am in a great mood. _____

_____

10. Flowers make me sneeze. _____

_____

_____

_____ AH-CHOoo

Lesson II-24: Lengthening Sentences by Using Prepositional Phrases (Varying Sentences)

To the Teacher

The use of prepositional phrases is another way for students to lengthen a basically short sentence. Phrases beginning with prepositions (*in, on, around, through, beside*) can add just a few words to make a sentence clearer and more interesting. The purpose of this lesson is to provide students with practice in adding prepositional phrases to a sentence.

To the Student

Today we're going to learn about lengthening a sentence by adding something called a prepositional phrase. That's a long word, isn't it? What's a preposition? Prepositions are words that help you know exactly *where* in position something is. Something might be in the cup, around the bend, over your head, beside the rock, or under your desk. Usually a prepositional phrase is three words and tells exactly where something is. It helps us pinpoint the location of something.

A little trick to help you remember prepositions is to think of something a mouse can do to a tree. A mouse can be up a tree, behind a tree, inside a tree, beside a tree, down the tree, around the tree, and over a tree.

Here is a sentence. See if you can add the prepositional phrase to the sentence to have it make sense.

The boy was looking for food. (**in the refrigerator**)
The boy was looking for food in the refrigerator.

Try this one:

The dog was running. (**to the house**)
The dog was running to the house.

One more: This one has two phrases to add.

The girl got wet. (**on the deck; in the water**)
The girl on the deck got wet when the boat in the water splashed her.

Worksheets

Answers to Worksheet II-24A:

Students' sentences will vary.

Answers to Worksheet II-24B:

Students' sentences will vary. Here are examples.

1. The mouse is running **on the wheel/in the cage.**
2. The monkey is hanging upside-down **in the tree.**
3. The dog is lying **beside the house.**
4. The little girl can run **up the hill.**
5. The happy cat is **on the table** drinking milk.
6. The beautiful horse jumped **over the fence** and went **into the woods.**
7. I have a pet puppy snuggling **inside my pocket.**
8. The busy ants crawled **under the napkin** to get some food.
9. I can tie this rope **around your feet** to make you hop!
10. I'll race you **down the hill.**

Follow-up Activity

Have a creative student or two make a poster showing some sample prepositions and prepositional phrases. (They can use the mouse and the tree example, if they like.) Highlight the words so students can easily refer to them when they are looking for a way to lengthen sentences.

II-24A. Add the Prepositional Phrase

Read each short sentence. Choose a prepositional phrase to lengthen the sentence and then write the new sentence.

1. The movie was boring. (at the theater, in the town, by the courthouse)

_____

2. The kitten was cute. (in the box, at the store, from the pound)

_____

3. The girl was crying. (by the pool, in the lake, at the school)

_____

4. I found a rock. (at the beach, in the sand, by the tree)

_____

5. The plane was yellow. (in the sky, at the airport, by the clouds)

_____

6. The flowers were pretty. (in the yard, by the bushes, behind the house)

_____

7. The boys won the game. (at our school, on our team, in the club)

_____

8. The pencils are broken. (in the can, on the desk, on the floor)

_____

9. The ant is busy. (in the yard, on the hill, beside the stick)

_____

10. I read the book. (from the library, in my desk, beside the window)

_____

II-24B. Writing a Sentence with a Prepositional Phrase

Look at these pictures. Write a sentence to go with each one using a prepositional phrase.

1. _____

2. _____

3. _____

4. _____

5. _____

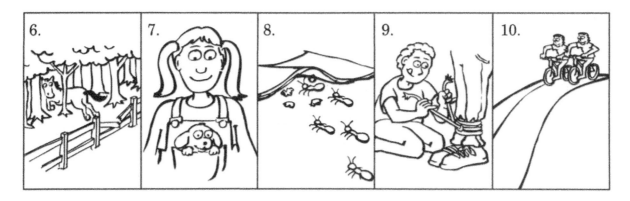

6. _____

7. _____

8. _____

9. _____

10. _____

Lesson II-25: Using More Specific or Varied Words

(Varying Sentences)

To the Teacher

Students tend to use simpler words at first until they become more comfortable with using specific, clearer words. They also tend to use the same word over and over instead of looking for synonyms for that word. The purpose of this lesson is for students to practice writing better sentences by using more specific or varied words when the same word or topic is used more than once.

To the Student

Here are some sentences about a dog. Read them/listen to them and tell me what you think:

> I have a dog. My dog is brown and white spotted. My dog has a curly tail that goes up over his back. I like to take my dog for a walk. Sometimes my dog and I go outside to play together.

How many times did I use the word "dog"? (5) There are other words that I could have used instead of using the word "dog" over and over." Take a look at this revision:

> I have a dog. My puppy is brown and white spotted. My little friend has a curly tail that goes up over his back. I like to take Spotty for a walk. Sometimes my buddy and I go outside to play together.

How many times did I use the word "dog" in that group of sentences? (just once) Did I know I was still talking about a dog in the other sentences? (yes) It makes more interesting reading if you can use different words instead of using the same word over and over. Why do you think it is a good idea to use "dog" in the first sentence, though? (It lets the reader know what you are writing about.)

In this lesson, you are going to work on rewriting sentences to make them more specific as you vary them.

Worksheets

Answers to Worksheet II-25A:

Students' sentences will vary.

Answers to Worksheet II-25B:

Students' sentences will vary. Here are some rewritten examples.

1. the pests, the unwelcome visitors, the insects
2. dripping wet, cold water, slushy drops
3. Shelley, the little girl
4. a banana, an apple, bunch of grapes
5. pants, shirt, socks
6. sit, read a book, listen to music

Follow-up Activity

Copy a page with a short story on it and have students count how many times a targeted word is used. Locate synonyms that the author may have used for the topic word. It may be hard to find an exact synonym for a specific word (e.g., grasshopper), but students can use either *more specific words* (long-legged hopper) or try the other extreme, using a very *general word* (e.g., bug). Be sure to spend time going over the examples with students so that they understand it is not "wrong" to use the same word over and over, but varying the usage (sometimes a more specific word, sometimes a more general word) makes it interesting and well-written.

II-25A. Choosing More Specific Words

Read each sentence. Change the boldfaced word or words to more specific, interesting words. Select one of the choices or create your own. Discuss why the choices are more specific than the boldfaced word.

1. I took my little **dog** for a walk. (puppy, poodle, cocker spaniel)

_____

2. She got many **toys** for her birthday. (dolls, balls, game)

_____

3. This **food** is great! (pizza, chocolate, spaghetti)

_____

4. We are going to the **south** on vacation. (Florida, Walt Disney World, Alabama)

_____

5. I broke my **leg**. (knee, shin bone, thigh bone)

_____

6. Let's play a game of **cards**. (War, Crazy 8's, Old Maid)

_____

7. My sister is crazy about **animals**. (horses, cows, chickens)

_____

8. Do you want to come over to **play**? (make a snowman, play basketball)

_____

9. I'm going to the mall with **my friend**. (Tommy, Brenda, Kirsten)

_____

10. My dad says we have to **work** outside this afternoon. (rake, mow, paint)

_____

Name _____ Date _____

II-25B. Varying Repeated Words

Read each group of sentences. Rewrite them so that the
same word is not repeated in the second or third sentences.

1. We were having a picnic outside when we were joined
   by **ants**. The **ants** crawled up our legs. We got mad
   when the **ants** tried to eat our food.

   _____

   _____

   _____

2. It began to **rain**. We got **rain** on our heads. We got **rain** on our backs. We got **rain** in
   our shoes.

   _____

   _____

3. I took **my sister** to the movies. I bought **my sister** some lemonade. **My sister** ate all
   of my popcorn.

   _____

   _____

4. It is healthy to eat **fruit**. You should eat a piece of **fruit** for breakfast. A piece of **fruit**
   makes a good snack. Reach for a piece of **fruit** when you are hungry between meals.

   _____

   _____

5. I slipped in a mud puddle and got **my clothes** all dirty. I got mud on **my clothes**. I got
   mud in **my clothes**. I got mud dripping down **my clothes**.

   _____

   _____

6. After school, Jeremy wanted to go home to **relax**. He wanted to **relax** outside on the
   porch. He wanted to **relax** where it was quiet. He wanted to **relax** where no one would
   bother him.

   _____

   _____

Lesson II-26: Changing the Position of Phrases
(Varying Sentences)

To the Teacher

Another technique that is helpful to teach varying the words in a sentence is to change the position of a phrase in a sentence. For example, the phrase "at night" could be placed at the beginning, middle, or end of a sentence to yield the following examples: ***At night,*** *I like to watch TV until I fall asleep. Sometimes I'm afraid **at night** so I leave a light on. We are always supposed to be quiet **at night**.* The purpose of this lesson is to provide students with practice in writing sentences with various placements of a phrase.

To the Student

With longer sentences, you can pick out a beginning, a middle, and an end. One way to vary your sentences is to practice changing these various parts of a sentence. If you are able to place a phrase in a specific part of a sentence (e.g., the beginning, the middle, the end), it shows that you are getting good at understanding how to put words together to make good sentences.

Try this phrase: "a little tadpole." Can you write three different sentences and put that phrase at the beginning of a sentence, somewhere in the middle of a sentence, and finally at the end of a sentence?

A little tadpole was swimming in the water.

I saw **a little tadpole** at the beach.

I wanted to catch **a little tadpole**.

You really have to think to be able to do this! But this will help you become a more creative writer.

Worksheet

Answers to Worksheet II-26:

Students' sentences will vary. Here are examples.

1. The big lion was roaring. I saw the big lion in the zoo. I would not touch the big lion.

2. A sunny day is nice for picnics. We enjoyed a sunny day after all the rain. Let's go outside on a sunny day.

3. Red jelly beans are great! Some people like red jelly beans, and some people don't. Please give me those red jelly beans.

4. Five dollars is not a lot of money. I wish I had five dollars to spend on candy. I lost five dollars.

5. The alarm clock went off in the morning. Turn off the alarm clock so I can get back to sleep. I broke the alarm clock.

6. In the corner is a little chair. Put the plant in the corner of the room. I put my books in the corner.

7. Nine o'clock is the time I go to bed. Everyone should be up by nine o'clock in the morning. It's almost nine o'clock.

8. A hamburger with cheese is my idea of a great lunch. I would like a hamburger with cheese to go, please! My sister can eat a hamburger with cheese.

9. My left foot hurts. A horse stepped on my left foot and it hurts! I can jump on my left foot.

10. Dinosaurs are really interesting. I think dinosaurs are great. I want to read more about dinosaurs.

Follow-up Activity

Beginning, Middle, and End Game: Write 20 phrases on individual slips of paper and put them into a bowl. On the board, make a scoreboard with 3 column headings: *Beginning, Middle,* and *End.*

Form two teams and have students alternate selecting phrases. One team chooses the phrase and gets to go first, selecting the position of the phrase (beginning, middle, or end). A team member writes (or orally states) a sentence with the phrase in that position. If done correctly, that team gets a point. The phrase goes to the opposite team, which must make a sentence putting the phrase in one of the other columns (beginning, middle, or end—whichever is unused). Depending on the phrase, it is sometimes difficult to come up with a smooth sentence using the phrase in specific spots! You may want to have a 30-second time limit per sentence to move the game along.

II-26. Beginning, Middle, and End

Write three sentences for each phrase. Try to write a good sentence that uses each phrase at the beginning, in the middle, and at the end.

1. **the big lion:** _____

_____

_____

2. **a sunny day:** _____

_____

3. **red jelly beans:** _____

_____

4. **five dollars:** _____

_____

5. **the alarm clock:** _____

_____

6. **in the corner:** _____

_____

7. **nine o'clock:** _____

_____

8. **a hamburger with cheese:** _____

_____

9. **my left foot:** _____

_____

10. **dinosaurs:** _____

_____

Lesson II-27: Combining Short Sentences
(and, but, so) (Varying Sentences)

To the Teacher

How many times have you read a student's work that is a collection of short choppy sentences? It is a more complex task for students to see the relationship between short sentences and correctly connect them into one better sentence. The purpose of this lesson is to provide students with examples and practice in how to connect short sentences using *and, but,* and *so.*

To the Student

Using and: When you are writing more than one sentence about something, it is better to combine the two short sentences into one really clear sentence. Here's an example: (write on the board)

The cat was white. The cat had a fuzzy tail.

Instead of using two sentences to give two details about the cat, let's say I just wanted to tell you two things about the cat using only one sentence. How could I do that?

The cat was white and had a fuzzy tail.

Using the word *and* is a good connecting word because it "ties together" the two details about the cat.

Practice using the word *and* to connect these pairs of sentences:

Tommy went to the movies. Tommy went to the store. (Tommy did both things, so let's not repeat that part. What are the two things he did? He went to the movies and he also went to the store. *Tommy went to the movies and the store.*)

Sara likes to ride horses. Sara also likes to jump horses. (Sara likes to do two things: ride horses and jump horses. Put them together: *Sara likes to ride and jump horses.*)

Using but: You can use the word *but* to connect two sentences if the two are related this way: The first sentence says something, but the second sentence brings up an opposite idea or a problem. Here's an example.

I want to do my homework. I'm too tired.

I want to do my homework, but I'm too tired.

The first part of the sentence tells what I want to do (my homework); the second part of the sentence considers why I don't want to do homework (I'm too tired). You will notice that when you connect these two sentences, you put a comma after the first part, and then the word *but.*

How would you combine these sentences?

I like dogs. I don't like dog hair all over my clothes. (I like dogs, but I don't like dog hair all over my clothes.)

Sandy wanted to watch TV. She couldn't find the remote control. (Sandy wanted to watch TV, but she couldn't find the remote control.)

Ed likes the big wagon. He doesn't have enough money to buy it. (Ed likes the big wagon, but he doesn't have enough money to buy it.)

Using so: Here's an example of how to combine two sentences using the word *so.*

I want to get an A on the test. I will study hard. (I want to get an A on the test, so I will study hard.)

The first sentence tells about something, the second sentence tells what to do because of the first one.

>   *Teresa had a cold. Teresa took some medicine. (Teresa had a cold, so she / Teresa took some medicine.)*

Remember that when you connect two sentences using *so*, put a comma after the first sentence, and then add the word *so* and the second sentence.

How would you combine these sentences?

>   *Alison didn't like her hair cut. She went back and had it done over. (Alison didn't like her hair cut, so she went back and had it done over.)*

>   *It was snowing really hard. We wore our winter coats to keep dry. (It was snowing really hard, so we wore our winter coats to keep dry.)*

>   *My grandmother is coming to visit. I better clean up my room. (My grandmother is coming to visit, so I better clean up my room.)*

Let's try some writing practice on combining sentences.

Worksheets

Answers to Worksheet II-27A:

1. Jenny is supposed to water the flowers and take out the trash.
2. Mark likes to read books and write letters.
3. It is raining and lightning outside.
4. A snake can eat mice and bugs.
5. Puppies need lots of sleep and a warm place to stay.
6. In the summer, we like to go water skiing and swimming.
7. I would like to eat a hamburger and French fries.
8. The man wore a black hat and a raincoat.
9. A hedgehog and a gerbil are little pets.
10. Amanda and Mindy are coming over.

Answers to Worksheet II-27B:

1. I wanted to go for a bike ride, but my bike has a flat tire.
2. A hedgehog is a cute pet, but it is hard to pet one.
3. We wanted to go swimming, but it was lightning outside.
4. I tried to win the race, but I could not beat Shelby.
5. Jane was supposed to go to the birthday party, but she forgot the address.
6. Mrs. Smith likes animals, but she is allergic to most of them.
7. I wanted to listen to the radio, but my grandmother wanted to talk to me.
8. Our plane left at 8 in the morning, but we did not get to the airport in time.
9. I wish I could lend you some money, but I do not have any.
10. The little boys wanted to build a model, but they did not have time to finish.

Answers to Worksheet II-27C:

1. I am really hungry, so I will eat a sandwich.
2. It is raining hard outside, so I will take an umbrella with me.
3. My glass is empty, so I will get a refill.
4. The trash is picked up on Thursday morning, so I will take the trash out on Wednesday night.

5. Tomorrow is Saturday, so we do not have school.

6. I cannot hear the music, so I will turn up the volume.

7. I have to get up early tomorrow, so I will go to bed early tonight.

8. A turtle is a good pet for a child, so I will get little Carla a turtle.

9. The door is wide open letting the wind in, so close it.

10. Tonya would like to use the computer, so she will wait in line for her turn.

Answers to Worksheet II-27D:

1. It is dark in here, so I will turn on the light.

2. I'm afraid of heights, but I'm not afraid of water.

3. Stanley likes to eat chocolate and pizza.

4. I wish I could tell you the answer, but I can't tell you what it is.

5. I'm afraid of heights, so I'm not going to jump in the pool.

6. I want these plants to grow, so I'm going to water them.

7. Alfred likes to help others and he likes to share things.

8. It is not nice to tease other people, so you should be careful what you say.

9. I wish I had a bird and five dogs.

10. I wish I had a horse, but I don't have a barn to keep a horse in.

Follow-up Activity

Be on the lookout for sentences containing the connecting words *and, but,* and *or*. As you examine them, have students try to separate the longer sentence into two smaller sentences. Have them start searching in their books (especially stories) and even in newspapers or magazines. Being able to separate the longer sentence into two smaller sentences will help students do the reverse—connect the two smaller sentences into a longer one.

II-27A. Combining Short Sentences with *and*

Read both sentences. Combine the two using the word *and*. No comma is needed.

1. Jenny is supposed to water the flowers. She is also supposed to take out the trash.

_____

2. Mark likes to read books. Mark likes to write letters.

_____

3. It is raining outside. It is lightning outside, too.

_____

4. A snake can eat mice. A snake can eat bugs.

_____

5. Young dogs need lots of sleep. Puppies need a warm place to stay.

_____

6. In the summer, we like to going water skiing. In the summer, we like to go swimming.

_____

7. I would like to eat a hamburger. I would like French fries.

_____

8. The man wore a black bat. He wore a raincoat.

_____

9. A hedgehog is a little pet. A gerbil is a little pet.

_____

10. Amanda is coming over. Mindy is coming over.

_____

Copyright © 2001 by John Wiley & Sons, Inc.

Name _____ Date _____

II-27B. Combining Sentences with *but*

Read the sentences below. Rewrite them, combining them into
one sentence using the word *but*. Don't forget the comma!

1. I wanted to go for a bike ride. My bike has a flat tire.

   _____

   _____

2. A hedgehog is a cute pet. It is hard to pet a hedgehog.

   _____

3. We wanted to go swimming. It was lightning outside.

   _____

4. I tried to win the race. I could not beat Shelby.

   _____

5. Jane was supposed to go to the birthday party. Jane forgot the address.

   _____

6. Mrs. Smith likes animals. Mrs. Smith is allergic to most animals.

   _____

7. I wanted to listen to the radio. My grandmother wanted to talk to me.

   _____

8. Our plane left at 8 in the morning. We did not get to the airport in time.

   _____

9. I wish I could lend you some money. I do not have any money.

   _____

10. The little boys wanted to build a model. The little boys did not have time to finish.

   _____

II-27C. Combining Sentences with *so*

Read the sentences. Combine the two sentences into one
sentence using the word *so*. Don't forget the comma!

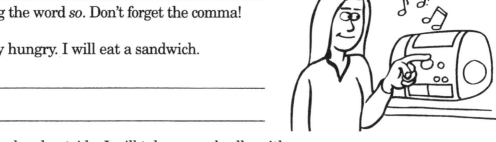

1. I am really hungry. I will eat a sandwich.

_____

_____

2. It is raining hard outside. I will take an umbrella with me.

_____

3. My glass is empty. I will get a refill.

_____

4. The trash is picked up on Thursday morning. I will take the trash out on Wednesday
night.

_____

5. Tomorrow is Saturday. We do not have school on Saturday.

_____

6. I cannot hear the music. I will turn up the volume.

_____

7. I have to get up early tomorrow. I will go to bed early tonight.

_____

8. A turtle is a good pet for a child. I will get little Carla a turtle.

_____

9. The door is wide open letting the wind in. Close the door.

_____

10. Tonya would like to use the computer. Tonya will wait in line for her turn.

_____

II-27D. Mixed Practice

Read the sentences below. Then rewrite them, combining them into one sentence using the connectors *and, but,* or *so.*

1. It is dark in here. l will turn on the light.

   _____

   _____

2. I'm afraid of heights. I'm not afraid of water.

   _____

3. Stanley likes to eat chocolate. He likes to eat pizza.

   _____

4. I wish I could tell you the answer. I can't tell you what it is.

   _____

5. I'm afraid of heights. I'm not going to jump in the pool.

   _____

6. I want these plants to grow. I'm going to water them.

   _____

7. Alfred likes to help others. Alfred likes to share things.

   _____

8. It is not nice to tease other people. You should be careful what you say.

   _____

9. I wish I had a bird. I wish I had five dogs.

   _____

10. I wish I had a horse. I don't have a barn to keep a horse in.

   _____

Name _____   Date _____

Lesson II-28: Using Commas in a List (Varying Sentences)

To the Teacher

The use of commas is sometimes confusing to students. In this lesson, students will be given practice in rewriting a sentence containing lists of items to include commas. **Note**: There are two basic ideas about the use of commas in a list. One way to look at a comma is as a replacement for the word *and*. In this respect, a sentence with a comma would read: *I like beans, carrots, corn and potatoes.*

The other common use of commas is simply to separate each item. In this respect, the same sentence would be punctuated: *I like beans, carrots, corn, and potatoes.*

Because there is some variation in the teaching of commas in a list, you should follow the format set at the school or district. In this lesson, for purposes of consistency, the comma will be used to separate each item on a list.

To the Student

Let's say you're going shopping for a party. What things would you need to get? (balloons, cake, silverware, wrapping paper, streamers, etc.) If you just made out a shopping list, you would write them in a row. But let's say you were writing a letter to someone and wanted to tell him or her what you were getting at the store. How would you put all of those items in a sentence? ("I'm going to the store to get balloons, a cake, silverware, etc.")

When you are writing about a list of things in a sentence, you will get to use a comma. A comma is used to separate the things you are listing. Take a look at these examples:

I like horses, dogs, cows, and cats.
How many kinds of animals do I like? (4)

We invited Tom, Jenny, Jamal, Casey, Shelby, and Frank to the party.
How many people were invited to the party? (6)

Now, I'm going to show why a comma is really important to help the reader understand what the writer is saying. Here is a sentence without the commas:

We invited Susan Ann Jenny Marie and Fred to the party.
How many people were invited? (possibly 5)

Now look at it:

We invited Susan Ann, Jenny Marie, and Fred to the party.
How many people were invited? (3—the girls use two names)

Now it's your turn to practice writing with commas and lists!

Worksheets

Answers to Worksheet II-28A:

1. I like to go skiing, horseback riding, sledding and canoeing.
2. Many people have visited Indiana, Illinois, and Michigan in the summer.
3. Sally likes to play cards, video games, jump rope, and hockey.
4. Do you like red, green, blue, or yellow socks?
5. The farmer had spotted cows, yellow chickens, a red dog, and a tan puppy.
6. Mom went to the store to get eggs, brownie mix, flour, and sugar.
7. I had to pick up my math book, my spelling folder, and my social studies homework.
8. I like science, reading, and math.
9. John's favorite basketball teams are the Bulls, the Lakers, and the Bucks.
10. Randy, John, and Tony are going to watch TV, play outside, go swimming, and hike in the woods.

Answers to Worksheet II-28B:

Part One:

1. Sue Ann, Sally, Tommy Lee, and Bobby went to the game.

2. We bought candy, apples, fruit, cupcakes, and donuts at the store.

3. I love buttered popcorn, strawberries, yogurt, and green beans.

4. The girls played with a red top, a jump rope, two sticks, and a puppy.

5. Dad likes to read books about running, football, baseball, field hockey, and basketball.

6. We went to visit Randy, Lizzie, Katie Sue, and Amanda.

7. We went to visit Randy, Lizzie, Katie, Sue, and Amanda.

8. Steve went to the store to get a basket, ball, clock, timer, apple pie, and orange juice.

9. Steve went to the store to get a basketball, clock, timer, apple pie, and orange juice.

10. Steve went to the store to get a basket, ball, clock, timer, apple, pie, and orange juice.

Part Two:

Students' sentences will vary.

Follow-up Activity

There are lots of things that can be grouped or listed. Challenge students to try to think of at least ten items that could go in each list. Then have them write two or three sentences telling something about the items on the list. For example:

a list of good places to eat—Pizza Hut, McDonald's, grandma's house, etc.

a list of unusual pets—raccoon, hedgehog, lizard, etc.

a list of favorite cars—Corvette, Camaro, Cadillac, Formula One, etc.

a list of who you would invite on a cruise to Walt Disney World—names of friends and family

a list of good hiding places in your house—basement, closet, attic, under the bed, etc.

II-28A. Rewriting Lists with Commas

Write these sentences placing commas between each item.

1. I like to go skiing horseback riding sledding and canoeing.

   _____

   _____

2. Many people have visited Indiana Illinois and Michigan in the summer.

   _____

3. Sally likes to play cards video games jump rope and hockey.

   _____

4. Do you like red green blue or yellow socks?

   _____

5. The farmer had spotted cows yellow chickens a red dog and a tan puppy.

   _____

6. Mom went to the store to get eggs brownie mix flour and sugar.

   _____

7. I had to pick up my math book my spelling folder and my social studies homework.

   _____

8. I like science reading and math.

   _____

9. John's favorite basketball teams are the Bulls the Lakers and the Bucks.

   _____

10. Randy John and Tony and going to watch TV play outside go swimming and hike in the woods.

    _____

II-28B. Use Commas Carefully

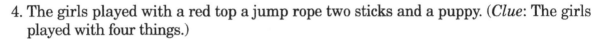

Part One: Each sentence is written without commas. Read the clue so you know how many commas are needed.

1. Sue Ann Sally Tommy Lee and Bobby went to the game. (*Clue:* Four kids—two girls and two boys—went to the game.)

2. We bought candy apples fruit cupcakes and donuts at the store. (*Clue:* We bought five things at the store.)

3. I love buttered popcorn strawberries yogurt and green beans. (*Clue:* I love four things.)

4. The girls played with a red top a jump rope two sticks and a puppy. (*Clue:* The girls played with four things.)

5. Dad likes to read books about running football baseball field hockey and basketball. (*Clue:* Dad likes to read about five sports.)

6. We went to visit Randy Lizzie Katie Sue and Amanda. (*Clue:* We visited four people.)

7. We went to visit Randy Lizzie Katie Sue and Amanda. (*Clue:* We visited five people.)

8. Steve went to the store to get a basket ball clock timer apple pie and orange juice. (*Clue:* Steve got six things at the store—including one kind of pie.)

9. Steve went to the store to get a basket ball clock timer apple pie and orange juice. (*Clue:* Steve got one toy, one kind of pie, and three other things.)

10. Steve went to the store to get a basket ball clock timer apple pie and orange juice. (*Clue:* Steve got seven things at the store.)

Part Two: Now it's your turn. Write a sentence that fits each description.

1. Write a sentence that names four people with whom you would like to go to the movies.

_____

2. Write a sentence that lists three of your favorite foods.

_____

3. Write a sentence that tells five places you would like to visit.

_____

4. Write a sentence that tells three games you like to play.

_____

5. Write a sentence that lists four things you would buy with $100.

_____

_____

Lesson II-29: Using a Comma When Addressing
Someone (Varying Sentences)

To the Teacher

Another common use of a comma is when someone is being addressed. For example, if a student is writing conversation to a person, a sentence might read: *John, please open the window.* In this lesson, the student is given practice in writing sentences that are addressed to another individual.

To the Student

Here's another use of the comma. When you are talking to someone and want to get his or her attention, you might use the person's name. For example:

John, come over here.
Sandra, would you please hand me that pencil?
Bob, I am talking to you!
Rover, I said to sit down!

It's the same in writing. When you are writing and directing your words to someone specific, you would probably use the person's name, then put in a comma, and then put in what you would want to say to that person (or dog or other character).

Let's try some examples. Where would you put a comma in these sentences? (write on the board)

> *Amanda please shut the window.* (After "Amanda")
> *Rick and Helen come over here right now.* (After "Helen")
> *Pete you open the door and Cathy you close it after everyone is out.* (After "Pete" and after "Cathy")

Some sentences use names, but they are not used to call attention to someone. For example: *Amanda shut the window.* That just tells what Amanda did; you are not instructing Amanda to shut the window. *Sandra will hand me the pencil.* That just tells what Sandra is doing. *Hand me the pencil, Sandra.* I'm still addressing or talking to Sandra, but this time it's at the *end* of the sentence. No problem—I'm still going to use a comma to separate my command to Sandra from her name. *Rick and Helen came over here right away.* That just tells what Rick and Helen were doing; I wasn't specifically talking to them. Do you understand the difference?

Now it's your turn to practice putting in commas in the right place.

Worksheets

Answers to Worksheet II-29A:

1. Beth, please turn in your homework on time.
2. Donald and Jake, I told you to come in the room quietly.
3. Come over here right now, Barney.
4. Would you like some candy, Carla?
5. Jeff, can you reach that light?
6. Mother, please let me stay up all night to watch movies.
7. Little Frog, jump for me!
8. I think it's time to wash the dishes, Max and Ellen.
9. Kate and Jillian, run upstairs and answer the phone.
10. Who has my purse Jessica?

Answers to Worksheet II-29B:

Read each sentence carefully. Some of them need commas to show the person who is being addressed or talked to. Some are just regular sentences and are telling what is happening. Add commas if they are needed.

1. —
2. Who would like to erase the boards, Mike and Fred?
3. Sandy, would you please give me your pencil?
4. Miguel, did you turn in your homework?
5. May I please see your assignment, Ellen?
6. Who wanted to borrow the calculator, Kyle and Jeremy?
7. Rover, I told you to sit down.
8. —
9. —
10. Kalim, did you turn in that basketball?

Follow-up Activity

Have each student ask a question of another student, beginning with the student's name. Have them write their questions on slips of paper. Randomly pull out slips of paper and have students ask questions of each other (and then answer them). Practice changing the position of the student's name (the beginning, the end, even in the middle if desired) and show how this would translate to a written sentence. Examples:

Jessica, how many cats do you have?

How many cats do you have, Jessica?

I wonder, Jessica, how many cats you have?

II-29A. I'm Talking to You!

Someone is being addressed in each sentence below. Read them carefully and insert a comma in the correct places.

1. Beth please turn in your homework on time.

2. Donald and Jake I told you to come in the room quietly.

3. Come over here right now Barney.

4. Would you like some candy Carla?

5. Jeff can you reach that light?

6. Mother please let me stay up all night to watch movies.

7. Little Frog jump for me!

8. I think it's time to wash the dishes Max and Ellen.

9. Kate and Jillian run upstairs and answer the phone.

10. Who has my purse Jessica?

Name _____ Date _____

II-29B. Am I Talking to You?

Read each sentence carefully. Some of them need commas to show the person who is being addressed or talked to. Some are just regular sentences and are telling what is happening. Add commas if needed.

1. George and Steve are running down the hall.

2. Who would like to erase the boards Mike and Fred?

3. Sandy would you please give me your pencil?

4. Miguel did you turn in your homework?

5. May I please see your assignment Ellen?

6. Who wanted to borrow the calculator Kyle and Jeremy?

7. Rover I told you to sit down.

8. Rover was supposed to sit down when I told him to.

9. Did Tricia find the scorecard after practice?

10. Kalim did you turn in that basketball?

Lesson II-30: Varying the Length of Sentences

(Varying Sentences)

To the Teacher

When students begin writing longer pieces, they will want to vary the sentences they use. Varying the style and length of sentences is what makes it more interesting to read, rather than having identical sentence patterns over and over. In this lesson, students are given practice in varying the length of their sentences.

To the Student

Here are some sentences about skiing that I would like you to read. Then give me your opinion about them. (Write these sentences on the board.)

I like to ski in the winter. Skiing is a fun sport to do. Many people enjoy skiing at ski resorts. It is fun to ski very fast.

What did you think? (probably OK—it tells about how someone feels about skiing) Did the sentences start with different starting words? (yes) Are they all complete sentences? (yes) Now I would like you to count how many words are in each sentence.

first sentence—7

second sentence—7

third sentence—7

fourth sentence—7

They all have the same number of words. There is nothing wrong with these sentences, but there is a way to make them a little more interesting. We are going to work on varying the length of your sentences.

Now read these sentences about skiing:

Most people like to ski in the winter when it is cold and brisk outside.

Skiing is the most fun when it's cold! Brrrr! I don't mind the cold. I love it!

When it is cold, I just ski longer and faster. The hot chocolate at the end of the day is worth waiting for. I love to ski.

Count the words in these sentences:

first—15	fifth—3
second—8	sixth—10
third—1	seventh—13
fourth—5	eighth—4

When you read these sentences, some are long, some are really short, some are just medium. It is a surprise to read because you don't know how long those sentences are going to be. The writer also used the word "Brrr." Is that really a word or is that a sound effect? Did you know exactly what the writer was thinking about? (being cold)

As you do more sentence writing, try to think about varying the length of your sentences.

Worksheets

Answers to Worksheet II-30A:

Students' sentences will vary.

Answers to Worksheet II-30B:

Students' sentences will vary.

Follow-up Activity

Divide into teams. Make cards with numerals 1–10 on them and shuffle the cards. Give students a pool of target words, such as weekly spelling words or vocabulary words. Have students from each team alternate drawing a number card. That indicates the number of words that the team must put into a complete sentence. You can award points (one per word) for successfully writing each sentence.

II-30A. Count My Words

Read each word or phrase below. Can you write a sentence that
contains exactly the number of words indicated? Give it a try!

1. the apple tree (10)

_____

2. my cat (7)

_____

3. black and white (15)

_____

4. Angela (5)

_____

5. hot (3)

_____

6. broken umbrella (8)

_____

7. lightning and thunder (11)

_____

8. sleeping puppy (9)

_____

9. long hair (5)

_____

10. piano lessons (6)

_____

Name _____ Date _____

II-30B. Short, Long, Longer

Write a sentence about anything you like that contains the following number of words. (For the short ones, you might want to use someone's name, a command, or a sound effect.)

1. (6) _____

_____

2. (5) _____

_____

3. (8) _____

_____

4. (2) _____

5. (5) _____

_____

6. (7) _____

_____

7. (3) _____

_____

8. (1) _____

9. (10) _____

_____

_____

_____

10. (6) _____

_____

_____

Lesson II-31: Paraphrasing (Varying Sentences)

To the Teacher

Paraphrasing is a particularly useful skill when students begin to write paragraphs with an introductory sentence and a concluding sentence that state basically the same information. Paraphrasing also involves using synonyms not only for words, but for entire thoughts. The purpose of this lesson is to give students practice in recognizing and generating paraphrased sentences.

To the Student

Pretend it's sunny and 100 degrees outside. What might you hear people say when they are talking about the weather? *Boy, it's really hot out! I think I'm melting! Get me to the pool before I melt on the sidewalk. The sun is really hot out today.*

All of those sentences are saying about the same thing—the person talking is really hot because of the sun. But people can use different words to convey the same message. It would be dull if everyone just said "It's hot outside." There are many more interesting ways to say "It's hot outside."

When you use different words to say the same thing, it's like using synonyms, only you are changing groups of words instead of simply one word. You are expressing the same idea, but you might use different words. Here are some more examples:

Alice ate everything on her plate in a hurry.
Alice devoured the food on her plate.

The dog went through the kitchen garbage.
The dog made a mess of the trash in the kitchen.

Tony fell off of his bike and hurt his knee.
Tony had an accident with his bike.

Can you paraphrase these sentences?

    Jenny loved to watch the fish swim in the bowls. (Jenny enjoyed looking at the aquarium.)

    Mike was really angry when his brother shoved him. (Mike got mad when his brother hit him.)

    The dog tracked in mud all over the kitchen floor. (The dog ran through the kitchen with dirty paws.)

Now it's your turn to practice recognizing and writing sentences that are paraphrased.

Worksheets

Answers to Worksheet II-31A:

1. a, c	3. b, d	5. c, d
2. a, b	4. a, c	

Answers to Worksheet II-31B:

Students' sentences will vary. Here are examples.

1. Puppies are fun pets for kids.

2. Grandma is a good cook.

3. A bee attacked Denise at the picnic.

4. Kelly gave her mother a nice bunch of flowers.

5. Alison is good with taking care of birds.

6. Dr. Smith looked at my teeth yesterday.

7. On Saturday, I'd like to go see a good movie.

8. Ricardo accidentally dropped his popcorn on the floor.

9. The boys colored a nice picture to give their aunt.

10. I need some help on this math paper.

Follow-up Activity

If you have some clever students, they can work on short plays to present to the class dealing with what people "really mean" when they say things. For example, if a teacher says, "Well, I think you could do better on this," she might REALLY mean, "You didn't try at all! Did you guess at ALL of the answers?" If your father says, "This room is a total disaster area!" he REALLY means, "You haven't cleaned this room in a month!" If the doctor says, "You may have a short wait until I can get to you," he REALLY means, "You'll be in this waiting room until midnight."

You get the idea! Students can have a lot of fun interpreting those comments we often give (and hear).

II-31A. What's Another Way to Say It?

Read each sentence. Then select the two best sentences below that paraphrase the meaning of the sentence. Write the letters on the line.

1. It was really cold outside today. _____

    a. My fingers were freezing outside.

    b. I wore a new coat to school.

    c. It felt like zero degrees today.

    d. It felt like 100 degrees outside today.

2. Tom doesn't like to eat vegetables. _____

    a. Beans and carrots are not on Tom's list of favorite foods.

    b. Tom doesn't care for vegetables.

    c. Tom only likes to eat ice cream.

    d. Tom likes to eat fruit and dairy products.

3. Jerry got a new bike at his birthday party. _____

    a. Jerry's parents are rich.

    b. Jerry got a wonderful present for his birthday.

    c. Jerry had a birthday.

    d. Jerry got a bike on his birthday.

4. Sara is always reading books about horses. _____

    a. Horse stories are Sara's favorites.

    b. Sara is a good horseback rider.

    c. Sara enjoys reading about horses.

    d. Sara is a good reader.

5. I played ball with my dog in the park. _____

    a. My dog likes to walk in the park.

    b. My dog ate my homework.

    c. My dog likes to play with a ball.

    d. My dog and I have fun in the park.

Name _____ Date _____

II-31B. Write a Paraphrase

Read each sentence below. Then write another sentence that means the same thing.

1. Children can have fun with new puppies.

_____

2. There are lots of good things to eat at Grandma's house.

_____

3. Denise got stung by a bumblebee at the picnic.

_____

4. Kelly picked flowers for her mother.

_____

5. Alison knows a lot about how to take care of birds.

_____

6. I had to go to the dentist yesterday.

_____

7. Let's go to the movies this weekend!

_____

8. Ricardo spilled popcorn all over Mom's new rug.

_____

9. Shane and William drew a picture for their aunt.

_____

10. I don't understand how to do this math.

_____

Lesson II-32: Legible Writing (Proofreading/Editing)

To the Teacher

While some students may have wonderful thoughts and wit, their handwriting may be so sloppy and difficult to read that the meaning of their great work of literature is lost simply because the reader can't figure it out. The purpose of this lesson is to have students identify elements of good handwriting (e.g., spacing, letter formation, neatness), make corrections in practice examples, and write acceptable sentences.

To the Student

I want you to read the most wonderful sentence I have ever run across! You'll love this! It will change your life! Here it is: (Write on the board illegible scribbling with smudges, erasures, etc.) Who can read it out loud so we can all enjoy it? (pause) No one? Why not? (can't read it, it's a mess)

When something is written like this, it's called... a mess! It's also called *illegible*. If something is important enough to be read by others, it should be written so that others can figure out what you wrote! I know that writing on a computer makes it a lot easier, but you will still have times when you must turn in writing samples with pencil (or pen) and paper. It is important for you to be able to write a *legible* sentence.

You are going to have some practice now in figuring out what makes a sentence legible, or readable, and then actually correcting and writing legible sentences.

Worksheets

Answers to Worksheet II-32A:

1. sloppy handwriting
2. no spacing
3. upper and lower cases mixed
4. cursive and printing mixed
5. messy—cross outs and rewriting
6. not on the line
7. size—some big, some small
8. slanted backwards and slanted forward—not consistent direction

Answers to Worksheet II-32B:

Students' sentences must be legible.

Answers to Worksheet II-32C:

Students' sentences must be legible.

Answers to Worksheet II-32D:

Students' sentences will vary.

Follow-up Activities

1. Collect writing samples from students' journals, written assignments, and daily sentence exercises. Use them as examples (anonymously) to have the class evaluate and revise them.

2. If certain students tend to make the same mistakes (forgetting to space, mixing up upper and lower cases, not staying on the line, etc.), call this particular problem to their attention and have them be on the "lookout" for this type of error. Be sure to compliment students when they have found, and then corrected, the problem!

3. It is helpful to save papers from early in the school year (or even from a previous grade) to compare with later efforts. There is usually some progress to be found!

Name _____   Date _____

II-32A. Can You Read This?

Read these sentences with your class. What is difficult
to read about each one?

1. Birds come in many colors.

2. Allbirdsarewarm-blooded.

3. Birds have feathers and Backbones.

4. Baby birds must eat their own weight in food a day.

5. Birds don't have teeth to chew up their food.

6. Birds swallow pebbles to grind up their food.

7. Birds ave bones that are very light.

8. Most of their bones are hollow.

II-32B. Make the Corrections

Rewrite each sentence from Worksheet II-32A, making corrections that will make the sentences easier to read.

1. _____

_____

2. _____

_____

3. _____

_____

4. _____

_____

5. _____

_____

6. _____

_____

7. _____

_____

8. _____

_____

II-32C. Writing Legible Sentences

Copy the sentences below. Use the checklist below to score your first effort. Make changes if needed. Practice scoring sentences written by classmates.

- Good handwriting (correct upper and lower cases, letters formed correctly)
  X = Good handwriting, O = Poor handwriting
- Spacing (stay on the line, space between words, sizes consistent within words)
  X = Good spacing, O = No spacing
- Neat (erased carefully, no write-overs) **X = Neat, O = Messy**

1. Not all birds can fly. (__/__/__)

_____

2. Penguins are birds that do not fly. (__/__/__)

_____

3. An ostrich can run very fast. (__/__/__)

_____

4. A hummingbird can fly backwards and straight up like a helicopter. (__/__/__)

_____

_____

5. Birds cannot fly without feathers. (__/__/__)

_____

_____

6. Some birds fly to a warmer climate in the winter. (__/__/__)

_____

_____

7. This journey is called migration. (__/__/__)

_____

_____

8. Birds know when they are supposed to come home. (__/__/__)

_____

_____

Name _____ Date _____

II-32D. On Your Own

Answer these questions/statements using complete sentences.
Remember to make your sentences legible so that the person
who reads them will have no trouble.

1. What is your middle name? _____

   _____

   _____

2. What is something you would give a dog to eat? _____

   _____

3. Tell about a good place to hide in your house. _____

   _____

4. What would be your wish on your birthday? _____

   _____

5. Write a sentence that starts with "Once upon a time." _____

   _____

6. Where would a magic carpet take you? _____

   _____

7. Describe your brother/sister/pet. _____

   _____

8. What would we find in your pocket? _____

   _____

9. What is the best thing about you? _____

   _____

10. Tell why your best friend is your best friend. _____

   _____

Lesson II-33: Capital Letters—Only When Necessary!

(Proofreading/Editing)

To the Teacher

Some students get careless with the use of capital letters. Some students tend to always capitalize B/b and D/d (perhaps to avoid the confusion that comes with reversing the lower-case letters). Even when students are aware that a sentence begins with a capital letter and recognize proper nouns, they will still sometimes throw in a capital letter for no apparent reason. The purpose of this lesson is to alert students to proofreading written work, specifically to be aware of the correct use of capital letters.

To the Student

(Write on the board)

I like to go to *School*.

I go to Riley Elementary *School*.

School is fun.

I think *School* is fun.

What word is in all four of these sentences? (school) You will notice that it begins with a capital S in all four sentences, but there might be a mistake here. Remember that every capital letter used has to have a specific reason. If there's no reason to give it a capital letter, the word doesn't get one.

Take a look at the first sentence. Is there any reason to capitalize school? (No, it's just referring to school in general.) Look at the second sentence. Is it okay to capitalize school here? (Yes, it refers to a specific school.) What about the third sentence? (Yes, capitalize but only because it is the first word in the sentence.) And the last one? (This word should not be capitalized because it refers to school in general, not a specific school; and since it's not the first word in the sentence, there's no reason to capitalize it.)

Now you are going to have some practice in proofreading sentences to see if the capital letters are used at the right time.

Worksheets

Answers to Worksheet II-33A:

1. —	5. —	9. sand, feet
2. desert	6. —	10. camel, very, pet
3. hump	7. camel, zoo, big	
4. stomach, water	8. feet	

Answers to Worksheet II-33B:

1. My Aunt Jessica has a birthday in June.

2. We will probably celebrate at Pizza Hut.

3. Aunt Jessica and Uncle Tom are really nice.

4. They live in Milwaukee, Wisconsin, on North Avenue.

5. They have two dogs named Barney and Bilbo.

6. We took a trip to Arizona one summer during vacation.

7. Aunt Jessica has a daughter named Beth.

8. We used to laugh at Beth because she fell down when she was a baby.

9. Now Beth is older and she goes to Clark School.

10. On Monday, we will both go to Wisconsin to visit our relatives.

Answers to Worksheet II-33C:

Students' sentences will vary.

Follow-up Activity

Capital Chaos: This is a simple game that takes some preparation, but can be played quickly once everything is made. Making the game is a valuable part of the experience.

Materials: Make cards (or assign students to help with category cards) for words that require a capital letter for these categories: names, places, states, cities, countries, holidays, months, days, specific landmarks (could be local sites, parks, etc.) and famous people. Have 10 cards for each category (total 100 cards). Write the word correctly (with a capital letter) on one side and incorrectly (lower-case letter) on the other side. It is very helpful to use 10 different colors for the categories.

Make a playing board for each student (4 players is probably the right number to have control of the game and move the action along). Any shape can work, but a "rainbow" with five hands or a "sun" with 10 spokes will work fine. The idea is to have a space for 10 cards to fit on the playing board. For the rainbow, two cards can fit on either end of each band; for the sun, the 10 spokes can each hold one card. Each of the 10 places for cards to go should be labeled to match one of the 10 categories of cards (names, places, cities, etc.), and that is where a card from each category should be placed.

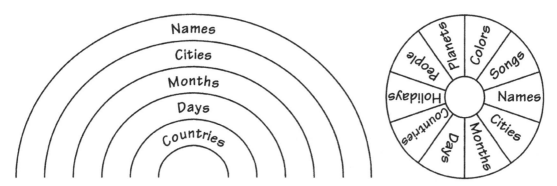

How to Play: The idea is for each student to fill up his or her playing board with 10 cards, one from each of 10 categories. The categories are all words that begin with capital letters (proper names, cities, places, etc.). Each category should have a designated spot on the playing board. The spot does not really matter because the player who fills his or her board first is the winner.

All of the 100 cards (10 each in 10 categories) are shuffled. The cards contain the target word spelled correctly with a capital letter on one side; the same word is written without a capital letter on the opposite side. The reason for this is that students must turn their cards to the capital side before putting it on the board. This helps students focus on the point of the game: The words must have a capital letter to be correct.

The dealer passes out one card to each student on each turn. The student turns the card to the capital side (sometimes it helps to have them say in unison: "Capitals up!"), reads the card (can be done silently), identifies the category, and places the card on the correct spot on the playing board. As students become more familiar with the pool of words and the position of the categories on their playing board, this can be completed faster and faster. If a student already has a card filling a category, the card is simply returned to the deck.

Play continues (it will go quickly at first) until one student has all 10 categories completely filled with a card (capital side up). If a head is declared "filled up" but a card is not turned to the capital side, remove the incorrect cards and keep playing. All cards have to have the capital side up to be correct.

Variations:

- Dealer can pass out 5 cards at a time to each student to move things along.
- A timer can be used to "rush" the pace of placing the cards to make it more chaotic (yes, this can be fun).
- Students can work in teams (two on a board), especially if there is a student who might need extra help in identifying a category.

Ideas for "Capital Chaos" Cards: Have a lot of extra blank cards so that mistakes can be quickly discarded. Some students will have trouble writing the words correctly (if you let the students make the game). Insist that the words be written clearly; otherwise, players will not be able to use them when they play the game. Sloppy handwriting is *not* acceptable. Also, capital letters must be clearly capitals—spacing and size have to be correct. This is a good exercise in legibility!

Names—names of students in the classroom, pets, teachers

Places—local library, name of a church, local park, state park, name of schools

States—your own state, surrounding states, famous states, states that have landmarks with which students are familiar

Cities—your own city, state's capital city, nearby cities, cities associated with colleges or sports teams

Countries—try to have students think about different languages, and then list the country in which that language is spoken (Japanese/Japan; Chinese/China; French/France; Spanish/Spain or Mexico)

Holidays

Months—select 10 months (maybe vote on which ones to use by how many birthdays are in a month)

Days—there are the 7 days in the week, but for the extra 3 repeat any of the days students select

Specific Landmarks—the Statue of Liberty, Space Needle, Eiffel Tower, etc.

Famous People—movie stars, singers, political people, other celebrities

Name _____   Date _____

II-33A. Give a Reason

Circle every capital letter in these sentences. It you can't give a specific reason for why each letter needs to be a capital, rewrite the sentence without the capital letter.

1. Camels live in dry lands such as Africa.

   _____

   _____

2. They travel very well across the Desert.

   _____

3. A camel has a Hump that can store fat.

   _____

4. They have a large Stomach that stores Water.

   _____

5. Water is important to the camel.

   _____

6. I saw a camel in the Milwaukee Zoo one summer.

   _____

7. The Camel in the Zoo was very Big.

   _____

8. Camels have very wide Feet with pads.

   _____

9. They won't sink into the Sand with the Feet.

   _____

10. I don't think a Camel would make a Very good Pet.

   _____

II-33B. Correct These Sentences

There are mistakes with capital letters in these sentences. Rewrite each sentence correctly. Remember that each capital letter has to have a reason.

1. My Aunt Jessica has a Birthday in June.

   _____

   _____

2. We will probably celebrate at Pizza hut.

   _____

3. Aunt Jessica and uncle Tom are really nice.

   _____

4. They live in Milwaukee, Wisconsin on north Avenue.

   _____

5. They have two dogs nameD Barney and bilbo.

   _____

6. We took a trip to arizona one Summer during vacation.

   _____

7. Aunt jessica has a Daughter named Beth.

   _____

8. We used to Laugh at Beth because she fell Down when she was a Baby.

   _____

9. Now beth is older and she goes to clark school.

   _____

10. On monDay, we will Both go to wisconsin to visit our relatives.

   _____

II-33C. Watch Your Writing!

Answer these questions. Add a third sentence to tell more.
Then check your work to make sure you used capital letters
appropriately.

1. What is the name of your pet? Where did you get your
   pet?

   _____

   _____

2. Who is your favorite TV person? Why do you like him or her?

   _____

3. What is the name of your city? What is something fun you would tell someone to do in
   your city?

   _____

4. What is your favorite day of the week? When do you get up in the morning on this day?

   _____

5. When is your birthday? How old were you on your last birthday?

   _____

6. What is a fun holiday in April? What is a good trick to play on someone on that day?

   _____

7. Who is your teacher? What is something funny that your teacher has done?

   _____

8. Who lives next door to you? What street do you both live on?

   _____

9. If you could visit another state, where would you go? What would you do?

   _____

10. If you could visit another country, where would you go? What would you do?

    _____

Lesson II-34: Editing for Punctuation (Proofreading/Editing)

To the Teacher

When proofreading work for punctuation, students should readily be aware of end punctuation (period, exclamation point, question mark). As they become better writers, they should look for correct use of commas (in a list, addressing someone) and quotation marks. The purpose of this lesson is to provide students practice in recognizing common punctuation errors, making appropriate corrections, and generating sentences free of these errors.

To the Student

When you are editing a sentence for punctuation, what do you think you should be looking for? (periods, question marks, commas, etc.) Basically, you are looking for the little marks that give clues as to how to read the words that are written. For example, how does a simple little comma change the meaning of this sentence:

> *Bob Tom and Mike would like to go canoeing with you.*

> *Bob, Tom and Mike would like to go canoeing with you.*

(In the first example, it sounds as though two people want to canoe with another person; in the second example, someone is talking to Bob, telling him that two people want to canoe with him.)

How does the end punctuation change the meaning of this sentence:

> *I am thrilled to be called into the office.*

> *I am thrilled to be called into the office!*

> *I am thrilled to be called into the office?*

(In the first example, the writer could be sarcastic—he or she is not really thrilled to be called into the office. In the second example, the writer really is excited about going to the office. In the third example, it sounds as though the writer is talking to someone, expressing disbelief that anyone would think he or she was happy about being called into the office.)

So you can see that punctuation is really important to a writer and to a reader. Use the clues on the worksheets to help you figure out what kind of punctuation is needed on the examples.

Worksheets

Answers to Worksheet II-34A:

1. need period instead of question mark
2. OK
3. OK
4. no comma
5. need comma after black
6. no comma
7. need comma and quotation mark
8. need comma instead of question mark
9. need period instead of question mark
10. OK
11. need comma instead of question mark
12. no comma, need period at end

Answers to Worksheet II-34B:

1. Mother, please shut the window.
2. Dave, please shut the window!
3. Go to the store and get oranges, apple pie, and a candy bar.
4. Jon said, "Let's go to the baseball game."
5. Janelle said, "I would like to go with you!"
6. Alex said, "Debbie, please stop screaming!"

Answers to Worksheet II-34C:

Students' sentences will vary. Here are examples.

1. Amy, go to the store and get me some apples, bananas, and pears.
2. Bob, sit down right now!
3. Jennifer, please pass me the corn.
4. My favorite pets are dogs, cats, horses, and hamsters.
5. Ellen said, "I just stepped on a nail!"
6. Jeff said, "Hello, Bob!"
7. Mom, would you get me a game, a jump rope, and a doll for my birthday?
8. Steve said, "Dad, would you take me camping?"
9. Sam, get over here!
10. Mother, I have homework in math, spelling, social studies, and science tonight.

Follow-up Activity

Have students look for examples in newspaper articles of the correct usage of these types of punctuation in everyday writing. Punctuation, especially quotation marks, can be somewhat confusing until it is readily understood by students. Give lots of proofreading practice with examples from anonymous student writing samples.

Name _____ Date _____

II-34A. Find the Punctuation Errors

Some of these sentences are written correctly. Others have one or more punctuation mistakes. Circle every punctuation mark. If the sentence is correct, write OK. If it is not correct, put an X on the incorrect punctuation.

1. We went to the pet store?

2. I saw lots of dogs, cats, and hamsters.

3. I said, "Wow!"

4. My mother told me to, look at the puppies.

5. The puppies were black brown, white, and spotted.

6. They were running, all over the cage.

7. My mother said You should not get a puppy."

8. Mother? please let me get a puppy.

9. Puppies are fun?

10. I will name the puppy Fred.

11. Fred? come over here.

12. I think, puppies are fun to have for pets,

II-34B. Correct the Punctuation Errors

Use the clues to correct the sentences below.

1. Mother" please shut the window? (*Clue*: You are talking to your mother and want her to shut the window because it is a little breezy outside.)

_____

_____

2. Dave? please shut the window, (*Clue*: You are talking to Dave and it is starting to look like a very bad storm is coming your way.)

_____

_____

3. Go to the store and get oranges, apple, pie, and a candy bar. (*Clue*: You are supposed to get three things at the store.)

_____

_____

4. Jon said. "Let's go to the baseball game. (*Clue*: Jon is talking and he is saying that he wants to go to the baseball game.)

_____

_____

5. Janelle said. I would like to go with you. (*Clue*: Janelle is talking and she is saying that she wants to go with you. She is very, very excited about going.)

_____

_____

6. Alex said? "Debbie please stop screaming. (*Clue*: Alex is talking to Debbie, asking her to please stop screaming. He is very angry with her.)

_____

_____

II-34C. Writing Sentences without Punctuation Errors

Write sentences that fit these descriptions.

1. You are talking to Amy and want her to go to the store to get three pieces of fruit.

   _____

2. You are talking to Bob and want him to sit down immediately.

   _____

3. You are talking to Jennifer and want her to pass you a plate of vegetables.

   _____

   _____

4. You are listing your four favorite pets.

   _____

5. Ellen is talking and she is saying that she stepped on a nail. She is very upset about it.

   _____

6. Jeff is talking and he is saying hello very loudly to a friend across the street.

   _____

7. You are talking to your mother, and want to ask her if she would get you three toys for your birthday.

   _____

8. Steve is talking to his father and he is asking if his father would take him camping.

   _____

9. You are calling to your dog who is running out in the middle of the road.

   _____

10. Kristine is telling her mother that she has homework in four subjects tonight.

   _____

   _____

Lesson II-35: Editing for Spelling (Proofreading/Editing)

To the Teacher

A first copy or rough draft may legitimately contain numerous spelling errors for the sake of getting ideas down quickly without worrying about details; however, students are responsible for making sure that steps are taken to edit their written work for spelling. Editing for spelling errors implies that students (a) will check each word carefully, (b) will recognize when a mistake has been made, and (c) will know how to correct those errors. The purpose of this lesson is to provide practice for students in these three areas of proofreading for spelling accuracy.

To the Student

Take a look at this sentence (write it on the board):

I took my kat and my dog for a wolk arnd the yrad.

What seems to be wrong with this sentence? (spelling errors) Let's underline each word as we read it. When you get to a word that you think might have a spelling mistake in it, let's put a little oval underneath it. (demonstrate)

I   took   my   kat   and   my   dog   for   a   wolk   arnd   the   yrad.
—   —   —   0   —   —   —   —   —   0   0   —   0

How many ovals do we have? (4) What those ovals are going to mean is that I strongly suspect or definitely know that there is a spelling mistake. If I know for sure that a word is spelled wrong, I am going to cross it out, correct it, and then X off the oval.

For example: I know that "cat" is spelled "c-a-t," so that one is easy to correct. (Make correction.) But let's say that I strongly suspect that wolk is spelled wrong. I'm going to go to a piece of scrap paper and try out some different spellings because I think I know what it is supposed to look like. Follow me to this little box… (Draw a little box on the board.)

Here I'm going to try some different spellings for "wolk." Let's see… Does wolk look right? No. What about walk? Yes, that one looks right. I'm sure now that the correct spelling is w-a-l-k. Now I'm going to cross off that one!

Let's go to "arnd." I know the word is supposed to be "around," but let's say I do not remember how to spell it. Let me try "the box." arownd—arond—arund… Hmmm… I don't know if I can figure this one out. What could I do now?

- Ask someone.
- Use a dictionary.
- Use my "personal dictionary" of commonly misspelled words.
- Check in my spelling book.
- Use a spell checker on the computer or word processor.
- Other ideas?

Let's say I used my spelling book and now I know that it is spelled: a-r-o-u-n-d. I can cross out the misspelled word and spell it correctly now. I can cross out the oval.

Now let's go to the fourth oval: yrad. I know this is supposed to be the word "yard." For some people, this might be an easy correction. For other people, you might have to go to the box and play around with it for awhile. (Demonstrate: yerd—yard.) Or it might be a word that you have to check further to figure it out.

Now let's rewrite the sentence without any spelling errors:

I took my cat and my dog for a walk around the yard.

Perfect! Now let's try practicing making spelling corrections! Remember, if someone else (such as a peer or your teacher) checks your work, that person may put an oval under the words that you should check. Ask yourself these questions:

1. Is it just a simple quick fix? (such as a mistaken letter written down hastily?)

2. Is it a word you need to play around with? (shuffle the letters to make it look right)

3. Is it a word you need to get further help with? (use a dictionary, ask someone)

Worksheets

Answers to Worksheet II-35A:

Part One:

1. My dadd and I went for a rid in the car. (dad, ride)
       O   O

2. Wee rolled down the windo. (We, window)
   O   O

3. Th breeze felt so goode (The, good)
  O   O

4. It mad my hair blow all ovr. (made, over)
    O   O

5. It is fun to rid on a sunny daye. (ride, day)
        O   O

Part Two:

1. My dad licks to drive fast. (likes)
       O

2. Hiz car is whit and blue with blak stripes. (His, white, black)
  O   O   O

3. My dog liks to ride in the car, too. (likes)
       O

4. He stiks his hed out of the window and barks. (sticks, head)
   O   O

5. People lik to see us go by. (like)
    O

Answers to Worksheet II-35B:

Part One:

1. family	3. together	5. choosing
2. because	4. shuffle	

Part Two:

1. brother	3. either	5. because
2. people	4. doesn't	

Answers to Worksheet II-35C:

1. information	4. people	7. wise	10. afraid
2. interesting	5. feathers	8. learn	
3. night	6. move	9. desert	

II-35A. Quick Fixes

These students were in a hurry and made some simple mistakes.

Part One: Look at the words marked with an oval. Can you spell them correctly?

1. My dadd and I went for a rid in the car. _____
   O   O

2. Wee rolled down the windo. _____
   O   O

3. Th breeze felt so goode. _____
   O   O

4. It mad my hair blow all ovr. _____
   O   O

5. It is fun to rid on a sunny daye. _____
           O   O

Part Two: Mark all mistakes with an oval. Can you spell the words correctly?

1. My dad licks to drive fast. _____

2. Hiz car is whit and blue with blak stripes. _____

3. My dog liks to ride in the car, too. _____

4. He stiks his head out of the window and barks. _____

5. People lik to see us go by. _____

II-35B. Play Around with These Words

Sometimes you need to see if a word looks right. These
sentences have words that need to be checked.

Part One: Circle the correct choice for the word marked
with an oval.

1. My famly likes to play games together.

   O   famely   family   phamily

2. We do this on a weekend becose we have the time.

   O   becase   because   becawse

3. It is fun to do something togeter.

   O   tagether   togehrer   together

4. My dad likes to shufle the deck of cards.

   O   shoffle   shutter   shuffle

5. We take turns chozing the games we want to play.

   O   choosing   chossing   choozing

Part Two: "Play around" with the marked words to rewrite them correctly.

1. My bruther sometimes gets mad if he doesn't win.

   O   _____

2. I told him that peeple don't like to play with poor losers.

   O   _____

3. You can't win all the time or that isn't fun ether.

   O   _____

4. My sister said she doezn't need to win all of the time.

   O   _____

5. We all just like to play becauz it's something we all enjoy.

   O   _____

II-35C. Get More Information

These sentences contain words that are a little more difficult to spell. You will probably have to use a regular dictionary, a personal dictionary, consult someone, use a spell checker, or use a spelling book. Rewrite the words correctly.

1. My class was reading a book that had a lot of informashun about birds.

    O

    _____

2. It was intresting to read about owls and other birds.

    O

    _____

3. Owls sleep during the day and hunt for their food at nite.

    O

    _____

4. Farmers and other peeple like owls when they eat insects.

    O

    _____

5. A mother owl might make a nest of grass or fethers.

    O

    _____

6. An owl cannot muve its head from side to side.

    O

    _____

7. Some people call the owl a very wize old bird.

    O

    _____

8. Another interesting bird to lern about is the ostrich.

    O

    _____

9. These birds live on the dessert and can go without water for a long time.

    O

    _____

10. Ostriches run around when they are afrade of things.

    O

    _____

Lesson II-36: Editing for Meaning (Proofreading/Editing)

To the Teacher

When students read a sentence they have written, many times they will read what they had *intended* to write. Hopefully the written and spoken words will match; but when they don't, there is an error that needs to be located and corrected. Sometimes students will add extra words, omit words, or mix up the order of words and still insist that the sentence makes sense. The purpose of this lesson is to provide practice for students in reading sentences correctly, determining whether or not the sentence makes sense, and then making appropriate corrections.

To the Student

(Write on the board)

> *My family and I went the Grand Canyon for vacation.*

I am going to read this sentence to you out loud: "My family and I went to the Grand Canyon for our vacation." Is that what you see? (no) What's wrong? (the words "to" and "our" are missing from the board) Sometimes when you read or write, you read the words as if you were saying them. If I were talking to you, I probably wouldn't say: *I am going lunch right now.* I would say: *I am going TO lunch right now.*

But when you write something, it is easy to skip over a word and miss it when you are reading it back! When you read, it is easy to slip in a word that you know is supposed to be there. But when you write, you might have to go back and check every single word to make sure that you didn't miss any.

Here are three kinds of mistakes to watch out for when you are proofreading your writing:

1. Adding a word (or words) that doesn't need to be there. *Example*: We took a nice vacation out **to the out** west to the Grand Canyon.

2. Omitting a word that should be there. *Example*: We took nice vacation out west. (We took **a** nice vacation…)

3. Mixing up words (right words, the wrong order, or starting one thought and then going off to finish another sentence—it just doesn't sound right!) *Examples*: Sandy and **friend her** went for a walk in the woods. Sandy and **her friend was named** Joan went for a walk in the woods.

Here is a way to proofread written sentences to make sure what you write and what you read match:

1. Read the sentence out loud very slowly, touching the first letter of each word as you read.

2. Read the sentence in a normal tone of voice, making sure the words say and express what you wanted to say or write.

3. If something doesn't sound quite right, draw a squiggly line under the part that needs to be examined more closely.

4. Try to figure out what doesn't look or sound right. Did you skip a word? Add a word? Mix up words?

Worksheets

Answers to Worksheet II-36A:

1. OK
2. *Read*: Sometimes a little bit of sand or dirt **gets** inside the shells.

3. *Read*: This little piece **of** sand **becomes the** beginning of a pearl.

4. OK

5. OK

6. *Read*: It **is** white **or a** very light color.

7. OK

8. OK

9. *Read*: They bring **in** oysters from the ocean and open them.

10. *Read*: They put in a little piece **of** sand, wood, or shell.

Answers to Worksheet II-36B:

1. There was a man named Eli Whitney who liked to make things.

2. When he was just a boy, he made a violin.

3. Later, as a man, he invented a machine called the cotton gin.

4. This machine helped farmers take the seeds out of cotton plants.

5. Before this, people took the seeds out by hand.

6. It would take fifty men to do as much work as the cotton gin.

7. Eli Whitney also had another invention.

8. A long time ago, guns were made by hand, not by machine.

9. Eli Whitney invented a machine that made parts for guns.

10. Now guns could be made faster and change parts easily.

Follow-up Activities

1. **Practice Sentence Reading:** Compile a list of ten sentences with lots of little words (*of, and, the,* etc.) and have students practice reading these "tricky" sentences carefully. Call their attention to the types of mistakes they may encounter. Award stars, points, or grades for perfect oral reading.

2. **Practice Proofing:** Compile written examples from the students of sentences with these types of errors—omitted words, extra words, and mixed-up words. Have students continually practice being on the alert for finding these types of mistakes and then making corrections. Be sure to keep student examples anonymous so students are not embarrassed.

II-36A. Listen and Read Carefully

Your teacher will read these sentences to you. Follow along to determine whether or not the words match with what is said. Make any corrections. If the sentence is correct, write OK.

1. Pearls are found inside oyster shells.

_____

2. Sometimes a little bit of sand or dirt inside the shells.

_____

3. This little piece sand becomes to the beginning of a pearl.

_____

4. The oyster does not push the little piece of sand out.

_____

5. Instead, the oyster covers it with a smooth covering.

_____

6. It white or it a very light color.

_____

7. This is how a pearl begins to grow.

_____

8. People today want to make pearls.

_____

9. They bring oysters from the ocean and open them.

_____

10. They put in a little piece sand, wood, or shell.

_____

II-36B. Find the Mistakes

Each of these sentences has at least one mistake—a word is missing, there is an extra word, or the words are mixed up. Find and identify the mistakes. Then write each sentence correctly.

1. There was man named Eli Whitney who liked make things.

_____

2. When he was just was a boy, he made a violin.

_____

3. Later, as a man, he invented a the machine called the cotton gin.

_____

4. This machine helped farmers take the seeds out cotton plants.

_____

5. Before this, people had to people took the seeds out by hand.

_____

6. It would take fifty men to do much work as the cotton gin.

_____

7. Eli Whitney also he had another invention.

_____

8. A long ago, guns were made by hand, not by machine.

_____

9. Eli Whitney invented machine that made parts for guns.

_____

10. Now guns could be made could be faster and change parts easily.

_____

_____

Lesson II-37: Editing for Overuse of "and"

(Proofreading/Editing)

To the Teacher

A very common error in writing is the overuse of the word "and" in sentences. This skill will be dealt with in greater detail in Section III when writing paragraphs; for now, students should be aware that the word "and" can correctly be used when referring to more than one person or actor (Tom and Bill), more than one action (laughing and running), the last item in a list (peas, carrots, and beans), and when two events are closely related (rented a video and got a pizza). The word "and" is probably overused if you have used it more than two times in one sentence or if you are really connecting short sentences to make one overly long sentence. The purpose of this lesson is to give students practice in correctly editing sentences involving the word "and."

To the Student

We are going to examine another common writing mistake. See if you can figure it out by reading and saying this sentence: (write on board)

I got a hamburger and a soda and French fries and a candy bar and a salad.

What do you think? (too many "and"s) How many times is the word "and" used? (4) This sounds like it could be a better sentence if it were a list. How could you rewrite this sentence to make it list the foods eaten?

I got a hamburger, a soda, French fries, a candy bar, and a salad.

There are certain "and" traps you have to watch out for. Make sure that you really need the word "and" before you use it and over use it. Take a look at the use of "and" in this sentence: (write on board)

Kristina and I went shopping at the mall and the next day I stayed overnight at Jean's house.

What's going on here? Are you talking about Kristina and I going to the mall or is the sentence about staying overnight at Jean's house? It's both events, but they don't really have anything to do with each other. They are not closely related. This would be better as two separate sentences. How could you rewrite this to make two sentences?

Kristina and I went shopping at the mall. The next day, I stayed overnight at Jean's house.

Let's try another example. Consider the use of the word "and" in this sentence: (write on board)

It was a sunny day and my brother and I went for a walk and it was nice outside and we caught some bugs and then it was getting dark and we went home and my mother ordered pizza for us and we ate the pizza and we got tired and we went to bed.

Wow! How many times was "and" used in that sentence? (10) Is this really even one long sentence or would it sound better to make it several shorter sentences? (several shorter) Where can we start breaking it up to make the sentences shorter, but still related to each other? Let's try it this way:

It was a sunny day. My brother and I went for a walk because it was nice outside. We caught some bugs. It was getting dark so we went home. My mother ordered pizza for us. We ate the pizza. We got tired and went to bed.

What changes did I make? I ended the first sentence after "sunny day," I kept the part about the brother and I walking. Why? Because it was nice outside. Those parts are closely related, so they can stay together. The part about the bugs can be a short sentence. Getting dark and going home are closely related, connected with "so." Mother ordering pizza and eating the pizza could be closely related, so that's another option for that part. Getting tired and going to bed are closely related, so that can be connected with "and" or you could change it to "so."

Remember, it is OK to use "and" (in general) when:

- You are identifying a group (more than one).
- You are identifying more than one action.
- You are listing things.
- You have two events that are closely related (in which case, you may also consider the words "because" or "so")

Ready for some practice?

Worksheets

Answers to Worksheet II-37A:

1. Some people who are blind use a guide dog to help them go places.
2. When we go to the zoo, I would like to see a camel, a zebra, and a snake.
3. After school, Karla and Jenny are going to run around the park. They will clean up their room tonight.
4. We saw a beautiful peacock. It had long bright feathers.
5. We saw a beautiful peacock with long bright feathers.
6. I want to order a pizza with pepperoni, ham, sausage, and green peppers.
7. Stacy and Elaine are best friends. They like to write plays, jump rope, and go swimming.
8. The pool is very cold today, so I am not going in.
9. Our class is going to earn money by collecting cans, glass, and plastic. We will take them to the recycling center.
10. We will take a picnic basket, a towel, suntan lotion, and a hat to the beach.

Answers to Worksheet II-37B:

1. John, Mike, and Fred went to the fair last night.
2. OK
3. OK
4. It started to rain, so they ran for cover. They went in the barn.
5. OK
6. The boys decided to run for the parking lot, so they put umbrellas over their heads. They ran for the car, but they still got wet.
7. The rain stopped soon, so the boys went back to the fair and rode more rides.
8. At night, there was a tractor pull, a country singing show, and a pig race.
9. OK
10. Next year, the boys will go with Annie, Kate, and Sarah. They will go on all the rides again.

Follow-up Activity

Provide students with clear examples of appropriate uses of the word "and" in a sentence. Make (or help students make) a poster to display in front of the classroom. Have students illustrate the sentences with cartoon drawings.

II-37A. Revising Sentences with "and"

These sentences all use the word "and" in a way that could be improved. Follow the clues to rewrite the sentences to make them better.

1. Some people who are blind use a guide dog and the dog can help them to go places. (*Clue*: Combine the two closely related parts.)

_____

2. When we go to the zoo I would like to see a camel and a zebra and a snake. (*Clue*: Make a list.)

_____

3. After school, Karla and Jenny are going to run around the park and they will clean up their room tonight. (*Clue*: Make two separate sentences.)

_____

4. We saw a beautiful peacock and it had long bright feathers. (*Clue*: Make two separate sentences.)

_____

5. We saw a beautiful peacock and it had long bright feathers. (*Clue*: Combine closely related parts.)

_____

6. I want to order a pizza with pepperoni and ham and sausage and green peppers. (*Clue*: Make a list.)

_____

7. Stacy and Elaine are best friends and they like to write plays and jump rope and go swimming. (*Clue*: Make two separate sentences. In the second sentence, make a list.)

_____

8. The pool is very cold today and I am not going in that pool. (*Clue*: Combine closely related parts.)

_____

9. Our class is going to earn money by collecting cans and glass and plastic and we will take them to the recycling center. (*Clue*: Make two separate sentences. In the first sentence, make a list.)

_____

10. We will take a picnic basket and a towel and suntan lotion and a hat to the beach. (*Clue*: Make a list.)

_____

II-37B. Revising Sentences with "and"

Some of these sentences use the word "and" too much; others are correct. Mark sentences "OK" if they do not need to be changed. Rewrite the ones that could better be combined by using a list, or a different connecting word, or making shorter sentences.

1. John and Mike and Fred went to the fair last night.

   _____

   _____

2. They rode the roller coaster, the tilt-a-whirl, and the Ferris wheel.

   _____

3. The boys ate hot dogs and played games on the midway.

   _____

4. It started to rain and they ran for cover and they went in the barn.

   _____

5. It rained hard and everything got wet.

   _____

6. The boys decided to run for the parking lot and they put umbrellas over their heads and they ran for the car and they still got wet.

   _____

7. The rain stopped soon and the boys went back to the fair and they rode more rides.

   _____

8. At night, there was a tractor pull and a country singing show and a pig race.

   _____

9. John, Mike, and Fred said that they still had a good time at the fair.

   _____

10. Next year, the boys will go with Annie and Kate and Sarah and they will ride all the rides again.

    _____

Lesson II-38: Editing for Interest (Proofreading/Editing)

To the Teacher

Even students are probably tired writing basic, boring sentences that simply fulfill the requirement of being "a sentence." How much more fun, challenging, and motivating it is to write a sentence that shows some thought and experimentation! The purpose of this lesson is to give students practice in rewriting basic, generic sentences to make them more interesting by adding details, choosing clearer words, or expressing a thought in a different, clever way.

To the Student

What is a sentence? (a complete thought, starts with a capital letter, ends with a period) Is this a sentence? (write on the board) *The dog chased the cat up a tree.* Well, it sounds like something that makes sense all by itself, there's a capital letter, there's punctuation at the end… I guess it's a sentence all right!

Now I'm going to make a few changes, right before your very eyes! (rewrite)

The big black mongrel chased the poor little kitten all over the yard before the kitten leaped into a tree, out of reach of the growling dog.

What do you think of that? (better) Why? (gives more details, it's longer, helps the reader picture exactly what the animals look like and what happened) I revised this sentence to make it more interesting by adding details.

A sentence doesn't necessarily have to be a lot longer to be more interesting. For example, let's change this: *I really hate cleaning my room.* to: *I despise cleaning my room.* What's the difference? I only changed two words into one. What makes it more interesting to read the second one? (the word "despise" is very strong) A sentence can be more interesting by choosing stronger words or words that make your details clearer.

Here's another way to make a sentence more interesting. I'm going to start with this basic sentence: (write on the board) *I could hardly wait to jump in the lake and go swimming.* Can you tell that the writer really wanted to go swimming? That's a fine sentence, but now I'm going to make it more interesting by saying it in a different way. Watch: *I felt like magnets were pulling me into the water!* Or *The most important thing in my life right then was getting in that lake!* Or *The lake was calling to me: "Jump in! Come on! Hurry!"*

All three of these sentences express the idea: The person really wanted to get in the water. But instead of saying it in an ordinary way, there are three kinds of clever or more interesting, surprising ways to say the same thing. Remember, *you* are the writer. You are going to use words with which you are familiar. Don't try to write like someone you are not— but experiment with saying things in a way that is comfortable to you!

Worksheets

Answers to Worksheet II-38A:

Students' sentences will vary.

Answers to Worksheet II-38B:

Students' answers will vary. Here are sample words.

1. am crazy about	5. blaring, deafening	9. sweet, loving
2. fascinating	6. obnoxious, whiney	10. speedy, swift
3. uninteresting	7. explode, dance, rocket around	
4. starving, ravenous	8. ecstatic, joyous	

Answers to Worksheet II-38C:

Students' sentences will vary. Here are examples.

1. I am absolutely crazy about horses.
2. When friends come over, Monopoly is the game we grab first.
3. The story I am reading works like a sleeping pill for me.
4. Stay out of my way! I'm heading for the refrigerator!
5. I have to get my earplugs when that song comes on the radio.
6. Someone around here is in the doghouse—really!
7. Watching kernels of popcorn explode is really fascinating for me.
8. I was so excited to get the birthday card, I jumped all over the room.
9. The kitten likes people so much, she attaches herself to your lap and won't move.
10. Kara runs like the wind.

Follow-up Activity

Continue to pull examples from students' writing activities and work together on revising them to make them more interesting. You may divide the class into small groups and have them come up with different revisions for the same sentence. It will be fun to compare and discuss their examples.

II-38A. Revising by Adding Details

Rewrite these ordinary sentences to make them more interesting
by adding details. If you need prompts, follow the questions that
are in parentheses.

1. It was such a windy day we couldn't keep our hats on. (*How
   strong was the wind? Where did the hats blow to?*)

   _____

   _____

2. We planted flowers in the garden. (*What kinds of flowers? What colors are the flowers?
   Did you work hard at planting the flowers? Where is the garden?*)

   _____

3. The puppy was sleeping on the rug. (*What does the puppy look like? What does the rug
   look like? Why is the puppy tired? Is the puppy dreaming?*)

   _____

4. I live in a red house. (*Where is the house? What does the house look like? Is the house in
   a park or forest or near a lake?*)

   _____

5. My sister and I ate a whole pizza by ourselves. (*How hungry were you two? What kind
   of pizza did you eat? Why were you so hungry? How did you feel afterwards?*)

   _____

6. We made a snowman. (*Who is "we"? How did you make the snowman? Was it cold outside?
   Was it snowing? Did you add anything to decorate the snowman?*)

   _____

7. Bobby fell off his bike and hurt his knee. (*What was Bobby doing on his bike? Can you
   describe the accident? How did his knee look?*)

   _____

8. Grandpa and I went fishing. (*Can you describe your grandfather? Where did you go
   fishing? What equipment did you take? Did you catch any fish?*)

   _____

Name _____ Date _____

II-38B. Revising by Using Different Words

Rewrite these ordinary sentences by changing the bold word
or words to a different, more interesting word or group of
words. You don't need to rewrite the entire sentence—just
the words indicated.

1. I **really like** horses.

   _____

   _____

2. "Monopoly" is a **fun** game.

   _____

3. The story I am reading is really **boring**.

   _____

4. I am **very hungry**.

   _____

5. That song on the radio is **really loud**.

   _____

6. My little dog has been very **bad** today.

   _____

7. I like to watch the popcorn **pop**.

   _____

8. The birthday card made me **happy**.

   _____

9. The kitten is very **friendly**.

   _____

10. Kara is a **fast** runner.

    _____

II-38C. Revising by Being Clever

This may be a challenging activity—but give it a try! Rewrite the sentences from Worksheet II-38B to make them clever, surprising, or more interesting in some way. Remember to keep the basic meaning the same, but change whatever words or phrases you want to.

1. I really like horses.

_____

2. "Monopoly" is a fun game.

_____

3. The story I am reading is really boring.

_____

4. I am very hungry.

_____

5. That song on the radio is really loud.

_____

6. My little dog has been very bad today.

_____

7. I like to watch the popcorn pop.

_____

8. The birthday card made me happy.

_____

9. The kitten is very friendly.

_____

_____

10. Kara is a fast runner.

_____

_____

Lesson II-39: Editing with Proofreader's Marks

(Proofreading/Editing)

To the Teacher

As soon as students begin writing, they will begin revising. These revisions may be simple, such as adding or deleting a word, or more complex, such as moving a sentence or rewriting a complete sentence. The purpose of this lesson is to familiarize students with common proofreader's marks, and then to provide practice for the student in revising sentences by following the proofreader's marks. A further purpose is to provide opportunities for students to use proofreader's marks in their own writing.

To the Student

Sometimes when you are writing, you may change your mind about what you've written. Perhaps you thought of a better word, or something you wanted to include in your sentence. Or, perhaps you realized that you made a mistake when you wrote the sentence and want to change it.

The more you write, the more you will find certain proofreader's marks helpful to you in your writing.

Let's take a look at some changes and marks you could make in your writing.

1. *Adding a Word or Words:* Let's say I want to write a sentence about my flowers, and I write this: (write on board)

   I have a flower garden.

Then I think about telling how "nice" my flower garden is, so I want to add the word "nice." I want to insert it after the word "a." I could mark the change this way:

   nice
I have a flower garden.
    ∧

That little mark is called a caret, and it tells the writer or proofreader to "add something and insert right here!"

Let's say I wanted to add "vegetables" to my garden sentence. I could mark the change this way:

    and vegetable
I have a nice flower garden.
      ∧

2. *Deleting a Word:* Now let's say I don't want to leave the word "nice" in that sentence. I would show that I want to delete that word by drawing a line through it.

   I have a ~~nice~~ flower garden.

Maybe I will want to delete a word, and then add a new word. I could do that like this, combining the delete and add marks:

    beautiful
I have a ~~nice~~ flower garden.
      ∧

3. *Capitalizing a Word:* A common mistake is forgetting to capitalize a word. I can show this by drawing three little lines under the letter that should be capitalized:

   m̲ike and i̲ went to m̲innesota.

4. *Indicating Lowercase:* The opposite mistake of forgetting to capitalize a word is using a capital letter when it should be a lower-case letter. I can show this by drawing a slanting line through the mistake.

 Mike and I went to MiNNesota.

5. *Transposing Words:* Sometimes if I'm in a hurry, I might mix up the order of a word or two. Perhaps I wrote: *I like black fast cars.* But I want it to say: *I like fast black cars.* I can show that I want to change the order of those words like this:

 I like black fast cars.

This is called transposing, and it means reversing the order because the words are mixed up.

6. *Adding End Punctuation:* Sometimes when I'm in a hurry, I make careless mistakes. I can show how to correct these easily. Let's say I forgot to put a period at the end of a sentence. I can show it like this:

 We went to the circus on Thursday⊙

If I forgot to put a question mark, it's the same idea:

 Will you go with me to the circus?

7. *Inserting a Space:* If I am careless with my handwriting, I might squeeze two words together when there should be a space in between. I can use this mark to show "insert a space." I just put the mark where the space should be.

 #
 We went to the zooand to the circus.

8. *Closing a Space:* A final mistake that I might make is leaving too much room between words or letters. I can show that I really intended to close this space by drawing lines that close it up:

 My big d og is my favorite pet.

Now it's your turn to have some practice in writing revised sentences!

Worksheets

Answers to Worksheet II-39A:

 like
1. I would ^ to go on a boat ride.

2. Maybe the will weather be nice tomorrow.

 not
3. I hope it is ^ rainy.

 Bob and I
4. We ^ will take our friends with us.

5. Don't forget to bring the picnic basket.

6. We should remember to ask aunt Jane to go with us.

7. I hope we can get the boat in to the water.

8. Maybe our father will be able to give us a hand.

9. i sure hope that we will have a good time.

10. It's al ways fun to go out on the Lake.

Answers to Worksheet II-39B:

best
1. My friend and I had an argument.

2. My friend's name is debbie.

3. Debbie and I ~~both~~ wanted to go to the movies.

4. i said that I wanted go to to the movies on friday.

5. Debbie wanted to *go* on saturday afternoon.

6. We just could not agree on what to do.

7. Finally, we decided to flip a coin.

8. Debbie won the toss, so we went the to movie on saturday.

Follow-up Activities

1. Have students make posters showing these common proofreader's marks along with examples. (You can use the guide sheet as an example.)

2. Have students randomly read and revise sentences that you have selected. Be sure to keep examples anonymous. Encourage students to use the proofreader's marks and use them yourself when you are editing students' work.

3. This activity can also be used on a daily basis as a morning warm-up activity with a sentence written on the board either (a) with the mistakes noted as evidenced by proofreader's marks, or (b) without the marks, but with apparent mistakes. Then have students show the corrections and rewrite the sentences.

Proofreader's Marks

1. insert   ∧   I have a ∧garden. *(nice)*

2. delete   —   I have a ~~nice~~ garden.

3. capitalize   ≡   alex and i

4. lowercase   /   went Home

5. transpose (change order)   ⎍⎍   little cute kitten

6. insert punctuation   ⊙   We went home⊙

7. insert a space   #   went#for a walk

8. close a space   ⌒   have a big d⌒og

9. add a comma   ⌄   Lori⌄ Wayne⌄ and Emily

10. add apostrophe   ⌄   Tyler⌄s toy

11. new paragraph   ¶   ¶ A long time ago there lived a young person

II-39A. Write the Revised Sentences

Use the proofreader's marks to rewrite these sentences as the writer intended them to be written.

1. I would to go on a boat ride.

2. Maybe the will weather be nice tomorrow.

3. I hope it is rainy.

4. We will take our friends with us.

5. Don't foRget to bring the picnic basket.

6. We should remember to ask aunt Jane to go with us.

7. I hop e we can get the boat in to the water.

8. Maybe our father willbe able to give us a hand.

9. i sure hope thatwe will have a good time.

10. It's al ways fun to go out on the Lake

Name _____ Date _____

II-39B. Add the Proofreader's Marks

Show the revisions for each sentence by using the correct proofreader's marks. Use the clues to help you.

1. My friend and I had an argument. (*Clue*: Add "best" in front of friend.)

   _____

2. My friend's name is debbie (*Clue*: Show that "debbie" needs a capital letter; insert a period.)

   _____

3. Debbie and I both wanted to go tothe movies. (*Clue*: Delete "both"; insert a space between "to" and "the.")

   _____

4. i said that I wanted go to to the movies on friday. (*Clue*: Show that "i" and "friday" need capital letters; show that "go" and "to" are transposed.)

   _____

5. Debbie wanted to on saturday afterNoon. (*Clue*: Show that "saturday" needs a capital letter; the "N" should be lowercase; and insert the word "go" after "to.")

   _____

6. We just couldnot agree on wHat to do (*Clue*: Insert a space between "could" and "not"; show that the "H" in "what" should be lowercase; and insert a period at the end.)

   _____

7. FinaLLy, we decided to flipa coin. (*Clue*: Show that the "LL" in "finally" should be lowercase; insert a space between "flip" and "a.")

   _____

   _____

8. Debbie won the toss, so we went the to movie on saturday. (*Clue*: Show that "the" and "to" are transposed; show that "saturday" needs to have a capital letter.)

   _____

   _____

Lesson II-40: Rough Draft and Final Copy

(Proofreading/Editing)

To the Teacher

Students may question the purpose of having a rough draft and then rewriting the whole thing a second time. Writing is not an activity that is completed correctly the first time; revision is an essential part of the "process" of creating a final product. Comparing this process to drawing is a good analogy—usually an artist makes a quick sketch to get proportion, placement, and basic ideas in place; then the drawing is finished by incorporating those changes. Likewise, the purpose of a rough draft is to "sketch" in the writer's ideas, making them easy to change and improve, resulting in a finished product. The purpose of this lesson is to provide students with a sketching/rough draft analogy and practice in determining what changes could be made in a rough draft to result in a more polished final copy.

To the Student

(Hold up a painting, poster, or drawing.) How do you like this? (Wait for comments.) Do you think the artist just sat down one day and drew or painted this? (probably not) What steps do you think the artist went through to make this beautiful drawing or painting? (had an idea, tried out some sketches, selected one he or she liked, worked on it for several days, etc.)

When you are thinking like a writer, which you have been doing, you are going through much the same process. Remember all the skills involved in making better sentences? You learned about choosing words carefully, using good handwriting on your work, editing your sentences for mistakes, and other skills. Very few people can just sit down at a desk and write or type a perfect piece of writing. Just like an artist, the writer gets an idea, "sketches it out" using words instead of a pencil or paint, and dabbles around with making changes until satisfied with the final product.

Today you're going to have practice in looking at some sentences that are considered "rough drafts." Sometimes these are called the "sloppy copy" or "first attempt" at writing. It is okay to make mistakes or changes on these first attempts. This is where you can be wild and creative. Then take some time and go through the different ways to edit a sentence to come up with something that is just right. *Remember*: The purpose of a rough draft is to *get your ideas down in writing*. You don't have to be perfect the first time; but you do have to make improvements so that your final copy is as close to perfect as you can get it.

Worksheets

Answers to Worksheet II-40A:

1. b	3. f	5. c
2. d	4. a	6. e

Answers to Worksheet II-40B:

Students' sentences will vary. Here are examples.

1. When I was 7, I had a frightening experience when I went shopping with my mother.

2. I remember going into a huge store.

3. As soon as we went in, I immediately found the toy department.

4. I jumped into a big red wagon and pretended to drive it.

5. Suddenly I realized that my mother was nowhere in sight.

6. I began to cry so loudly that people ran up to me wondering what was the matter!

7. My mother heard my screaming and came running right up to me.

8. I learned my lesson after that: Stay with my mom.

Follow-up Activities

1. As a class activity, take a sentence for consideration and have the class critique it in terms of all the different ways of editing a sentence. Model ways to make changes in the sentence, freely adding, deleting, and changing words in the sentence to improve it. Point out to students that simply changing things does not necessarily improve it; the point of revising something is to make it better, not just different.

2. As always, take student writing examples and discuss how students used rough-draft changes to make sentences better. Ask for student volunteers to express their ideas for how they improved their sentences.

II-40A. From Rough to Real

See if you can match the rough draft sentences on the top with the final products on the bottom. Look for changes that the writer wanted to make. Write the letters on the lines next to the sentences.

My sister and I

sunny nice?

1. ~~We~~ went ~~walking~~ in the woods one day.   _____

gorgeous? beautiful?

2. It was a ~~sunny~~ day.   _____

were scared

3. We ~~heard~~ a strange noise.   _____

4. At first I thought it was geese honking.   _____

I realized it was

5. ~~It turned out to be~~ my dad honking ~~the~~ horn of ~~his car~~   _____

My sister and I   *leave*

6. ~~We knew~~ it was time to ~~go.~~   _____

thought?

a. At first, I thought the honking was from a group of geese.

b. My sister and I decided to stroll through the woods one sunny day.

c. Then I realized that it was my dad honking his car horn.

d. It was sunshiny and beautiful outside.

e. My sister and I realized that it was time to head for home.

f. We were startled when we heard a strange noise.

Name _____ Date _____

II-40B. Your Turn

Here are some writer's word "sketches" of sentences. See if you can improve them using the writer's ideas (look for the clues) and your own.

1. When I was ~~little,~~ I remember shopping with my mom.

_____

I remember
2. We went into a (big store).

_____

Right away
3. I found the toy department and took off.

_____

red   fun? pretending
4. I sat in a wagon and had ~~a great time~~.

_____

realized mom was gone
5. I looked around and couldn't find my mom.

_____

scream? panic?
6. I started to ~~cry really loudly~~!

_____

and came up to me
7. My mom was right there.

_____

my lesson   my
8. I learned (to stay with her after that.)

_____

_____

_____

Lesson II-41: The Editing Team (Proofreading/Editing)

To the Teacher

Having students work in groups to edit their own (or sample) pieces of writing is a wonderful way to involve students in a team approach to editing. By assigning students a specific job and then rotating these positions, students will take a turn at closely evaluating writing samples from different "angles." One approach is to assign students to a team with a specific role, title, and editing task. In this lesson, students are introduced to this team approach to editing.

The five members of a team (adapt as necessary to your needs) are:

1. *The Capital Queen or Capital King*—This person is assigned the job of editing work for correct use of capital letters.

2. *The Punctuation Prince or Princess*—This person checks end punctuation, commas, and quotation marks (and any other types of punctuation that may have been taught to the class).

3. *The Official Word Counter*—This person counts the number of words in a sentence (assuming an assignment might be to write a longer sentence), also checks for making sure there are no extra words, omitted words, or repeated words.

4. *The Handwriting Analyzer*—This person ensures that the handwriting is legible, spacing between words is adequate, and letters are formed reasonably well.

5. *The Spelling Wizard*—This person is the human spellchecker; makes sure words are spelled correctly or sends back questionable words for rechecking.

These positions can be assigned randomly and held for several days while editing writing. It is important that positions are changed so that each member of the editing team gets a chance to view the writing from each perspective.

To the Student

You are now well armed with skills for editing pieces of writing that you have written or that others have written. It is now time to become part of a team. There are so many things to look for when you are editing writing—if you work together on a team, each member can look for something specific. Then when each of you has evaluated the writing and made suggestions, you can be pretty sure there are no mistakes and the writing is as good as it can be.

Here are five jobs or positions that you might be called upon to do while we are group editing some writing.

1. The first job is that of the *Capital Queen or King*. This person looks out for capital letters. He or she has to make sure the words that need to be capitalized *are* capitalized. This person also has to make sure there aren't capital letters where there should be lower-case letters. For example, the Capital Queen or King would have a lot of work to do in this sentence: (write on board or prepare sample page)

   on monday maRy and jane went to parK city to get BoBBy and his aunt Jane to take Her to chicaGo.

Wow! How many mistakes can you find in that sentence? (14) How could a Capital Queen or King rewrite that?

   On Monday Mary and Jane went to Park City to get Bobby and his Aunt Jane to take her to Chicago.

Much better! Who thinks they would be a good Capital Queen or King?

2. Another very important editing job is that of the *Punctuation Prince or Princess*. This person has to watch out for end punctuation (periods and exclamation points and question marks), commas in a list, commas when you are talking to someone, and quotation marks. A Punctuation Prince or Princess would have a lot of work to do on this sentence: (write on board or prepare sample page)

Mary would you please get me a pencil a pen a crayon and a ruler.

How many mistakes did you find in that sentence? (5) How would the Punctuation Prince or Princess rewrite that sentence?

Mary, would you please get me a pencil, a pen, a crayon, and a ruler?

3. A third job is that of the *Official Word Counter*. When you were younger, you may have written short sentences. Now, though, you know how to lengthen sentences by adding details, telling more, and using different words. Not every sentence has to be really long, but too many short sentences are not interesting to read.

Pretend you are the Official Word Counter. How many words are in these sentences? (write on board or prepare sample page)

In the morning, we ran through the woods.

One day Philip and his friend Molly decided to explore the old cave.

It rained.

I thought about writing a letter, but I decided to call instead.

Did you get these numbers? (8, 13, 2, 12) It is important in this job to count carefully. You don't have to rush, but read the sentence while you are counting and make sure there aren't missing words, extra words, or words out of order!

What would an Official Word Counter do with these sentences? Count the number of actual words, but then in parentheses write the number of words you think there should be to make a good sentence. (write on board or prepare sample page)

In morning, we got out of bed. (6 words, but "the" is missing—need 7)

One day, Phil and Molly they went in a cave. (10, but "they" is extra—should have 9)

The dog chased the cat went outside. (7 words, but it looks like it needs "and it" or else omit the word "went" to have it make sense)

4. A fourth job is that of the Handwriting Analyzer. This person makes sure the handwriting on the paper is easy to read, that there are spaces between each word, and the actual letters (whether printed or in cursive) are written reasonably well.

If you have the job of Handwriting Analyzer, what comments might you make about these sentences? (these might be best displayed on a prepared sheet to distribute to students)

(the letters are sloppy and there is no spacing)

(the letters are difficult to read)

5. A final important editing job is that of the *Spelling Wizard.* This person's job is to make sure the words are spelled correctly. This person can use a spellcheck or a dictionary if not completely sure how some words are spelled. It is important that the Spelling Wizard doesn't do all of the corrections by herself or himself; it is more important that the Wizard finds the mistakes and returns the work to the original writer to correct. The Spelling Wizard can use a wavy underline to indicate words he or she thinks should be rechecked for spelling.

How could a Spelling Wizard edit these sentences? (write on board or prepare sample page)

Meny people went with us to the stor.

I think we shud always rember to close the windos.

Worksheet

It will take same preparation to put the editing team into production. You may want to have students design logos, business cards, posters advertising their services, hats or crowns, and so on to get them into the spirit of working as a team. Depending on the number of students to be involved, it might be easier to have them work in pairs for each of the jobs.

To get them started, you might assign all students a similar task, such as using a weekly spelling list to write ten sentences. Have them leave their names off their work so everything will be edited anonymously. Select a set of papers (possibly three to start with) and then have the students on the Editing Team evaluate only their own task for each sentence. Once they have indicated the corrections (different colored pens might be useful), they should initial the paper and pass it on to the next group. When all five members of the Editing Team have evaluated the sentences, it is time to discuss it publicly. Each person on the team should give his or her comments and improvements. No one—either the writer of the sentences or the editor who may have missed an error—should be put down for making a mistake. This is a time for learning, for honing skills, and for practicing!

Answers to Worksheet II-41:

1. Capitals are OK; punctuation is OK; 8 words; handwriting is OK; 1 misspelled word

2. 1 capital error; punctuation is OK; 14 words; handwriting is OK; 1 misspelled word

3. Capitals are OK; punctuation error—needs ?; 10 words; handwriting is sloppy, not spaced well; no misspelled words

4. Capitals are OK; punctuation is OK; 6 words, but 1 is missing, should be 7; handwriting is OK; 1 misspelled word

5. 1 capital error; punctuation is OK; 9 words; handwriting is hard to read; no misspelled words

6. Capitals OK; punctuation OK; 9 words; handwriting is reasonably OK; 1 misspelled word

Follow-up Activity

Depending on the success and the interest level in the Editing Teams, this could be a weekly project for a class to continue. Make sure students serve on different committees so they have a chance to do each kind of job.

Name _____ Date _____

II-41. Sample Sentences to Edit

The Members of this Editing Team Are:

Capital King/Queen _____

Punctuation Prince/Princess _____

Official Word Counter _____

Handwriting Analyzer _____

Spelling Wizard _____

Spelling words for the lesson:
soft low wonder world same tame

1. Jane heard a soft voice outsid the window. _____

_____

2. I put the dog's bowl down low so my dog buddy cold reach it. _____

_____

3. Do you ever wonder why the sun is so hot . _____

_____

4. Meny people have traveled around world. _____

_____

5. my cosin has the same name as my dad . _____

_____

6. Is that horse tame or will she bit me ? _____

_____

Section III
Writing Paragraphs

Lesson III-1: Sandwiches and Paragraphs

(The "Sandwich" Model for Paragraphs)

To the Teacher

A paragraph is a group of sentences, related in some way, that provides more information than is possible in a sentence. One model that is helpful to students to guide them in recognizing parts of a paragraph (and later writing a paragraph) is that of comparing the basic structure of a paragraph to that of a sandwich: the bun (topic sentence, concluding sentence); the lettuce, meat, and other condiments (details); and seeds on the bun (title). The purpose of this lesson is to provide this model to students.

To the Student

You have had a lot of practice in writing good sentences; now it is time to expand your skills to writing paragraphs. Paragraphs are more than just a group of sentences, one after the other. A paragraph has some sort of structure that shows how the sentences are related to each other to make a paragraph.

For example: (write on the board)

I have lots of animals. We went to the zoo on Friday. If it is sunny tomorrow, we might go swimming. John called Linda in the afternoon. My dog needs a bath.

There are several sentences in this example, but most of them don't have anything to do with each other. This is not a paragraph. Now examine this one: (write on the board)

I have lots of animals. I have nine cats who live outdoors. I also have a few dogs who live in the house. Down at the barn, we have some horses. There are always plenty of animals around my house.

All of these sentences are talking about something. What? (animals) This is an example of a paragraph. All of the sentences are related to talking about one thing.

One way to help you recognize and write a paragraph is by having a model to follow. One model is called a Sandwich Model.

When you look at a sandwich, it has a top and a bottom. The bun might be cut in half to form the two parts, and the two parts are different in some ways (the shape, the thickness), but they are also quite similar (made from the same piece of bread) and have a lot in common. Their functions, however, are different—the bottom part might hold things up, whereas the top part helps to keep it together and easier to hang on to. You can have a sandwich with only a bottom part (called an "open-faced sandwich"), but it would be hard to have a sandwich without a top part!

In the same way, you can think of a basic paragraph as having a "bun" or a top and bottom (in this case, beginning and ending) part. The first and last sentences of a paragraph are going to be similar in some ways, but have different functions. The top bun represents the start of your paragraph, or the topic sentence. The bottom bun helps hold everything together. In a paragraph, the last sentence is similar to the first in that it retells the topic.

In the middle of a sandwich is all the good stuff! Maybe you like your sandwiches with cold ham or slices of roast beef (or both), plus some mayonnaise, mustard, maybe a pickle or two! Whatever you put into your sandwich is what you like about a sandwich! Taken in pieces, it's just little bits of food—a pickle here, a slice of lunch meat there... but put together, it's a sandwich!

In a paragraph, the "good stuff" is all of those sentences that you put into your paragraph to add details. It makes your paragraph more interesting and spices it up!

Worksheet

Answers to Worksheet III-1:

1. Horses OOOO

(I love horses) Horses are beautiful animals. They can run fast and jump over fences. It's fun to take care of horses. Many people like to own horses. (I think horses are wonderful animals.)

2. Homework OOOO

(Students should not have any homework.) People are very busy at night. Kids are tired after working at school. Sometimes children have piano lessons and clubs to go to. (I don't think we should have homework.)

3. Summer OOOO

(My family had fun this summer.) First we took a trip to the ocean. Then we went sailing on our new boat. My sister and I played in the swimming pool. (We had a great summer this year.)

4. My Dog OOOO

(My dog is not very smart.) I tried to train him to roll over. He decided to sit instead. He won't fetch balls when you throw them to him. Most of the time he just likes to sleep. I don't know if he knows his name, because he won't come to me. (I think my dog is not very bright.)

Follow-up Activities

1. Have students construct models of a sandwich out of various types of media—construction paper, clay, Styrofoam, etc. Students can be creative with this! As they create their models, remind them to connect the model in their mind with the purpose of making the model: understanding a paragraph!

2. You may also want to make a poster depicting the parts of a paragraph written in the appropriate spots on a sandwich. Display it in front of the class, particularly while you are working on paragraph writing.

III-1. Recognizing Parts of the "Sandwich" Model

Each paragraph below contains the "sandwich" parts. Can you identify the seeds, the top and lower buns, and the details in each? (You can draw the "seeds" by the title, draw the "bun" around the topic and concluding sentences, and underline the "condiments" or details.)

1. **Horses**

I love horses. Horses are beautiful animals. They can ran fast and jump over fences. It's fun to take care of horses. Many people like to own horses. I think horses are wonderful animals.

2. **Homework**

Students should not have any homework. People are very busy at night. Kids are tired after working at school. Sometimes children have piano lessons and clubs to go to. I don't think we should have homework.

3. **Summer**

My family had fun this summer. First we took a trip to the ocean. Then we went sailing on our new boat. My sister and I played in the swimming pool. We had a great summer this year.

4. **My Dog**

My dog is not very smart. I tried to train him to roll over. He decided to sit instead. He won't fetch balls when you throw them to him. Most of the time he just likes to sleep. I don't know if he knows his name, because he won't come to me. I think my dog is not very bright.

Lesson III-2: Writing a Topic Sentence

(The "Sandwich" Model for Paragraphs)

To the Teacher

The first part of writing a paragraph (using the "sandwich" model) is coming up with a good topic sentence. The other parts of the paragraphs will be based primarily on this sentence. The purpose of this lesson is to have students practice writing a topic sentence, given a general subject.

To the Student

The topic sentence is the most important sentence in your paragraph, because it lets the reader know right away what you are going to be discussing and a little bit about how you are going to proceed with your comments about it. A title, on the other hand, is very general and may not tell the reader where you are going with your comments. For example:

> **Title:** *Rockets*   **Topic Sentence:** *One day my brother and I decided to build a rocket.*
>
> **Title:** *Grooming a Dog*   **Topic Sentence:** *You might think it is easy to groom a dog, but it involves a lot of different things.*

Now let's concentrate on writing a good topic sentence. Here are some examples of topic sentences that make the reader interested in knowing more. (Write on the board)

1. I had a wonderful surprise on my birthday. (I wonder what the surprise was. What did he/she get or do?)

2. My favorite animal is a camel. (That's an unusual choice. I wonder what it is about a camel that the writer likes.)

3. I love winter! (Why? Is the writer going to tell us what he or she likes to do? Does he or she like snow?)

4. There was a mystery in our house last night. (What? What happened? I have to know!)

5. No one has ever seen a dog like mine. (Oh, really? What is so unusual about the dog?)

6. My father likes to do magic tricks. (What kinds of tricks does he do?)

All of these examples prompt the reader to ask questions about what is coming next. These topic sentences don't give away the whole paragraph, yet they let the reader know that something worth reading is coming up.

Worksheets

Answers to Worksheet III-2A:

1. b	3. a	5. b
2. a	4. b	6. a

Answers to Worksheet III-2B:

Students' sentences will vary. Here are examples.

1. We took a wonderful trip to the Grand Canyon.

2. Betsy proved she was a great friend to me one day.

3. On my last birthday, I was really surprised.

4. My favorite animal is not a cat or a dog, but an unusual animal called a chameleon.

5. Skiing might be fun, unless you have an accident like I did.

6. I am a fabulous cook when it comes to pizza.

7. If you want something to read for fun, try the Harry Potter books.

8. I love to paint sunsets.

9. Of all the chores there are, I hate taking out the trash the most.

10. I have the most unusual sister on the planet.

Follow-up Activities

Have students share and discuss the various topic sentences they came up with for the same basic subject. Discuss what possible questions are raised by the topic sentence and why the reader would want to keep on reading.

Name _____ Date _____

III-2A. Choose the Better Topic Sentence

Which of these sentences would make the better topic sentence for the subject given? Remember to look for something interesting that would make the reader want to find out more.

1. Subject: **Plants**

   a. My mother likes to grow plants in the summer.

   b. My mother makes our front yard look like a jungle with all the plants she grows there.

2. Subject: **Airplanes**

   a. Airplanes have always been interesting to me.

   b. I like airplanes.

3. Subject: **Roller Coasters**

   a. I like to think I am an expert on how to ride a roller coaster.

   b. I have ridden on many roller coasters.

4. Subject: **Computer Games**

   a. There are a lot of computer games available.

   b. Some computer games are really tricky, but fun to play.

5. Subject: **Visiting Relatives**

   a. It's boring to visit relatives.

   b. Visiting relatives may not be thrilling, but sometimes you have to do it.

6. Subject: **Swimming Lessons**

   a. Swimming lessons are my favorite lessons of all.

   b. You can take swimming lessons at the high school.

III-2B. Writing a Topic Sentence

Write a topic sentence about each of the following subjects.
Remember to make it interesting and try to give the
reader a reason to keep on reading to find out what
happens.

1. a trip you have taken

_____

_____

2. a friend who did something nice for you

_____

_____

3. a surprise someone gave you

_____

_____

4. a favorite animal

_____

_____

5. an accident you have had

_____

_____

6. something that you are really good at doing

_____

_____

7. a good book to read

_____

_____

8. something you like to do

_____

_____

9. something you hate to do

_____

_____

10. how you feel about your sister/brother/pet

_____

_____

Lesson III-3: Adding Details

(The "Sandwich" Model for Paragraphs)

To the Teacher

After students have identified or written a good topic sentence, it is time to add the "meat" or details to the paragraph. In this lesson, students are given practice in identifying appropriate details to support or clarify the topic sentence.

To the Student

You can think of your topic sentence as the top piece of the bun in your sandwich model. We are going to deal with the bottom bun a little bit later, so don't worry about that right now. What we are going to do is finish making the sandwich.

Going along with the sandwich model, what are some things you might add to a sandwich to make it taste good? (lettuce, cheese, meat, ketchup, mustard, pickles, etc.) There are lots of little things you can put together to spice up your sandwich.

When making a paragraph, these ingredients are the details. They tell more about the topic sentence: They give more information, clarify some things about your topic, and in general make your paragraph readable and interesting.

After you have your topic sentence, think of some questions that readers might want to have answered. You can add details that answer these questions as well as add details that explain more about your topic.

Worksheets

Answers to Worksheet III-3A:

Students' questions will vary. Here are examples.

1. What kind of plants does she grow? What do the plants look like? Why does she grow so many plants?

2. When did you start liking airplanes? What about airplanes is interesting to you? Have you flown in an airplane?

3. What games are tricky? Are there ways to win the game? What makes them fun to play?

4. What do you think is the "way" to ride a roller coaster? What roller coasters have you been on? Have you been on a lot of them?

5. When have you visited relatives? What did you do that made it bearable? Did anything fun come out of a visit?

6. Why do you like swimming lessons? What other lessons have you taken that aren't so much fun?

Answers to Worksheet III-3B:

Students' answers will vary.

Follow-up Activities

Have students work in small groups to generate questions that would help enhance a topic sentence. You may wish to write topic sentences on strips of paper and distribute them to the small groups. After working on their questions, groups can write short paragraphs incorporating the details.

III-3A. Identifying Questions to Add Details

Here are topic sentences from Lesson III-2. What are some questions a reader might be interested in knowing regarding the subject?

1. My mother makes our front yard look like a jungle with all the plants she grows there.

   _____

   _____

   _____

   _____

2. Airplanes have always been interesting to me.

   _____

   _____

   _____

3. Some computer games are really tricky, but fun to play.

   _____

   _____

   _____

4. I like to think I am an expert on how to ride a roller coaster.

   _____

   _____

   _____

5. Visiting relatives may not be thrilling, but sometimes you have to do it.

   _____

   _____

   _____

6. Swimming lessons are my favorite lessons of all.

   _____

   _____

   _____

III-3B. Adding Details to the Topic Sentence

Now that you have questions to guide you, practice adding some details to each topic sentence to make your paragraph.

1. My mother makes our front yard look like a jungle with all the plants she grows there.

   Detail: _____

   _____

   Detail: _____

   Detail: _____

2. Airplanes have always been interesting to me.

   Detail: _____

   Detail: _____

   Detail: _____

3. Some computer games are really tricky, but fun to play.

   Detail: _____

   Detail: _____

   Detail: _____

4. I like to think I am an expert on how to ride a roller coaster.

   Detail: _____

   Detail: _____

   Detail: _____

5. Visiting relatives may not be thrilling, but sometimes you have to do it.

   Detail: _____

   Detail: _____

   Detail: _____

6. Swimming lessons are my favorite lessons of all.

   Detail: _____

   Detail: _____

   Detail: _____

Lesson III-4: More Practice in Adding Details

(The "Sandwich" Model for Paragraphs)

To the Teacher

Some students my need additional practice in grasping the idea of adding appropriate details to expand a topic sentence. The purpose of this lesson is to provide that additional practice.

To the Student

Today you're going to have more practice in adding details to a topic sentence for a paragraph. I'm going to show you a paragraph with details, and have you give me a question that is answered by the detail.

I had a wonderful surprise on my birthday. (That's the topic sentence.)

I walked into my house and found a room full of people. (What question would that answer? Where did you get your surprise?)

My friends yelled, "SURPRISE!" (What did the people do when you went into the room?)

There were balloons everywhere. (What did the room look like?)

Mom had a cake for me with my name on it. (Did you have a surprise cake, too?)

Worksheet

Answers to Worksheet III-4:

Students' questions will vary. Here are examples.

1. My favorite animal is a camel.

    I used to visit a camel in our local zoo. (*Where did you see a camel?*)

    He was named Sydney. (*What was the camel's name?*)

    It was fun to watch him walk around. (*What did the camel do that was interesting?*)

    He had a big hump on his back and long whiskers on his nose. (*What did the camel look like?*)

2. I love winter!

    In the winter, we get to go skiing. (*What do you do in the winter?*)

    There is a big hill in our backyard for sledding. (*Where do you go sledding?*)

    Ice skating is fun, too. (*What else do you do?*)

    We always make a big snowman for the front yard. (*How else do you have fun in winter?*)

3. My family had a great vacation last year.

    We got in an airplane and flew to Hawaii. (*Where did you go on vacation?*)

    My brother and I learned to surf. (*What did you do?*)

    It was sunny every day. (*What was the weather like?*)

    We got to swim in the ocean. (*What else did you do?*)

4. No one has ever seen a dog like mine.

    He has long, thick fur on his body. (*What does your dog look like?*)

    His tail curls up over his back. (*What is his tail like?*)

One eye is blue and one eye is brown. (*What is unusual about his eyes?*)

One ear stays up and the other flops down. (*What do his ears look like?*)

5. (My father likes to do magic tricks.)

He can have you pick a card and tell you what it is. (*What tricks does he do?*)

He can make two short pieces of rope into one long one. (*What other tricks does he do?*)

One day he pulled a quarter out of my sister's ear. (*Any more tricks?*)

Follow-up Activity

Collect students' examples of paragraphs they are working on. Read or display these and have students speculate on what questions are answered by the details. Continue to "prompt" students, if necessary, to think of questions.

Name _____ Date _____

III-4. Questions for the Details

Read each paragraph. Mark the topic sentence with a big "bun" around it. Write out a question that is answered by the details in the paragraph.

1. My favorite animal is a camel.

   I used to visit a camel in our local zoo. _____

   _____

   He was named Sydney. _____

   It was fun to watch him walk around. _____

   He had a big hump on his back and long whiskers on his nose. _____

2. I love winter!

   In the winter, we get to go skiing. _____

   There is a big hill in our backyard for sledding. _____

   Ice skating is fun, too. _____

   We always make a big snowman for the front yard. _____

3. My family had a great vacation last year.

   We got in an airplane and flew to Hawaii. _____

   My brother and I learned to surf. _____

   It was sunny every day. _____

   We got to swim in the ocean. _____

4. No one has ever seen a dog like mine.

   He has long, thick fur on his body. _____

   His tail curls up over his back. _____

   One eye is blue and one eye is brown. _____

   One ear stays up and the other flops down. _____

5. My father likes to do magic tricks.

   He can have you pick a card and tell you what it is. _____

   He can make two short pieces of rope into one long one. _____

   One day he pulled a quarter out of my sister's ear. _____

Lesson III-5: Writing a Concluding Sentence

(The "Sandwich" Model for Paragraphs)

To the Teacher

After students are familiar with identifying and writing a topic sentence and details, they are ready to put in a concluding sentence (the "bottom bun"). Basically, a concluding sentence summarizes the contents of the paragraph or restates the topic sentence in slightly different wording. The purpose of this lesson is to provide practice for students in identifying and writing concluding sentences for a paragraph.

To the Student

In going along with the "sandwich" model for paragraphs, we have the top bun, and then we added some ingredients to make the sandwich tasty. Now it is time for the bottom bun; the bun that helps hold everything together. A good paragraph will have a concluding sentence that will restate or summarize the topic sentence.

The tricky part of writing a concluding sentence is thinking of another way to say what you said in the topic sentence without using exactly the same words. You have to paraphrase or summarize the contents of the paragraph.

For practice, see if you can match the topic sentence listed below with a concluding sentence. (write on board)

1. I love horses.

2. We should not have any homework.

3. My family had fun this summer.

4. My dog is not very smart.

a. We had a great summer this year!

b. I think horses are wonderful animals.

c. I think my dog is not too bright.

d. I don't think we should have homework.

You should have matched: 1—b, 2—d, 3—a, 4—c. How are the sentences in each pair alike? (basically they say the same thing, just use different words) *Remember:* When you write a concluding sentence, it is similar to the topic sentence in that it is basically repeating the same information, just using different words.

Worksheets

Answers to Worksheet III-5A:

1. d	4. c	7. j	10. i
2. e	5. b	8. h	
3. a	6. g	9. f	

Answers to Worksheet III-5B:

Students' sentences will vary. Here are examples.

1. My mother thinks she is the Queen of the Jungle.

2. I really enjoy learning about airplanes.

3. It's fun to learn how to play the tricky computer games.

4. I am the expert on roller coaster riding.

5. It's not always fun, but it's good for you.

6. When it comes to lessons, give me swimming!

Follow-up Activity

The actual writing of a concluding sentence that matches the topic sentence may require a lot of practice before students catch on to the idea of paraphrasing. Continue to give examples of how there are different ways to say the same thing. Have students try using the concluding sentence *first* in their paragraph to see if the paragraph still makes sense.

III-5A. Match the Sentences

Below are some topic sentences. Match an appropriate concluding sentence to each and write the letter on the line.

1. We took a great trip to California.   _____

2. My best friend is Karen.   _____

3. One summer my friend bought me a wonderful gift.   _____

4. My favorite animal is a chicken.   _____

5. I broke my collarbone one winter.   _____

6. I am the world's best sleeper.   _____

7. I love the story *Black Beauty*.   _____

8. I enjoy making pizza for my family.   _____

9. I hate to do chores around the house.   _____

10. Sometimes I think my sister is from another planet.   _____

a. I loved the thoughtful gift from my friend.

b. I always think of my broken collarbone every winter.

c. Chickens are pretty neat animals.

d. I highly recommend California as a great place to visit.

e. You would really like Karen, too.

f. Chores are a real pain!

g. I wish I could get an award for sleeping.

h. Pizza-making is my specialty.

i. I wish my alien-sister would go back to Mars.

j. *Black Beauty* is a wonderful story to read.

III-5B. Writing a Concluding Sentence

Below are some topic sentences for which you have already written details. Now you are to write a good concluding sentence for each. You might want to refer back to the details that you wrote for each topic sentence in Lesson III-3 to give you some ideas.

1. My mother makes our front yard look like a jungle with all the plants she grows there.

_____

_____

_____

2. Airplanes have always been interesting to me.

_____

_____

_____

3. Some computer games are really tricky, but fun to play.

_____

_____

_____

4. I like to think I am an expert on how to ride a roller coaster.

_____

_____

_____

5. Visiting relatives may not be thrilling, but sometimes you have to do it.

_____

_____

_____

6. Swimming lessons are my favorite lessons of all.

_____

_____

_____

_____

Lesson III-6: More Practice in Writing Concluding Sentences (The "Sandwich" Model for Paragraphs)

To the Teacher

Some students may need additional practice in writing concluding sentences. The purpose of this lesson is to provide that additional practice.

To the Student

Remember that when you write a concluding sentence for a paragraph, you are going to go back to the topic sentence and in some way try to restate what you already said. You want the basic meaning to be the same, but you want to use different words.

Worksheets

Answers to Worksheet III-6A:

1. b   2. c   3. b   4. a   5. c

Answers to Worksheet III-6B:

Students' sentences will vary. Here are examples.

1. Many things frighten me when I'm home alone.

2. Bob was completely covered with mud.

3. It can be very destructive to experience an earthquake.

4. A veterinarian does many things with animals.

Follow-up Activity

Go over students' ideas for concluding sentences on these two worksheets and have students discuss how they thought of ways to restate the topic sentences. Even changing just a few simple words will make the sentence sound a little different.

III-6A. More Concluding Sentences

Read each short paragraph and highlight the topic sentence. Then select an appropriate concluding sentence for each and write its letter on the line.

1. It's not very hard to make an ice cream sundae. You have to get all of the ingredients, such as the ice cream, whipped cream, hot fudge, and perhaps some nuts. Some people like to put everything in a special ice cream dish. After you scoop out the ice cream, just add all of the toppings.

   Best concluding sentence: _____ a. Eat everything before it melts.

   b. It's easy to do this.

   c. Don't forget to add the nuts.

2. There are a lot of things to do on a hot day. Some people might like to go to the beach. Other people like to sit in an air-conditioned room and read a book. Maybe you would like to drink something cold.

   Best concluding sentence: _____ a. Turn up the air conditioner.

   b. Try to survive the heat.

   c. There are many ways to survive the heat.

3. My younger sister will not quit talking. She has learned that she gets lots of attention by talking. She talks to people she doesn't know. She yaks on the phone whenever it rings. She even goes up to people in the store and tries to talk to them.

   Best concluding sentence: _____ a. My sister is a nuisance.

   b. My sister talks all the time.

   c. My sister should be quiet.

4. We had an unwelcome visitor to our house. First we noticed that many cans were tipped over. Then the bag of cat food was opened and eaten. There were little footprints all around the front yard. We think we saw a hairy creature run away when we turned on the outdoor light.

   Best concluding sentence: _____ a. We hoped the raccoon would not come back.

   b. We wanted to use the cat food.

   c. The hairy creature was a raccoon.

5. I love to ride my bike. I ride in the park. I ride through the neighborhood. Sometimes my dad goes with me and we go on long rides through the country. Long rides are the best.

   Best concluding sentence: _____ a. I like to ride with my dad.

   b. I am a good bike-rider.

   c. It's really fun for me to ride my bike.

Name _____ Date _____

III-6B. Write a Concluding Sentence

Read each paragraph. Highlight the topic sentence. Read the details and then write a concluding sentence that retells the topic sentence.

1. I get scared when I am home alone at night. Shadows on the wall seem like monsters. Every noise makes me think someone is coming into the house. I want to turn on every light in the house.

_____

_____

_____

2. Bob made a mess when he played in the mud with his friends. He had mud on his clothes. There was mud on his face and hands. His shoes were covered with mud. There was even mud in his hair.

_____

_____

_____

3. Earthquakes can cause a lot of damage. Buildings can be knocked down. Roads can be broken up. Sometimes people are killed because of things that have fallen. Earthquakes can cause fires which cause more problems.

_____

_____

_____

4. A veterinarian has an interesting job working with animals. One day he or she might give an injection to an elephant at a zoo. Another day the vet might take care of a sick bird. Some vets have to figure out a special diet for unusual animals from other countries.

_____

_____

_____

Lesson III-7: Putting a Title to Your Paragraph

(The "Sandwich" Model for Paragraphs)

To the Teacher

Sometimes a paragraph grows from being prompted by a title; sometimes the title is the last piece you add to your paragraph. In "Sandwich" model, the title is likened to the little "seeds" on top of the bun of the paragraph. They represent a little hint about what the paragraph will be about. The purpose of this lesson is to have students practice writing appropriate titles for paragraphs.

To the Student

After you have finished writing your paragraph, there is one more thing you need to add: a title. In general, a title is short, usually just a few words, and gives the reader a hint as to what the paragraph is about. It is not a complete sentence.

Sometimes you might be given the title first, and then be asked to write a paragraph about the title. Some examples are:

A Rainy Day—What would you expect to find in this paragraph? (something that happened on a rainy day, some rainy day activities, etc.)

My Favorite Birthday—What might this be about? (a particular year that was memorable, a surprise party, etc.)

My Dog—What information would most likely be in this paragraph? (the name of the dog, what he/she looks like, why the writer likes the dog, etc.)

Most of the time your title should be short and to the point. Otherwise, you are probably turning your title into a topic sentence. What do you think about these titles?

A Very Scary Night When My Friends Came Over and We Stayed Up All Night (too long; should probably be turned into a topic sentence)

A Day (doesn't give enough information; what kind of day? a long day? a fun day?

A Fire in Our Basement (this is a good one; will probably reveal a dramatic story)

My Aunt Sarah (this one is fine; we know it will give details about the aunt)

My Smart Brother and Going to the Mall (are topics related? sounds as though the writer is talking about two different things—better choose one or the other)

Now it's your turn. You'll have some practice in selecting good titles for paragraphs and then writing your own paragraph titles.

Worksheets

Answers to Worksheet III-7A:

1. b   2. c   3. b   4. a   5. c

Answers to Worksheet III-7B:

Students' titles will vary. Here are examples.

1. Airplanes   3. My Cat Fuzzy   5. Colors
2. Funny Todd   4. Riding the Roller Coaster

Follow-up Activities

1. **Add a Title:** Write a short paragraph (or have students contribute their paragraphs) each day on the board and have students practice writing an appropriate title for the paragraph.

2. **Add a Paragraph:** Write an intriguing (or just general) title on the board and have students write a short paragraph using the title as their idea for a topic. Discuss the relatedness of a title and the paragraph that goes with it.

III-7A. Good Titles

Read each paragraph and then select a title that indicates what the paragraph is about without being too long, too short, or off the subject. Write the letter on the line.

1. We had too many trees in our yard. There were so many trees, you could hardly walk to the mailbox. One day some men came and chopped them down. Now we have just enough trees in our yard.

   Best title: _____
   a. Walking to the Mailbox
   b. Too Many Trees
   c. Men Who Chop Trees

2. My mother did not want to get glasses. She thought glasses would make her look old. She didn't want to have to remember where she put them. She thought they were too expensive. She had lots of excuses for not getting glasses.

   Best title: _____
   a. Excuses, Excuses
   b. I Forgot My Glasses
   c. My Mother and Her Glasses

3. I should not have gotten up this morning. I was late for school. I did not have time for breakfast. I forgot my homework. I did not remember to bring a pen. I got in trouble at lunch. I should have stayed in bed.

   Best title: _____
   a. Forgetting My Homework
   b. A Bad Day
   c. Bad

4. The house next door caught on fire. We heard the fire trucks coming in the middle of the night. Firefighters climbed the ladders and rescued the neighbors. The flames were so hot we could feel them from our house. The smoke was black and smelled bad. It was scary watching the house burn.

   Best title: _____
   a. A Burning House
   b. Fire Trucks
   c. Smoke and Fire

5. A map can be very helpful when you are trying to find a place. You have to know how to read the directions: north, south, east, west. It helps to know where you live on the map so you can figure out where you're going. Some maps show railroad tracks and cities. It is useful to have a map when you travel.

   Best title: _____
   a. Many Maps
   b. North, South, East, West
   c. Helpful Maps

Name _____   Date _____

III-7B. Add a Title

Read each paragraph. Write a good title for each.

1. Title: _____

I love airplanes. I collect model airplanes. I have posters all over my room of airplanes. I always wanted to ride in an airplane. Airplanes are my favorite thing.

2. Title: _____

Todd is a funny boy. He is always able to make people laugh. He can do funny tricks. He has a great sense of humor. Everyone likes funny Todd.

3. Title: _____

My favorite cat is Fuzzy. She mostly sleeps all day. Sometimes she will play with a ball of yarn. She likes to hunt birds outside. I like Fuzzy a lot.

4. Title: _____

I had a great time on the roller coaster. At first I was really scared because it seemed so high. People were screaming. The noises were so loud. I didn't think I would like it, but then I got on it. It was so much fun I wanted to ride again and again. I loved riding the roller coaster.

5. Title: _____

I think about colors. Black makes me think sad thoughts. My favorite color is red because it makes me think about Valentine's Day. I like green, too, because that is the color of summer grass. Yellow is like the sunshine. I enjoy thinking about all the different colors.

Lesson III-8: Evaluating a Paragraph

(The "Sandwich" Model for Paragraphs)

To the Teacher

Students should now have had quite a few opportunities to recognize and write topic sentences, details, concluding sentences, and titles. The purpose of this lesson is to offer practice paragraphs for students to evaluate. The students should recognize the components and determine whether or not they are interesting and appropriate.

To the Student

Let's review the "Sandwich" model of a basic paragraph. What is the top bun compared to? (the topic sentence) What fills up the sandwich? (the details) What's at the bottom to keep it all together? (the concluding sentence) What are the seeds on the top bun? (the title)

We are going to add just one more thing to remember about a written paragraph. When you write a paragraph, the first line is *indented*, or moved in a little bit. This will be very helpful when you start writing longer pieces that have several paragraphs. Be sure to notice in the paragraphs you see today that the first line is indented.

Now you are going to have some practice in evaluating a paragraph. See if you can pick out the parts of the paragraph and evaluate them to decide whether or not they are interesting, contribute to the paragraph, and are well-written.

Remember (write on board):

Parts of a Basic Paragraph

1. Title—short, makes sense

2. Topic Sentence—interesting, tells what you will be writing about

3. Details—add to the topic sentence

4. Concluding Sentence—retells the topic sentence

Worksheet

Answers to Worksheet III-8:

1. a. yes   b. yes   c. 6   d. no, not the one about swimming

2. a. it sounds like a whole sentence rather than a short title
   b. My Nightmare/My Nightmare in the Day
   c. 8
   d. no
   e. That was my nightmare in the day.

3. a. it's a little long
   b. An Unusual Bird
   c. 6
   d. yes, the one about the aunt
   e. yes

Follow-up Activity

Copy and hand out the "Paragraph Checklist." Make sure students read and understand the various components. Then have students pair up and take turns explaining each element to each other. They can use the practice paragraphs to illustrate the components, if desired.

Paragraph Checklist

1. Title

- should be short, not a complete sentence

- capitalize the important words

- tells about the topic

2. Topic Sentence

- indent first line

- tells what the paragraph will be about

- interesting, makes the reader want to read on

3. Details

- answer questions the reader might have about the topic

- adds interesting things about the topic

4. Concluding Sentence

- retells the topic sentence in different words

III-8. Evaluating Practice Paragraphs

Read the following paragraphs and evaluate them. You may want to use this checklist:

Does the paragraph have a title?

Does the paragraph have a topic sentence?

Is the topic sentence interesting?

Do the details tell more about the topic?

Are the details interesting?

Does the paragraph have a concluding sentence that retells the topic sentence?

1. The Ice Cream Disaster

I had a terrible time with my ice cream cone. It was a very hot day. I like to swim on hot days. The ice cream melted all over my hand. Then some of it got on my brand new shirt. A boy knocked into me and the rest of it fell on the ground. It was not a good day for eating an ice cream cone.

a. Does the title tell about the paragraph? _____

b. Does the topic sentence match the concluding sentence? _____

c. How many detail sentences are there? _____

d. Do all of the details go with the topic? _____

2. One Day I Had a Nightmare

Most people have nightmares at night, but not me. I had a nightmare in the middle of the day. I was sitting in my living room, just watching TV. There was a knock on the door. I went to answer it. A person in a clown mask was at the door. I screamed! Then the clown pulled off the mask. It was just my brother trying to be silly.

a. What do you think of the title? _____

b. How could you improve the title? _____

c. How many detail sentences are there? _____

d. Is there a concluding sentence? _____

e. What concluding sentence could you write? _____

3. The Talking and Singing Bird Named Zippo

Zippo was a very unusual bird. Zippo was able to talk. He was also able to sing. When people saw Zippo, they tried to make him answer their questions. One day my aunt came to visit me. Zippo only talked when he wanted. There aren't many birds rare and different as Zippo.

a. What do you think of the title? _____

b. How could you improve the title? _____

c. How many detail sentences are there? _____

d. Should any details be removed? _____

e. Is there a concluding sentence? _____

Lesson III-9: Writing a Descriptive Paragraph

(Types of Paragraphs)

To the Teacher

There are several specific "types" of paragraphs with which students should become familiar. Students should be able to identify and write sample paragraphs that are descriptive, express an opinion, inform, explain, narrate, and persuade. In this lesson, students are given guidelines for identifying a descriptive paragraph and then practice in writing one.

To the Student

There are several different types of paragraphs, and each serves a specific purpose. You have completed lessons on writing a "basic" paragraph, which is simply one that has the elements of what would most likely be found in a good paragraph: a title, a topic sentence, relevant details, and a concluding sentence. If you are comfortable with the format of a "basic" paragraph, now we as writers can close in on writing even more specifically. There are six specific types of paragraphs that you will be focusing on during the next set of lessons.

The first specific paragraph type is a *descriptive* paragraph. This is one that simply describes something. What sense (hearing, seeing, taste, etc.) am I appealing to in these sentences? Listen:

The black mother cat was followed by three tiny little gray kittens. (*sight*)

The cat yowled and screeched and howled all night long. (*hearing*)

The baseball hit me so hard on the arm I could hardly lift it the next day. (*feeling*)

I got one whiff of Grandma's apple pie baking in the oven and I could not leave the kitchen. (*smell*)

Wow! That lemon is sour! (*taste*)

When you write a descriptive paragraph, keep in mind that you can use all of the senses to help your reader understand what you want to say about something. To get you going, think about how you would describe the following, and try to use words that convey the five senses:

Today's weather

The inside of your desk or bookbag

Your bicycle

Sledding

Your dog

What you had for breakfast

Worksheets

Answers to Worksheet III-9A:

1. a. seeing b. bands, stretching c. probably

2. a. seeing, hearing, touch b. made up c. color patterns in fur, long whiskers, fluffy tail, etc.

3. a. feeling, taste b. sick c. probably

4. a. seeing, feeling b. loves it c. going really fast, crashing, flying up in the air, hitting the ground

Answers to Worksheet III-9B:

Students' answers will vary.

Follow-up Activities

While focusing on this theme (descriptive paragraphs), provide students with a title each day that they should develop into a descriptive paragraph. You might also want to indicate on which sense you want them to focus. Rather than go with the obvious (rainbow/color, food/taste, etc.), try having them write descriptive paragraphs that appeal to different senses. For example: What sounds do you hear in the park? What colors stand out when you look at your food? etc.

III-9A. Examples of Descriptive Paragraphs

Read the sample paragraphs that describe something. Identify the topic sentence, details, concluding sentences, and to what senses the writer is appealing.

1. The Rainbow

I saw the most beautiful rainbow in the sky. There were bands of the seven different colors. They stretched from one side of the sky to the other. I could see each color very clearly. The white clouds were in the background, behind the shiny rainbow. It was gorgeous.

a. What sense does the writer appeal to? _____

_____

b. How did the writer describe the rainbow? _____

_____

c. The writer didn't list the colors of the rainbow. Do you think that would have improved the paragraph?

_____

_____

2. My Cat Teddy

My favorite pet is my cat, Teddy. He has long black and white fur. He loves to purr. You can hear him purr all the way across the room. His fur is soft and silky. Sometimes he stretches and makes his back arch high above his head. That's my cat-pal.

a. What senses does the writer use? _____

_____

b. Is "cat-pal" a real word or one that the writer made up to fit the paragraph?

_____

_____

c. If the writer wanted to explain more about what Teddy looks like, what other details could he add?

_____

_____

III-9A. Examples of Descriptive Paragraphs (continued)

3. The Flu

It is no fun to have the flu. You might think it's great to have a day off from school, but having the flu will make you think twice about that. Your head hurts. Your stomach hurts. Your legs hurt. Even your eyes hurt. Nothing sounds good to eat. Even watching TV isn't fun because all you can think about is how bad you feel. Even a phone call from your best friend won't get you out of bed. The only fun about having the flu is getting over it!

a. What senses does the writer use to describe the flu? _____

_____

b. How did this paragraph make you feel? _____

_____

c. Did you feel sorry for the writer? _____

_____

4. Sledding Down Twister Hill

Sledding down Twister Hill is thrilling fun! You have to drag your sled all the way up to the top of the hill, but once you're there, it's all downhill after that. The more kids you can pile on the sled, the better. You can go really fast as long as you make the turns and stay on when you hit the bumps. Sometimes you go so fast the wind whips in your face and it stings. There is a huge bump at the bottom that you start thinking about from the very top of the hill. It gets closer… closer… closer… and then you're THERE! Everyone has to close their eyes because you don't actually want to see yourself crash. The bump makes you fly up in the air for several seconds before you know you're going to come down and hit the ground. You do and it hurts but it's fun! There's no thrill like Twister Hill!

a. What senses does this paragraph use? _____

_____

b. How does the writer feel about sledding on Twister Hill? _____

_____

c. What words let you know that it is exciting for the writer? _____

_____

Name _____ Date _____

III-9B. Writing a Descriptive Paragraph

Select several of the following topics for descriptive paragraphs. Identify the elements of the paragraph and try to appeal to at least one sense in each. Use another sheet of paper for your paragraphs.

DESCRIBE...

A winter day

Your favorite pizza

Your best friend

A pony

A sports car

A superhero

A cartoon character

The inside of your bedroom closet

Decorating for a surprise party

Your favorite holiday

Your house

A snowflake

Your earrings/other jewelry

The view from your window

Lesson III-10: Writing an Opinion Paragraph

(Types of Paragraphs)

To the Teacher

Another type of paragraph that students should learn to write is that of expressing an opinion about a subject. Students should take a position on a topic and give reasons why they feel a certain way about that topic. Everyone is entitled to his or her own opinion, of course, but expressing that opinion clearly and logically will carry more weight than simply stating an opinion without any clear reason. The purpose of this lesson is to provide practice for students in identifying and writing opinion paragraphs.

To the Student

(List on the board some popular musical groups) OK, what do you think about this group's music? (probably students will offer different opinions) Well, some of you seem to think the music is good. Others of you think the music is awful. Who is right? Who is wrong? Sometimes there isn't a right or a wrong to something; there is just a reaction to something that expresses how you feel. How you feel about something or what you think about it is your opinion.

Another type of paragraph that you will practice writing is an **opinion** paragraph. In this type of paragraph, you will give your opinion about something—that would be in the topic sentence—and then your reasons for why you feel that way—the details.

What do you think about having to wear a seat belt in the car? (listen to ideas) What would be some reasons why someone might think this was a bad idea? (tight, takes time to put it on, etc.) What are some reasons why this might be a good idea? (saves lives in accidents, keeps kids from moving around in the car, etc.)

There are many subjects that cause different opinions to be expressed. Some people might feel very strongly that something is right or wrong (legalization of certain drugs, abortion issues, gun control, etc.). Other people might feel we don't know enough about a certain subject to really give a definite opinion, but still have some ideas that they want to express.

Why is your opinion important? (because you are important, what you think will guide what you do, many people who feel the same way can influence others to think like them, etc.) Why is it important to be able to express your opinion clearly? (shows that you gave it some thought, people will listen to something that seems to make sense)

Some clues to recognizing an opinion paragraph are the words: "I think…" "I feel that…" and "it seems to me…" These words are insisting that something is right or wrong, but they convey the message that this is what the writer thinks.

Are these opinion sentences?

I think girls are treated better in school than boys. (opinion—someone might disagree)

It is sunny out today. (check the weather—is it?)

My last name is Smith. (this can be checked)

I don't like my first name because it is dumb. (this is an opinion—her parents might disagree)

No one should be allowed to have a gun under any circumstance. (opinion—people would disagree—what about hunters?)

This class is really boring. (well… someone might like it!)

When you express your opinion, you can follow the same "Sandwich" model: state your opinion in the topic sentence, give support for what you think in the detail sentences, and then restate your opinion in the concluding sentence.

Worksheets

Answers to Worksheet III-10A:

Students' paragraphs will vary.

Answers to Worksheet III-10B:

1. Not a clear paragraph; the writer rambles all over and doesn't give good reasons for why cats are the best pet; not very convincing

2. It's a pretty good paragraph—good topic and concluding sentences; the writer explains why it is so hard for him/her to keep a secret; good reasons

3. Interesting topic sentence and some good reasons—working hard, motivation, etc.; but it gets a little unrealistic when writer suggests $1,000 for every A!

Answers to Worksheet III-10C:

Students' paragraphs will vary.

Follow-up Activity

What I Think About…: Every morning during these lessons on opinions, write a somewhat controversial title for students to work on during the day. It may be a topic of interest in your school or your community. Have students practice expressing their opinions on these topics.

It will be interesting to tally the results of each topic to see if the majority of students feel a certain way about an issue. Don't forget to discuss the supporting reasons that are given for each opinion.

III-10A. Finish the Paragraph

Several students began paragraphs to express their opinions about something. You have their topic sentence to start with. Pretend you are that student (even if you don't really agree!) and finish each paragraph! Don't forget to give it a title. (Use the back of this sheet if you need more space for your paragraph.)

Every student should have his or her own computer at school.

_____

_____

_____

_____

The school lunches at our school are incredible. _____

_____

_____

_____

Girls should be allowed to play any sport that boys play. _____

_____

_____

_____

The most interesting show on TV is the nightly news. _____

_____

_____

_____

I don't think children should be paid for getting good grades. _____

_____

_____

_____

Name _____ Date _____

III-10B. Evaluate These Paragraphs

Students wrote the following paragraphs to express an opinion. Read the paragraphs carefully. Keep these questions in mind as you comment about each paragraph:

Does the topic sentence express an opinion?	**Does the paragraph help you understand the writer's feelings?**
Did the writer give good, understandable reasons supporting his or her opinion?	**What do you think of the paragraph in general?**

1. **The Best Pet**

    The best pet anyone could have is a cat. Cats are really pretty. When they have their claws, they damage furniture by scratching on it. I have five cats. I like my cats. I don't know why, I just do. Cats are the best.

_____

_____

_____

2. **Surprise Party**

    I think it's really hard to keep a secret about a surprise party. When I know something special is going to happen for somebody, I want to tell them so I can help make them feel good. I also think about the fun that we're going to have, and I can't think of anything else. I know it's important to not give it away, so I try to talk about something else. It sure is hard to keep a surprise party a secret.

_____

_____

_____

3. **Money for Grades**

    I think kids should be paid for good grades. We work hard to get good grades and we should be rewarded. Some kids who don't care would work hard if they knew they would get money. Parents might have to pay for a tutor to help their children anyhow, so why not just pay the children to learn it the first time? I think we should each get at least $1,000 for every A we get on anything. We need money!

_____

_____

_____

III-10C. Write an Opinion Paragraph

It's your turn! Write a paragraph (with all the parts) that expresses your opinion about the following subjects. (Your teacher will tell you how many paragraphs to work on.)

How you feel about a certain sport (swimming, baseball, tennis, football, etc.)

What animal makes a good pet

What school rules or policies should be changed

Why kids should/should not have to do chores at home

How to get kids to work harder in school

Why big families are fun

What I think about "zero tolerance" for _____

The best place to go on vacation

Why older sisters/brothers are great

What I think about smoking

_____

_____

_____

_____

_____

_____

_____

_____

_____

_____

_____

_____

_____

_____

_____

SchoolRules

I. No running in the halls.

II. No chewing gum

III. No cheating

IV. Do not be tardy

V.

Lesson III-11: Writing a Narrative Paragraph

(Types of Paragraphs)

To the Teacher

A narrative paragraph is another useful type of paragraph for students to become familiar with. A narrative is simply telling about something, usually an event that happened to someone or to yourself. In this type of paragraph, students can bring their own experiences to the page, and be somewhat creative in their writing. The purpose of this lesson is to provide practice for students in writing narrative paragraphs.

To the Student

Who did something interesting or unusual last night or last weekend? Tell us about it. (Give students an opportunity to relate their stories.)

If I wrote down everything you just said, I would have written a narrative. You told us about an event or an experience in your own words. Another way to remember what's a narrative is by thinking about going to a play and hearing a voice tell the audience what is going on. That's a narrator. The narrator is speaking to the audience to tell them about the events they are seeing.

An important thing to remember about a narrative paragraph is that you tell either your own story or someone else's story. If you tell the story from your own perspective, you would use the word "I" throughout your paragraph. If you are telling an event about someone else, you would often use the words "he," "she," or even "they" when you write about it.

When you write a narrative paragraph, one thing that might be a little different is your concluding sentence. Instead of retelling the topic sentence, you might change or update your concluding sentence to tie the whole paragraph together because you are telling an event or a story. That might mean you write something that is similar to the first sentence, but without having the same meaning. Some examples on the worksheets will help you understand this.

Here are some activities to help you become familiar with writing narrative paragraphs.

Worksheets

Answers to Worksheet III-11A:

Students' titles will vary.

Answers to Worksheet III-11B:

Students' paragraphs will vary.

Follow-up Activity

Have students share their narrative paragraphs by reading them out loud to each other and to the class. They might enjoy illustrating their paragraphs, especially as they are written about personal events. Through drawing, the students can try to capture what they experienced or felt during this event.

Name _____   Date _____

III-11A. Write a Title

Read each paragraph and write a title that best tells about it.

1. _____

I had a great time in Cleveland last weekend. I went with my family, which is one thing that made it fun, because my family is a lot of fun. We went to the Rock and Roll Hall of Fame, which is a museum that has a lot of rock-and-roll music and things to look at. We went to eat at McDonald's which was fun, too, but you can eat at a McDonald's anywhere. We saw a baseball game there, too. Cleveland was fun.

2. _____

I did not want to go to camp. I promised my parents I would clean the whole house if I didn't have to go. I begged them to let me stay home. When I knew I would have to go anyway, I packed my suitcase full of comic books and candy bars. I was so afraid no one would talk to me. I knew there would be mosquitoes and bugs, and I sure didn't like that. After I was there for one hour, I changed my mind. The kids were really friendly and asked me to join them on a hike right away. The beds were soft. Having a lot of candy bars made me quite popular. I decided that camp was not so bad.

3. _____

Tommy had a great idea. He wanted to start a club at school for kids who liked to draw. He decided to ask some local artists to come to the club meetings to show kids ways they could learn to draw better. It was a great success. The kids drew pictures to decorate the halls of their school. Some of them took them to nursing homes to hang up for the residents there. A lot of the kids learned how to draw better because of the older kids and adults who helped them. Tommy's idea was a very good one for a lot of people.

Name _____ Date _____

III-11B. Write a Narrative Paragraph

Choose from the follow ideas or add your own. Practice writing narrative paragraphs about these subjects. Remember that you don't always have to use "I" when you tell your story; try using another person's perspective on some of these.

a trip to an interesting place

how it feels to walk through the woods

a time when you were scared

a mistake you or someone else made

when you broke a bone or were injured

what you would do on a snow day

a problem you or someone else solved

a trick you played on someone else (or that someone else played on you)

a sporting event you went to

a special time you spent with someone you care about

_____

_____

_____

_____

_____

_____

_____

_____

_____

_____

_____

_____

_____

_____

_____

Lesson III-12: Writing an Informative Paragraph

(Types of Paragraphs)

To the Teacher

As students begin to do more writing in school, they will have to do "reports" in which they provide written information about topics. The purpose of this lesson is to give examples and practice for students in recognizing and writing informative paragraphs.

To the Student

How many breeds of dog can you name? (Allow students a moment or two to begin listing breeds.) Can you think of certain characteristics about a particular breed? In other words, what is something that breed is known for? (German shepherd—guide dog, labrador retriever—hunting, etc.) If I wanted to learn about dogs, I might ask each of you to select a breed and find out more about that specific breed. By searching for information on a breed, each of you would be looking for similar information (e.g., where the breed originated, how tall the dog gets, what the dog would look like), but the actual information that you find would be different.

When the purpose of your writing—or, in this case, your paragraph—is to find and tell information about a topic, you are writing an **informative** paragraph. Your purpose is to inform, or teach, the reader about your topic.

When you are writing to provide information, here are some guiding question words that will help you seek out specific details:

What? What do you already know about a greyhound, for example? What are they used for?

When? When did greyhounds become popular as pets?

Where? Where can you find a greyhound?

Who? Who might have information about adopting a greyhound?

How? How do greyhounds learn to race?

Try to formulate some questions that you would like to answer in your paragraph. This is the detail information that will make your informative paragraph interesting to read.

Later, you will learn how to turn these questions into paragraphs when you are doing longer writing projects. For a simple paragraph, however, you may want to focus on answering only one of the questions that you come up with about your topic.

Worksheets

Answers to Worksheet III-12A:

Students' answers will vary. Here are examples.

1. *Title*: Money in the Colonies

   Questions: What kind of money did the colonies have? How was the money system different between colonies? What problems did all of the different money types cause?

2. *Title*: Many Uses for Reindeer

   Questions: What are reindeer used for in Lapland? How do reindeer serve the same purpose as other animals?

3. *Title*: A Famous President

   Questions: What do we know about Abraham Lincoln as president? What did he do during the Civil War? How did he die? Why is he famous?

Answers to Worksheet III-12B:

Students' paragraphs will vary.

Follow-up Activity

Informative paragraphs can serve as "mini-reports" for students, especially those in the younger grades. Allow time to showcase the students' findings by having them volunteer to read their paragraphs to the class. They may also want to supply a visual aid, such as a drawing, poster, pictures of a person, etc. Discuss what question(s) were answered in the paragraph and what possible other questions could have been included. At this point, it should be kept simple. More formal, lengthier reports will come soon!

III-12A. Examining Informative Paragraphs

Each paragraph below is providing information about a topic. After reading each, write an appropriate title for each paragraph and write at least one question that each paragraph answers.

1. *Title*: _____

When our country was very young, each colony that formed America had its own money. Each colony had different coins. It was confusing because some of the coins were not even the same size as others. Some had different shapes. Not all of the coins had the same value as each other. When people traveled between colonies, they had to be able to use different coins. All of the different types of money made things very confusing.

Questions: _____

_____

_____

2. Title: _____

In Lapland, reindeer have many uses. They can pull sleds just like horses. Their skin is used to make clothing for the people. They also provide milk for the people. Reindeer are very useful in the cold country of Lapland.

Questions: _____

_____

_____

3. Title: _____

Abraham Lincoln is one of the best-known presidents of the U.S. He was president during the very hard times of the Civil War. He is known for freeing the slaves during that time. He was very tall and had a beard. We often see pictures of him wearing a tall black hat. We probably remember Abraham Lincoln as the president who was shot in a theater. He was a kind, honest man. Abraham Lincoln was a very famous man.

Questions: _____

_____

_____

III-12B. Writing an Informative Paragraph

Below is a list of sample topics that might help you think of something to write about for an informative paragraph. Your class may add more to the list. Select ones that interest you and practice writing informative paragraphs. Remember to think of questions that would interest your readers.

Our state bird, flag, motto, etc.

A famous person (celebrity, president, person from history, current famous person)

What early automobiles looked like

Types of bears

Something about your favorite type of car

Breeds of dogs, cats, horses, fish

Types of elephants

Inventions and inventors

Native American tribes

Making coins

How a volcano erupts

Why it's fun to collect coins/stamps/dolls, etc.

History of our school

The plot of a story/book/movie/play

Life in the 1950s

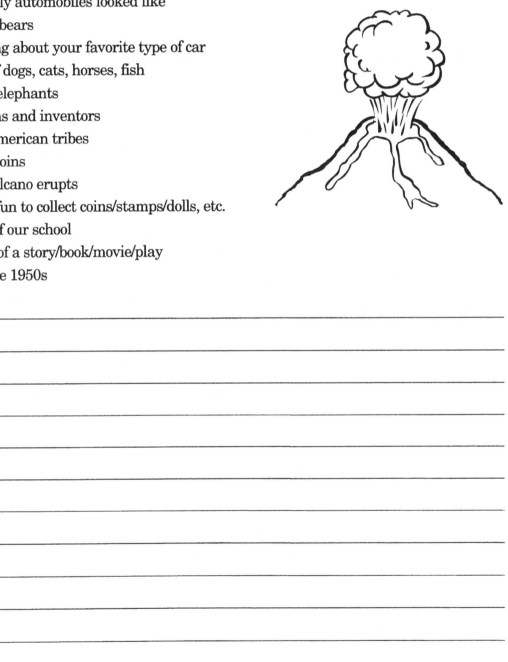

_____

_____

_____

_____

_____

_____

_____

_____

_____

_____

_____

_____

Lesson III-13: Writing a How-to Paragraph

(Types of Paragraphs)

To the Teacher

Writing instructions for how to do or make something is another type of paragraph with which students should become familiar. Giving good directions involves writing clearly; putting steps in logical, sequential order; and writing so that the reader can understand and perform the task. The purpose of this lesson is to provide practice in organizing and writing steps to complete a task.

To the Student

If I asked you how to make chocolate chip cookies, who could help me out? (Have students offer steps for making cookies.) Is this a clear explanation of making cookies? (Read slowly or write on the board.)

1. Get the stuff.

2. Put it together.

3. Bake it.

4. Eat it.

What do you think? Would you really know how to make chocolate chip cookies if that is all you had to go on? (no—not specific, not clear) How could we fix this up to make it clearer?

1. Get the stuff. (What stuff? The ingredients? Do we need to list the ingredients?)

2. Put it together. (What does "put" mean? Stir? Chop? Throw it in a bowl?)

3. Bake it. (At what temperature? For how long?)

4. Eat it. (Is this really part of "making" the cookies?)

Those directions aren't really so clear or specific as they could be. What do you think of these directions? (Read slowly or write on the board.)

1. Go to the store.

2. Go in the store.

3. Get a shopping cart.

4. Get chocolate chips.

5. Get brown sugar.

6. Get white sugar.

7. Get flour.

Whoa! Let's just stop there! Where is this heading? What's wrong with these directions? (way too specific, takes too long to get through the task) Let's look at one more example. What do you think of this set of directions? (Read slowly or write on the board.)

1. Gather the ingredients for the cookies.

2. Get out the utensils you need for cooking.

3. Put flour, sugar, and butter in a bowl.

4. Put spoonfuls of the dough on a cookie sheet.

5. Put the chocolate chips in the bowl and stir them into the dough.

6. Put the cookies in the oven.

7. Oh, I forgot to tell you—turn on the oven to 350 degrees.

8. Add vanilla, water, and an egg to the dough in the bowl.

What's wrong with these directions? (out of order—the writer should have told you to turn the oven on first, put the ingredients in the bowl before you put them on a cookie sheet in the oven)

Well, what guidelines should we look for when listing steps for how to do something?

1. Make sure the steps are clear to read.

2. Make sure the steps are specific, but not overly detailed.

3. Make sure the steps are in the right order.

When you write a how-to paragraph, it will be easier if you write out the steps first. Then you can easily turn the steps into the details of your paragraph.

Worksheets

Answers to Worksheet III-13A:

Order of steps: 4, 1, 2, 6, 3, 7, 5

Students' paragraphs will vary.

Answers to Worksheet III-13B:

Students' answers will vary.

Follow-up Activities

1. **Writing to an Alien:** Tell students they are to write a letter or paragraph to an alien from another planet who does not understand our ways of doing things. Have students select a simple human activity (riding a bike, brushing teeth, eating breakfast, etc.) and explain this task in simple terms that an alien would be able to understand.

2. **Oral Presentations:** Students can further this experience by reading their paragraphs out loud to each other or to the class. Have students give constructive comments to help improve the paragraphs. Students can enhance their presentations by adding a poster that may demonstrate steps of a task, give an actual demonstration, or videotape each other and then replay them to see how clearly they were presented.

Name _____ Date _____

III-13A. How to Make Brownies

Below are some steps for making brownies. First put the steps in the right order. If they are not clearly written, rewrite them to make them clear. Then rewrite the sentences to make a how-to paragraph. Remember to put in a title, topic sentence, and a concluding sentence.

Step _____ Pour the mixed-up brownies from the bowl into a pan.

Step _____ Turn on the oven to 300 degrees.

Step _____ Get the brownie mix, an egg, and vegetable oil while the oven is heating up.

Step _____ Let the brownies cool before cutting them into squares.

Step _____ Mix the ingredients in a large bowl.

Step _____ Decorate the brownies with colored frosting when cool.

Step _____ Put the pan into the oven for 25 minutes.

Title: _____

Topic sentence: _____

_____

Details: _____

_____

_____

_____

_____

_____

_____

_____

_____

Concluding sentence: _____

_____

III-13B. Practice Writing How-to Paragraphs

Choose from the following topics (or add your own). Remember to write the steps for each task clearly, specifically, and in the right order.

how to make an ice cream sundae

how to make a pepperoni pizza

how to draw a bird/dog/ house/horse/car

how to ski down a hill

how to groom a horse/dog

how to braid hair

how to dive into a pool

how to pitch a softball

how to make a code

how to plant flowers

how to make a cherry cola

how to make a gum-wrapper chain

how to do tricks on a skateboard

how to water ski

how to videotape with a video camera

how to kick a football

how to ride a bike/scooter

how to in-line skate

how to make a snowman

how to bake a cake

_____

_____

_____

_____

_____

_____

_____

_____

_____

_____

_____

_____

Lesson III-14: Writing a Persuasive Paragraph

(Types of Paragraphs)

To the Teacher

The final paragraph type that students will learn is that of writing a persuasive paragraph. In this paragraph, students attempt to persuade the reader to do something, feel a certain way, or react in a way that the writer wants the reader to react. A good persuasive paragraph will not only reflect the writer's opinion on a topic, but will also give reasons that try to "sway" the reader to agree with the writer. The purpose of this lesson is to provide practice for the student in evaluating and writing persuasive paragraphs.

To the Student

If I told you I could be persuaded into giving this class an extra recess, how would you try to persuade me? (Have students give suggestions—get all their work done, promise to behave, bring you flowers, whatever!) Which of your reasons do you think I would listen to? (the ones that make the most sense)

When you write a **persuasive** paragraph, it is somewhat similar to the opinion paragraph in that you want to convince someone else to agree with your opinion. It is a little trickier, however, because you not only have to express your opinion, but you also have to try to get the writer to agree with your opinion.

Let's say you wanted to persuade your parents to take a trip to Walt Disney World. Which of these reasons might be persuasive?

- Tell them you will do a written report for your class. (maybe—it's educational)

- Promise you will not fight with siblings on the trip, during the trip, or after the trip. (this might work—parents like peaceful families)

- Tell them you will take them to France next year. (unlikely that kids will have enough money to carry this out)

- Promise to be good for the rest of your life. (this is very vague—and unrealistic)

- Insist you will do research on other things to do in Florida that your parents might enjoy. (this is good—parents might be more likely to go if there are things they want to see along the way)

You can see that your persuasive reasons have to suggest something you could really carry out and something that would appeal to the people you are trying to persuade.

When you write a persuasive paragraph, start with a topic sentence that states your position, give convincing arguments to support your topic, and then have a concluding sentence that restates your position.

Worksheets

Answers to Worksheet III-14A:

1. a. yes, they both refer to going to the beach
   b. temperature, crowds, important to spend time together
   c. yes, these are good reasons
   d. probably

2. a. the topic sentence states the position well; there is no concluding sentence
   b. tickets are on sale, prepared for the noise and parking, timing is good, etc.
   c. $100 a ticket is still very expensive; referring to the loud noise probably won't be persuasive—it will call attention to a potential problem; it's not likely they'll be able to go backstage

    d. the parking problem solved by taking the bus; the concert being on Friday won't affect getting up early the next day

3. a. yes

    b. the size of the dog, protection from strangers, teaching responsibility

    c. Dad is allergic to them, the family already has cats

    d. eliminate the weak reasons; add more that emphasizes how a dog would improve the family situation

Answers to Worksheet III-14B:

Students' paragraphs will vary.

Follow-up Activity

Letters to the Editor: Have students collect and read letters written to the local newspaper editor. These are examples of community issues that concern people enough to write to the editor for publication. Discuss the reasons that are given to support the positions stated by the writer of the letter.

Name _____ Date _____

III-14A. Evaluating a Persuasive Paragraph

How effective do you think these persuasive paragraphs are? Read them and answer the questions that follow.

1. **The Beach**

I think our family should go to the beach this weekend. First of all, it's going to be over 90 degrees so it will be very hot. The water will feel wonderful. Also, a lot of people are out of town this weekend, so it won't be very crowded. It's important, too, for families to do things together, so that's another reason why we should go. We should go to the beach this weekend.

a. Does this paragraph have good topic and concluding sentences? _____

_____

b. What reasons does the writer give to support his or her opinion? _____

_____

c. Would these reasons persuade someone to go to the beach? _____

_____

d. Would these reasons be convincing to you if you were the parent? _____

_____

2. **The Rock Concert**

I think our family should go to a rock concert this weekend. The tickets are on sale and they are only $100 a piece which is a lot cheaper than some other concerts. We can take earplugs so we won't damage our hearing. We can take the bus so parking won't be a problem. It doesn't matter if it is a late concert, because the next day is Saturday, so we can sleep in. We might be able to go backstage to meet the band and get autographs after the concert. Mom and Dad will appreciate our music if they hear it often enough.

a. Does this paragraph have good topic and concluding sentences?

_____

b. What reasons does the writer give for why the family should go to the concert?

_____

c. How persuasive are those reasons? _____

_____

d. Which reasons are the most persuasive? _____

III-14A. Evaluating a Persuasive Paragraph (continued)

3. **Why We Need a Dog**

I think our family needs to get a dog. If we get a little dog, it won't cost much to feed it. It can sleep in my bedroom, because Dad is allergic to dogs. A dog will bark when strangers come and will protect us. Even though we have five cats, a dog will get used to them and they will all get along. We can take turns taking it for walks every day, and that will teach us responsibility. This family needs a dog.

a. Does this paragraph have good topic and concluding sentences? _____

_____

b. What reasons are the most persuasive? _____

_____

c. What are some problems this family would have with a dog? _____

_____

d. How could you improve this paragraph?_____

_____

III-14B. Practice Writing Persuasive Paragraphs

Below are some topics that could be developed into persuasive paragraphs. Select several from below (or add to the list) and write paragraphs that will persuade the reader to agree with you.

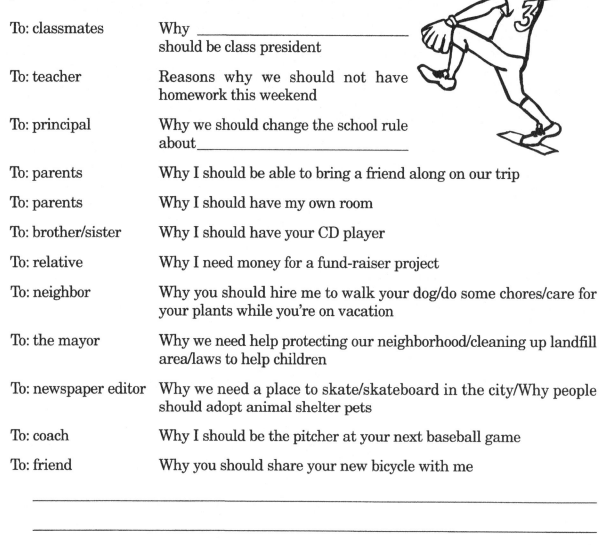

To: classmates   Why _____ should be class president

To: teacher   Reasons why we should not have homework this weekend

To: principal   Why we should change the school rule about_____

To: parents   Why I should be able to bring a friend along on our trip

To: parents   Why I should have my own room

To: brother/sister   Why I should have your CD player

To: relative   Why I need money for a fund-raiser project

To: neighbor   Why you should hire me to walk your dog/do some chores/care for your plants while you're on vacation

To: the mayor   Why we need help protecting our neighborhood/cleaning up landfill area/laws to help children

To: newspaper editor   Why we need a place to skate/skateboard in the city/Why people should adopt animal shelter pets

To: coach   Why I should be the pitcher at your next baseball game

To: friend   Why you should share your new bicycle with me

_____

_____

_____

_____

_____

_____

_____

_____

_____

Lesson III-15: Review of Paragraphs (Types of Paragraphs)

To the Teacher

This lesson provides a review of the six types of paragraphs that have been studied. In this lesson, students are to read sample paragraphs and identify which type of paragraph it represents, evaluate each, and write a paragraph of each type.

To the Student

Let's review the different types of paragraphs you have written so far.

1. **Descriptive paragraph**: appeals to the senses; tells what something looks like, sounds like, feels like, etc.

2. **Opinion paragraph**: expresses an opinion about a topic; gives reasons why this opinion is important and valid

3. **Narrative paragraph**: tells about an event

4. **Informative paragraph**: gives information about a topic

5. **How-to paragraph**: lists steps for how to accomplish a task

6. **Persuasive paragraph**: tries to convince the reader to agree with the writer's opinion

Here is some practice in identifying, evaluating, and writing these types of paragraphs.

Worksheets

Answers to Worksheet III-15A:

1. how-to   3. descriptive   5. narrative

2. persuasive   4. informative   6. opinion

Answers to Worksheet III-15B:

Descriptive:

1. seeing, hearing

2. yes

Opinion:

1. yes, he thinks spring is the best season

2. very good reasons that appeal to him

3. may or may not, but you don't have to because it is an opinion

Narrative:

1. a raccoon visiting the barn

2. yes, you can follow the story easily

Informative:

1. starfish

2. yes

3. perhaps

How-to:

1. make hot chocolate

2. yes

Persuasive:

1. not taking other people's medicine

2. it can be harmful to take someone else's medicine and to mix medicines

3. yes

Answers to Worksheet III-15C:

Students' paragraphs will vary.

Follow-up Activity

Have students work on writing paragraphs about other topics that can be written from different perspectives (six different ways using six paragraph types). Examples may include:

Sports—how to play a certain sport, why the sport is fun, why it is the "best" sport, etc.

Television show—why a certain show is appealing, what happened in an episode of the show, why everyone should watch that show, etc.

Working for an allowance—why this is good for kids, how you can do jobs to save money, a time when you were working and something odd happened, etc.

Spending time with a grandparent—why you should do this, how to make it enjoyable, a time when you did something with Grandma, etc.

III-15A. Identifying Paragraph Types

Read the following paragraphs and identify which paragraph type it represents:

| Descriptive Opinion Narrative Informative |
| How-to Persuasive |

1. _____

It's easy and fun to make hot chocolate. First, you heat some water until it is very hot. Meanwhile, open the hot chocolate packet and dump it into a cup. When the water is hot, add it to the mix and stir it. Add marshmallows if you like. Then drink it and enjoy it.

2. _____

People should not share their medicine with other people. When you take medicine, it is for your own sickness or problem. The wrong medicine might make another person sick. Also, mixing different kinds of medicine might cause a reaction that will be harmful. Medicine is for the individual only, not to share.

3. _____

It was a stormy day. The dark clouds came rolling in across the sky. The wind was blowing so hard it knocked over small trees and signs. The lightning and thunder boomed and made us jump in fright! What a storm we had!

4. _____

Starfish are very interesting creatures. Starfish are not really fish, although they live in the water. They are shaped sort of like stars, but they have arms that come out in different directions. They have an eye at the end of each arm. If they lose an arm, they will grow a new one. It is fascinating to learn about starfish.

5. _____

One day I had a surprise visitor in the barn. It was dark and I opened the door slowly. Something scurried past me, almost touching my legs. I thought it was my cat, but it seemed bigger. I switched on the light and saw the back end of a fat raccoon running out the door. I don't know who scared who, but we both were surprised.

6. _____

I think spring is the best season of the year. Plants and flowers begin to bloom and look so beautiful. The weather starts to get warmer and you can do more outside. It stays light longer, so you can stay up later to play outside. When it's spring, you know that summer and summer vacation are right around the corner. That's why I think spring is the best season.

III-15B. Evaluating Paragraphs

Read each paragraph on Worksheet III-15A again and answer these questions regarding the paragraphs.

Descriptive paragraph

1. What senses does this paragraph appeal to?

   _____

2. Does the writer do a good job of explaining what a stormy day is like?

   _____

Opinion paragraph

1. Does the writer state his or her opinion clearly? _____

2. Does the writer give good reasons to support his or her opinion? _____

3. Do you agree with this opinion? _____

Narrative paragraph

1. What event or story does the writer describe? _____

2. Is the event clearly explained? _____

Informative paragraph

1. What topic is the writer writing about? _____

2. Does the writer give interesting information about this creature? _____

3. Did you learn anything that you didn't know before? _____

How-to paragraph

1. What task does the writer tell you how to do? _____

2. Are the steps clear and in order? _____

Persuasive paragraph

1. What is the writer's opinion that he or she wants you to agree with? _____

2. What reasons does the writer give? _____

3. Are these convincing reasons? _____

III-15C. Writing Paragraphs

You are going to work with only one topic, but write six different types of paragraphs about the same topic. As you write each paragraph, remember to use the characteristics of the paragraph type that you are working on to complete the paragraph.

Topic: **Brushing Your Teeth**

Paragraph 1: **Descriptive paragraph**

> Write a paragraph that describes your toothbrush and toothpaste.

Paragraph 2: **Opinion paragraph**

> Write a paragraph that tells why you think brushing your teeth daily is important.

Paragraph 3: **Narrative paragraph**

> Write a paragraph that tells about a time you brushed your teeth on a plane, in a lake, or some other unusual place.

Paragraph 4: **Informative paragraph**

> Write a paragraph that explains (by giving reasons) why brushing teeth is healthy.

Paragraph 5: **How-to paragraph**

> Write a paragraph that lists the steps for how to brush your teeth.

Paragraph 6: **Persuasive paragraph**

> Write a paragraph that tries to convince the reader to brush his/her teeth every day.

Lesson III-16: Ways to Organize Multiple Paragraphs
(Multiple Paragraphs)

To the Teacher

A short paragraph can convey only a small amount of information. When students are ready to incorporate more information into their work, they will need to write lengthier documents that involve more than one paragraph. The purpose of this lesson is to introduce students to several ways to organize writings that have multiple paragraphs.

To the Student

If I asked you to write down everything you know about _____ (select a popular topic) in a paragraph, would you be able to do it? (probably not—it would make a very long paragraph) When you have a lot to say, you will need to use more than one paragraph to say it. This helps the reader follow your organization and understand what you think is important.

A very common way to organize information for a report is using an **informative** format. You are primarily writing to provide information for the reader. For example, if I were writing a report on ten different breeds of dogs, I would probably write an introductory paragraph (which compares with the topic sentence), and then have ten paragraphs (one each about the breeds I have selected), and then end with a concluding paragraph (which compares with the concluding sentence).

But if I were writing a story about what happened one exciting day, I would want the reader to know about the different events in the order they happened. This is a **sequential** format. With this format, I would start out with my introductory paragraph and then use paragraphs to tell each step of the event. I would use words such as *first, next / then, later*, and *finally* or *at last* to help guide the reader through my piece. These are clue words that indicate the order of events. This type of organization works well with how-to reports if you are explaining how to do something in a particular order.

A third way to organize multiple paragraphs is by **comparing and contrasting**. This format is useful when you are writing about two different things and you want to write about how they are alike (comparing) and how they are different (contrasting). For example, I might want to discuss how cats and dogs are alike and different. Or I might compare how my mother and father are alike and different. In this type of writing, I would start out with my introductory paragraph telling the reader what I am going to compare and contrast, and then use the following paragraphs to alternate between the two things I am comparing.

A fourth way to organize longer writing is by starting with a **topic** and then providing **support** for that topic. This can be used when you express an opinion and then support it with details. It can be used with persuasive writing as well.

Here is some practice for you in identifying how these formats can be used in writing multiple paragraphs.

Worksheets

Answers to Worksheet III-16A:

1. topic-support 2. sequential   3. informative   4. compare/contrast

Answers to Worksheet III-16B:

1. compare/contrast	5. topic, support	9. topic, support	13. sequential
2. informative	6. compare/contrast	10. informative	14. informative
3. sequential	7. sequential	11. sequential	15. compare/contrast
4. informative	8. sequential	12. compare/contrast	16. topic-support

Follow-up Activity

Begin to collect students' writing samples that lend themselves to these different organization formats. You may want to make large envelopes for display in a prominent place in the room and have students sort their writings by format and place them in the correct envelope. In this way, you will readily have an assortment of examples to read and discuss with students.

Name _____ Date _____

III-16A. Recognizing a Format

Below are diagrams of several formats for organizing multiple paragraphs. Write the format that best shows how the paragraphs are organized.

1. _____   2. _____

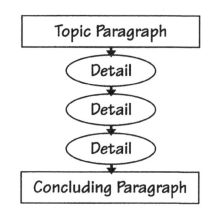

| Topic Paragraph |
| Detail |
| Detail |
| Detail |
| Concluding Paragraph |

| Topic Paragraph |
| Event—what happened first |
| What happened next |
| What happened last |
| Concluding Paragraph |

3. _____   4. _____

| Topic Paragraph |
| Information |
| More information |
| Concluding Paragraph |

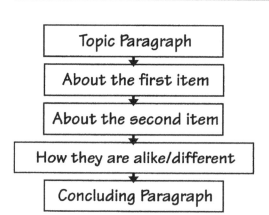

| Topic Paragraph |
| About the first item |
| About the second item |
| How they are alike/different |
| Concluding Paragraph |

Explain why you selected the diagrams.

Name _____ Date _____

III-16B. Identify the Format

Below is a list of topics and ideas that a student might write about. Identify which format (informative, sequential, compare/contrast, and topic, support) would be most appropriate for each. Put an X under your choice and explain your reasons on another sheet of paper.

	informative	sequential	compare/contrast	topic, support
1. How Frogs and Toads Are Alike				
2. What to Feed a New Puppy				
3. How to Build a Birdhouse				
4. All about Lizards				
5. Why I Should Have My Own Room				
6. Alligators and Crocodiles				
7. My Busy Weekend				
8. The Life of a Butterfly				
9. Reasons Why Our Team Needs New Uniforms				
10. History of Baseball				
11. How to Adopt a Pet				
12. What's Worse, Hurricanes or Tornadoes?				
13. My Trip to Mammoth Cave				
14. How to Skate Backwards				
15. Sports for Girls and Boys				
16. Why Our School Needs a New Mascot				

Lesson III-17: Writing an Informative Report

(Multiple Paragraphs)

To the Teacher

Writing reports is probably one of the most common written assignments that students will be working on for school projects. Knowing how to create a well-written, organized report is an essential skill for students. The purpose of this lesson is to assist students in organizing information for the purpose of writing a report. The format used will be the **informative** format.

To the Student

When you are asked to write a report about a certain topic, it's best to organize your thoughts first. Once you have a direction in mind, or know where you are going with your thoughts, it's easier to stay on task and have a clear plan for what you want to say. The task of writing will be so much easier once you have your plan in mind and are able to just stick with it!

In this lesson, you will be working on developing and writing a "simple" report, that is, a short report that will consist of only a few paragraphs. The important thing for you to learn is to make your plan and stick with it. Later you will be given further guidelines on writing a more extensive report, but for now, your goal is simply to generate several paragraphs that relate to your topic. Let's get started!

1. First of all, you need to *select your topic*. Let's say your teacher asks you to write a simple report on a wild animal. Let's select the fox as an example. You know some things about foxes already; perhaps you know what they look like, where they live, and what they eat. But there is so much information about foxes! Think of all the books and articles in encyclopedias about foxes. If you wanted to know all about foxes, it would take you a long, long time.

2. Keeping in mind that you want to write about foxes, you can proceed to the second step: *narrow your topic*. Think about what might be interesting to learn about regarding foxes, but something that is not so extensive. Are you interested in how foxes raise their young? Or perhaps you are interested in how foxes communicate with each other. One way to get ideas for narrowing your topic is by getting some books and materials and looking through them. As you explore the topic, what are some things that catch your attention? If you already have some materials in front of you, you are ready to start narrowing your idea. You can always find additional sources to add to your report, but right away make sure you have something to get you started. Let's say you want to write your simple report on the body of a fox.

3. The next step is to *gather information* about your topic. You will want to find details that you can expand into paragraphs. One way to picture this is by making a "web"— put your topic in the middle of the web and extend lines from the web that indicate what your ideas or details are. (see example) Now go looking for information that gives details about your topic.

4. Now you can begin to *organize* your information. Maybe you were not able to find a lot of information

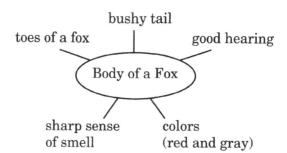

about the colors of the fox, so go ahead and eliminate this one. You can jot down notes right on your "web" sheet about these details. Perhaps you want your first paragraph to be about the toes, and then go right around to the tail, hearing, and then the sense of smell. You can number your details so you will remember the order in which you want to write about them.

5. Now, start writing. This is your rough draft exercise. It's time to start changing your "web word" into paragraphs. In this step, you will *expand your writing*—the words will become sentences, the sentences will become paragraphs. Just follow the order of the "sandwich" paragraph that you are so familiar with. Your topic paragraph is the middle of the web—the body of the fox. Your paragraph is going to introduce the readers to the interesting body of the fox. Now extend your details—each detail coming out of the web is going to be a separate paragraph. At this point, your paragraphs can be quite short—even two or three sentences are fine. Finally, don't forget to write a brief concluding paragraph that is similar to your topic paragraph.

6. Finally, go through your *proofreading* process by examining the paragraph for all of the little things that are so important—watch for capital letters, punctuation, good handwriting, perfect spelling, and varied sentences.

7. Recopy your rough draft into *final form*. This should represent your best effort. Of course, you can add extras to your report such as pictures, diagrams, even a nice cover, and so on.

Now let's do some practice in writing a simple report that follows the informative format.

Worksheets

Answers to Worksheet III-17A:

1. too general

2. probably too specific

3. just right—probably would contain information about the different roles of the parent elephants and the babies

4. OK—would probably talk about the various features of a frog: legs, voice, etc.

5. too general—where would you begin?

6. interesting, good topic

7. interesting, would be able to find lots of information

8. too general

9. probably too specific

10. too general

11. very informative

12. good, specific enough

13. too specific—after you list the colors, what more is there to add?

14. good and interesting, lots of information available

15. good and interesting

16. specific

17. too general

18. specific enough

19. specific enough

20. good and specific

Answers to Worksheet III-17B:

Students' answers will vary.

Answers to Worksheet III-17C:

Kinds of Frogs

There are many different kinds of frogs around the world. There are several kinds of frogs that are found in the United States and Canada.

One kind of frog is called the true frog. These frogs live in or near water. They have long hind legs with webbed feet. There are more than 20 of these kinds of frogs in the United States. They include the bullfrog, the green frog, and the wood frog.

Another kind of frog is the tree frog. As you can probably guess, these frogs live in trees. They are small frogs. They are less than 2 inches long.

There are other frogs in the United States, too. They include the narrow-mouthed toad, which has a very small mouth. Another kind is the tailed frog. This frog lives in mountain streams.

You can see that there are many types of frogs. The United States and Canada are home to lots of different frogs.

Follow-up Activity

Assign students a topic to work on for their informative report. You may want to have students work in pairs, at least initially. Make sure they follow the steps on the checklist so that they turn in a "web," a rough draft, and a final copy.

Keep a running list of informative topics that work well with this format. Examples include:

- anything to do with lifestyle or anatomy of animals
- places to visit in certain states or areas of the country
- inventions and how they were created
- products from a state or country
- symbols that are included on the state flag
- parts of a car, ship, rocket, or other vehicle
- unusual habits of some birds

Name _____ Date _____

III-17A. Selecting and Narrowing Topics

Here we sample topics for writing an informative report. Some are too general (there are volumes of information out there!), some are too specific (there may not be much information at all), and others are "just right." Indicate what you think about each of these topics.

	too general	too specific	just right
1. The Planet Earth			
2. An Elephant's Toenail			
3. An Elephant's Family			
4. Parts of a Frog			
5. The United States			
6. Places to Visit in Arizona			
7. The Five Senses			
8. Flowers			
9. One of the Rings around Saturn			
10. Flavors of Ice Cream			
11. Equipment on a Fire Engine			
12. Different Uses for Horses			
13. Colors of the Rainbow			
14. Some Inventions of Thomas Edison			
15. Famous Landmarks in Washington, D.C.			
16. Crops of Hawaii			
17. Cats			
18. Care of Kittens			
19. Things to Do at Sea World			
20. Different Rooms at the White House			

Select two or three of the "too general" topics. How could you revise them to be "just right"?

_____

_____

_____

_____

Name _____ Date _____

III-17B. Writing a Rough Draft

Below is a "web" that a student has started on frogs. The student has already jotted down some facts to go with the details about the topic (kinds of frogs) and is beginning to organize the information. Help this student begin writing a rough draft that includes this information.

True Frogs
- live in or near water
- 20 kinds live in the United States
- include bullfrogs, green frogs, wood frogs
- long hind legs
- webbed feet

Tree Frogs
- live in trees
- are less than 2 inches long

Common Kinds of Frogs

Other Frogs
- narrow-mouthed frogs (have little mouths)
- tailed frogs (live in mountain streams)

Topic sentence: _____

Add another sentence: _____

_____

Next paragraph: _____

_____

Second paragraph: _____

_____

Third paragraph: _____

_____

Concluding paragraph: _____

_____

_____

III-17C. Rough Draft and Final Form

Here is a rough draft for the frog report. Pay attention to the proofreader's marks and rewrite this in final form.

kinds of frogs

There are meny different kinds of frogs around the world. There are several kinds of frogs that are found in the United states and canada.

One kind of frog is called the true frog these frogs live in or near the water. They have long hind legs with web bed feet. There are more than 20 of these kinds of frogs in the U.S. They include the bull frog, the green frog, and the wood frog.

Another kind of frog is the Tree frog. As you can probly guess, these frogs live in trees. They are small frogs. They are Less than 2 inches long.

There are other frogs in the united states, too. They include the narrow-mouthed toad, which has a very small mouth. Anuther kind is the tailed Frog. This frog lives in mountain streams.

¶ You can see that there are meny types of frogs. The United states and Canada are home to lots of different kinds of frogs.

Lesson III-18: Writing a Sequential Report

(Multiple Paragraphs)

To the Teacher

Another way to organize multiple paragraphs is by **sequential (or time) order**. When writing about something that takes place over time, it is logical to arrange the paragraphs in terms of what happened first, later, at the end, and so on. The purpose of this lesson is to provide practice for students in arranging paragraphs in sequential order and then to assist students in writing a short document in sequential format.

To the Student

A second way to organize a document that has several paragraphs is by arranging them in sequential order. In this format, you would write about something that happens in a certain order. This would be appropriate for writing about what you did during a day (starting out with the morning, going through the events of the day, etc.), or telling about the life of your dog (when he was a puppy, when he went to dog training school, what he does now as an adult, etc.), or writing about what happened in a certain event such as taking a trip (preparing for the trip, what you did on the trip, when you came home, etc.). The things you write about sequentially are things that happen in a certain order.

When you write sequentially, you might use these words to help organize your writing: *first, next, and then,* and *finally,* or *at last.* This will help the reader follow your thoughts.

Here is a diagram that shows how to organize a simple report using this format:

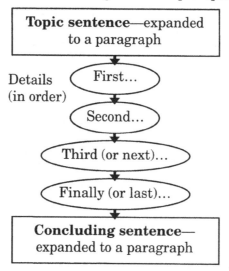

Let's take the life of a frog as an example. Here is how you could write a simple report on the life of a frog using the sequential format.

1. First, just as in the informative format, you need to *select a topic* that interests you. We will choose frogs for this example.

2. Second, you will *narrow your topic* to something that is more specific. Again, this is the same as in the informative format.

3. The third point is different. Now you are ready to *list the steps of your topic in order.* Ask yourself. What happens first? What next? After that? and so on. It is important

that you list what happens in the order they happen. With the frog example, the steps might include:

1. starts as an egg

2. becomes a tadpole

3. becomes an adult

4. Your information is easy to organize, because it should already be in the order you need. You can go right on to the next step, *expand your writing*. Now it is time to complete your paragraphs in order by adding information. Here you would add information about what the egg looks like, how many there are, etc.; what a tadpole stage looks like, growing legs, losing a tail, etc.; and finally describing an adult frog. This is still the rough draft stage, so feel free to make changes.

5. Continue with the *proofreading* process, as in the other format.

6. Recopy your rough draft with changes into *final form*. Add pictures and other "extras" if you choose.

Now let's do some practice in writing a simple report that follows the sequential format.

Worksheets

Answers to Worksheet III-18A:

1. yes	5. no	9. yes	13. no	17. no
2. no	6. yes	10. yes	14. yes	18. yes
3. yes	7. no	11. yes	15. yes	19. yes
4. yes	8. no	12. no	16. no	20. no

Answers to Worksheet III-18B:

Students' rough drafts will vary.

Answers to Worksheet III-18C:

Early Life of Benjamin Franklin

Benjamin Franklin had an interesting early life. He did many things before he became a famous American leader.

Benjamin Franklin was born in Boston, Massachusetts, in 1706. He was the 15th child in a family of 17 children. His father owned a candle shop.

Mr. Franklin attended school in Boston for only two years. He loved to read. He had to drop out because his father could not afford to send him. Then he worked for his father in the candle shop.

Benjamin Franklin worked as an apprentice for his brother as a printer. He also wrote newspaper articles. When he was 17, he ran away to Philadelphia.

He worked for a printer in Philadelphia. Later he wrote and published his own newspaper. He always believed that hard work is the key to success.

Benjamin Franklin was a hard worker who tried many things in his early life. He later became a famous American.

Follow-up Activity

Have students continue to practice writing simple reports using the sequential format. Keep a running list of topics that lend themselves to this format. Examples include:

- any kind of tour of a place or building
- relating an event that takes place over a day, week, or other time period
- writing person's history
- changes in body as an animal or insect grows
- explanation of how to do or make something (involving steps in sequential order)

III-18A. Selecting Topics for the Sequential Format

Remember that the sequential format is useful for writing about things that happen in a certain order. Which of these topics would be appropriate for the sequential format? Write "yes" or "no" on the lines.

1. How to Make an Ice Cream Sundae   _____

2. Different Kinds of Ice Cream   _____

3. My Early School Years   _____

4. The Life of Thomas Jefferson   _____

5. Parts of a Butterfly   _____

6. The Life Cycle of a Butterfly   _____

7. Products of France   _____

8. Famous Cities in France   _____

9. My Trip to France   _____

10. What I Did on Saturday   _____

11. How to Make a Model Car   _____

12. Thoughts about Swimming   _____

13. Different Kinds of Rocks   _____

14. The Adventure of the Lost Dog   _____

15. U.S. Presidents in My Lifetime   _____

16. My Favorite Sports   _____

17. The Different Rooms in Our House   _____

18. From Kitten to Cat   _____

19. A Walk Along the River   _____

20. All about Lightning and Thunder   _____

III-18B. Writing a Rough Draft

Below is rough draft of a simple report on Benjamin Franklin. Help this student complete the rough draft by using the information that is already in sequential order.

Topic: Benjamin Franklin

Narrowed topic: Franklin's early years

Early life:	• born in Boston, Massachusetts • born Jan. 17, 1706 • 15th child of 17 children
Student:	• worked in father's candle shop • had to drop out of school when father couldn't afford to send him • loved to read
Apprentice:	• worked for his brother who was a printer • ran away to Philadelphia at age 17 • wrote newspaper articles
Printer:	• worked as a printer in Philadelphia • began publishing his own newspaper • believed in hard work to be successful

Topic sentence: _____

_____

Add another sentence: _____

_____

Paragraph about early life: _____

_____

Paragraph about being a student: _____

_____

Paragraph about being an apprentice: _____

_____

Paragraph about being a printer: _____

_____

Concluding paragraph: _____

_____

III-18C. Rough Draft and Final Form

Here is the rough draft for the report on Benjamin Franklin. Pay attention to the proofreader's marks and rewrite the report in final form.

early Life of Benjamin Franklin

Benjamin had an interesting early life. He did many jobs things before he became a famus american Leader.

Benjamin Franklin was born in Boston, massachusetts, in 1706. He was the 15th child in a family of 17 kids. His father had a candle shop.

Mr Franklin went to school in boston for only two years. He loved to read books. He had to drop out becos his father could not afford to send him. Then he worked for his father in the candle shop.

Benjamin Franklin worked as an apprentice for his brother as a Printer. He also wrote newspaper articles. When he was 17, he ran away to philadelphia.

He worked for a printer in Philadelphia. Later he wrote and published his newspaper. He always believed that hard work is the key to success

Benjamin Franklin was a hard worker who tryed many things in his early life. He later be came a famos american.

Lesson III-19: Writing a Compare/Contrast Report

(Multiple Paragraphs)

To the Teacher

Sometimes the best format to use when writing is that of comparing and contrasting two or more things. In this type of organization, two events, places, people, or other items are compared (in terms of how they are similar) and/or contrasted (focusing on the differences). The purpose of this lesson is to provide practice for students in determining the appropriateness of this format for given topics as well as to help students practice looking for similarities and differences.

To the Student

A third way that might be helpful in organizing your paragraphs is the format of comparing and contrasting. This method views two (or possibly more) separate things, and studies how they are alike and different. This format would be helpful in comparing different pets (cats and dogs), deciding which vacation resort is nicest (Hawaii or the Bahama Islands), which sport is more exciting (baseball or football), or discussing how girls and boys view the same issue with different outlooks (a particular book or movie).

Usually you will compare two things, but it is certainly possible to use this format when you are considering an issue that has more than two points of view. (For example, you might compare cats, dogs, and gerbils in terms of which is the best pet, or compare five different movies to judge which is the most exciting.)

Here is a diagram that shows how you can organize your information for a simple report using the compare/contrast method:

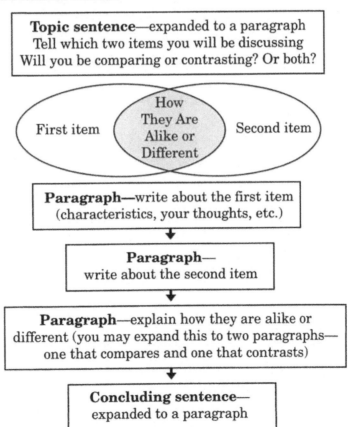

Topic sentence—expanded to a paragraph
Tell which two items you will be discussing
Will you be comparing or contrasting? Or both?

First item — How They Are Alike or Different — Second item

Paragraph—write about the first item (characteristics, your thoughts, etc.)

Paragraph—write about the second item

Paragraph—explain how they are alike or different (you may expand this to two paragraphs—one that compares and one that contrasts)

Concluding sentence—expanded to a paragraph

Let's take a comparison between frogs and toads as an example. Here is how you could write a simple report comparing these two animals.

1. First, *select the two items* you are going to consider. In this report, we are going to be writing about frogs and toads.

2. Second, *decide if you are going to compare, contrast, or do both* in your report. Depending on the length of your report, you want to stick with only one consideration. In our example, we will consider how frogs and toads are alike and different.

3. Now you are ready to *gather your information* on both sides. List the facts and details that you want to include in your report for both items. For example:

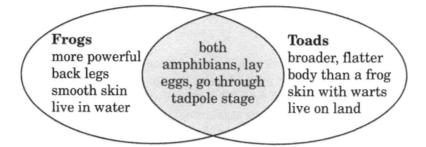

4. Now you are ready to start your *rough draft*. In your topic paragraph, let the reader know two things you are investigating and what you are going to do about them (compare? contrast? both?).

In your next paragraph, tell about the first item. (what you want to write about frogs) In the following paragraph, tell about the second item. (what you know about toads) In the paragraph after that, point out how they are different. In the next paragraph, point out how they are alike. Finally, write your concluding paragraph.

5. Continue with the *proofreading* process.

6. Recopy your rough draft into the *final form*, and add pictures or other "extras" if you choose.

Now it's your turn to practice writing a simple report that follows the compare/contrast format.

Worksheets

Answers to Worksheet III-19A:

1. no	5. yes	9. yes	13. no	17. yes
2. yes	6. yes	10. yes	14. no	18. yes
3. yes	7. yes	11. yes	15. yes	19. no
4. no	8. no	12. no	16. yes	20. yes

Answers to Worksheet III-19B:

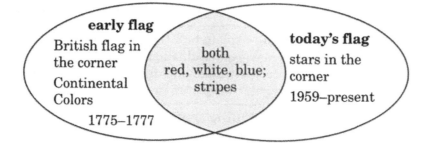

Answers to Worksheet III-19C:

Comparing Two Flags

The first U.S. flag is similar in some ways to the flag we have today. In some ways, they are different.

The first flag flew from 1775 to 1777. It was called the Continental Colors. In the corner was a square that looked like the British flag. This was because our country was closely tied to the British at that time.

Our flag today has been flying from 1959 until now. It has 50 stars in the upper corner. Each star represents one of our 50 states.

Both flags are red, white, and blue in color. They both have red and white stripes on them. Both flags have something in the upper corner that is important to the country. One helps us remember being British and the other helps us remember our 50 states.

Our flag today has some similarities to the first American flag. It's important to remember that we are a different country now than we were back then. This shows in our flag.

Follow-up Activity

1. This format may be one of the most difficult for students to use easily. You may wish to use the image of "zigzagging" between the two items that are going to be compared, especially if students are comparing and contrasting them. It may be helpful to have students make a diagram that can be placed on a bulletin board, using circles to represent each item that is considered. You can actually use colored yarn to "chart" the path of the report, back and forth between the two items.

2. As with the other formats, begin collecting lots of examples of simple reports that work well with the compare/contrast format.

Name _____ Date _____

III-19A. Selecting Topics for the Compare/Contrast Format

When you are comparing or contrasting items, you need to have at least two that have something to do with each other. Which of these topics would be appropriate for using the compare/contrast format for writing? Write "yes" or "no" on the lines.

1. Cats and Rocks _____

2. Cats and Dogs _____

3. Swimming and Jogging _____

4. Lakes and Swimming _____

5. How Parents Treat Girls and Boys _____

6. Thoughts about Different Sports _____

7. Christmas and Hanukkah _____

8. Why I Like My Computer _____

9. Different Kinds of Computers _____

10. State Flags _____

11. Different Breeds of Dogs _____

12. Watching a Tadpole Grow into a Frog _____

13. How to Make a Snowman _____

14. Having a Snowball Fight _____

15. Who Can Make the Most Unusual Snowman _____

16. How Two Great Inventors Were Alike _____

17. Which Is More Fun—Roller Coasters or In-line Skating _____

18. Math and Reading _____

19. How to Play a Good Trick on a Friend _____

20. Having a Big Sister and a Little Sister _____

Name _____ Date _____

III-19B. Writing a Rough Draft

Below is a rough draft of a simple report that compares and contrasts some United States flags. Help this student complete the rough draft by using the information.

Topic: U.S. flags

Narrowed Topic: comparing the first American flag (in 1775) with today's flag

Two item to compare:

early flag	both	today's flag
British flag in the corner	red, white, blue; stripes	stars in the comer
Called Continental Colors 1775–1777		1959–present

Topic sentence: _____

_____

Add another sentence: _____

_____

Paragraph about early flag: _____

_____

_____

Paragraph about today's flag: _____

_____

_____

Paragraph about how they are alike: _____

_____

_____

Concluding paragraph: _____

_____

_____

III-19C. Rough Draft

Here is a rough draft for the simple report on the early and present American flags. Rewrite this rough draft in final form.

comparing two flags

The first u.s flag is similar in some ways to the flag we
have. today In some way*s* they are different.

The first flag flew from 1775 to 1777. It was called the
continental colors. In the corner was a square that looked like
the flag British. This was becos our country was closely tied
to the British. at that time

Our flag today has been flying from 1959 until ~~today~~ now. It
has 50 stars in the upper corner. Each ~~of the~~ star*s*
represents one of ~~the~~ our 50 states.

Both flags are red, white, and blue in color. They both have
red and white stripes on them. ~~and~~ both flags have some thing
in the upper #corner that is important to the country. One
helps us remember being british and the other ~~one~~ helps us
remember our 50 states.

Lesson III-20: Writing a Topic-Support Report

(Multiple Paragraphs)

To the Teacher

Another example of a way to write a simple report with multiple paragraphs is by organizing the information according to a main topic supported by details. This method is also useful for expressing an opinion (supported by reasons) or writing a persuasive document (supported again by arguments). The purpose of this lesson is to provide practice for students in recognizing this format and writing a short report.

To the Student

You have already had some practice in giving an opinion and then coming up with good reasons to support your opinion. Let's say I said that Pizza Barn is the best place to eat in town. What might some reasons be to support that statement? (good food, good service, good prices, good location, etc.) You would expect my reasons to make sense, right? If I said that Pizza Barn was the best place because my aunt lives next door or because the door is painted red… well, those reasons don't seem to have anything to do with why it is a good restaurant.

When you write to convince your reader of something, you are going to start with your topic sentence—make it clear to the reader what your position is—and then support that topic with logical, convincing reasons or details.

The format you will use when you write papers that try to convince someone else of something is called the **topic-support** format. This simply means that you start with your topic clearly stated and the rest of your document is organized with details to support that topic.

Here are the steps to writing a document using this format:

1. *Select your topic.* For example, try to think of something you feel very strongly about. This will make your arguments much more convincing! Let's work through the example of year-round schooling. This is the general topic you are going to think about.

2. *Choose your position* on this topic. Do you agree or disagree? There are reasons pro and con for year-round schooling. Perhaps you need to find out more information about the topic before you can truly decide how you feel. Let's decide that you are going to take the position that year-round school is a great idea.

3. Once you have chosen your position, *write details* that support your position. Each detail will be developed into a paragraph. Make sure your details give good reasons that accurately support your position. Some reasons that support year-round schooling might include: you can take vacations at different times during the year, you won't forget so much because you're in school longer without breaks, it's helpful for parents who work year-round.

4. Now it's time to *organize your details*. You might want to start with the strongest reason first and then add other relevant details. For our example, you might want to start with the educational reasons and then put the vacation idea at the end.

5. Once you have your organization plan, continue to *expand your writing* to form paragraphs. This is your rough draft stage, so don't worry about making mistakes. Get your ideas down. At this point, you may decide to eliminate some reasons that aren't so powerful. You might also clarify your details with examples to support the way you think.

6. Now go through the *proofreading* process.

7. Finally, recopy your rough draft into *final form*, adding any "extras" to make your paper more interesting or believable.

You can think of a diagram for this format in this way:

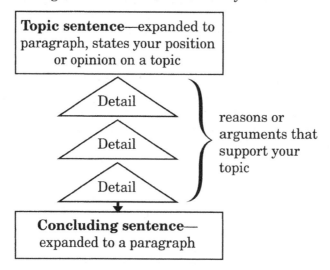

Now let's take time to practice recognizing and writing reports that follow the topic-support format.

Worksheets

Answers to Worksheet III-20A:

1. yes	5. yes	9. no	13. no	17. yes
2. yes	6. no	10. yes	14. yes	18. no
3. no	7. yes	11. no	15. no	19. yes
4. yes	8. no	12. no	16. yes	20. no

Answers to Worksheet III-20B:

Students' rough drafts will vary.

Answers to Worksheet III-20C:

A Community Problem

There is too much litter in our community. This is becoming a terrible problem that we should correct.

There is always a lot of trash in the city park. If you walk on the roads, you can see how much paper and garbage is thrown in the park.

People who go to the park for ball games throw their cans on the ground. They should put them in the trash instead. It makes the park look messy.

There should be a penalty for people who litter. They should have to pay a fine. They should also have to pick up trash so they can see how much better it looks with the trash gone.

We can have a nice clean park if we work on this problem. We don't want litter in our community.

Follow-up Activity

Have students take opposing sides on topics, and go back and forth reading their papers and expressing their positions. Encourage students to evaluate very carefully the reasons given for each position. Even if someone doesn't agree with a certain position, there may be some reasons that are quite supportive and make sense. While it is important to pick a position and follow through on that, it is also of educational benefit to be open-minded and realize that there are valid reasons on the opposing side as well.

Name _____ Date _____

III-20A. Selecting Topics for the Topic-Support Format

Your topic should be something about which you have strong feelings. Which of these topics below would be appropriate for the topic-support format? Write "yes" or "no" on the line.

1. Why All Parks Should Be Free _____

2. Dog Owners Should Clean Up After Their Dogs _____

3. Many Kinds of Dogs _____

4. Our Football Team Needs New Uniforms _____

5. Everyone Should Come to the Fun Fair _____

6. The Big Sale at the Mall _____

7. Why You Should Come to the Big Sale _____

8. Three Ways You Can Show Your School Spirit _____

9. How to Make Jewelry _____

10. There Are Too Many Fund-Raising Activities _____

11. Rules for Sailing _____

12. A Beautiful Day on the Beach _____

13. A Story about a Storm _____

14. Why We Should Help the Poor _____

15. Dangers of Tanning _____

16. People Need to Stay Out of the Sun _____

17. Littering Is a Community Problem _____

18. Our Trip to the Zoo _____

19. Exotic Animals Do Not Make Good Pets _____

20. Ways to Cheer Up a Sick Friend _____

III-20B. Writing a Rough Draft

Here is a rough draft of a student's report about littering. Help the student complete the rough draft.

Topic:	Littering in the Community
Position:	There is too much litter
Details:	There is litter in the community park
	People throw cans around at the ball games
	There aren't enough trash cans in public places
	We need more signs that talk about the problem of littering
	People who litter should be fined

Topic sentence: _____

_____

Add another sentence: _____

_____

Detail: _____

_____

_____

Detail: _____

_____

_____

Detail: _____

_____

_____

Detail: _____

Concluding paragraph: _____

_____

_____

III-20C. Rough Draft and Final Form

Rewrite this rough draft on littering by making the proofreading changes.

A community problem

Their is to much litter in our community. This is becoming a terrible problem that we ~~need to~~ should correct.

There is always a#lot of trash in the city park. If you walk on the roads, you can see how much garbage and paper is thrown in the park.

the
People who go to park for ball games throw their cans on the ground. They shold put them in the trash instead. it makes the park look messy.

There should be a ~~fine~~ penalty for people who litter. and they should have to pay a big fine. They should also have to
looks
pick up trash so they can see how much better it ~~is~~ with the trash gone.

We can have a clean nice park if we work ~~hard~~ on this problem. We don't want litter in our Community.

Section IV

Other Types of Writing Activities

Lesson IV-1: Elements of a Story (Writing a Story)

To the Teacher

Once students become proficient with the shorter writing activities, they may feel ready to tackle a larger project—that of writing a short story. This allows them more freedom to develop their characters, elaborate their descriptions, and move a plot along in different ways. The purpose of this lesson is to introduce students to the very basic elements of a story: plot, characters, and setting.

To the Student

What's the best story you ever read? (Allow for discussion.) When you were younger, what stories did you like your parents to read to you? (common bedtime stories) They probably did not read a huge chapter book to you before bedtime, but I bet they read a story that could be finished in a few minutes (so hopefully you would fall asleep).

You probably have some books that you are reading or you like to read. What you are going to be working on is *not* writing a book, but writing a short story. A story could be turned into a book, if it was long enough and had enough to tell to make it that long. But to begin with, you are going to have the opportunity to write a short story.

There are some terms and ideas about a short story with which you need to become familiar. These are the **elements** of a story. All stories will have these elements, so you can look for them when you read, and make sure you include them when you write.

First of all, every story has a **plot**. This simply means "what happened" in the story. You can string the events together to retell the story. For example, what's the plot of *Little Red Riding Hood*? Basically, a little girl goes through the woods and is stopped by a wolf who tries to trick her. She outsmarts the wolf and wins in the end. You will notice that I left a lot of the actual story out of that brief plot. A plot is just the outline of what happens in a story.

Another element is that of the **characters** in the story. Someone or something has to do something to make the story. Maybe the characters are people (such as in fairy tales). Maybe the characters include animals (again, fairy tales). Perhaps there is a story about a boy and how much he loves his dog. The plot would be telling about what he and his dog did together; the characters are the boy and his dog.

Even before you write your story, you can decide on the **setting** of the story. This tells when and where the story takes place. For example, a story about dinosaurs could be set in an unknown land and it would have been a long time ago. A story about the Civil War could be set in the South and would have been in the mid-1800s. When you decide to write your own story, you might want to pick a setting that you are familiar with (your school, your neighborhood, a beach you have been to) and a time that makes sense. It would be difficult to write about something that happened 100 years ago if you don't know anything about that time period.

Let's see if you can identify these elements of a story. Here's some practice.

Worksheets

Answers to Worksheet IV-1A:

1. setting	4. plot	7. setting	10. setting	13. character
2. character	5. character	8. setting	11. plot	14. plot
3. character	6. plot	9. character	12. setting	15. plot

Answers to Worksheet IV-1B:

Students' charts will vary.

Follow-up Activity

Silly Stories: Have three envelopes, each containing pieces of papers with sample characters, settings, and plots written on them. They do not have to go together logically! Have students work in pairs to create silly stories to tell to the other groups by pulling out one of each element and composing a simple, silly story.

Name _____   Date _____

IV-1A. Identify the Element

For each example below, write the term that describes it: plot, character, or setting.

1. a beach in Hawaii   _____

2. a tall man with a mysterious face   _____

3. a raccoon   _____

4. hiking along the Grand Canyon   _____

5. twins   _____

6. twins who try to fool people by switching places   _____

7. a big house where twins live   _____

8. the sun rising early in the morning   _____

9. a paramedic   _____

10. a hospital   _____

11. an ambulance pulling up to the emergency room   _____

12. the top of a huge mountain covered with snow   _____

13. an alien with two heads   _____

14. uncovering clues to find out who stole the gold   _____

15. opening a box to have a snake jump out   _____

Name _____ Date _____

IV-1B. Putting the Elements Together

Complete the chart below by outlining a possible story. Some of the elements are missing.

Character	Setting	Plot
An evil scientist	_____	_____ _____
_____	A dark cave in Africa	_____ _____
_____	_____	Hiding from aliens who want to eat humans
A baby	_____	_____ _____
_____	The principal's office	_____ _____
_____	_____	Having a surprise party
A movie star	_____	_____ _____
_____	An amusement park	_____ _____
_____	_____	Being chased by a tiger

Lesson IV-2: Using Dialogue (Writing a Story)

To the Teacher

Students will probably include conversation in their stories. The purpose of this lesson is to demonstrate the use of dialogue between characters, in particular, the use of quotation marks and new paragraphs.

To the Student

When you write your story, you will probably have your characters talk to each other. When you put this in writing, there are specific ways to show talking to each other, or **dialogue**.

1. **Using Punctuation/Quotation Marks.** You may still remember the lesson on writing sentences with quotation marks (see Lesson II-14). If not, some review may be appropriate. The important thing to remember is that the words said by a character need to be marked by quotation marks at the beginning of what is said, and a comma and then quotation marks at the end. The first word said should start with a capital letter. For example:

    The hungry lion said, "I am going to eat you!"

    I was afraid when I heard the voice call out, "Who are you?"

    "Stop right there, young man," my mother said.

2. **Alternating Paragraphs.** When you include dialogue in your story, you have to remember an additional rule: Every character's dialogue will be a new paragraph. Even if the character only says one word, that still has to be a new paragraph. Remember, that means you have to indent each new paragraph as well. For example:

    The lion and the zebra ran into each other in the jungle one morning. "Hello there, Mr. Zebra," said the lion.

    "Hello," said the zebra to the lion.

    "What are you doing?" the lion asked. He wasn't sure what the zebra was up to, so he thought he would ask.

    The zebra answered, "I'm doing what zebras do. Running away from lions!" And he did.

3. **Split Dialogue.** When the dialogue is split, you still have to remember to include every word that is said in quotation marks. For example:

    "I'm surprised to see you," said the man, "but I'm happy that you're here."

    "If you wait a minute," called my mother, "we can catch up to you."

    "I think," the teacher said, "we should go outside."

Here is some practice in identifying and using dialogue.

Worksheets

Answers to Worksheet IV-2A:

One day a little boy decided he was going to ran away. He asked his mother if she thought that was a good idea. "Mother, I am leaving home." the boy said.

"Why are you leaving?" asked his mother. "Aren't you happy here?"

"Yes, I'm happy," said the boy. "But I need more adventure in my life. Things are just too boring here."

The mother smiled at the little boy. "If you are bored, maybe you should help your brother clean out the garage," she said.

Answers to Worksheet IV-2B:

Bobby and Tina decided to have a race. "I'm faster than you are," said Bobby.

"No, you're not," said Tina. "I'm faster than all of the boys in the class."

Bobby laughed. "You are not," he said. "I think I can beat a girl like you."

That really made Tina mad. She decided to challenge Bobby to a race. "Let's have a race," she said. "I will race you to the other end of the playground and back. What do you think about that, Bobby?"

Bobby laughed again. "It's a deal," he said. "Let's race, Tina."

"Yes, let's race," said Tina.

Follow-up Activity

Use old books or reproduce short stories that have two characters conversing. Give students two different colors of crayons or highlighters (one for each character) and have them practice underlining or highlighting the conversation between the two characters.

Name _____ Date _____

IV-2A. Add the Punctuation

Below is a portion of a short story that includes dialogue. Add the appropriate punctuation. The number next to each line indicates how many marks need to be added.

One day a little boy decided he was going to run away. He asked his mother **(0)**

if she thought that was a good idea. Mother, I am leaving home the boy said. **(3)**

Why are you leaving? asked his mother. Aren't you happy here? **(4)**

Yes, I'm happy, said the boy. But I need more adventure in my life. Things **(3)**

are just too boring here. **(1)**

The mother smiled at the little boy. If you are bored, maybe you should **(1)**

help your brother clean out the garage, she said. **(1)**

Name _____ Date _____

IV-2B. Rewriting Dialogue

Below is a conversation between two characters. The punctuation is correct, but the dialogue needs to be separated by paragraphs. Rewrite the short story using paragraphs to show dialogue.

Bobby and Tina decided to have a race. "I'm faster than you are," said Bobby. "No, you're not," said Tina. "I'm faster than all of the boys in the class." Bobby laughed. "You are not," he said. "I think I can beat a girl like you." That really made Tina mad. She decided to challenge Bobby to a race. "Let's have a race," she said. "I will race you to the other end of the playground and back. What do you think about that, Bobby?" Bobby laughed again. "It's a deal," he said, "Let's race, Tina." "Yes, let's race," said Tina.

_____

_____

_____

_____

_____

_____

_____

_____

_____

_____

_____

_____

_____

_____

Lesson IV-3: Plot: Beginning, Middle, and Ending

(Writing a Story)

To the Teacher

The plot of a story can be roughly divided into three parts: a beginning, a middle, and an end. The purpose of this lesson is for students to practice recognizing and outlining a basic story plot with these three parts.

To the Student

When you are ready to start writing your story, you should think about your plot—what is going to happen in the story. Stories should have three parts—a beginning, a middle, and an end. Here are some specific details that each part should contain.

1. **The Beginning:** The first part of your story should introduce the characters, the setting, and let the reader know what the plot is going to be about. For example, after reading the beginning of a story, we might know that you are writing about two children who live in a neighborhood who want their parents to get them a pet.

2. **The Middle:** In this part of the story, the plot comes to a climax, or high point. The characters have started doing things to move the plot along and the reader is interested in knowing what might happen. In our example, the children might try various ways to get their parents to get them a pet. Will it work? Will their ideas convince their parents to give in?

3. **The Ending:** Finally, the plot is worked out and the reader is ready to say goodbye to the characters. The reader has the answers to the questions that were formed in the middle. In the example, yes, the parents agreed to a lizard for pet. The reader is left satisfied that he or she knows how everything turned out.

Worksheets

Answers to Worksheet IV-3A:

1. a. middle	2. a. ending	3. a. beginning
b. beginning	b. beginning	b. ending
c. ending	c. middle	c. middle

Answers to Worksheet IV-3B:

Students' answers wil vary.

Follow-up Activity

Using the Beginning/Middle/Ending format, have students reread familiar short stories and practice summarizing the plot to fit into the three parts. Demonstrate how the characters and plot are introduced in the first section. Have students form a question regarding the plot, especially in the middle section. Discuss how stories can end, usually resolving the conflict neatly.

IV-3A. Beginning, Middle, and Ending

Read these examples that summarize a portion of a story. Decide whether each example is from the beginning, middle, or ending of a story.

1. The Candy Makers

a. The girls have so many orders for candy, they can't keep up with them and are running to the store to buy candy to sell. _____

b. We meet Charlotte and Brooke, two girls who want to make money selling candy to people. _____

c. Charlotte and Brooke decide that they have had enough of the candy business and quit. _____

2. Stray Dog

a. The dog is finally caught and adopted by a family. _____

b. A thin, ragged dog is running around a neighborhood eating garbage. _____

c. People in the neighborhood try to catch the dog by various tricks, but they are having a hard time. _____

3. Canoe Disaster

a. A group of kids at camp want to go canoeing on a hot day. _____

b. Everyone pulls the canoe out of the water and trudges back to camp, all wet and freezing. _____

c. Someone starts rocking the canoe and it tips over, spilling everyone into the water. _____

IV-3B. Outlining a Plot

Below are some sample plots you could turn into a short story. Select one and complete the rest of the worksheet to give your ideas for a beginning, a middle, and an ending.

Two children accidentally find and open a magic box.

A mysterious man turns out to be a famous movie star hiding from the public.

A community welcomes a new family from another country.

Animals on a farm want to change places with each other.

A circus clown decides he wants to tame a lion.

Beginning—What characters are in your story? What is the story going to be about?

Middle—What's the main problem that the characters are trying to resolve? What are some ways that they are working on the problem or what are they doing? What questions does the reader want answered?

Ending—How is the problem worked out? What happens to each of the characters?

Beginning

Middle

Ending

Lesson IV-4: Character Development (Writing a Story)

To the Teacher

When writing a short story, the reader will need to know about the characters who "perform" in the story. The student should be able to provide some depth to important characters by giving each a name, personality, physical characteristics, and other features that are important to the story. The purpose of this lesson is to provide examples of these features, and practice in identifying and developing characters in a short story.

To the Student

Another important aspect of your story is what you do with the characters in your story. Here are some ways to help you "develop" your characters, or in other words, make them believable to yourself and your readers.

First, of course, you must decide which characters will be in your story. Are you going to have several important people? Are you going to write something like a fairy tale that might have talking animals? Be clear in your mind who your characters will be. It is helpful to draw pictures or cut out people from magazines who resemble your characters so you can keep them in mind while you are writing. At this point, you might want to give each of your characters a **name**.

To further develop your characters, complete their profile by thinking about what they look like physically. Do you want your children to be tall? Short? Have long hair? Have a skinned knee? Do you want the clown in your story to have a red ball on his nose? Should the dog be a collie? Think about what your characters will **look** like.

Finally, give your characters (at least the major ones) a **personality**. This will tie in with your plot. Do you want the father in the story to be funny and happy? Do you want the teacher to be strict? Should the puppy constantly be getting into trouble? You might include physical **skills** in this section, too. Is the man going to be athletic? Is the girl a fast runner? As you look at the pictures of your characters, jot down words that describe the personality of each. It is important to remember that even if you don't specifically write about these personality traits in your story, you will improve your descriptions by thinking about them. The words you use will tend to reflect the personalities you have given the characters.

Worksheets

Answers to Worksheet IV-4A:

1. looks	6. name	11. looks
2. name	7. name	12. looks
3. personality	8. personality	13. personality
4. personality/skill	9. looks	14. name
5. looks	10. personality/skill	15. looks

Answers to Worksheet IV-4B:

Students' answers will vary. Here are examples.

1. Spike was the meanest dog on the block. He was as black as coal.

2. My Aunt Lydia is a sweet lady. She is always ready to give someone a fresh cookie when they visit.

3. Tony had bright red hair. He was sometimes given the nickname "Carrot Top" but he liked to be called that. He actually liked to eat carrots.

4. Once there was a huge grey elephant named Tiny. The elephant had huge ears that

flapped. He had wrinkly skin and big toenails.

5. George was the tallest boy in the class. He was an excellent basketball player. Everyone wanted him on their team because he was a good player.

6. Jenny and Benny were twins who looked exactly alike. They both had black hair and blue eyes. They both were tall and thin. But they were different because Jenny was outgoing and Benny was very shy.

Follow-up Activities

1. **Character Development:** Have students select a favorite character from a book that they have read. Have students copy or draw a picture of the character and then practice describing (verbally and in writing) the traits that describe that character.

2. **Describing Me:** Students can also practice character development by applying these techniques to themselves or to each other (being careful not to hurt others' feelings or to be cruel in any way about others' physical appearance). Emphasize the positive!

Name _____ Date _____

IV-4A. Name, Looks, or Personality/Skills?

Read each sentence and decide how it helps to develop the character's personality for a reader. Does the detail tell about the character's name, how the character looks, or describe the personality/skills?

1. The little puppy was covered with tiny black dots. _____

2. Once upon a time there were twins named Kameel and Tanya. _____

3. The teacher was the nicest anyone in the school had ever known. _____

4. Albert was the smartest boy in the class. _____

5. Sarah's horse was a huge black mare with a star and four white socks. _____

6. The green space alien was called Stargazer-451. _____

7. Amos was named after his great-grandfather. _____

8. The dog bared his sharp teeth and growled at us as we walked by. _____

9. Karla had long red hair that she always wore in a braid. _____

10. No one else could run faster or jump higher than Sammy. _____

11. The little boy's face was dotted with orange freckles. _____

12. Johnny's father is tall and handsome. _____

13. Grandma was the sweetest, kindest lady on the block. _____

14. We named our new bunny Hopper. _____

15. Hopper likes to wiggle his little pink nose back and forth. _____

IV-4B. Developing a Character

Practice writing several sentences that develop these characters. Add details that name or tell more about the physical looks and personality/skills of each.

1. a black dog named Spike (*add personality*) _____

_____

_____

_____

2. a sweet aunt (*add name*) _____

_____

_____

3. a red-haired boy (*add name and personality*) _____

_____

_____

4. a friendly elephant (*add looks and name*) _____

_____

_____

5. George (*add looks and personality*) _____

_____

_____

6. twins named Jenny and Benny (*add looks and personality*) _____

_____

_____

Lesson IV-5: A Checklist for Writing a Short Story

(Writing a Story)

To the Teacher

A lot of preparation time can be spent in thinking about a good plot, creating interesting characters, and so on; but at some point, the story actually has to be written! The purpose of this lesson is to provide suggestions for students to help them start, work on, complete, revise, publish, and celebrate their story.

To the Student

Let's say you have decided on the plot for your short story: You are going to write a mystery about a missing book in a classroom that finally turns up in a new boy's desk. Everyone accuses the boy of stealing until someone else confesses and everyone becomes friends and learns about forgiveness. Let's say you have selected some interesting characters and chosen the classroom for your setting, and now you are ready to go! Ready to write! Right?

Well, sometimes it's really difficult to "get going," even if you have your ideas in place and have your story organized on a web or a plot outline. It helps if you have a really good introduction or beginning sentence. This will get the reader interested, and if you are excited about your story, it will help you get started and know how to proceed.

Let's take a look at a checklist that you can follow to help you get going on your story. It combines the characters, setting, and plot outline, but adds other details that will help your story take off.

Worksheet

Worksheet IV-5 is a checklist students can use to help them write a short story.

IV-5. Checklist for Writing a Short Story

☑ Have your basic plot (with beginning, middle, and ending) clear in your mind. Know your characters (What are they like? What do they look and act like?). Select your setting.

☑ Start your story with a good sentence that will get the reader interested. For example:

> *No one thought anything out of the ordinary was going to happen on this boring June day.*
>
> *Martha usually had great ideas, but this one was the best!*
>
> *If you go into the blue house on the corner, you will never be the same again.*

Fred and Tom were good friends who did a lot of things together, but most of them ended with the boys in trouble.

☑ Use the beginning of your story to identify the characters, let the reader know the setting, and get the reader interested in the plot.

☑ The middle part of your story should keep the plot moving. Don't drag out the events too long. Somewhere in the middle you should have the "high point" or most important, exciting part of the story. This should leave the reader very interested or "breathless" for a moment. What will happen? What will they do?

☑ Remember to use separate paragraphs for dialogue between characters.

☑ As you come to the ending of your story, tie up the "loose ends." Make sure the reader knows how the plot ends (answer all of those questions from the middle) and what you have done with the characters.

☑ The very last line of your story should wrap up the whole story by powerfully telling us how things ended. You might get an idea of how to end your story by going back to your first line. For example:

> *The boring June day turned out to be a day no one in town will ever forget.*
>
> *Once again, Martha had done it!*
>
> *We are all thankful for that little blue house on the corner.*
>
> *Fred and Tom will never learn their lesson about staying out of trouble.*

☑ Consider your first effort a **rough draft**. Don't be afraid to make changes on this copy. Don't forget to add pictures or sketches if you want!

☑ Now it is time to **publish** your story so that others can read it. Think about how you can make your final copy something that others can read and enjoy. Are you going to handwrite it? Are you going to type it or use a word processor? Don't forget to add a cover—probably with an illustration to go with it.

☑ You're finished! Now it is time to **celebrate** your work. You can do this in lots of different ways. Maybe your entire class will have a party with people reading the stories out loud to small groups. Maybe you can have a story exchange, where you trade books with another person. Your class can have a book display where others can come and see what kind of stories you have written. A class library is a nice idea for storing those finished books. Be creative and be happy that you have completed a thoughtful project!

Lesson IV-6: Writing a Book Report

(Writing for School Projects)

To the Teacher

A common school project is writing a book report, which can take many forms. The purpose of this lesson is to provide students with a typical format for a written book report and then to provide practice in completing the requirements.

To the Student

One of the most common written assignments you will have at school is that of a written book report. The advantages of a written report over an oral or display or other creative form include (1) many people can read your report at different times (and some may be further interested enough to read the book), (2) it provides a structured presentation style (so that all book reports follow the same pattern), and (3) it allows for a long-term written record of which books were read and what you, the evaluator, thought of each.

There are many types of formats for writing a book report, but most of them will have certain common characteristics. What do you think should be included in a book report? (author, title, evaluator's opinion, etc.)

The worksheet gives one possible format for completing a book report. Let's take a look at it.

Worksheet

Worksheet IV-6 shows a sample book report form.

Follow-up Activities

1. Obviously, this can be a very long book report if students answer each of the ten questions with a sentence or two. Depending on the grade level and writing ability of the students, you may have students answer only a few of the questions or have them select three or four that they would like to answer.

2. If students read the same book (either as a class or in small groups), they can break up the questions among themselves and turn in a complete report together.

   An alternative is to have the entire class read the same book and then answer the questions in small groups. Compare and discuss the responses to the questions.

Name _____ Date _____

IV-6. Sample Book Report Form

Part I: Basic Information

Title of the Book: _____

_____

_____

Author:_____

Illustrator (if included): _____

Type of book: (fiction/nonfiction): _____

Category (mystery, short story, sports, jokes, historical fiction, humor, etc.):

_____

Number of Pages: _____

Part II: Character, Setting, and Plot Information

Answer the questions using complete sentences.

  1. Who were the major characters?_____

  _____

  _____

  2. What was the setting?_____

  _____

  _____

  3. What was the basic plot? (Do NOT give away the ending!) _____

  _____

  _____

  _____

  _____

  _____

  _____

Name _____ Date _____

IV-6. Sample Book Report Form (continued)

Part III: Reviewer's Opinion

Answer these questions using complete sentences. You do NOT have to write paragraphs.

1. Who was your favorite character and why? _____

_____

_____

_____

2. Were there any characters you did not like? Why? _____

_____

_____

3. Was there a character that you wish you knew more about? What would you like to know?

_____

_____

_____

4. What was the most exciting part of the book? _____

_____

_____

_____

5. What was your favorite part of the book? _____

_____

_____

_____

_____

IV-6. Sample Book Report Form (continued)

6. Did you like how the author ended the story? Why? _____

_____

_____

_____

_____

7. Would you recommend this book to your friends? Why or why not? _____

_____

_____

_____

8. Who (what kind of people) would like to read this book? _____

_____

_____

9. What, if anything, surprised you about the story? _____

_____

_____

_____

10. Would you like to read other books by this author? Why or why not? _____

_____

_____

_____

Lesson IV-7: Writing an Essay Response
(Writing for School Projects)

To the Teacher

A common school activity, especially for the upper elementary grades, is that of responding to an essay question. This is particularly common in subjects such as Social Studies, Science, and perhaps Reading/Literature in which material is taught and then a thoughtful synopsis of the material is required. The purpose of this lesson is to provide practice for the student in following a step-by-step procedure for answering an essay question.

To the Student

In some subjects, particularly social studies or science, you may run into essay questions at the end of a chapter or perhaps on a test. These questions might ask you to summarize key points of something you have read. When you answer an essay question, more than a very short "yes" or "no" is required. A good response shows that you understand the question, have thoughtfully considered your answer, and are able to put that answer in clear writing.

Here are some steps that will help you answer an essay question. For an example, let's say you have been doing some reading about pioneers. In your reading, you have learned that the pioneers were very self-sufficient by taking care of their food and clothing needs. You learned about some specific ways the pioneers took care of themselves.

Your essay question is:

What are some ways that early pioneer families took care of their needs?

1. First, show that you understand the question by turning it into a simple statement. For example:

   Early pioneer families had to take care of their own basic needs.

2. Next, provide details or examples that support your statement. For example:

   Pioneer families took care of their food needs by growing their own vegetables. They also learned ways to preserve food by drying meat or keeping it in a smokehouse. They were also able to hunt nearby animals for food. They took care of clothing in the same way. They would use skins or fur of animals to keep warm. They also made cloth from wool or cotton.

3. Last, summarize your answer very simply. For example:

   The pioneers were very resourceful in taking care of themselves.

The most important thing, of course, is to make sure you KNOW the answer to the question. You can't really write a good response if you don't know the answer.

Worksheets

Answers to Worksheet IV-7A:

Students' answers will vary.

Answers to Worksheet IV-7B:

Students' answers will vary.

Follow-up Activities

1. **Advance Preparation:** Before you teach or discuss a particular topic, write a possible essay question that will be a good summary of the material. Then, as you teach the material, call attention specifically to details that would be good support for an essay

response. You may even have students highlight specific phrases or details that would be helpful to them. The idea is to thoroughly prepare students for the task of writing a clear essay response.

2. **Oral Preparation:** Before a good response can be written, the students must completely understand the question and their answers. Have students practice saying their answers before they write them. They might practice with a partner, rehearsing what they want to write.

Name _____ Date _____

IV-7A. Writing an Essay Response

Below is a short report on home safety. Read the report and then use the information to write a good essay response on a separate sheet of paper.

Home Safety

Did you know that about half of all accidental injuries occur in the home? There are many needless accidents that occur simply because of carelessness. If people were more careful, these accidents and even deaths could be prevented.

One cause of accidents is due to falls. People can slip on loose rugs, waxed floors, or even ice in the front yard. When you don't pick up objects on the floor, this is another possible cause of a fall. Bathrooms are particularly dangerous areas, especially when getting out of the tub or shower. Simply turning on a light in a dark hallway is one easy way to prevent a fall.

Burns are another cause of accidents. Hot or burning objects include pans on the stove, cigarettes, logs in a fireplace, or lanterns. Again, there are simple ways to prevent these burns from occurring. Turn the handle on a hot pan towards the back of the stove, not the front. Make sure the fireplace has a safety grate in front of it.

Another safety problem involves poisoning. Young children can get into unlocked medicine cabinets and possibly eat pills or medicine that can be harmful. Look in your garage. Do you see cleansers, paints, or plant sprays there? These are all potential dangers. It's a good idea to have a first-aid kit handy in case of accidental poisoning.

Answer one or more of the following essay questions:

1. What are some possible home safety problems?

2. What are some ways to protect yourself and your family from home dangers?

3. How can someone prepare for home accidents?

Name _____ Date _____

IV-7B. More Practice in Writing Essay Responses

Here is another example of a short report with essay questions. Use another sheet of paper for your answer.

The Skeleton

All animals with a backbone, and that includes people, have a skeletal system. That means you have a skeleton inside of you. This is a collection of bones that serves many purposes. Your skeleton gives you a shape by supporting the rest of your body, allows you to move, and protects your vital organs such as your heart.

There are over 200 bones in the human body. There are sixty-four bones just in your hands and arms! Bones provide calcium and sodium to the blood. They also hold protein and contain bone marrow, which helps form your blood.

Have you ever broken a bone? You probably went to a doctor who took X-rays of the broken bone. You may have been able to see a crack (called a fracture) on the X-ray. The doctor may have put you to sleep while he or she reset the bone and put a cast on your arm or leg. In about six weeks, the bone heals and is as strong as ever.

Answer one or more of the following essay questions:

1. What purposes does the skeleton serve?
2. How are bones important to the human body?
3. What happens when a bone is broken?

Lesson IV-8: Keeping a Journal (Writing for School Projects)

To the Teacher

Keeping a journal can be a wonderful writing activity, especially if students are having "fun" responding to creative, thought-provoking questions or statements. There are many sources available that contain lots of possible stimulating questions to which students can respond even on a daily basis. The purpose of this lesson is to provide students with some possible journal topics and response ideas.

To the Student

Keeping a journal can be a lot of fun. It can serve as a way to collect your thoughts, informally write down things you are thinking about, and even just have fun playing with words. If you keep a journal on a daily basis, it is also very interesting to go back to the beginning from time to time to see how you felt about something several weeks ago.

A journal can be like a dairy—in which case you might decide it is personal and no one else should read it without permission. But a journal can also be something that is open for everyone to read. You need to decide which type of journal you would like to keep.

The really good thing about a journal is that there are no specific rules—unless specified by your teacher. Perhaps you have to write at least three to five sentences each day. Maybe you need to also keep track of the day, the weather, and specific class activities. You might enjoy reacting to a "Question of the Day." This is your opportunity to respond in your own unique way!

Worksheets

Answers to Worksheet IV-8A:

Students' journal entries will vary.

Answers to Worksheet IV-8B:

Students' journal entries will vary.

Follow-up Activity

Obviously, having students start and maintain a journal is an excellent way for them to do some informal daily writing. You might think about your requirements for the journal—providing some sort of structure (even though it can be creative) will help students know how to organize this activity.

- Do you want students to write a certain number of sentences?
- Is the journal private or public?
- Do you want students to exchange journals and comment on each others' responses?
- Can they add drawings, doodles, and other items to their entries?
- Are you interested in their spelling or can they write mainly for content?

There are many resources available for generating writing ideas, but you will probably have success and greater interest by having students contribute to their own thought-provoking (or even funny) questions.

Name _____ Date _____

IV-8A. Sample "Questions of the Day"

Respond to a different question each day. Share your
answers with classmates to see how different people
responded to the same question.

1. What would you do if you were invisible for a day?

2. Who would you rather change places with: your
   father or your mother?

3. What is your favorite animal and why?

4. What is the most surprising thing about you?

5. How do you make your favorite dessert?

6. When was the last time you got in trouble? What were the consequences?

7. What always makes you laugh?

8. What is something you feel very strongly about?

9. Do you wish the weather would always be cold or always be hot?

10. Who would you like with you on a desert island if you knew it would only be for a day?
    What about for a year?

11. What are three things you can't live without?

12. What would your teacher say about the condition of your bedroom?

13. If you could rename yourself, what name would you choose?

14. What is your favorite sport?

15. How does the color *red* make you feel like?

16. Who is better at sports—boys or girls?

17. If you could only speak 20 words a day, what would you say today?

18. What is the scariest movie you have ever seen?

19. Would you like to be President of the United States?

20. What are 15 things that start with the letter "A"?

21. If people had three eyes, where would the third eye be?

22. What would you like to be doing 10 years from now? What about 20 years from now?

23. What is one school rule you'd like to add for your school?

24. If there was a fire in your house, what three things would you grab first?

25. What famous person do you think you look like?

26. What's the best joke you heard this year?

Name _____ Date _____

IV-8B. Sample Journal Entries

Here are some sample entries from students' journals. The only requirements were to write between 3 and 5 sentences for each. Discuss which entries you like the best and tell why. Is there a right/wrong answer? How would *you* answer the question?

If you had $100, what would you do with it?

(Sarah) If I had $100, I would put it in the bank and get interest on it. I think that saving money is really important. I wouldn't put it under my mattress, because my little brother would probably snoop around and find it and take it.

(Ellen) If I had $100, I would spend it as fast as I could. I'd buy some new clothes, a lot of candy, and I'd buy my mom a manicure. Maybe I would save a dollar, but probably not.

(Tom) $100 is not a lot of money. I couldn't buy anything good with it, like a bike or a four-wheeler. I'd probably just give it to my mom to keep for me.

(Rick) I would give $100 to the poor people so they could have something to eat. I would get the money in $5 bills so a lot of people could have some of my money. It's good to help people.

_____

_____

_____

_____

_____

_____

_____

Lesson IV-9: Writing a Letter (Writing for School Projects)

To the Teacher

At some point in every student's school writing career, he or she will be faced with the task of writing a friendly letter. The purpose of this lesson is to introduce students to the basic parts of a letter (heading, greeting, body, closing, signature), have them recognize the parts, and write a letter. For the sake of simplicity, students will use a simple block style of organizing the letter.

To the Student

What's the best thing you could possibly find in your mailbox? (Allow time for responses—probably some involve getting money in the mail or winning something.) Most people enjoy getting a letter from someone. Although more and more people are using computers to communicate with each other, it is still important and useful to know how to write a letter.

There are several parts to a letter:

1. **Heading:** The heading of a letter includes three lines: Your street address should be on the first line, your city and state (separated by a comma) should be on the second line with the ZIP Code, and the third line is the date. Write out or abbreviate the month, then the number of the day, then a comma, and then the year. Start writing the heading on the left side of your paper. For example:

   151 Valley Road

   La Porte, IN 46350

   June 7, 2001

2. **Greeting:** This part of the letter is where you greet the person to whom you are writing. Most often you will simply write: "Dear _____(Somebody)," but there are other possibilities ("Hello, Grandmother," or "Greetings, Friend").

3. **Body:** The body is the part of your letter where you give your message to the reader. You will probably have several paragraphs. The first one might ask how the person is, what he or she has been doing, and so on. The other paragraphs might contain information about what you are doing, the purpose of your letter, and ask some questions so the person has a reason to write back.

4. **Closing:** This is a short phrase, such as, "Yours truly," "Love," or "Sincerely," that indicates you are just about ready to end your letter. Follow the short phrase with a comma.

5. **Signature:** This is where you sign your name. Leave about four lines between the closing and the signature. If you are using a word processor or typewriter, you should type your name, but then actually get a pen and write your name above it.

These are the main parts of a basic letter. When you are writing a friendly letter, it is sometimes fun to add a "**P.S.**" to the letter. This might be a quick closing thought, usually something not too serious, that comes at the very end of your letter. It is not necessary, but it is fun and informal to include when you write a letter to a good friend.

Worksheets

Answers to Worksheet IV-9A:

1. closing   2. body   3. heading   4. greeting   5. signature

Answers to Worksheet IV-9B:

Students' letters will vary.

Answers to Worksheet IV-9C:

Students' letters will vary.

Follow-up Activity

Pen Pals!: Form a connection with another school, possibly in another state or even in another country. This is a wonderful opportunity for students to get to know people who are similar in some ways to them, who may share interests and ideas, but may differ in geographical locality and other ways. This also provides a very "natural" purpose for students to write letters back and forth.

IV-9A. Identifying the Parts of a Letter

Below are the parts of a friendly letter that Susan wrote to her friend Denise. The parts are all mixed up. Can you identify the heading? greeting? body? closing? signature?

1. _____

   Your friend,

2. _____

   How are you doing? Do you think you will be able to go to camp with me this summer? I sure hope you can go. We had so much fun last year. Remember the hike we took in the woods and how funny it was when we discovered we were picking poison ivy?

3. _____

   598 N. Main Street
   Elko, NV 89801
   March 22, 2001

4. _____

   Dear Denise,

5. _____

   Susan

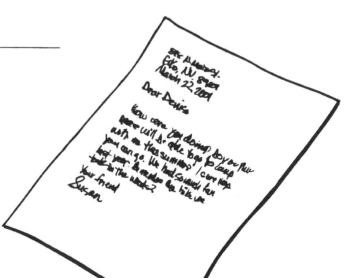

Name _____ Date _____

IV-9B. Writing a Friendly Letter

Here are the instructions for writing a letter to a friend. Follow the prompts to write a basic friendly letter on another sheet of paper.

1. **Heading:** Write your street address on the first line; your city, state, and ZIP Code on the second line; and today's date on the third line.

2. **Greeting:** You are really good friends with this person, so use a simple "Dear" greeting and add his or her name. Don't forget the comma at the end.

3. **Body:** Write two paragraphs. In the first paragraph, ask your friend some questions. You might want to ask about what he or she is doing, how school is going, or if he or she has seen a movie that you like. In the second paragraph, tell your friend what you are doing.

4. **Closing:** Choose a closing that you feel comfortable with. Girls might like to use "Love" if it is a close friend. You could even use "Goodbye for now" if you like that one.

5. **Signature:** Leave some space and then write your name at the bottom. You probably don't have to put your last name, because if you are writing to a friend, the friend will know who you are by your address.

6. You can add a P.S. if you have another last-minute thought!

Name _____ Date _____

IV-9C. Writing a Letter

Here are some possibilities for writing a letter to someone. Choose one or more and work on a good basic letter. (Feel free to add your own ideas as well.)

1. Write a letter to a relative, thanking that person for a birthday or holiday gift.

2. Write a letter to your family, asking them to tell you what they would like to do for a summer vacation or project.

3. Write a letter to a favorite celebrity (singer or movie personality), telling him or her what you think of his or her work.

4. Write an imaginary letter to Santa Claus, telling him why you deserve a lot of presents for Christmas.

5. Write a letter to your last year's teacher, reminding him or her of some of the fun things you did in class.

6. Write a letter to a teacher whom you may have *next* year, warning him or her about the upcoming class!

7. Write a letter to the mayor (or other city official) of your town, explaining how people your age feel about their community.

8. Write a letter to your local newspaper editor, telling about some need you have noticed in your town.

9. Write a letter to someone you admire, detailing what it is that you like about him or her.

10. Write a letter to someone who has been kind to you, thanking him or her for the deed of kindness.

11. Write a letter to a neighbor, volunteering to help him or her in some project that might require extra people.

12. Write a letter to someone who is sick or in the hospital, encouraging that person to feel better.

13. Write a letter to your brother or sister, giving some kind of welcome advice.

14. Write a letter to a local business, asking for information about what services or products it is associated with.

15. Write a letter to your school's principal, indicating your ideas for generating more "school spirit."

Lesson IV-10: Writing Definitions (Writing for School Projects)

To the Teacher

In subjects such as Science, Social Studies, and Literature, students come across certain vocabulary words that are important to know. One way that we as teachers hope students will come to understand and use the words is by writing definitions. It is a fairly straightforward task to *copy* definitions; but it is a much more beneficial learning task to have students *paraphrase* definitions in their own words. The purpose of this lesson is to provide practice in simplifying and writing definitions.

To the Student

When you are studying subjects such as Science and Social Studies, you probably have to be familiar with certain terms or vocabulary words. If you see a list of terms, such as at the beginning of a chapter, usually they are listed in bold print and are followed by a definition. What does the definition tell you? (It explains what the term means.) Why do you think it is important to understand the definition? (So that when you see the word in the text, you will know what it means.) After the definition, there may be a brief explanation of how the word is used or what it means in practical life.

You may be keeping a notebook that lists the words you need to know, along with their definitions. Sometimes, however, the definition might be a little lengthy to copy! For example:

> **Fluoride:** *A compound of the chemical element fluorine.* Fluorides help to maintain calcium deposits in hard tissues of the body. The addition of fluorides to water supplies seems to help prevent tooth decay. Fluorides may also play a role in the prevention and treatment of osteoporosis.

The vocabulary word, or term, is in boldface type. The definition follows in italics. After that is a brief description of what the word means in practical life.

Now, it would be easy enough to copy everything above. Do you think it would help you remember the term and the definition? If you are good at memorizing words, this might be a way to help you. But if you are like most people, it's easier to remember something if you understand it well enough to put it into your own words or can associate it with something you are familiar.

Let's go back to fluoride. You probably brush your teeth with toothpaste that has fluoride in it. Maybe you have watched commercials that advertise how great the toothpaste is because it contains fluoride and the children who brush with it faithfully do not get cavities. They don't get cavities because the fluoride contains calcium and that helps the teeth stay hard. It protects them. So, how could you say (and write) that easily? Let's try:

> **Fluoride:** *A substance that contains calcium, which helps make bones hard.*

You might be tempted to write: "**Fluoride:** *Something that helps keep your bones hard,*" and that is OK except watch out for using words like "something." Whenever you can, try to be as specific as you can. Instead of the word "something," you can use the words "a substance." It sounds more precise and is actually more accurate.

Here is some practice in simplifying and writing definitions.

Worksheets

Answers to Worksheet IV-10A:

1. a   2. b   3. c   4. b   5. c

Answers to Worksheet IV-10B:

Students' definitions will vary.

Follow-up Activity

As you assign students the tasks of finding, copying, simplifying, and writing definitions for various subjects, remind them to use words that are meaningful to them. At the same time, their definitions must be accurate. Offer the students lots of practice in writing acceptable definitions for the terms with which they must be familiar.

IV-10A. Simplifying Definitions

Here are some definitions of words associated with the digestive system. Pick a simpler definition from the choices below each and write it on the line. Discuss as a class why you chose the answers you selected.

_____ 1. **digestion:** *the process by which food is broken down physically and chemically so that the nutritional elements it contains can be absorbed*

    a. the body's way of making food ready for the body to use

    b. the way you eat

    c. how the body's organs are lined up inside you

_____ 2. **molars:** *strong, broad-crowned teeth at the back of the mouth that grind food into small particles*

    a. big teeth in the back of your mouth

    b. teeth in the back of your mouth that grind up food

    c. something in your mouth

_____ 3. **saliva:** *a fluid that enters the mouth cavity from three glands and contains an enzyme that converts starch into simple sugars*

    a. spit

    b. something like water in your mouth

    c. special fluid from glands in your mouth that helps break down food

_____ 4. **epiglottis:** *a flap of cartilage and membrane that helps to shut the windpipe while food is swallowed*

    a. something that stops food from going down the wrong tube

    b. a little flap like a trapdoor that stops food from going down the windpipe

    c. a thing that helps you swallow food properly

_____ 5. **esophagus:** *a short length of tube between the lower pharynx (throat) and the stomach, lubricated by mucus*

    a. something that connects two parts of the digestive system

    b. a short tube that floats food down to the stomach

    c. a short tube that connects the throat and the stomach

Name _____ Date _____

IV-10B. Writing Definitions

Simplify these definitions for terms that have to do with the human eye.

1. **eye:** *a spherical organ of the human body that connects with the brain to allow vision*

   _____

   _____

   _____

2. **cornea:** *the bulging, transparent front of the outer layer of the eyeball*

   _____

   _____

   _____

3. **sclera:** *the outer ("white") layer of the eye that is opaque to light*

   _____

   _____

   _____

4. **retina:** *a layered network of nerve cells that line the inside of the back of the eyeball*

   _____

   _____

   _____

5. **pupil:** *a hole surrounded by a muscular diaphragm (the iris) through which light enters*

   _____

   _____

   _____

Lesson IV-11: Writing Spelling Words in Context

(Writing for School Projects)

To the Teacher

How many times have you told students to "Use each of your spelling words in a sentence" as part of the weekly spelling assignment? Students may have written sentences using the spelling word somewhere in the sentence, but whether or not it was a valuable learning experience was doubtful. The purpose of this lesson is to demonstrate sample spelling activities that help students combine using words in context with other writing elements.

To the Student

You are probably familiar with how to use your spelling words in a sentence. If, for example, you have the word "animal," what would be an appropriate sentence for that word?

I have a large animal at my house.

Would you like a new animal?

What's wrong with this sentence:

Tell me how to spell the word animal.

In that sentence, you couldn't tell if the writer knew what the word meant or not. When you want to clearly show the meaning of a word, you have to use the context to show what the word means. One way to test for this is to leave out the key word and see if you can figure it out from the rest of the sentence.

I have a large _____ at my house.

Well, it could be a table. It could be a car. We don't know if it's an animal or not. It's the same with the next sentence:

Would you like a new _____?

It could be a wool coat. It could be a house. Again, we don't really know.

When you carefully use context, it helps the reader know what the word means. Here are some sentences that use context to demonstrate that the word *animal* is the missing word.

I saw a very strange _____ in a cage at the zoo.

We went into the jungle to take a picture of a very unusual _____.

I love dogs, but tell me which is your favorite _____.

All of those sentences are much clearer in helping the reader know that the word is *animal*.

Here are some practice spelling activities that will help you provide a clear context for each word.

Worksheets

Answers to Worksheet IV-11A:

1. a   2. b   3. a   4. b   5. b

Answers to Worksheet IV-11B:

Students' answers will vary.

Answers to Worksheet IV-11C:

Students' sentences will vary.

Follow-up Activities

1. **What's My Word?:** Have students write sentences for spelling words, but leave an actual blank in the sentence where the targeted word should be. Have students make an answer key (on the back or upside-down) and then exchange their papers. Students will be able to provide feedback on the accuracy and clarity of the sentences with blanks. It's not so easy as it seems!

2. **Two in One:** Have students practice writing sentences that contain two spelling words. The words have to be used grammatically correct in the sentences. For example: *read* and *steal*…

 I love to *read* so much, I think I might have to *steal* that book you're reading.

Name _____ Date _____

IV-11A. Writing Clear Sentences for Spelling Words

Here is a sample of words. Which sentence below better uses context for that word? Write your answer on the line.

_____ 1. **Art**

> a. My favorite school subject is art because I love to draw and paint.
>
> b. I love it when we have art.

_____ 2. **Barking**

> a. There is too much barking outside at night.
>
> b. What are the dogs barking at?

_____ 3. **Start**

> a. We were all very nervous at the start of the race.
>
> b. I hope the play will start soon.

_____ 4. **Farmer**

> a. It is a hard job to be a farmer.
>
> b. A farmer must take care of fields, animals, and crops.

_____ 5. **Sparkler**

> a. I like to see the sparkler.
>
> b. We had fun lighting the sparkler with a match and watching it fizz.

Name _____ Date _____

IV-11B. Your Turn

Write a sentence for each spelling word below. Remember to use context so that if you deleted the word, the reader could still figure out what it was.

torn   corner   forward   bored   thorn

1. _____

_____

_____

2. _____

_____

_____

3. _____

_____

_____

4. _____

_____

_____

5. _____

_____

_____

Name _____   Date _____

IV-11C. Context and More!

Are you ready for something new? You are going to write a sentence for each spelling word, but this time each sentence must include something else. Watch for the clues to write your sentences. An example is given.

> **reach** (*include a list*): I am going to *reach* for the shelf with the beans, tomatoes, and corn on it.

1. **beach** (*include a city*): _____

   _____

2. **teacher** (*include a proper name*): _____

   _____

3. **deep** (*include the name of an ocean*): _____

   _____

4. **feather** (*include two color words*): _____

   _____

5. **head** (*include an animal*): _____

   _____

6. **dread** (*include the word **monster***): _____

   _____

7. **health** (*include a quotation*): _____

   _____

8. **sea** (*include adjectives that describe the sea*): _____

   _____

9. **leather** (*include a list*): _____

   _____

10. **read** (*include a compound word*): _____

   _____

Lesson IV-12: Writing a Current Events Summary
(Writing for School Projects)

To the Teacher

Students may be asked to write a summary of a news event as part of a current events unit or ongoing Social Studies assignment. The purpose of this lesson is to provide a format for writing a short summary of a news article.

To the Student

You may be studying current events in some classes. What does this mean? (things that are going on right now) What are some examples of current events? (local news, state news, nationwide happenings, etc.) Why do you think it might be important to know what's going on? (so that you are aware of changes that might affect the individual; also helps to be aware of world events because they will affect the individual's life as well)

You will probably find helpful current events articles in your local newspaper, or even a newspaper that keeps you informed on world events such as *USA Today*. There are also news articles in magazines. Of course, you can get the news by watching television or listening to the radio, but we are going to concentrate on written articles so that you can analyze them and summarize them.

The purpose of summarizing an article is to get to the heart of the article without repeating all the details. Basically, when you write a summary, you should include the following information:

- **Source:** What is the newspaper?
- **Date:** When was this article written?
- **Headline:** This will indicate what the article is about.
- **Information:** Certain questions will most likely be asked or answered in the article. You may not find all of them, but some of them will apply. These are: Who? (What person or group is the article about?) What? (What happened? What is the problem or situation? For what reason did the writer write this article?) Where? (What place is involved?) When? (Is there a certain time that an event will take place or already took place?) How? (How will something be accomplished?) Why? (Why is this a problem or why is this of interest to people?)
- **Response/Opinion:** Why did you select this article? Why was it interesting to you? What comment or reaction do you have to the information in the article?

Worksheets

Answers to Worksheet IV-12A:

Students' summary sheets will vary.

Answers to Worksheet IV-12B:

Students' summary sheets will vary.

Follow-up Activities

1. **Current Events Bulletin Board:** Create an ongoing bulletin board in an area of your classroom. Have students turn in article summaries on a regular basis, and then select and highlight one or two each week. You may choose volunteers who would like to read and then lead a brief discussion of the events that they wrote about. Use the reproducible summary sheet (Worksheet IV-12C) for this activity.

2. **Follow a Story:** In some cases, a current event may be reported by a newspaper over several days or weeks (in contrast to a one-time event). If you have the space, you may designate one wall as a timeline to follow the course of the story over several weeks. (This is a particularly appropriate activity in an election year.)

Name _____ Date _____

IV-12A. Sample Article Summary

Read the news article and complete the summary sheet below.

Source: LaPorte Herald-Argus

Date: July 24, 2000

Headline: _____

_____

Information:

Who? _____

_____

_____

What? _____

_____

_____

Where? _____

_____

When? _____

_____

How? _____

_____

Why? _____

_____

Response/Opinion: _____

_____

_____

_____

3rd Disney park planned in Calif.

ANAHEIM, Calif. (AP)—A third Disney theme park is in the works here.

The still-unnamed park would be built on 89 acres next to 45-year-old Disneyland, on property already controlled by the Walt Disney Col., Cynthia Harriss, president of The Disneyland Resort, said.

The park, scheduled to be completed by 2010, may house water rides based on the movies "The Little Mermaid" or "Winnie the Pooh." It will also have a shopping mall and hotel.

According to the Los Angeles Times, the cost may rival the $1.4 billion spent on Disney's California Adventure, a 55-acre theme park adjacent to Disneyland scheduled to open in February 2001.

IV-12B. More Practice

Here are two additional news articles that provide current event information. Read each and complete the form. (See Worksheet IV-12C.) You may not have information for all of the items, but complete as much as you can. The information is from the newspaper *The LaPorte Herald-Argus* on Monday, July 24, 2000.

Report: Millions of African children will lose at least one parent to AIDS

DURBAN, South Africa (AP)—Nearly 28 million children in Africa will have lost at least one of their parents to AIDS by the year 2010, causing a social nightmare for these countries for decades, according to a report released today.

"The HIV pandemic is producing orphans on a scale unrivaled in history," said Susan Hunter, an author of the "Children on the Brink 2000" report by the U.S. Agency for International Development. A summary was released at the 13th International AIDS Conference.

Currently there are nearly 16 million children who have lost at least one parent to the disease. About 90 percent of these orphans are in sub-Saharan Africa.

By 2010, about one in three children in Namibia, Swaziland, Zimbabwe and South Africa will have lost a parent, most of them to AIDS.

Famine, wars and other disease outbreaks often cause a large increase in orphans, but those are short-term calamities that quickly end, Hunter said. AIDS will continue to create millions of new orphans for decades.

Throughout the developing world, at least 44 million children will have lost at least one parent, 30 million of them to AIDS, according to the report.

The estimates do not include children born with the virus that causes AIDS, since most of them will likely die before they reach age 5.

The orphans will strain the resources of families, communities and governments, said John Williamson, the report's other author.

"AIDS is changing the social landscape in the most affected countries," he said. "It's creating an unprecedented set of child-welfare problems."

Children whose parents become ill often leave school because they are forced to care for them or get a job to support the family, Hunter said.

Vietnam vet represents 1960s on stamp

The world has gotten a lot smaller for a Beaver County, Penn., man since he learned that a 33-year-old image of him jumping off a helicopter in Vietnam has been chosen to represent the war on a U.S. postage stamp.

"People have come up to me and congratulated me. And a woman hugged me in Wal-Mart the other day," said Jim Patton, a 53-year-old general laborer. Patton said he led a rather simple and anonymous life until a few weeks ago, when news about his appearance on the stamp began to spread.

The picture featuring Patton was chosen last year to represent America's involvement in the Vietnam War. The Vietnam War stamp appears on a sheet with several other 33-cent stamps commemorating the 1960s.

His image is immortalized with pictures of Neil Armstrong's footprints on the moon, Martin Luther King Jr., the Barbie doll and New York Yankee Roger Maris hitting his 61st home run.

Beaver Postmaster Charles Nowry said the 1960s collection had suddenly become popular in his post office.

"It's created quite an interest," Nowry said. "I have people specifically asking for the '60s stamps. You hear it from veterans and from everyone else. That picture is getting quite a lot of press."

It seems everyone wants to talk about the stamp that shows Patton, who was getting ready to jump from a helicopter landing skid, and two other members of the U.S. Army's 1st Squadron, 9th Cavalry, 1st Cavalry Division (Airmobile), when they arrived in Chu Lai in the spring of 1967.

Patton had been in Vietnam for less than a week when Sgt. 1st Class Howard C. Breedlove, an Army reporter, snapped the now famous photo.

Name _____ Date _____

IV-12C. Current Events Article Summary

Source: _____

Date: _____

Headline: _____

_____

Information:

Who? _____

_____

What? _____

_____

Where? _____

_____

When? _____

_____

How? _____

_____

Why? _____

_____

Response/Opinion: _____

_____

_____

_____

_____

_____

_____

Lesson IV-13: Writing a Math "Story" Problem and Math Log (Writing for School Projects)

To the Teacher

It is helpful to integrate writing with content area subjects whenever possible. This can be done, even in Math, by having students write story problems and/or maintain a simple math log. The purpose of this lesson is to provide practice for students in writing Math-related activities such as creating math story problems and maintaining a math log.

To the Student

Sometimes your Math lesson is rather straightforward; it consists of performing math operations (such as adding, subtracting, multiplying, and dividing) on numbers that are given to you. But another type of math exercise that you have is sometimes called "story problems" or "word problems." In this type of exercise, you can't just look at the numbers; you have to read the problem to figure out what you are supposed to do. For example, here are some straightforward math problems:

$4 + 7 =$ _____ $8 \times 3 =$ _____ $9 - 5 =$ _____

Here are some story problems:

Guilliame has 3 stamps. Each stamp costs 33 cents. How much does he spend on the stamps? (*You have to multiply the number of stamps times the cost of each stamp.*)

Amanda has $1.00. She wants to buy a candy bar for 45 cents. How much will she have left? (*Subtract 45 cents from $1.00.*)

It can be fun to write a story problem. You can create your own characters, even give them personalities, and proceed to set up a math problem for someone else to solve.

Steps involved to help you write a good math story problem include:

1. Decide on your math operation (e.g., adding, subtracting, multiplying, dividing).

2. Write out the exact math problem that you want someone to solve (e.g., $74 + 59 = 133$) and make sure your answer is correct!

3. Create a situation (with characters) that fits the numbers.

4. Write a short math story that weaves the numbers into the story.

Example:

1. multiplication

2. $5 \times 7 = 35$

3. Five children, each has 7 cookies, they want to combine their cookies into one big batch

4. Grandma Smith has 5 grandchildren. She wants each of them to bring a different kind of cookie to her 80th birthday party. Each child brings 7 cookies to the party. They put them all into a big tub. How many cookies are in the big tub for her party?

Worksheets

Answers to Worksheet IV-13A:

Students' math stories will vary.

Answers to Worksheet IV-13B:

Students' math logs will vary.

Follow-up Activities

1. **Expanded Story Problems:** Depending on the math ability of your students, math story problems can be expanded to include virtually any type of operation. They can become quite complex as the characters buy new things (addition), lose them (subtraction), double the price (multiplication), have a party and divide their toys (division), and even calculate the cost (money). Be sure students write out the operations and the answer before writing the story.

2. **More Math Trivia:** Students may include math or number trivia as part of their math journals. Students might find interesting numbers that can be incorporated into their logs. For example, what is the population of your state? How many quarters would it take (stacked on top of each other) to make a pile one inch high? How much money would that be?

IV-13A. Examples of Math Story Problems

Here are some hints to help you write an interesting math story problem. Use the clues to finish each problem.

1. **Arguing over Candy**

   Decide on your math operation: division

   Write out the problem and solution: 40 divided by 8 = 5

   Create a situation: There are 40 pieces of candy in a bag and 8 hungry children

   Write the story:

   _____

   _____

   _____

   _____

2. **Collecting Stuffed Teddy Bears**

   Decide on your math operation: addition

   Write out the problem and solution: 11 + 7 + 4 = 22

   Create a situation: A girl collects stuffed Teddy bears and gets them from three relatives for her birthday

   Write the story:

   _____

   _____

   _____

   _____

3. **Losing My Marbles**

   Decide on your math operation: subtraction

   Write out the problem and solution: 23 − 14 = 9

   Create a situation: Joe has a bag full of marbles and doesn't notice a little hole. The marbles drop out of the hole.

   Write the story:

   _____

   _____

   _____

   _____

Name _____ Date _____

IV-13B. Keeping a Math Log

A math log can consist of virtually anything that is applicable to your understanding of math. Below is a sample list of items that could be maintained in a math journal. Your teacher will let you know if you should maintain a daily or weekly log.

Vocabulary words: Define boldfaced terms that are introduced and used in chapters from a math book (e.g., fraction, numerator, denominator, equivalent).

Ideas: Write the key ideas about a math lesson (e.g., fractions are simply cutting things into pieces; equivalent fractions mean both fractions are the same).

Pictures: Make illustrations, drawings, or sketches to help remember key ideas (e.g., a pizza can represent fractional parts; a spilled water bucket can represent subtraction).

Sample test items: Write an example of a problem that would likely be on a test. Continue to review these items.

Specific problems: If there were a certain problem or concept that was difficult, put *** by it and continue to work through and study this type of math problem, especially when reviewing for a test.

Daily grades, test grades: Keep a running record of assignments completed, scores, and anything that is graded. This will help indicate which type of items are mastered and which may need more work.

Math jokes, riddles, puzzles: Include your favorites! It might be fun to have a puzzle of the week.

Attitude: Some students find math particularly challenging—in a negative way! Occasionally write positive math statements about what you are doing in math and how you feel about your learning.

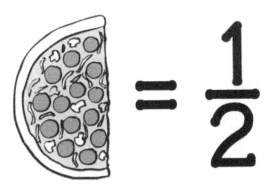

Lesson IV-14: Writing an Interview (Writing for School Projects)

To the Teacher

At some point, students may be required to interview someone as a source of information for a report or presentation. Rather than ramble through a discussion that may provide interesting, but irrelevant, information, students who are well-prepared with focused questions can conduct an interview that will result in needed information without wasting a lot of time. The purpose of this lesson is to provide guidelines for a student to conduct and write an interview.

To the Student

If you wanted to find out what the Vietnam War was like, what might you do? (check old newspapers, read a book, talk to someone) Do you know of any people who might have been involved in that conflict? Who? (students may name parents, relatives, etc.) Why would talking to someone who had been directly involved be a good source of information? (that person would have first-hand knowledge or experience and could provide insights because of his/her connection)

One way to get information from someone is to conduct an interview. How do you think this is different from just sitting down and talking to someone? (more focused, the interviewer would ask questions)

What kinds of questions do you think you would ask someone if you were interested in learning about his/her war experiences? (where he/she served, some events that happened, what he/she felt like) Are there some questions that you should NOT ask? (if he/she went crazy, if he/she hurt anyone or enjoyed hurting someone, etc.) These are inappropriate, very personal, and not relevant to the topic.

Today you are going to work on interviewing skills and then practice writing your information so that it is useful to you.

Worksheets

Answers to Worksheet IV-14A:

1. a. yes	b. yes	c. no	d. yes	e. no
2. a. no	b. yes	c. no	d. yes	e. no
3. a. yes	b. yes	c. no	d. yes	e. no

Answers to Worksheet IV-14B:

Students' questions will vary.

Answers to Worksheet IV-14C:

Students' answers will vary.

Answers to Worksheet IV-14D:

Students' answers will vary.

Follow-up Activity

Have students practice "mock" interviews by practicing with each other. The purpose is to help students prepare questions and record responses quickly to keep the interview moving smoothly. When students interview each other, they might include 5–10 questions, such as:

- How long have you lived in this city/attended this school?
- Have you ever lived anywhere else?

- What do you like about this school?
- What are some things you like to do after school?
- How many people are in your family?
- Do you have any pets?
- What are your hobbies?
- What is your favorite subject at school?
- Do you have a favorite book? Why?
- Have you traveled to any other states?

Name _____ Date _____

IV-14A. Appropriate Questions

Pretend you are interviewing people to get information on certain topics. Select which questions would be relevant and appropriate to your search, and write "yes" on the line. Write "no" for the ones that are off the subject or not appropriate to ask.

1. Interviewing Mrs. Kim about how to cater a meal for a wedding party

    a. How do you know how much food to order? _____

    b. How much might it cost to serve a meal to 100 people? _____

    c. Have you ever given anyone food poisoning? _____

    d. How did you get started in the catering business? _____

    e. Do you sometimes forget to wash your hands before you serve the food? _____

2. Interviewing Dr. Sharma about cosmetic surgery

    a. How much does a nose job cost? _____

    b. How much training do you have to have to do surgery? _____

    c. Have you ever done surgery on anyone we know? _____

    d. What types of cosmetic surgery do you do? _____

    e. Do you ever faint during surgery because of the blood? _____

3. Interviewing Sally Greenbaum about her experience working in an orphanage in Haiti

    a. How do the children get assigned to the orphanage? _____

    b. How does working with the children make you feel? _____

    c. Could you give me copies of the children's photos for my report? _____

    d. Are there any especially happy experiences that you could tell me about? _____

    e. Did you get airsick on the flight to Haiti? _____

Name _____ Date _____

IV-14B. Thinking About Your Interview

Write five appropriate and relevant questions for the following interviews. Then decide on a person who would be most helpful to interview. (It need not be a specific person; choose a likely "type" or person in an appropriate career or situation.)

Interview One: You are doing a report on making TV commercials.

Someone to interview: _____
Questions:

1. _____

_____

2. _____

_____

3. _____

_____

4. _____

_____

5. _____

_____

Interview Two: You are doing a report on travel to Japan.

Someone to interview: _____
Questions:

1. _____

_____

2. _____

_____

3. _____

_____

4. _____

_____

5. _____

_____

IV-14B. Thinking About Your Interview (continued)

Interview Three: You are interested in clothing and fashion from the 1970s.

Someone to interview: _____

Questions:

1. _____
_____

2. _____
_____

3. _____
_____

4. _____
_____

5. _____
_____

Name _____ Date _____

IV-14C. Your Interview

Select a topic you would be interested in learning more about. Then follow the steps to set up your interview.

1. What is a topic you would be interested in learning more about?

   _____

2. What type of person or career would be helpful to learn about this?

   _____

3. Who is a person involved in this topic who would be able to give you information?

   _____

4. List several questions you would like to ask this person:

   _____

   _____

   _____

   _____

5. Make contact with this person to set up a meeting. Include the time and place. Let the person know about how much time you will need to conduct the interview.

   Date: _____   Time: _____

6. While you are interviewing the person, have your questions ready and JOT DOWN the person's answers. Do not copy what he/she says word for word, as this will take a long time. You may want to tape record your interview (with the person's permission) and write the responses later.

Interview notes: _____

_____

_____

_____

_____

_____

Name _____ Date _____

IV-14D. Writing the Interview

After you have compiled your information, you are ready to write your interview. Use the following format to share your information in writing.

My topic was: _____

I interviewed _____

on _____

I asked _____ (give number) questions about my topic. I wanted to know:

_____

_____

_____

_____

I found out: _____

_____

_____

_____

_____

After doing this interview, I learned: _____

_____

_____

_____

_____

_____

_____

_____

Lesson IV-15: Taking Class Notes (Writing for School Projects)

To the Teacher

When you are conducting a lesson, it would be wonderful to think all your students are listening to your every word; jotting down the main ideas and key details in neat, concise handwriting; and organizing their notes in such a fashion that they can easily find them at a moment's notice. It would be wonderful, but highly unlikely! The purpose of this lesson is to provide exercises for students in taking class notes that will be retrievable and useful.

To the Student

Sometimes when you are in class, your teacher might say something like, "This is really important; be sure to remember this," or "Pay close attention to the list on page 37 of your book." These are hints that you need to especially remember those points. Because not everyone has an excellent memory, it is good to be able to take notes.

Taking notes does not mean you write down every single word your teacher says or copy every paragraph out of the book. Why rewrite everything that is already written? When you take notes, you should be writing down the *most important* details or points that are covered. Then when you study your notes, you can spend the time on this condensed version of the material.

For example, let's say you are listening to your teacher talk about the Pony Express. What notes would you take on the following?

"I am going to tell you some things about the Pony Express, which was a mail delivery service back in the 1860s. I would like you to remember a little bit about how the system worked, where the mail went to and from, and why it ended.

"The Pony Express was a mail service for the Old West. It started in 1860, and the purpose was to carry mail on horseback across the plains from St. Joseph, Missouri, to Sacramento, California. The people who started this service wanted to prove that this could get the mail delivered faster than the system of using stagecoaches. The riders changed horses every 50 miles, stopping at relay stations to hop on new, fresh horses. Then they rode at top speed from one station to the next. At the new station, the next horse was saddled and ready to go. The rider would jump from his horse, grab the mail bag, and was on his way within two minutes.

"At first it took riders about ten days to make the trip from Missouri to California. Later trips were made in eight or nine days. The riders carried guns and a knife to protect themselves from attacks by the Indians or bandits. They rode day and night, in good weather and bad.

"The Pony Express ended in 1861, after only a year and a half of operation. The reason? The telegraph! Telegraph service was now available, coast to coast, so important information could be sent along the wire."

Complete these notes:

1. The Pony Express was a _____ service. (*mail*)

2. It started in _____ and ended in _____. (*1860, 1861*)

3. The mail went from _____ to _____. (*station, station* OR *Missouri to California*)

4. The riders changed horses every _____ miles, stopping at _____. (*50 miles, relay stations*)

5. It took about _____ days to make the trip. (*10*)

6. To protect themselves, the riders carried _____. (*guns and knives*)

7. The Pony Express ended after only _____ years in operation. (*1-1/2*)

8. The main reason it was no longer needed was because of the _____. (*telegraph*)

Worksheets

Answers to Worksheet IV-15A:

1. Robert Peary 2. North Pole 3. third 4. weather, lack of supplies 5. 5

Answers to Worksheet IV-15B:

Students' notes will vary.

Follow-up Activity

Prompted Notes: Pass out an incomplete outline to students as you give specific lessons. As you go over your notes for the lesson, give strong hints to students to record phrases or words that complete the outline. You can leave out a word or two or make a short list (if you are going to be giving several examples). In this way, students can follow along with where you are in the lesson and hopefully will listen more carefully to find the key words that go in the blanks. Using prompted notes can help students focus on what are the main ideas and begin to jot down words instead of trying to write complete sentences.

It is very important to let students know ahead of time what details they will be expected to commit to memory or to take notes on. You can tell them ahead of time or use a partially completed outline. At times, it is helpful to give examples to elaborate on a point, but make sure students know you are giving "extra" information to help them learn, not that you expect them to remember every detail from the example.

IV-15A. Listening and Note Taking (prompted)

Here is a short lesson to read/listen to. Try to remember the important points.

"An important explorer in American history is Admiral Robert E. Peary. I would like you to remember what he is best known for and be able to tell a little about the hardships he and his men faced on their trips.

"Robert E. Peary was born in 1856 and died in 1920. He was an explorer of the Arctic region, and became famous for his discovery of the North Pole.

"Peary was interested in exploring the artic regions of the Earth. He had already been in charge of expeditions to northern Greenland and became familiar with polar regions. His goal was to get to the North Pole.

"His first expedition for that purpose, starting in 1897, took four years, but he did not succeed. He set out again in 1905, but hardships forced him and his crew to turn back about 200 miles from the pole. He wrote books that told about their adventures. Perhaps you can imagine what it would be like to be in an area where the temperatures can fall to 90 degrees below zero in the winter. Finally, in 1908, he set out again. It was a difficult trip and his crew members, one by one, turned back as they ran out of supplies. When he finally reached the pole, only four Eskimos and his black servant, Matthew Henson, were with him."

Notes:

1. An important American explorer was _____.

2. He is best known for his discovery of the _____.

3. He got to this area on the _____ attempt.

4. Some of the hardships were _____ and

    _____.

5. When he finally reached his goal, there were _____ other people with him.

Name _____ Date _____

IV-15B. Listening and Note Taking (without Prompts)

Here is a lesson on bees. Take notes at the bottom to remember these important points: (1) the role of the queen bee, and (2) the other types of bees in the hive and their roles.

"Thousands of bees live together in a single hive. The family of the bees is very well organized. Each type of bee has a specific purpose.

"There is only one queen bee in each family. This bee is the largest and lays hundreds of eggs.

"The father bees are called drones. They don't do any work. After the baby bees are hatched, the drones are killed because there is not enough food for everyone.

"The other bees in the hive are called the workers. They guard the queen bee and care for the babies. They also gather food for the whole hive. They store the food for the winter in the honeycomb."

Now take notes to record the key points:

_____

_____

_____

_____

_____

_____

_____

_____

_____

_____

_____

Lesson IV-16: Completing an Assignment Sheet

(Writing for School Projects)

To the Teacher

There are many classroom and schoolwide systems in use for helping students to record and monitor their many assignments. The record-keeping form is important, but students must be able to notate their assignments on that form in order to keep track of what the assignment is and whether or not it is completed or needs to be done. The purpose of this lesson is to provide a sample assignment monitoring sheet and exercises in recording sample assignments.

To the Student

Why do you think it is important to keep track of your assignments? (so you know what books you have to take home; so you know when an assignment is due) Sometimes using a weekly calendar or even a daily assignment sheet can really help you organize your assignments. But it will only be helpful if you actually use it and keep referring to it throughout the days or weeks.

When you write down your assignments, it is helpful not only to know what specific pages to read, questions to answer, or problems to solve, but also to have a record throughout the year of what topics you studied.

Here are some sample ways to record an assignment:

"For social studies, read Section 1 and answer questions 1–4 at the end of the chapter." *Write*: Soc. Stud.—Sec. 1, Qus. 1–4

"In science, read the directions for Experiment #1 and bring 3 balloons and a clothespin to school for Thursday's class." *Write*: Sci.—Exp. #1, ** 3 balloons, 1 clothespin for Thurs.

"For homework in math today, do all of the odd problems on page 45. That would be starting with 1 and ending with 31." *Write*: Math—p. 45 (1–31, odd)

"For general music, listen to the Beethoven tape and write down the titles of the music." *Write*: Music—listen to tape, write titles

It is also helpful to make a notation of when you have completed the assignment. You could do this by putting a small "X" in the corner of the square. Some people might want to cross out the entire box, but this would cover the assignment. You might have a reason to go back to the assignment to recheck what it is; if it's covered, you can't read it.

Another helpful notation is to indicate which subjects need to go home for homework. If you haven't finished the assignment in school that day, you should check your assignment sheet before you leave to see which assignments/books need to be finished at home. You could do this by making a large star * next to those assignments that need to go home.

Worksheets

Answers to Worksheet IV-16A:

Students' sheets will vary. Here is an example.

	Class	Assignment	Due:	Done (X)	Take Home(*)
Date: 10/12/01		**Day of the week:** Tuesday			
1st Hr.	Science	Ch. 2, qus. 4–6, pen	10/13		
2nd Hr.	Math	TEST 10/14, review	10/14		book*
3rd Hr.	P.E.	run mile	today		
4th Hr.	S.S.	2 cur. events, sum. for each	10/13		
5th Hr.	Read/Lit.	2 bks-rockets (bring to class)	10/15		
6th Hr.	Art	report (fam. artist)-color prints to class/computer	10/18		report*

Answers to Worksheet IV-16B:

Students' assignment sheets will vary.

Answers to Worksheet IV-16C:

Students' assignment sheets will vary.

Follow-up Activity

Spend time teaching students how you want them to complete the assignment sheets. As a class, you may want to decide what symbols you will use to designate a test, a report due, a guest speaker, or other special assignments or days. It is best to *keep it simple!* The sheet will be used only if it is perceived as being useful; and it will be useful if students can quickly and easily use it to track their assignments. You may even incorporate a mini study skills unit in your classroom (for any class) in order to make sure students work on this skill and to convey to them the importance you yourself place upon this.

Name _____ Date _____

IV-16A. Completing an Assignment Sheet

Use the informtion below to complete this sample assignment sheet. Use today's date.

Date:_____ Day of the week:_____

	Class	Assignment	Due	Done (X)	Take Home(*)
1st Hr.					
2nd Hr.					
3rd Hr.					
4th Hr.					
5th Hr.					
6th Hr.					

- Your first-hour class is Science. Your assignment is to read Chapter 2 and answer questions 4, 5, and 6 at the end of the chapter. The assignment has to be written in pen. It is due tomorrow.

- Your second-hour class is Math. You are having a test in two days, so your assignment is to review all of your math notes for the chapter. You think you better remember to take your book home so you can study tonight.

- Third-hour is P.E. You are supposed to run a mile when you get home as part of your physical fitness unit.

- Fourth-hour is Social Studies. You need to bring in two current events articles and write a summary for each. This is due tomorrow.

- Fifth-hour is Reading and Literature. You need to go to the public library to check out two books on rockets. You are supposed to bring the books to class on Friday.

- Last hour you have Art. You already wrote part of a report on a famous artist, but you have to collect some color prints of his/her work and bring them to class by next Monday. You think you might want to revise your report and then do some checking on the computer to find pictures of art work.

Name _____ Date _____

IV-16B. Your Own Assignment Sheet (Daily)

Complete the following assignment sheet using your own school information. You might want to make some changes to make the sheet fit your specific needs.

Today is: _____ The date is: _____

Subject	Assignment	Materials Needed	Due	Finished?	Comments

Name _____ Date _____

IV-16C. Your Own Assignment Sheet (Weekly)

Sometimes it is easier to keep track of your assignments if you can see the entire week at a glance. Again, make changes, if desired, to fit your needs.

Week of _____   T = test   R = report   HW = homework

Subject/Class	Monday	Tuesday	Wed.	Thurs.	Friday

Lesson IV-17: Taking a Phone Message

(Practical Writing Activities)

To the Teacher

There are many practical everyday activities that require some degree of writing proficiency. The purpose of this lesson is to provide practice for students in taking a phone message.

To the Student

When the phone rings at your house, who runs to answer it? If you don't have an answering machine, a person is going to have to pick up the receiver to see who the call is for. Even if you have an answering machine, if the person who is supposed to receive the call isn't there, someone will have to write down the message.

What information is important when taking a phone message for someone? (who the message is for, who is calling, what time the person called, the message itself)

Let's say you answer the phone while your mother is out shopping and get the following message:

"Hi, is your mother home? She's not? Well, would you give her a message for me, please? Tell her this is Mrs. Smith and I'll meet her for lunch tomorrow at the Red Barn at noon. Don't forget to let her know!"

Which of these would make the best message?

1. Mom, some lady will meet you for lunch tomorrow.

2. Mrs. Smith wants to eat lunch.

3. Mom, meet Mrs. Smith at Red Barn at 12:00 tomorrow.

Obviously, number 3 has all of the required information. The only part that might be a little clearer is the word "tomorrow." If you don't put the date somewhere on the paper and the message is misplaced for a day, the person reading won't know when "tomorrow" is.

Here is some practice in taking phone messages.

Worksheet

Answers for Worksheet IV-17:

Students' messages will vary. Be sure important parts are included.

Follow-up Activity

"It's for You!": Students can have a lot of fun with this activity by making up their own phony phone calls pretending to be a celebrity, cartoon character, superhero, or other creative individual. Have students work with partners to take turns giving a message and writing down the message. ("Robin called for Batman to let him know that the oil change on the Batmobile is finished.")

IV-17. A Message for You

Practice writing the important parts of these messages.

1. A man called for your father at 2 in the afternoon. He wanted to let your dad know that he is going to be dropping off a package at 6 tonight.

   _____

   _____

2. The dry cleaner's called to let someone in your family know the dry cleaning order is ready to be picked up.

   _____

   _____

3. Your family's dental office called to remind your sister of her appointment tomorrow at 3 o'clock for a cleaning. She should bring her insurance card with her.

   _____

   _____

4. Mrs. Alexander called for your mother to tell her that the rerun of the quilting show she wanted to see will be shown at 8 tonight.

   _____

   _____

5. Your brother's friend, Michael, called to remind him about football practice on Saturday at Grant Park at 8 in the morning.

   _____

   _____

6. The gas station called to let your parents know there is an opening for an oil change this afternoon at 4 if they can get the car in right away.

   PHONE MESSAGE
   WHILE YOU WERE OUT
   TO: _____
   CALLER: _____
   TIME: _____
   MESSAGE: _____
   _____
   _____

Lesson IV-18: Making a List (Practical Writing Activities)

To the Teacher

There are all kinds of lists that students (and even adults) can make. These include: guest list, shopping list, holiday/birthday list, a list of needed materials, and a list of brainstormed ideas. When making a list, a student should look for the best way to organize the information on that list to make it as useful as possible. The purpose of this lesson is to give students practice in making various lists and organizing the information as efficiently as possible.

To the Student

If I asked you to make a list of all the students in this class, how could you go about doing that? In other words, what are some ways you could organize that information to make sure you didn't miss anyone? (list the names alphabetically, list all boys and all girls, go around the room following a seating chart, etc.) There are lots of ways to possibly organize that information.

Let's say you were going to the grocery store and your parents wanted you to get about 20 different items. What would be some ways the grocery list might be organized? (in order of how you would find the things in the store—aisle 1, aisle 2, and so on; or in order of what's most important or needed—bread and milk first, then nonessential things listed later)

Let's try another list. Make a list of things you would like for your birthday. Your friends at school and your wealthy relatives are interested to know what you would like. How could you list those items? (might want to put a check mark next to the things you especially would like; make a separate list to circulate to friends who may not have a lot of money)

Here are some more lists for you to organize.

Worksheet

Answers to Worksheet IV-18:

Students' lists will vary.

Follow-up Activity

Brainstorming is a form of listing information. Rather than make a calculated, organized list, students can make "quick lists" by brainstorming—simply generating and writing down ideas quickly and easily. The ideas can be evaluated and discarded later, but the point of brainstorming is to get down creative thoughts in a flurry!

The idea of making lists quickly can be fun when it is done in groups or with a time limit. Tell students that they have 30 seconds in which to list everything they can think of in a category. For example: Write down everything you can think of that has four legs; how many things you can list that are red; list all of the girl names that start with "M"; jot down things you would find in a school lunch box, etc.

IV-18. Lists and More Lists

Read the following situations that ask for a listing of people or things. Decide on the best way to organize the list. Discuss your ideas with each other.

- materials you need to have a party at your house

- people who are in your class/club/group/scouting den/team, etc.

- animals that would make a good pet

- books you would like to read

- materials you need to make a poster for school about a foreign country

- food you want for the meal you are going to cook for your family

- chores you have to do

- your favorite TV shows

- your family members

- the childhood diseases you have had

- your favorite famous people

- people invited to your pool party

- things you need to take to the beach

- what you need to spend the night at a friend's house

- all the states you have visited

Lesson IV-19: Writing Directions or Instructions

(Practical Writing Activities)

To the Teacher

Students may be in a situation where they have to write clear directions for others. This may include directions for how to get to their home, to school, to a sports event, or other place. They may need to write directions for how to operate something (a computer game, a lawn mower), how to feed the dog when the family is on vacation, or even how Mom wants the flowers to be watered. The purpose of this lesson is for students to practice recognizing and writing clear directions that will enable others to understand and perform the task.

To the Student

When your family goes away on vacation or business, I bet your parents have to leave a list of instructions for other people to follow while they are gone. What are some jobs someone might have to do to help out when your family is away? (water the flowers, bring in the mail, feed the pets, etc.)

What would you think if you were supposed to help out your neighbors while they were away and these were your instructions:

1. Put the mail where it's supposed to go.

2. Water the flowers enough but not too much.

3. Find the dog's food and give her some.

4. Get the key and lock the door when you leave.

What would be some problems with those instructions? (Where does the mail go? No place was specified. How much water is just right? Where is the dog's food? How much does she get? Where is the key to lock the door?) Obviously, these written instructions aren't going to help too much.

What are some ways to make your instructions clear? How could you rewrite those instructions to make them easy to understand? For example:

1. Get the mail and put it on the kitchen table.

2. Water all of the flowers from one big watering can.

3. The dog's food is in the kitchen closet with a cup inside. Give her one full cup in the morning.

4. We will give you the key before we leave. Lock the door and keep the key until we get home.

When you give directions for how to get somewhere, you will need to remember these points:

- Where is the person starting from?

- Try to use street names or landmarks that don't move or change.

- It is sometimes helpful to tell how many miles apart things are or how long you would expect it to take to arrive.

Here are poor directions for getting to my house:

Go down that main road in town.

There's a black car parked on the corner lot. Turn there.

Keep going until you see my dog tied outside.

Here are better directions for getting to my house:

From your house, drive on North Avenue for three blocks until you get to the stoplight. Turn left (that's Main Street) and go four more blocks. When you pass the yellow house on the corner, count 2 more houses. That's mine—white with red trim.

Worksheets

Answers to Worksheet IV-19A:

Students' answers will vary.

Answers to Worksheet IV-19B:

Students' answers will vary.

Follow-up Activity

Community Map: Students who would like to go beyond this activity may want to create a community map. They can label specific streets and directions on this map, but more important they can draw houses, buildings, parks, and other points of interest for your town or community. From a student's point of view, the most important features might be the local skating arena, the pizzeria, where to get used comics, the baseball field, and the computer games store. By drawing and making a map, students can begin to visualize the layout of the town and where these points of interest are in relation to each other. Students can practice actually writing directions for how to get from one place to another using street names and other clues that don't change.

Name _____ Date _____

IV-19A. Writing Directions for Doing Something

Here are some ideas for writing directions or instructions for someone to follow. Choose several and practice writing out the steps. Exchange your list with someone else to see how clear your directions were.

- How to find a game on your computer
- How to win a game on your computer
- How to take care of your pet while you're away
- How to change a tire on your bike
- How to set the timer on the VCR to record a program
- How to set the stopwatch
- How to operate the lawn mower
- How to make your family's favorite pie or dessert

- What to do with the garbage on trash day
- How to design a web page
- How to paint the walls in your bedroom
- How to plant summer flowers
- How to clean the bird cage/cat box/back yard
- How to make the bed
- How to play a really fun card game

_____

_____

_____

_____

_____

_____

_____

_____

_____

_____

_____

_____

_____

Name _____ Date _____

IV-19B. Writing Directions for Getting Somewhere

Here are some ideas for writing directions or instructions for someone to follow that will help them get somewhere or find a place. Remember to begin with a starting place. Write the steps carefully and then exchange your list with someone else to see how clearly you explained how to get there.

- How to get to your school
- How to get to your house
- How to get to a baseball or sports field
- How to get to a friend's house
- Where to go to look in your house to find the games
- Where to put everyone's clothes after they are washed
- Where to dump the trash
- Where to go to walk the dog
- Where to meet your friends at the county fair

- How to get to your lessons (piano, karate, art, etc.)
- How to get to the nearest food store
- How to get to the best place to skateboard
- How to get to the community park/pool/picnic area
- How to get to the movie theater
- Where to go in the local department store to find the specific school supplies you want

_____

_____

_____

_____

_____

_____

_____

_____

_____

_____

_____

Lesson IV-20: Writing Notes on a Calendar

(Practical Writing Activities)

To the Teacher

Another practical writing activity is for students to maintain a personal calendar. As students become older, it seems their extracurricular schedules become fuller and more complicated! Teaching students to maintain a "social" calendar is something their parents will probably appreciate as well. The purpose of this lesson is to provide sample activities for students to record on a calendar.

To the Student

What are some activities in which you are involved? (scouting, sports, church youth group, music lessons, etc.) How in the world can you or your parents keep track of all those appointments? (write them on a calendar or daily reminder) Unless you have a personal secretary, it can become quite a job to remember all the things you are supposed to do. One helpful suggestion is to use a calendar to record your appointments and activities.

You can use your own "shorthand" system to code your appointments. For example, you can use "doc" for a doctor's appointment, "den" for a dentist appointment, G/S for a Girl Scout meeting, FB for a football practice, and so on. The important thing is to remember your codes!

You might also want to make note of special days on your calendar. Maybe your best friend's birthday is coming up and you want to remember to send a card. Or perhaps you have a big test or report due and you want to make sure you are prepared.

You will be using a practice calendar to help record some appointments for a pretend student. Then you can use a regular calendar to start making notes for your own appointments.

Worksheets

Answers to Worksheet IV-20A:

Students' calendars will vary. Here is an example.

Answers to Worksheet IV-20B:

Students' calendars will vary.

February 2001

Sun.	Mon.	Tues.	Wed.	Thurs.	Fri.	Sat.
				1	2	3 BB game Chi
4 CH 6-8 pm	5	6	7 B/S 4 pm	8	9	10
11 CH 6-8 pm	12	13	14 VAL-Skat 7 pm	15	16 Allen	17
18 CH 6-8 pm	19	20 Den 5:30	21 B/S 4 pm	22 Mom-B.	23 Math T! MILW ←——→	24
25 CH 6-8 pm MILW	26	27	28 B/S 4 pm			

Follow-up Activities

1. A social/appointment calendar is somewhat different than a school/assignment calendar, and it may be confusing to try to combine the two on one. Explain to students that the assignment calendar is really for school projects, but that the social calendar is for events and activities that are usually "outside" of school. When there is a big test or school project due, however, this should be included on the main calendar.

2. Some students may enjoy making their own monthly calendars. This can be done simply by using blank paper and decorating the calendar with stickers, drawings, and even glitter. Students can also use programs available on a computer to design their own. Students may be more likely to use a calendar when they feel "ownership" in creating it.

IV-20A. Practice Calendar

Here is a calendar for the month of February. Record Bob's appointments on the calendar. Use codes that make sense to you and to other people.

February 2001

Sun.	Mon.	Tues.	Wed.	Thurs.	Fri.	Sat.
				1	2	3
4	5	6	7	8	9	10
11	12	13	14	15	16	17
18	19	20	21	22	23	24
25	26	27	28			

He has Boy Scout meetings every Wednesday after school at 4 o'clock except for the second Wednesday.

His mother's birthday is February 22nd.

He has a dentist appointment on Tuesday, the 20th, at 5:30.

There is a big test in math on Friday, the 23rd, that he wants to study for.

On the last weekend in February, he is going to visit his cousins in Milwaukee. He will leave Friday after school and come back Sunday night.

There is a Valentine's Day party at the skating rink at 7 P.M. on that holiday.

Every Sunday night he has church youth group activities from 6–8 P.M.

His best friend Allen is coming to spend the night on Friday the 16th.

There is a basketball game on Saturday the 3rd in Chicago.

Name _____ Date _____

IV-20B. Your Own Calendar

Copy or design your own personal calendar on another sheet of paper. Practice writing your personal appointments on the appropriate days. Here are some activities you might want to include:

- Doctor's appointments
- Dentist's appointments
- Scout meetings
- Sports events
- School activities
- Holidays
- Birthdays of family members

- Birthdays of friends
- Dates when school projects are due
- Days when you will be gone or out-of-town
- Days when you have special jobs to do (taking care of someone's pets)
- Parties you are invited to
- Dates when you are supposed to pick up something (film, medicine, supplies)

Use the space below to make notes of these special activities before writing them on your calendar.

_____

_____

_____

_____

_____

_____

_____

_____

_____

_____

_____

_____

_____

Lesson IV-21: Completing a Form (Practical Writing Activities)

To the Teacher

At many points during a school career, the student will have to fill out a simple form that requires basic information. It is important for the student to realize what information is being requested and to clearly and completely provide the information. The purpose of this lesson is to provide practice for the students in completing simple informational forms.

To the Student

Before you go on a field trip, what does your parent or guardian have to sign? (a permission slip) What's the purpose of that? (so that everyone involved knows and agrees that the student is going on this trip) What specific questions or information might be included on a field trip form? (name of doctor, parent's work number, last date of tetanus shot, etc.) Why do you think that type of information is important? (for emergencies)

Sometimes there are forms that *you*, not your parents, have to fill out. Can you think of any? (forms requesting class information, book order forms, reading contest forms, etc.) What are some questions that would likely be on these forms? (name of the book, number of pages, price of the book, teacher's name, etc.)

It really is important that *you* provide the correct information for these questions. Here are some practice questions or items requesting information that you might have to fill out:

1. **Name:** If it requests full name, write your first name, middle name, and last name. If it requests last name first, then of course, you have to write your last name, then a comma, and then your first name.

2. **Address (Street, City, State, ZIP Code):** This is self-explanatory. For the street, write down the numbers that go with your street. If you have a post office box, write that on this line. For city, write the city you live in. For state, check to see how many blanks or boxes there are. If there are only two, then use the postal code for your state which is only two letters. Both letters should be capitalized. For the ZIP Code, most likely you will have a 5-digit number, although you might know the extra four.

3. **Doctor's Name, Address, Phone:** This information is needed in case of a medical emergency. Don't just write the doctor's last name; use the courtesy title of "Dr." and then write his/her last name. Make sure you know or can find out your doctor's office address and telephone number. Make sure you use the area code for the phone number, especially if you are taking a field trip and might be going some distance.

4. **Parent's Name, Address, and Work Number:** Most likely you will need to list the name of at least one of your parents or your guardian. If you do not live with both parents, you might need to know the street address and telephone number of each parent. Make sure you know where this person works (that means the name of the business and the address) and the telephone number. You might need to include an extension number. That means the additional number that someone would ask for to be connected with another office (where your parent works).

5. **School Name, Address, Phone, Grade, and Class:** When you write out the name of your school, remember to use the full name (not just what you call it or shorten it to), full address, and complete phone number. For your grade, you would just write in the number (e.g., 5th, 6th). The class might refer to your teacher. In that case, write your teacher's title (Mr., Miss, Ms., Mrs.) and last name. If there is more than one teacher with the same last name in your school, check with him/her to find out the initial of the first name or whatever system is used in your school to distinguish between them.

6. **Sex:** This means male or female. Use "M" if you are a boy; "F" if you are a girl.

7. **Date of Birth:** Write down the date you were born, including the year. This is usually abbreviated by using three numbers: the month, the day, and the last two digits of the year you were born (2/24/91).

8. **Book Title:** Just write the title of the book you are ordering or reporting. If there is more space to write down more books or items, but you only want one, just leave the spaces blank.

9. **Quantity:** For a book order, you might need to write how many of each book you would like to order. For example, if you and your sister each want a copy of the same book, the quantity would be "2."

10. **Total:** When you are ordering several items, you will have to list the amount of each separate item. Usually at the bottom there will be a space to add up the amount (order total) of everything that you ordered. You may also have to include shipping and taxes. The order total is simply the total price of everything you ordered.

11. **Parent or Guardian Signature:** This means you have to take the form home and have your parent or guardian sign the sheet, then return it to school. This is so your responsible adult knows what is going on and can help provide emergency information.

There will be other information on forms, depending on the purpose of the form. If you don't understand what information is requested, be sure to ask someone.

Worksheets

These worksheets provide practice forms for students to fill out. If students don't understand what information is requested, they should ask you for help.

Answers to Worksheet IV-21A:

Students' forms will vary.

Answers to Worksheet IV-21B:

Students' forms will vary.

Answers to Worksheet IV-21C:

Students' forms will vary.

Follow-up Activity

Begin collecting sample forms to use with students from time to time. Specific trips will request specific information that addresses the needs of the situation (e.g., for a party, who will bring the punch? Who will bring napkins?) As you and your students begin to pay attention to the information requested, take a moment to discuss what is needed for an appropriate response.

IV-21A. Basic Information Form

Name:_____

Address (street, city, state, ZIP Code):

_____

_____

_____

Date of Birth:_____ Sex: _____

Home Telephone: (_____) _____

Father's Name: _____

Father's Place of Work: _____

Father's Work Address: _____

_____

_____

Father's Work Telephone: (_____) _____

Mother's Name: _____

Mother's Place of Work: _____

Mother's Work Address: _____

_____

_____

Mother's Work Telephone: (_____) _____

Number of Brothers: _____ Sisters: _____

Your Current Grade in School:_____

Your Teacher's Name: _____

IV-21B. Completing a Book Order

Let's say that you want to order three books: *Molly's Adventure* ($4.95), *Tony and the Magic Truck* ($3.50), and *Fast Fred* ($2.95). You also want to order a race car poster ($2.00). Complete this order form:

Name: _____

School Name: _____

School Address:

_____

_____

_____

Teacher: _____

Grade: _____

• •

Book Title:	**Quantity**	**Amount**
_____	_____	$ _____
_____	_____	$ _____
_____	_____	$ _____
_____	_____	$ _____
_____	_____	$ _____
_____	_____	$ _____
_____	_____	$ _____

Other Items:	**Quantity**	**Amount**
_____	_____	$ _____
_____	_____	$ _____
_____	_____	$ _____
	Total:	$ _____

IV-21C. Field Trip Form

Let's pretend your class is going on a field trip to the Community Historical Museum next Friday.

Name: _____

Teacher: _____

Grade: _____

Date of Field Trip: _____

Destination: _____

• •

Your Doctor's Name: _____

Office Address:

_____

_____

_____

Your Parent's Name: _____

Parent's Work Telephone: (_____) _____

In case your parent cannot be reached, give a name and telephone number of another person to call in case of an emergency:

(Name) _____

(Telephone) (_____) _____

• •

_____
Signature of Parent or Guardian

Lesson IV-22: Writing/Completing an Invitation

(Practical Writing Activities)

To the Teacher

Students may have birthday party or class play invitations, or want to invite the community to tour their classroom. In each case, students will have to provide specific information for the recipient to read and clearly understand. The purpose of this lesson is to provide practice in writing or completing an invitation.

To the Student

Let's invite the community to visit our classroom to see the great book reports you just did! (Allow time for groaning.) Well, if we *were* going to send out an invitation, what kind of information would be needed? (who will receive the information, time, date, place, other specifics, etc.)

Whenever you are inviting someone to attend something, there are certain pieces of information you need to include. Here are some examples:

- **Event:** Is it a party? Is it an open house? What are you celebrating or inviting someone to see? Be sure to indicate if it is a SURPRISE!
- **Time:** Do you want everyone there right at 3 o'clock? Does it go until 5 o'clock? Is it an open house (people can drop in) or do you want everyone to stay the entire time?
- **Date:** Write the day and the date of when the event will take place.
- **Place:** Put the address of where people should go. If it's a party, is it at your house or someplace else? Be specific.
- **Other information:** List any specific items that your guests should bring. If it's a pool party, remind them to bring a towel, sunscreen, and a swimming suit. If it's a slumber party, should your guests bring money to go to a movie?
- **R.S.V.P.:** This indicates that you want your guests to call you or your parents to let them know if they are coming or not. After you write the letters R.S.V.P. (which is an abbreviation for the French words *répondez s'il vous plaît*), write the telephone number they should call.

Worksheet

Answers to Worksheet IV-22:

Students' invitations will vary.

Follow-up Activity

Half the fun of having a party, program, or other event is designing the invitation. With the help of computer graphics (or even just a few colored markers), students can create and design their own imaginative invitations. This also helps students organize their drawings and writing. (Aha! Sounds like a rough draft might be handy here!) Students will also enjoy seeing their own work being reproduced and used in such events as a student-designed program/cast list for a play, a written guided tour of a class museum, etc.

Name _____ Date _____

IV-22. You Are Invited!

Design your own invitation to a real or imaginary event. You may want to design a cover for your event. Be sure to include information that is necessary for someone to know exactly what to expect! Choose from the following ideas or make your own.

- surprise birthday party
- a birthday party at a video arcade
- horseback riding party
- a pool party
- a class play
- a school holiday program
- a Mother's Day breakfast

- a Father's Day brunch
- the community to tour the new school
- all parents to attend the "Holidays Around the World" program
- all parents of first graders to come to the Native American program
- all parents to come to and help at the Fun Fair

Use the space below for your rough draft. Then put your final invitation on a new sheet of paper.

Lesson IV-23: Writing a Thank-you Note

(Practical Writing Activities)

To the Teacher

A simple thank-you note is a nice way to acknowledge a kindness or courtesy. Here is an opportunity not only to incorporate writing into daily life, but also to teach the importance of being sincerely grateful to others. The purpose of this lesson is to provide students with opportunities to write thank-you notes.

To the Student

When was the last time you had to write a thank-you note? (after a birthday party, a holiday, etc.) Who did you write to and what did you say? (allow time for examples) Did someone "make" you write the notes? Was it hard to think of what to say?

It is very polite to write a thank-you note to someone who has given you a gift or money. Think of the time the person spent shopping for you, wrapping the gift, or even just tucking some money into a card. That person did something specifically for you. It is courteous to write a short thank-you to that person. It doesn't have to be long; in general, you can just say "thank you," acknowledge what the gift was (money or a specific present), and add a sincere personal note that expresses something more. You might tell what you will do with the gift, where you will wear the clothes, how nice it was of the person to think of you, and so on. It is really important to be *sincere* as well as polite. This means that even if you don't especially like the bright green pajamas with the little yellow ducks on it that your grandmother bought for you, you should still be thankful that she thought about you and took the time to get you something. You may not sincerely like the gift, but you should thank the giver.

You can also write a thank-you note to someone who has done something nice for you or provided you with a service that was exceptionally welcome. For example, perhaps you visited a friend and the neighbors took you out on their boat for three hours and taught you how to water ski. It would be courteous to thank them for their time and the attention they gave you. It is also appropriate to write a thank-you note if you are visiting someone and that person went out of his or her way to give up a bedroom, take you out to eat, or spend extra time with you.

You don't have to write thank-you notes for everything, of course. Sometimes people are pleasant and you would be overdoing it to write a thank-you note for every little thing. But when someone has been especially kind to you, it is always appreciated to receive a little note.

Worksheet

Answers to Worksheet IV-23:

Students' thank-you notes will vary.

Follow-up Activities

1. **Volunteer Thank-you Notes:** Some schools may have a "volunteer recognition" breakfast or brunch. Have your students design paper placements that not only have a picture drawn by each student, but also show generic thank-you notes. Again, the services performed could be general (reading to the students, tutoring, helping out at parties, etc.), but students could write specific thank-you notes right on the placement.

2. **Specific Class Thank-you's:** When you have a guest speaker or someone who has

taken the time to spend with your class, have the students work together to write a sincere note to send to the person. Although this may seem like a chore at first, students will come to expect to write these notes often as the opportunities come up. Again, these are opportunities to teach good social skills as well as practical writing skills.

IV-23. Thank You!

Here are some examples of situations for which a thank-you note would be appreciated and acceptable. Choose several that interest you (or add to the list) and write a brief note for practice. You may want to actually send a thank-you note to someone who has done something for you.

Thank your grandparent for the birthday money

Thank your grandparent for the new football

Thank your aunt for the new clothes she sent you

Thank your uncle for the CD he bought you

Thank your neighbor for taking care of your cat while you were on vacation

Thank your teacher for the holiday gift she gave you

Thank your friend for the birthday gift

Thank your older cousin for taking you to the movies

Thank your school bus driver for candy bars she gave everyone

Thank your friend's mother for picking you up after school when you needed a ride

Thank the people who returned your missing puppy

Thank the man who fixed your bicycle

Thank the person who helped you with your science project

Thank the paramedics who helped you when you broke your arm

_____

_____

_____

_____

_____

_____

_____

_____

_____

_____

_____

_____

Lesson IV-24: Addressing an Envelope
(Practical Writing Activities)

To the Teacher

Students will need to know how to address an envelope so they can mail their thank-you notes to the proper recipients. Addressing an envelope is also a necessary skill for mailing letters to pen pals, requesting information, sending an order for books or magazines, and writing letters home from camp. The purpose of this lesson is to provide practice in addressing an envelope.

To the Student

After you have written a thank-you note, you could just hand it to the person, but more likely you will mail the letter, especially to someone who lives out of town. There is a standard form that is used to address envelopes.

First, your return address goes in the upper left corner of the envelope. This consists of three lines:

Your name (first and last)

Your street

Your city, state, and ZIP Code

The purpose of the return address is to let the recipient of the letter know who it is from, but also to let the mail carrier know where to return the letter in case there is a problem delivering the letter. Maybe the address was written incorrectly or is too difficult to read; perhaps you forgot to put a stamp on or there's insufficient postage; or maybe the person moved and did not leave a forwarding address. In any case, write your return address on the envelope (or order preprinted stickers).

It is usually best to use a pen, rather than a pencil, to write the address, because the numbers and letters can become smudged when handled.

The name (first line) and address (second and third lines) of the person or company to whom you are sending the letter goes in the center of the envelope. Try to line up the three lines so that they are aligned on the left side. Some guidelines direct you to use all capital letters in the address; however, as long as the information is correct, the letter will be delivered. You can single-space the lines in the return address; double-space the lines in the main address.

Here is an example of an addressed envelope to a person:

Amy Smith
1234 North Street
Richmond, KY 40475-9432

                              Steven Carter
                              5678 South Avenue
                              Folsom, LA 70437

Worksheet

Answers to Worksheet IV-24:

Check to see that students' envelopes are correctly addressed.

Follow-up Activities

1. **Personal Address Book:** Some students may enjoy writing and could benefit from organizing and maintaining a personal address book. Whether they make one or purchase one, students can begin keeping track of friends, relatives, and other people with whom they may correspond regularly.

2. **Funny Addresses:** Around the Christmas holidays, it is fun for students to write letters to "Santa Claus." Usually these letters are designated for delivery somewhere around the North Pole. Students may also enjoy creating fictitious addresses for cartoon or imaginary characters.

If students create addresses for animals, where might a walrus live? On Tusk Avenue. How about an ant? On Hill Street. Or a dolphin? On Flipper Drive. Have students make up their own addresses for select groups of animals, famous people, etc. Some students may even want to design their own postage stamps!

IV-24. Addressing an Envelope

Have students practice writing their return address on pieces of paper the size of envelopes. When writing the main address on the envelope, students might benefit from a lightly drawn pencil mark indicating the left margin of the three lines. This can then be erased after students have written the address.

Address an envelope to the following people:

Mrs. Debbie Armstrong, P.O. Box 21, Columbus, OH 43271

Dr. Fred Peters, 107 W. Main Street, Des Moines, IA 50368

Alan Mongori, 20 Grand Boulevard., Roanoke, VA 24022

Mr. Steven Terpstra, 225 Eaton Street, Bedford Park, IL 60638

Kirsten Morrison, 1227 Green Drive, New York, NY 10020

Lesson IV-25: Writing a Poem (Creative-Writing Activities)

To the Teacher

Poetry is a style of writing in which the words are organized in a structure different from a story or a letter. The words and thoughts follow a pattern that is organized in verses, or short divisions of sentences. A poem can fit many styles. It can be as simple as two lines that rhyme or as complex as an entire story complete with plot and characters. It is helpful if students have been exposed to a number of different poets and styles of poetry before attempting to write their own poems. The purpose of this lesson is to provide a framework for students to write simple poems.

To the Student

We are going to be working on writing some poems. First of all, what is poetry? Can anyone recite an example of a poem? (Wait for examples.) What do you think of when you hear or recite a poem? (rhythm of the words, rhyming words) When you think of a song, can you see how just the words of a song are like a poem? They probably flow easily and have a rhyme at the end. For the simple poems you will be writing, there are two main things to look for:

1. the number of syllables in each line

2. the last word in each line

When you write your poem, you will want to have the same number of syllables in each line. When you are reading the poem, you can hear how the words flow—almost like a song. You don't have to have the exact number, but you should stay pretty close.

When you think of a poem, you probably think of words that rhyme as your first clue. If you have a line for your poem, start with that and then come up with a list of words that rhyme with the last word in the first line and use that to get you thinking about how your second line should go. For example, if your poem starts out like this:

One day I took a little walk (*Think*: There are 8 syllables in that line and it ends with the word *walk*.)

Now, for your second line, you will want to write a sentence that has close to 8 syllables and ends with something that rhymes with *walk*. What are possibilities? (*Chalk, talk, hawk, squawk*, etc.) What could you write? How about:

I did not really want to talk.

Or

I looked ahead and saw a hawk.

Or

I turned to hear a quiet "squawk."

Each of these second lines could steer your poem in a different direction! Where will you end up? Is your poem going to be about how you wanted a quiet day? Or what happened when you followed the bird? Or is it about your surprise to find a baby bird?

It's important you understand that all poems do not have to rhyme, although this is a common characteristic of a poem. Watch for the rhyming pattern, too; the rhyme may be in every other line, instead of lines that are said next to each other.

There really aren't too many rules for a poem. Poems can be written about feelings, something you see, something funny—anything you would write a paragraph or story about. The difference, however, is that you want to condense what you put into a poem so that you are saying what you want to say in fewer, very careful words.

For example, let's say I wanted to express this feeling about my dog:

> *I adopted a sad little beagle from the animal shelter. As soon as I saw Abby, I knew she was the dog I wanted. She had sad brown eyes and a tail that wagged so slowly and hopefully, I knew I had to take her home with me.*

Now I'm going to put the same feelings into a poem:

> *A long and lonely row of pets.*
>
> *Unwanted, sad, alone and yet*
>
> *I knew within a steel home*
>
> *I'd find a friend to call my own.*
>
> *I saw her bright and hopeful face.*
>
> *I stooped to see her in her place.*
>
> *Her eyes lit up and I could see*
>
> *The beagle was coming home with me.*

Do you see the pattern in the poem? What do you notice about the first two lines? (They have the same number of syllables and sort of a rhyming word at the end.) Does this pattern hold true for the next two lines? (Yes, both have 8 syllables and rhymes at the end.) How about the next two? The last two? (Pretty much—you have to say "beagle" fast to make it fit!)

How is the feeling expressed differently in the poem? Why wouldn't you just read the paragraph about the dog? (The poem reflects more thought and creativity; it's harder to make everything fit and still keep the feeling.)

Poems may require a bit more effort and are harder to write than just sitting down and putting your thoughts on paper, but that's what makes them fun! They are a challenge—almost like a puzzle to try to get everything to fit the pattern and still clearly express your thoughts and feelings.

Are you ready to write some poetry?

Worksheets

Answers to Worksheet IV-25A:

Students' lines will vary.

Answers to Worksheet IV-25B:

Students' poems will vary.

Follow-up Activities

1. **Poetry Show:** Have students write short poems and illustrate them on posters. You might stage a class performance in which students have an informal poetry reading. Display the posters on a bulletin board. You may even have a "poetry week" in which this type of writing is the primary writing theme.
2. **Poems and Poets:** Have students discover poetry by directing them to popular poets (e.g., Shel Silverstein, Dr. Seuss) and some of the classic poems. Encourage them to read humorous poems as well as more traditional poetry to understand that poetry is fun!
3. **Favorite Poems:** Have students tackle the task of finding out their parents' and grandparents' favorite poems. Form a class collection and take turns sharing the familiar or favorite poems of others. Add to a class collection by having students keep an eye open for poems they encounter in their personal readings.
4. **Poetry in Songs:** Many songs started out as poems, and then were set to music. If your students have favorite singing groups, take a moment to focus on the lyrics of a popular or favorite song and analyze how the words, syllables, and rhymes are like a poem.

Name _____ Date _____

IV-25A. Add a Last Line

Here are some partially written poems. Add your own last line! Remember to keep the flow of words to match the lines (same number of syllables, or at least close) and add a word that rhymes.

1. **Chores**   *There's nothing I hate doing more*
Than wasting a day on a boring chore.
My mom says I have to grab a broom

_____

_____

2. **Eating Lunch**   *I love my breakfast, every day,*
It's food I love to munch.
But sometimes school gets in my way

_____

_____

3. **My Sister**   *I have a little sister.*
Her name is Kathy Sue.
And I would like to tell you

_____

_____

4. **Saturday**   *My favorite day in the whole long week*
Is the day I get to snore and sleep.
On Saturday you'll find me in my bed

_____

_____

IV-25B. Write a Short Poem

Here are some beginning lines you could use to turn into a short poem. Try some of these and then work on your own. Remember, write a poem that makes sense—don't just throw words together that flow and rhyme but don't really say anything!

- When the sky is blue…
- My friend is the best friend I ever had…
- I love the quiet of the night…
- Trains, trains, I love the trains…
- Do you ever become scared at night?…

- I saw a pretty butterfly…
- Wishes, millions of wishes…
- I love to sing, I love to dance…
- Will you go with me?…
- If I had a dollar for every dream…

Use the lines here to brainstorm your ideas before you write your final copy.

_____

_____

_____

_____

_____

_____

_____

_____

_____

_____

_____

_____

_____

_____

_____

_____

Lesson IV-26: Writing a Song (Creative-Writing Activities)

To the Teacher

Is there a budding songwriter in your class? Students may enjoy taking their poems to a new level—that of adding music to make it into a song. The purpose of this lesson is to expose students to the connection between words of a poem and adding the element of music to make a song.

To the Student

Think about one of your favorite songs. (You can hum it if you like.) If you think about it, a song is really some sort of poem or group of words set to music. You might remember the tune more than the words, but there is something about a song that makes the words and music fit together. Is a particular song your favorite because of the music? Or because of the words? Or both? Think about how the words and music go together to make the song just right. When you think of a lullaby, for example, you would probably find words that are soft and gentle and soothing to go with the music. But if you think of a loud rock song you like, the words might be more dramatic and powerful. Again, the words and music should go together somehow.

Have you ever thought about writing a song? You might want to start with the words, and then a tune to go with it. Perhaps you would use a tune that is already a song (such as "The Farmer in the Dell" or "Hokey Pokey") and add your own words. It can be really fun to write silly songs or camp songs, just changing the words to meet your needs.

Here are some activities to get you started on the road to fame… or, just fun!

Worksheet

Answers to Worksheet IV-26:

Students' songs will vary. An idea for "The Teacher in the School" is: the teacher takes a student, the student takes a parent, the parent takes the school board, etc.

Follow-up Activity

Work together to come up with words for a class song. Start with a familiar song and then try to incorporate things you have done in your class this year or people who are in your class with specific traits. (Be sure students do not mind being "teased" about some characteristic, e.g., red hair, always forgetting lunch money, etc. Get students' permission.)

IV-26. Changing Words to Familiar Songs

Start with the tune to these familiar songs. Change the words to make them fit a different situation. These are all examples of what you can do to make them school situations. Use the lines to brainstorm your ideas before you write your final copy.

Tune: "The Farmer in the Dell"

Change the words to fit: "The Teacher in the School"

_____

_____

_____

Tune: "I'm Dreaming of a White Christmas"

Change the words to fit: "I'm Dreaming of a Homework-Free Weekend" or "I'm Dreaming of a Christmas Vacation"

_____

_____

_____

Tune: "Happy Birthday to You"

Change the words to fit: "Happy Saturday to You"

_____

_____

_____

Tune: "Jingle Bells"

Change the words to fit: "Tardy Bells"

_____

_____

_____

Tune: "Rock Around the Clock"

Change the words to fit: "Study Around the Clock"

_____

_____

_____

Lesson IV-27: Writing a Classified Ad

(Creative-Writing Activities)

To the Teacher

When students get older, they may truly need to write a classified ad to submit to a newspaper to sell something. As students, however, they can still practice the "basics" of writing a simulated ad. The ad must be clear, not too wordy, and provide the important information for buying/selling the item or service. The purpose of this lesson is to give students practice in identifying and writing clear ads.

To the Student

Think about your closet in your bedroom. I'll bet there is something in there that your mother would like you to get rid of; something that possibly someone else would want. You can sell items that are still of value in a **classified ad**. These are ads that you usually have to pay for per word, so you don't want them to be too long. Now think about that item. How would you go about writing an ad to sell it? What information would be important to catch someone's attention?

Who has an example? (tennis racquet, game, old bed, etc.) Let's take a game and work with that.

What do you think of this ad:

For sale: Old Monopoly game. It has most of the pieces, but some are lost. The box itself is in good condition. We had to tape the edges shut. I would like to get some money for the whole game. Call me if you are interested.

What could be improved in that ad?

- *Length*—too long, doesn't need to be complete sentences; if you are paying for the ad by length, you would want to keep it short
- *Too much information*—you don't have to tell about the missing pieces or taping the edges; you can inform interested people about the details when they call
- *Cost*—doesn't tell how much the person wants for it; will you take an offer?
- *Contact*—doesn't tell who to call or what the number is

How could we rewrite that ad to make it better? Here's an example:

For sale: Old Monopoly game, good condition. $2 or best offer. Call Pete at 555-1212.

Now it's your turn to practice revising and writing some classified ads.

Worksheets

Answers to Worksheet IV-27A:

Students' ads will vary. Here is what each ad needs for improvement:

Answers to Worksheet IV-27B:

Students' ads will vary.

Follow-up Activity

Funny Ads: Let students have some fun with pretending to sell things they probably really could not get away with selling—their younger brother, their parent's car, their used toothbrush, etc. Students may come up with some creative ideas for making these items sound appealing!

IV-27A. Revising Classified Ads

Here are some classified ads that could use improvement. Rewrite each one to make it shorter, clearer, or more complete.

1. For sale: color television. Comes with a VCR and a remote control. Does not come with a table. $100. Call me at 555-2775.

   _____

   _____

   _____

2. Free: two 8-week-old boxer puppies.

   _____

   _____

3. Tennis racquets for sale. $50 or best offer. Or $100 for the best one. $35. Phone 555-2002 after 3 p.m.

   _____

   _____

   _____

4. For sale or trade: bowling ball. It is black and round and has holes. $15. Call 555-2222.

   _____

   _____

5. For sale: Schwinn bicycle in good condition. Blue, 16", new tires, lights, and horn. Comes with a helmet. Ridden only on weekends on smooth roads. Call 555-3567.

   _____

   _____

   _____

6. Babysitting services available. $2/hr. for first child, $1/hr. for each additional child. References available.

   _____

   _____

   _____

IV-27B. Write a Classified Ad

Now it's your turn! Write an ad to sell each of the following items or services.

1. 5 black-and-white kittens

_____

_____

2. lawn-mowing services

_____

_____

3. paperback books (either sell or trade)

_____

_____

4. a used guitar in good shape

_____

_____

5. running shoes, size 6, never used

_____

_____

6. tutoring, any subject, $3/hour

_____

_____

7. set of encyclopedias, missing a few volumes

_____

_____

8. twin beds, mattresses, box springs, and frames, $100

_____

_____

9. a used computer

_____

_____

10. a two person tent

_____

_____

Lesson IV-28: Writing a Commercial Ad

(Creative-Writing Activities)

To the Teacher

A classified ad is primarily written to sell an item or offer a service. Students can expand this advertising skill by writing an ad to inform the public about their wonderful product and how it will appeal to the masses. The purpose of this lesson is to provide activities for students to design a commercial ad to advertise a product or service.

To the Student

(Hold up a magazine.) I have in my hand a magazine. It has a lot of news articles and information about people in it, but you know what? There is a lot of advertising in this magazine as well. I bet you are familiar with some of these ads and the slogans or even songs that go with them. (Page through and call attention to some of the more obvious ones.)

There are people who get paid a lot of money to write these commercial ads! What do you think makes them appealing? (interesting pictures, catchy phrases, words that tell how wonderful the product is)

You already know about how to write a clear classified ad. Now here is your chance to really put some creativity into another type of ad—this type is a commercial ad, and the purpose is to attract the attention of the reader to get him or her to take a look at the product. The ad will tell why this is a good product and why you and everyone else would want it! Perhaps it's a good value for the money; perhaps you need one to think you are popular and cool; or perhaps it's something that will make you feel good! For whatever reason, there is something about a good commercial ad that will make the reader want to buy the product or service.

What kind of words or persuasive arguments might you use to try to convince someone that he or she needs the following items or services?

Lawn mowing service (cheap, fast, careful job, has own equipment)

New car (good gas mileage, will attract attention, has TV inside)

Computer (good value for the money, will help your children do well in school)

Running shoes (good support for your feet, on sale this week)

Piano (beautiful piece of furniture, good sound)

Video camera (takes great pictures, easy to carry, helps you have wonderful memories)

Are you ready to write a commercial ad?

Worksheet

Answers to Worksheet IV-28:

Students' ads will vary.

Follow-up Activity

Students may get commercial ad ideas from looking through magazines, of course, but also from the Yellow Pages. There are lots of cute, quick ways to catch someone's attention. As a class project, you might assign each student (or assign pairs) a product or service and then have them design their own ads. Students will really get into making their washing machines and dryers sound like sports cars!

IV-28. You've Gotta Get One of These!

Pretend you have a great invention or idea! How are you going to convince others that they need this? Design your own commercial ad to sell it to the public! Use the space below for your brainstorming ideas before you prepare your final copy.

Some points to consider:

- Have an attractive picture of the item.
- Put in a slogan or motto.
- Tell the reader why he or she needs this.
- Use different types of print.
- Emphasize what a good value this is.

Lesson IV-29: Writing a Travel Brochure

(Creative-Writing Activities)

To the Teacher

Another outlet for creative writers is that of preparing a travel brochure, either for a real or imaginary place. Students will have to use colorful language to describe the beauties and attractions of the country or place they are highlighting. They will also have to write persuasively to appeal to the reader to visit their spot. The purpose of this lesson is to provide a framework for students to write a sample travel brochure.

To the Student

What is the greatest, most attractive, most fun place you have ever been to? (Listen to opinions.) What made the spot so wonderful? (what they did, what it looked like, the weather, etc.)

If you wanted to advertise this place to attract others to come visit, what are some things you might include in a travel brochure about it? (how much it costs, what you will get to do, where the good shopping is, etc.)

I want you to pretend that you are a travel agent. Your job is to create a travel brochure that will tell others about some place you would like them to visit. Maybe you have actually been somewhere and can honestly describe it and explain what there is to do there. Or, perhaps you would like to create a vacation dreamplace and pretend there are wonderful things to do there.

Follow the suggestions on the list of information you might want to include on your travel brochure.

Worksheet

Answers to Worksheet IV-29:

Students' brochures will vary.

Follow-up Activities

1. **Travel Brochures:** Collect travel brochures from a travel agency to demonstrate to students the different ways that can appeal to vacationers (eye appeal with great pictures, writing that is bold and stands out, etc.). You might want to assign a particular destination to each of several groups of students and have them rework a travel brochure to make it appealing to kids rather than to adults.

2. **Travel Fair:** After students have completed their travel brochures, set up individual booths and have a "travel fair" in which they display and talk about their brochures. Some might enjoy orally trying to promote their spots and try to entice others to come visit their booth. (Some will probably try to sell time shares!)

IV-29. Take a Trip!

Design a travel brochure that will invite others to come visit your travel spot. Think about the following ideas and information you might want to include on your brochure. Then design an attractive cover and other illustrations to make your travel brochure appealing. Use your imagination!

Travel destination (real or imaginary): _____

_____

_____

_____

Things to do (shop, swim, hike, play games, etc.): _____

_____

_____

_____

How much it costs (daily/weekly): _____

_____

_____

_____

What the weather is like (sunny, cold, windy, etc.): _____

_____

_____

_____

What the hotels/rooms/campgrounds are like (luxurious, rustic, compact, etc.): _____

_____

_____

_____

Who to contact for more information (555-4FUN, travel agent, etc.):_____

_____

_____

_____

Lesson IV-30: Writing a Cartoon Strip

(Creative-Writing Activities)

To the Teacher

Many students enjoy reading comic books. The pictures and action add a dimension to reading that appeals to students. Some students may enjoy trying to create a brief comic strip. Creating a comic strip may be a good paired activity, because some students are skilled at drawing and others may have clever ideas for the plot or dialogue. The purpose of this lesson is to introduce students to some elements of preparing a comic strip.

To the Student

Who likes to read comic books? Which are your favorites? (Allow time for opinions.) Why is it fun to read a comic book? (pictures show the action, they are funny, short, etc.) Do you ever read the comics in the newspaper? Which ones do you enjoy the most? Why?

Writing, as you know, can take many forms and one of them is writing a comic strip. Some of you are good at drawing, and some of you are clever with thinking up funny stories. If we can put these skills together, I bet you can come up with some very interesting comics.

There are a few things you need to know to help organize yourself and your ideas for writing a comic strip:

- Make sure you have your story idea well in mind. You might find it easier to draw the pictures first and then add the dialogue. Or you might find the opposite to be easier—writing the conversations between the characters and then drawing pictures.

- Each panel of the comic strip is a small event or part of the story. It's like the beginning, middle, and ending of a story, only you can make it longer if you like to add extra events.

- All of the words in the "balloons" are words spoken by the characters. The balloon acts like quotation marks.

- It is fun to add sound effects to your pictures. You can write the words (e.g., Thud, Pow! Boink), but make sure you don't put them in the balloons unless they are words spoken by the characters.

- Many comics are supposed to be funny, so go ahead and draw humorous characters with funny facial expressions and silly conversation. Enjoy writing it so that someone else will enjoy reading it!

Worksheets

Worksheet IV-30A:

Cut out an example of a comic strip from a colored Sunday paper edition. Have students discuss the questions about the comic strip.

Worksheet IV-30B:

Students' comic strips will vary.

Worksheet IV-30C:

Students' comic strips will vary.

Follow-up Activities

1. **Finish the Comic:** Students might enjoy completing the dialogue to cartoon strips where the words have been erased, covered, deleted, or somehow missing! After they

fill in what they think is a logical dialogue, reveal the original cartoonist's dialogue and see how close they came.

As a variation, you might keep the dialogue balloons but erase or delete the pictures. Have students come up with their own ideas for drawings that would convey the same message.

2. **Comic Exchange:** Students (individually or in pairs) should display and share their comic strips with each other. They may want to say a word or two about inspirational ideas that made their comics different or unique.

3. Have some students who really enjoy writing and drawing comic strips to create a comic book.

IV-30A. Analyzing a Comic Strip

Look at the comic strip your teacher has brought to class.

1. How many panels are in the comic strip?_____

2. How does each panel show an event in the comic strip?

   _____

   _____

3. Is there humor in the strip? Do you think it is funny? _____

   _____

4. How does the cartoonist use the drawings to make the comic strip fun and interesting?

   _____

   _____

5. Do you think the cartoonist wrote the dialogue first or drew the pictures first?

   _____

   _____

6. Is it easy to figure out what the characters were saying?_____

   _____

   _____

7. Has the cartoonist used any sound-effect words? If yes, are they effective?

   _____

   _____

   _____

IV-30B. Writing the Dialogue

Here is a partially completed comic strip. Add your own words to fit the pictures.

IV-30C. Writing and Drawing a Comic Strip

Now it's your turn to write a short comic strip. Use the space below to make rough sketches of the characters' positions and their dialogue so you know everything will fit within each panel. When ready, draw your final copy. Think about: What's the comic strip about?... What are my characters going to look like?... What are my characters going to say?

Lesson IV-31: Writing a Greeting Card

(Creative-Writing Activities)

To the Teacher

There are cards for nearly any occasion these days! Although it is getting easier and easier to buy one or make one on a computer, there is something personal about actually writing the words yourself. The purpose of this lesson is to provide students with ideas for writing several types of greeting cards.

To the Student

What was the last card you received from someone? (birthday card, get-well card) Have you ever gotten a card that someone made, either by computer or by drawing something and writing the words? How did you like it?

Today there are cards for almost any occasion. Can you think of some reasons why people send greeting cards? (birthday, get well, graduation, wedding, stay in touch, moving to a new house, etc.)

For this project, you are going to make a greeting card to send to someone and you can pick the occasion. Maybe you want to congratulate someone for getting a new puppy. Maybe your sister deserves a card of recognition for being part of a winning volleyball team. Or perhaps you would like to send a card to a sick person in a hospital who needs some cheering up. You select the occasion.

Usually a card will have something pretty or eye-catching on the front. You might also put part of your message on the front. ("Happy birthday to…" or "Congratulations for…") You can put your message on the inside. You might feel like writing a poem or maybe just a few words that express how you feel. If you make it personal (only for the person who is receiving the card), that person will know you took some time to make him or her feel very special.

Here are some ideas for making a greeting card.

Worksheet

Answers to Worksheet IV-31:

Students' cards will vary.

Follow-up Activity

The next time students go to the grocery store, have them go to the greeting card section and try to count how many different types of greeting cards they can find. It is amazing how many cards there are for very specific, unusual situations (Happy Birthday to Stepmother, Congratulations on New Puppy, etc.).

IV-31. A Card for You

Think of a person for whom you would like to make a card. Then think of an occasion (special day, special event, any reason at all) to send the card. Make an eye-catching cover for the card, write an appropriate message inside, and don't forget to sign your name! Use the space below for your rough draft before putting together your final card.

Some ideas…

Happy birthday	I love you
Congratulations	Please write to me
Missing you	Let's get together soon
Hoping you feel better	Remember a time when we had fun
Hope you have a nice day	Sorry to hear you're sick
Good luck	Hope your operation goes well
Want to let you know I'm thinking of you	You are a wonderful friend
Thanks for helping me	

Lesson IV-32: Writing a Joke or Riddle Book

(Creative-Writing Activities)

To the Teacher

Another fun writing project is that of collecting and writing jokes or riddles and compiling them into a book. This not only helps students with the actual writing process, but also helps them organize their writing. The purpose of this lesson is to provide ideas for students to make their own joke/riddle books.

To the Student

What's the best joke you've heard recently? (Allow time for joke-telling.) Can you think of different types of jokes or riddles? (elephant jokes, blonde jokes, knock-knock jokes, etc.).

You may have seen joke books available at the library. There are lots of books like these that contain jokes, riddles, cartoons, funny poems, and other pieces of writing that make you laugh. What I would like you to do is work on making your own joke or riddle book. Search through several books that contain this kind of material and select the ones you really like. Copying them and putting them together in a book is a way to keep a record of the things you think are funny. It's also something you can pull out when you feel the need to entertain others!

There are lots of sites on the Internet that have riddles and jokes that you might find funny, so check them as well.

Worksheet

Answers to Worksheet IV-32:

Students' jokes will vary.

Follow-up Activity

Some of the jokes and riddles lend themselves to a "stand-up" comedy routine. Students may want to memorize and "perform" some of these jokes with a partner in front of the class or as part of a comedy show.

For example, one student could hold up a poster holding the riddle question, and the second student could run onto the stage with the poster delivering the punch line. Students can embellish their theatrics by making "applause" signs, having canned laughter, and using sound effects.

IV-32. Joke Collection

There are many categories of jokes. As you look through different books and magazines, you might want to "collect" certain kinds of jokes and riddles, and categorize them in your joke/riddle book. Don't forgot to illustrate your book!

Here are some examples of joke types:

Doctor jokes	Riddles
Elephant jokes	Brain teasers
Jokes involving people's names	One-liners
Puns	Knock-knock jokes

Use the space below for notes about your joke collection, organizing the jokes, etc.

_____

_____

_____

_____

_____

_____

_____

_____

_____

_____

_____

_____

_____

_____

_____

_____

Lesson IV-33: A Written Time Capsule

(Creative-Writing Activities)

To the Teacher

A time capsule is an interesting way to preserve memories. Usually, a time capsule consists of artifacts from a certain time period that are then preserved in a box or other "capsule," buried or hidden somewhere, and then reopened at a later date. For a writing activity, students may write down their present thoughts, events of the day, and other informal pieces of writing that will be fun to forget and then rediscover. The purpose of this lesson is to provide students with ideas for compiling a personal time capsule.

To the Student

Does anyone know what a time capsule is? (Allow time for ideas.) Basically, a time capsule is a piece of the past, with things from that period of time preserved in a box or capsule. Time capsules are then sealed and opened years later.

When you think of a time period, for example, the 1950s, what comes to mind? (poodle skirts, Elvis Presley, rock and roll, etc.) If you were going back into time, let's say into the 1950s, what things might you find? You probably have seen some movies that show what life was like at that time. If you were opening a time capsule from the 1950s, you would pull out things that were popular at that time. You might find some records (explain what a 45 is!), a picture of Elvis Presley, saddle shoes, and other things that were common back then.

If you were going to make a time capsule of this year, what are some popular things right now that you might include? (singing groups, a computer, Harry Potter books, videos of movies, etc.)

For a writing activity, I would like you to collect some of your personal writing samples to put into your own personal time capsule. You might want to keep it sealed for a year, two years, or even longer. You will be surprised at what you were thinking about or thought was "cool" now, when you look back at it later.

Worksheet

Answers to Worksheet IV-33:

Students' answers will vary.

Follow-up Activity

Obviously, this writing activity should be followed up by the actual making of a time capsule! Each student may bring in a shoe box or larger box that can hold the treasures of his or her immediate life. Decide where the boxes will be stored (at home or at school), have a "sealing ceremony," and plan to have a ceremony when the boxes are reopened. Choose a date (either in one year or longer if you will remain in contact with the students) and write it down where you won't forget! Some things to include in a time capsule:

photographs of the student, his or her friends, and family	a ribbon, medal, certificate, or other honor that was achieved
a recent report card	a CD or tape of a popular musical group
a favorite book	list of best-selling CDs
news articles about what's going on in the world	list of most popular movies
a popular teen magazine	a newspaper from the community
	a television guide from the week

IV-33. Time Capsule Writing Ideas

These are some pieces of writing you might want to include in your personal time capsule:

What grade you are in, your teacher, and about your class

Who your best friends are and what you like to do

Your favorite movie, book, songs, TV show, etc.

A bit about your family—ages of your brothers and sisters and what they do

About your pets

What you think about school

What you think you will be doing 10 years from now

Things you really like

Things you don't like

What is happening in your community, your state, the country, the world

The headlines from your local paper for one week

How expensive things are: milk, a gallon of gas, a pencil, a car, etc.

Popular fads—what people wear, what their hair is like, popular phrases, slang words, etc.

What presents you got on your last birthday

Places you have traveled to

What you would spend $100 on

Your biggest worries

Your great accomplishments

How your favorite sports teams are doing

How do you think you'll feel when you open your time capsule? Jot down your thoughts.

_____

_____

_____

_____

_____

_____

_____

_____

Lesson IV-34: Writing a Skit or Play

(Creative-Writing Activities)

To the Teacher

A final creative-writing activity is that of writing a skit or play. Students may really get involved in the writing and then performing of a piece of drama they have created. The purpose of this lesson is to provide ideas for writing a short play.

To the Student

How many of you have ever been in a play? You probably have taken part in a school play at some time, and maybe some of you have actually performed in a play where you had to memorize lines, get up in front of an audience, and perform! When you are acting in a play, most likely you are following the written lines the playwright has written unless it is an improvisational skit, in which there are no set lines. The characters in that case just do something called ad-libbing, which means they make up their lines as they go.

It's fun to perform in a play, but it's also a lot of fun to write a play or a short skit for which you are the author. When you are writing the play, you control the actions and the dialogue of the characters. You make things happen!

You are going to have an opportunity to write a play. Here are some guidelines that will help you get started.

1. **Organizing the Setting, Characters, Scenes, and Props**

   The setting—Where does your play take place, what time period does it take place in? Is there a specific day and time (summer in New York City, a Sunday afternoon)?

   List of characters—Who are the major and minor characters in the play? Write a short synopsis of who each character is and his or her importance to the play (Mrs. Smith—the mother of the children; Aunt Jane—the mother's sister; Isabel and Frank—the twins who live next door, etc.).

   Scenes—How many different scene changes will be in your play? If it is only one short skit, you have only one scene; but if you are writing a longer play, you have a change of scene several times. Number these scenes and explain what they will look like (Scene 1—the Smith kitchen; Scene 2—outside on a street; Scene 3—the classroom). If you perform the play, you will want to make a background scene to go with each. You can use the same scenes again, but make sure you number them. For example, if Scene 4 takes place back in the kitchen, you would use the same setting for Scene 1.

   Props—You might need different props to go with the different scenes. For each scene, make a list of possible props that you will need (Scene 1—kitchen table, pitcher of milk, glass, apron; Scene 2—tree, background of houses in a row; Scene 3—student desk, portable chalkboard, calendar).

2. **Writing the Play**

   There is a specific style that you can use to write the words for your play. In general, start with the scene at the top. Number the scenes (if you have more than one), and write a word or two that describes the setting.

   Scene 1—The Smith Kitchen

   When the characters speak, write the words they will be saying after their name. Use a colon after you list the name.

   Mary: Good morning, everybody.

   You will want to let the actors know how you want them to perform the words. You should write your directions in parentheses. These directions are not read out loud; they are clues for the reader or actor.

> *Mary: (wiping her forehead, very tired) Good morning, everybody.*

Do you see how the clues help you picture the character and how the actor will say the words? You can also give directions for what the actor should do.

> *Mary: (wiping her forehead, very tired) Good morning, everybody. (She pulls out a chair and slumps into it.) Well, it's a good morning for everyone but me.*

These directions tell the actor that Mary is in a bad mood and is very tired.

Let's do some activities to help you get ready to write your own play.

Worksheets

Answers to Worksheet IV-34A:

Students' skits will vary.

Answers to Worksheet IV-34B:

Students' plays will vary.

Follow-up Activity

Check your school and local libraries for books for children with skits and plays. By reading the plays, students will gain a "feel" for what a play looks like and sounds like. Students will enjoy performing these written plays.

If the skits and plays are well done, have students take turns being a director and having other students act in their plays. This is a good test of how well the directions are written. It is also a confidence-building activity for students to "see" their work performed by others.

Books for Children's Skits and Plays:

Boiko, Claire. *Children's Plays for Creative Actors* (1997). Boston: Plays, Inc.

Kamerman, Sylvia E. (Editor) *The Big Book of Large-Cast Plays: 27 One-Act Plays for Young Actors* (1994). Boston: Plays, Inc.

Kamerman, Sylvia E. (Editor) *The Big Book of Skits: 36 Short Plays for Young Actors* (1996). Boston: Plays, Inc.

Miller, Helen Louise. *Everyday Plays for Boys and Girls* (1986). Boston, MA: Plays, Inc.

Miller, Helen Louise. *First Plays for Children* (1996). Boston, MA: Plays, Inc.

Miller, Helen Louise. *Special Plays for Holidays* (1986). Boston, MA: Plays, Inc.

IV-34A. Write a Skit

Write a one-scene skit. Here are some ideas. Don't forget to think about the setting, characters, scene, and props. Jot down your notes on the lines below.

Mom and Dad arguing about how to cook a steak on the grill

Babysitting for a little child who is a "wild thing" and will not behave

Driving in the family car on a long trip when everyone is crabby

Trying to behave at a piano recital when you have an itch and want to laugh

Two people who both want to operate the remote control for the TV

Doing everything you can to avoid going to the dentist

Dressing up a dog and trying to pass him off as a new student in school

A slumber party where everyone is telling ghost stories

Trying to sneak a bad report card past your father who is reading the newspaper

Cleaning up the house in a hurry before your very picky grandmother and grandfather arrive in 10 minutes unexpectedly

_____

_____

_____

_____

_____

_____

_____

_____

_____

_____

_____

_____

_____

_____

_____

IV-34B. Write a Play

Are you ready to try something longer? Decide on a plot for a play with several different scenes. Remember to use parentheses to let the reader/actor know how you want them to perform your lines. Jot down your notes on the lines below.

Here are some ideas for a play:

A new student comes to school, seems snotty and different at first, then students realize he/she is just shy. They join together to win the big contest against another school.

Children in a family want a pet, so they try out different kinds. They go through trials with different animals that are difficult (an elephant, a cow) until they finally decide that a puppy is best.

People in a town are afraid of a strange woman who moves into an old, deserted house and brings strange things into the house. Then they learn she used to work for a circus and these are things from her previous house.

Two kids decide they are going to make a lot of money having a lemonade stand in the summer. But by the time they buy everything they need and drink all of the lemonade, they end up going swimming instead.

A girl discovers that her dog can talk and has a opinion about everything, which embarrasses the girl when she takes the dog shopping, to a very elegant party, and to school.

A family goes to a very fancy restaurant. No one can figure out what is on the menu, so they send one member at a time to go to a bookstore down the street to look up everything in a foreign language book while the waiter brings them the different foods.

_____

_____

_____

_____

_____

_____

_____

_____

_____

_____

Notes

Notes

Notes

Notes

Notes

Notes

Notes

Notes

Notes

Notes

Made in the USA
Monee, IL
15 August 2021